The Complete Book of Activities, Games, Stories, Props, Recipes, and Dances

By Pam Schiller and Jackie Silberg

Illustrations: Richelle Bartkowiak, Deborah Wright

Dedication

To baby Evan whose life, I hope, is filled with the magic of stories.
—Pam Schiller

To all of the wonderful teachers in my early years who encouraged me to sing and dance and play and read and be joyful!
—Jackie Silberg

Acknowledgments

To Kathy Charner, my wonderful editor and friend who makes my books very special.

To Leah and Larry Rood, my publishers who believe in what I do.

To all of the teachers and parents who keep encouraging me to keep writing.

To all of the Gryphon House staff who keep everything running smoothly and make the books so beautiful.

—Jackie Silberg

The Complete Book of
Activities, Games, Stories, Props, Recipes, and Dances
for Young Children

Pam Schiller

Jackie Silberg

Illustrated by Richelle Bartkowiak and Deborah Wright

gryphon house®, *inc.*

Beltsville, MD 20704

OVER **600** selections

Copyright

Library of Congress Cataloging-in-Publication Data

Schiller, Pamela Byrne.
    The complete book of activities, games, stories, props, recipes, and dances / by Pam Schiller and Jackie Silberg; illustrations, Deborah Wright, Richelle Bartkowiak.
      p.cm.
    Includes index.
    ISBN 978-0-87659-280-9
    1. Early childhood education--Activity programs. 2. Games. I. Silberg, Jackie, DATE- II. Title.
LBII39.35.A37S34 2003
372.21--dc21

2002151426

Bulk purchase

Gryphon House books are available at special discount when purchased in bulk for special premiums and sales promotions as well as for fund-raising use. Special editions or book excerpts also can be created to specification. For details, contact the Director of Marketing.

Disclaimer

The publisher and the authors cannot be held responsible for injury, mishap, or damages incurred during the use of or because of the activities in this book. The authors recommend appropriate and reasonable supervision at all times based on the age and capability of each child.

Every effort has been made to locate copyright and permission information.

Gryphon House is a member of the Green Press Initiative, a nonprofit program dedicated to supporting publishers in their efforts to reduce their use of fiber-sourced forests. This book is made of 30% post-consumer waste. For further information visit www. greenpressinitiative.org.

Table of Contents

Introduction

How many times have you desperately searched for just the right story to reinforce your theme? When is the last time you wanted to play a game but couldn't quite remember how the game is played? How many times have you misplaced the recipe for your favorite no-bake cookies? Well, look no more. *The Complete Book of Activities, Games, Stories, Props, Recipes, and Dances* is an instant resource, filled with what you need for the classroom. This book contains over 600 curriculum enhancers and to make it even easier, it is organized to help you find exactly what you need quickly.

Teacher–Made Activities and Props

This section of the book includes more than 100 simple teacher-made games, props, and activities. Most are quick to make and easy to use. They can be used in the same way as the games. This section also includes a few extra pages for you to add your own ideas.

Games

Games are part of every early childhood curriculum because they serve two important purposes: they allow children to build skills, and they help channel the tremendous excess of energy that is part of childhood. How many times do you think of a game that will work well for teaching a specific skill or to enhance a theme and then get stuck because you can't quite remember the directions? How many times do you get stuck because you can't think of just the right game? *The Complete Book of Activities, Games, Stories, Props, Recipes, and Dances* also includes a broad selection of partner games, individual games, and group games.

Stories

This book contains more than 150 stories that are a combination of fables, folktales, traditional stories and rhymes, and stories and rhymes written by the authors. The stories are in a variety of formats: listening stories, action stories, prop stories, rebus stories, puppet stories, and flannel board/ magnetic board stories. The variety of formats serves two purposes: they stimulate children's interest, and they offer different aspects of support for the development of literacy.

Action Stories

Action stories allow the children to participate physically in the story. For example, "Candy Land Journey" takes the children on a pretend trip to a land of caramel rivers and peppermint stepping stones, or in "Marley Markle," children are instructed to pat their heads when they hear the words "good dog" and shake their finger when they hear the words "bad dog." By encouraging children's physical participation, action stories help build children's listening skills and their comprehension skills at the same time.

Flannel Board/Magnetic Board Stories

Another type of story in this book is flannel board/magnetic board stories. These stories are a great alternative to regular storybooks. The greatest benefit of these stories is that they allow children to retell the story in their own words or to make up a new story using the same story characters. This is particularly easy for children when they are retelling familiar tales like "The Three Bears." Flannel board stories also provide a format that allows the teacher to easily modify story vocabulary or to enhance the story line itself as she tells it in her own words.

Listening Stories

Listening stories help children develop their attention spans and offer the opportunity to create their own mental images of characters and actions in the story. Some of the listening stories in this book are specifically designed to help children sharpen their listening skills. For example, in "My Grandmother's Garden," children are instructed to say "ah-h-h-h" each time they hear the word "roses."

Prop Stories

Prop stories use concrete props such as bags, apples, clothing, and so forth to help tell the story. This type of story presentation provides just enough visuals for the listener to get the general idea but leaves plenty of room for imagination. Another advantage of prop stories is that they are easy for the children to retell by themselves. The props provide clues as to what part of the story comes next.

Puppet Stories

Puppet stories are always fascinating to children. They provide countless opportunities for building children's language development and confidence in their speaking ability. Puppets also allow children to become familiar with story characters in a more concrete way. When children retell stories using the puppets, they generally begin to add their own concepts into the personality of the character. Often, the personality of the character will be the basis on which children will develop new stories. The puppet stories offered in this book encourage the use of a variety of different types of puppets such as plate puppets, stick puppets, sock puppets, and bag puppets.

Rebus Stories

Rebus stories help children begin to build the feel of reading. A combination of words on sentence strips and picture cards are used to tell the story. Children may not yet be ready to read the words but the picture cards provide a way for the children to participate in reading the story. This process helps children feel the power of being able to unlock written text. In the story of "Susie Moriar," children can use both the picture cards and the predictable rhyming text as tools to open the door to reading.

The variety of stories will not only strengthen children's learning, but also will be used to support the themes in your curriculum. Each story has suggestions for thematic connections. You will find a chart on pages 16-18 that suggests stories for some typical early childhood themes. Many stories fit into several themes. Children need to hear stories again and again, so repetition actually helps the learning process. Every time children hear a story they gain something new from the experience. Use the stories as many times as they fit into your curriculum.

Arts and Crafts Recipes

Over the years, early childhood teachers have developed a number of recipes for arts and crafts materials. Some recipes were developed to save money on store-bought playdough or fingerpaint. Other materials were developed because they have a particular appeal to children, such as Goop and Gak. Teachers continue to use these recipes every day. *The Complete Book of Activities, Games, Stories, Props, Recipes, and Dances* offers 50 of these recipes. Take a look—you may find some recipes you've never seen before or the one you have been looking for and thought you'd never find.

Food Recipes

It's fun to eat and even more fun to cook what you eat. Children love to do things they see adults doing, and cooking offers an opportunity to do something "real." Cooking is probably one of the best examples of a single learning experience that integrates a number of literacy, math, and social skills. The recipes in this book offer creative suggestions ranging from simple to challenging. With over 100 to choose from, you are sure to find some to enhance your curriculum.

Dances

Children love to dance. They are developing coordination and rhythm, and dancing is a great way to practice what they are learning. The repetition in most dances is a perfect ingredient for strengthening those all-important brain connections for balance, coordination, and agility. The dances presented in this book are simple dances that are easy for children to learn.

We hope that you enjoy *The Complete Book of Activities, Games, Stories, Props, Recipes, and Dances* and that it provides hours of learning and fun for the children in your care.

16

Thematic Chart

The following chart demonstrates how to use this book to round out any curriculum. The far-left column contains a few of the common themes used in early childhood classrooms. The remaining columns identify the activities, games, stories, recipes, and dances that go with that theme. See the Theme Connection Index on page 619 for a complete list.

Theme Connection	Activities / Props	Games	Stories	Dances
Self-Esteem	Body Outline Puzzles Feely Box Sensory Glove Sound Canisters Aroma Canisters Smell Puffs Sound Match-Ups Tactile Cylinders Tactile Box Twister	Tightrope Walking Think, Pair, Share Tummy Ticklers Name Game 2 Back-to-Back Building Back-to-Back Lifts Fact or Fantasy Fitness Patterns Follow the Leader Yeah or Yuck	The Many Faces of Me I Can, You Can My Body Talks My Shadow My First Day of School The Lion's Haircut Photo Puppet Stories	Dance, Thumbkin, Dance It's a Simple Dance to Do Put Your Little Foot Hokey Pokey Tooty-Ta
Friends	Find a Friend Game Can Telephones Classroom Photo Album Classroom Photo Baggie Book Finger Pal Puppets Scavenger Hunt Yes/No Questions	Where, Oh, Where is Pretty Little Susie? Back-to-Back Building Back-to-Back Lifts Cooperative Musical Chairs Tug of Peace Think, Pair, Share Copycat Don't Let the Ball Fall Fact or Fantasy London Bridge Name Game 2 One Elephant The Quiet Game Straw Structures Three-legged Movements	Smart Cookie's Best Friend, Gabby Graham Mr. Wiggle and Mr. Waggle The Zebra on the Zyder Zee The Lion and the Mouse Sam and Pam The Ant and the Dove Issun Boshi Little Red Hen The Parade	Bunny Hop The Chicken Hansel and Gretel: A Dance of Opposites Circle 'Round the Zero Skip to My Lou Square Dance Where, Oh, Where is Pretty Little Susie? Old Joe Clarke Put Your Little Foot

Shapes	Sand Combs Shadow Match Apple Shape Puzzles Ball Chute Felt Books Bowling Pins Box Guitars Box Train Coin Coverup Color Hoops Paper Bag Blocks Puzzle Box Match-Ups	Ping Pong Toss Circle Relays Bean Bag Game Ball Rolling Bead in a Bucket Bead Pick Up Block Busters Don't Let the Ball Fall Hopscotch Hula Hoop Hop Think, Pair, Share Walk a Crooked Line	Tillie Triangle Smart Cookie's Best Friend, Gabby Graham A Special Surprise Perky Pumpkin's Open House	Square Dance Shape Dancing Circle 'Round the Zero
Music	Drums and Drumsticks Thumb Harp Tone Bottles Box Guitars Jingle Blocks Kazoos Wind Chimes 2 Canister Bell Rhyming Words Musical Chairs	Name That Tune Tone Bottles Hot and Cold Cooperative Musical Circle The Freeze Hot Potato Hummers Musical Ball Musical Chairs Musical Hide and Seek Name That Tune Sound Patterns	This Old Man is Rockin' On The Traveling Musicians Okki-Tokki-Unga The Calliope Sing a Song of Opposites The Color Song The Gunny Wolf On Top of Spaghetti The Three Bears Rap	Top Hat Tappers The Twist The Stroll The Macarena Use any dance with this theme
Transportation	Prop Boxes Box Train Garages	Heel to Toe Heel to Toe Race Che Che Koolay	The Zebra on the Zyder Zee The Little Spaceman Little Engine Ninety-Nine The Wheels on the Bus I Saw A Ship A-Sailing	Helicopter Ride Jim Along Josie The Stroll Walk, Along, John

Thematic Chart (continued)

The following chart demonstrates how to use this book to round out any curriculum. The far left column contains a few of the common themes used in early childhood classrooms. The remaining columns identify the activities, games, stories, recipes, and dances that go with that theme. See the Theme Connection Index on page 619 for a complete list.

Theme Connection	Activities / Props	Games	Stories	Dances
Insects	Bug Eyes Cup Puppets Apple and Worm Match Game Dancing Spiders	The Little Ants Spider Walk Inch Worm Relays Caterpillar, Caterpillar, Butterfly (See Duck, Duck, Goose)	Little Caterpillar The Little Ants Metamorphosis The Ant and the Grasshopper Fuzzy Caterpillar Ms. Bumblebee Gathers Honey The Ram in the Chili Patch	Waggle Dance Shoo Fly Skip to My Lou

Activities & Props

Apple and Worm Match Game

Cut three apple shapes from red construction paper. Cut one hole in the first apple, two holes in the second apple, and three holes in the third apple. Cut six worms from green, yellow, or brown construction paper. Encourage the children to match the worms to the holes.

Theme Connections

Apples
Counting
Food
Insects
Numbers

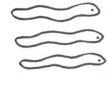

Apple Picking Sorting Game

Draw an apple tree on a piece of poster board. Cut large and small apples from construction paper and laminate them. Glue a piece of Velcro to the back of each apple and a corresponding piece of Velcro to the tree. Stick apples on the tree. Invite children to pick the apples and sort them into categories of big and little. Provide a couple of baskets to hold the sorted apples.

Theme Connections

Apples
Food
Growing Things
Nature
Opposites

Apple Shape Puzzles

Cut apple shapes from red construction paper. Laminate them and cut them into simple puzzle pieces.

Theme Connections

Apples
Shapes

Aroma Canisters

Soak cotton balls in scented oil. Put the cotton balls inside a margarine tub with holes poked in the lid. Make sure lids are taped or glued on securely. Scented oils are available at most candle and craft stores. Chamomile, orange, and lavender are soothing scents.

Theme Connections

Senses

Baby Bells

Sew a jingle bell to a piece of elastic or a child-size scrunchie that will fit loosely around wrists and ankles. Make sure the bell is sewn on securely. Encourage children to wear the bells when they dance.

Theme Connections

Senses

Baggie Fish

Cut fish shapes from acetate. Let the children take three fish and color them with markers. Help them scoop 1 cup of blue hair gel into a zipper-closure plastic bag and then place their three fish inside the bag. Make sure bags are securely closed. Change

the number of fish in the bags based on numbers you are studying.

Theme Connections

Colors
Counting
Fish
Numbers

Ball Chute

Cut a hole through a small cardboard box so that you can fit a paper towel tube through it diagonally. Roll a small ball through the paper towel "chute."

Theme Connections

Balls
Shapes

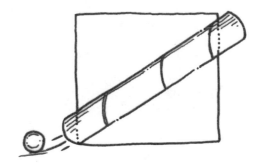

Ball Scoop

Cut the bottom and half of the sides (up to the handle) out of an empty, clean, plastic bleach or similar type bottle to make a scoop. Teach the children how to catch balls in the scoop.

Theme Connections

Balls
Movement

Beanbag Babies

Cut two identical animal shapes from washcloths. (You can find patterns in simple coloring books or use those included in this book as flannel board pieces.) Sew the two pieces together, leaving about 1" open. Fill the "animal" about ¾ full of dried beans and then stitch it closed.

Theme Connections

Animals

Bell Bags

Fill small envelopes with jingle bells. Put one bell in one envelope, two in the next, three in the third, four in the fourth, and five in the last. Seal all the envelopes and invite the children to arrange the bags from the softest sound to the loudest sound.

Theme Connections

Opposites
Senses

Bird Feeders

■ Pinecone

Spread a thin layer of peanut butter on a pinecone and then roll it in birdseed.

■ Milk Carton

Cut a hole in the sides of a milk carton (paper or plastic), stopping about 1" from the bottom, and pour birdseed inside. You might also cut holes to slide a plastic straw through to give birds a place to stand. Hang bird feeders outside with yarn, string, or wire.

Theme Connections

Birds
Food
Nature

Blue Bird

Cut strips of paper (about 2" x 11") in pairs of different colors to represent wings. Invite each child to pick the color of wings and consequently "bird" he or she wants to be. Pin the paper strips with safety pins to the shoulders of each child to make "wings." Ask the class to join hands and form a circle and then raise their arms to create arches that will represent windows. Change the color of the bird in each verse as you sing or chant the words below. Children with wings of the color mentioned in the chant "fly" in and out of the "windows."

Blue bird, blue bird,
Through my window. (all blue birds fly through the windows)

Blue bird, blue bird,
Through my window.

Blue bird, blue bird,
Through my window,
And sit up on my bed. (blue birds go back to their places in the circle)

Red bird, red bird,
Through my window... (all red birds fly through the windows)

Theme Connections

Colors
Senses

Body Outline Puzzles

Trace around the perimeter of the body of one of the children. Cut the body outline into a puzzle, keeping the major body parts intact. Give a puzzle piece to each of the children. Have them put the body outline puzzle together one piece at a time. Discuss body parts as they are added to the puzzle.

Theme Connections

Parts of the Body

Bottle Rollers

Fill clear plastic half-liter bottles with colored water (use food coloring). Add some interesting items to look at such as beads, seeds, aluminum confetti or sequins, or small plastic animals. Glue the lids on securely. Encourage children to roll the bottles across the floor. They will love watching the movement of the items inside the bottle.

Theme Connections

Colors
Senses

Bound Books

■ **Baggie Books**

Make baggie books by stapling five zipper-closure bags together across the bottom (the "unzipped" side) and placing a piece of tape over the staples. Let the children draw illustrations for the book on paper cut to fit inside the bags.

■ **Cereal Box Books**

Cut off the front panels of cereal boxes. Punch two holes in the sides and attach book rings.

■ **Felt Books**

Take five felt squares and sew them together on the left side to make a book. Cut felt scraps into geometric shapes and place them in a sandwich bag with a zipper top. Children can create objects, make sets, or reproduce patterns on the blank pages with the felt shapes.

■ **Greeting Card Books**

Cut off the fronts of old greeting cards. Lay the cards on construction paper, trace around them, and then cut out to use as the backs of the books. Cut paper to fit inside the books, and then staple it between the card and construction paper.

■ **Photo Books**

Make photocopies of photos you have collected. Cut them out and glue them onto 4" x 5" pieces of construction paper. Place photos in zipper-closure plastic bags, two photos back to back in each bag. Staple all the bags together at their "unzipped" ends (so you can open them). Use colored tape to cover the staples.

■ **Stapled Books**

Fold two pieces of paper in half and staple. Use tape to cover the staples.

Theme Connections

Holidays
Self-Esteem
Shapes

Bowling Pins

Collect several potato chip cans. Paint them or cover them with colorful contact paper or construction paper. If you need to weight them, drop a few small stones into each one. Make sure the lid is glued or taped on securely.

Theme Connections

Movement
Shapes

Box Guitars

Stretch rubber bands around empty shoeboxes. Use rubber bands of different widths and lengths to get a variety of tones and pitches.

Theme Connections

Music
Shapes

Box Train

String several empty cereal boxes or milk cartons together with yarn. Decorate the boxes, if desired.

Theme Connections

Shapes
Transportation

Braided Wig

Cut the feet off of a pair of pantyhose. Slit each leg of the hose into three sections. Braid the three pieces on each leg to make pigtails. Tie ribbon around the end of each braid. Show the children how to put the waistband of the pantyhose around their head to create a wig.

Theme Connections

Humor
Parts of the Body

Bug Eyes

Cut out two connected sections of a Styrofoam egg carton. Cut a hole in the bottom of each section. Attach 8" pipe cleaners to each side of the section to make a pair of glasses. Encourage the children to decorate the Bug Eyes with sequins, tempera paint, scraps of fabric, rickrack, and so forth.

Theme Connections

Humor
Insects
Senses

Can Telephones

Punch a hole with a nail or an ice pick in the bottoms of two tin cans (frozen juice cans work well, too). Be sure that the cans have no sharp edges. Cut a piece of string about 6' long. Run one end of the string through the hole in one can and tie it off. Run the other end of the string through the other can and tie it off. Now you are ready to stretch the string between the two cans and show children how to talk into one can to a friend who is listening on the other end.

Theme Connections

Friends
Senses

Canister Bell

Place a jingle bell inside an empty film canister. Make sure you tape or glue the lid on securely.

Variation

Make "jingle blocks" by placing jingle bells in empty tissue boxes and cover the opening with duct tape. Cover the entire container with colorful contact paper.

Theme Connections

Music
Senses

Catch the Pumpkin

Give the children orange beanbags or beanbags with a felt pumpkin attached with Velcro or a safety pin. Have the children toss their pumpkins in the air and see how many times they can "catch the pumpkin."

Theme Connections

Holidays
Movement
Pumpkins

Classroom Photo Album

Buy an inexpensive photo album and fill it with photos of the children and teachers in your class. Use photos you take in the classroom and others that families are willing to give you.

Theme Connections

Families
Friends
School
Self-Esteem

Classroom Photo Baggie Book

Make photocopies of photos you collected from families. Cut them out and glue them onto 4" x 5" pieces of construction paper. Place photos in zipper-closure plastic bags, two photos back-to-back in each bag. Staple all the bags together at their closed ends (so you can open them). Use colored tape to cover staples.

Theme Connections

Families   School
Friends   Self-Esteem

Coin Cover-Up

Put about 8" (20 cm) of water in a plastic tub or bucket. Place a quarter on the bottom in the center. Give each child a penny. Invite them to drop their pennies into the water one at a time. The object is to completely cover the quarter with pennies.

Theme Connections

Shapes

Color Hoops

Place colored cellophane or plastic wrap in embroidery hoops. Encourage the children to look through the hoops to see what happens to the world around them.

Variation

Cover one end of an empty toilet paper tube or paper towel tube with colored cellophane or plastic wrap. Secure with glue or masking tape.

Theme Connections

Colors
Shapes

Concentration Games

Make two photocopies of 6 to 8 selected patterns, or use stickers. If using photocopied patterns, color them, cut them out, glue them to 3" x 4" index cards, and laminate them. If using stickers, simply apply them to the 3" x 4" index cards and laminate. To play the game, shuffle the cards and place them face down in a series of rows. Each player turns over two cards at a time to find a matching pair of cards. When a player turns over a matching pair of cards, he or she collects those cards and gets to take an extra turn. The player with the most matching pairs wins.

Theme Connections

Use with any theme

Dance Streamers

Cut a variety of colors of crepe paper streamers into 18" strips. Cut a paper plate into four pie-shaped wedges. Give each child a wedge and some streamers to glue or tape to the outer edge of the wedge (plate). Attach the point of the wedge to a tongue depressor.

Encourage the children to dance creatively with their streamers.

Theme Connections

Colors
Movement
Shapes

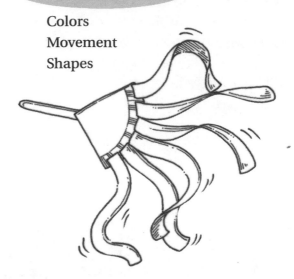

Dancing Spiders

Twist four 8" pipe cleaners together in the middle to make eight spider legs. Attach a 12" piece of elastic string to the middle. Encourage the children to hold the unattached end of the elastic string and bob it up and down to make their spiders dance.

Theme Connections

Insects

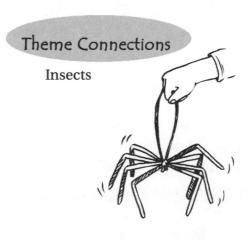

Dice

Cut cubes from a sponge. Use a permanent marker to make dots on each side of the cubes to replicate dice. The great thing about these dice is that they don't make any noise when they are rolled.

Theme Connections

Counting
Numbers
Shapes

Dippity-Do® Bottles

Fill an empty clear plastic soda bottle with Dippity-Do® or other clear hair gel. Add some sequins, buttons, or other interesting items and then glue the lid on the bottle. Encourage the children to observe the items in the bottles. What happens when you wiggle the bottle? Roll the bottle? Turn the bottle upside down?

Theme Connections

Senses
Shapes

Diving Gear

Make a diving tank out of an empty 2-liter soda bottle. With a glue gun, glue elastic onto the bottle to make shoulder straps (adults only). Make goggles by cutting two sections of an egg carton from the rest of the carton. Cut an eyehole in the bottom of each section. Attach elastic for a headband. Provide swimming fins to complete the diving gear.

Theme Connections

Boats and Ships
Occupations

Dog and Bone Match Game

Make 5 to 10 photocopies of the patterns on pages 304-305. Color them, cut them out, write the numerals 1-5 (or, depending on the abilities of the children, 10) on the collar tags. Then make 1-5 (or, depending on the abilities of the children, 10) dots on the bones, laminate them, and cut around the edges of the mouth of each dog. If you use brown paper or tag board you will have less

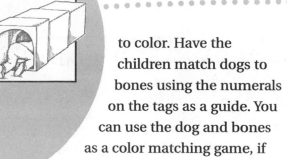

to color. Have the children match dogs to bones using the numerals on the tags as a guide. You can use the dog and bones as a color matching game, if you prefer.

Theme Connections

Colors
Counting
Dogs
Numbers

Dot Croquet

Make a set of croquet tunnels by cutting wide arches into both long sides of shoeboxes. Place one dot on the top of the first box, two dots on top of the second box, and so on. Arrange the boxes in any order on the floor. Encourage the children to use an empty paper towel tube or wrapping paper tube to hit a Ping-Pong ball or tennis ball through the boxes, beginning with the box with one dot and moving through the others in order.

Theme Connections

Balls
Counting
Movement

Dreidel

Collapse the top of a pint-size milk carton to make a square box. Cover the box with paper. Draw an "X" on the top and bottom of the box to create a center spot. Push a pencil through the center of the carton. Write the dreidel letters, "G," "H," "S," and "N" on each of the four sides of the box (see p. X for game directions).

Theme Connections

Alphabet
Counting
Holidays
Numbers

Drums and Drumsticks

Stretch canvas or heavy-duty plastic over the open end of a box or similar container. Stretch it tight to get the best sound and tape it securely. You can also make drums by turning over any box or similar container and encouraging the children to beat on the bottom. Drumsticks can be made by cutting a cardboard coat hanger tube in half or by wrapping one end of a ½" dowel rod with masking tape or duct tape.

Theme Connections

Music

Egg Carton Shake

Write the numerals 1, 2, 3, three times each in the sections of an egg carton. Paste a picture of a dog in one of the remaining sections, a cat in another, and a bird in the last. Invite the children to place a button in the egg carton, close the lid and shake. Then ask the children to open the lid and see where the button has landed. If it is on a numeral, ask the children to name the numeral. If it is on one of the animals, ask the children to make that animal's sound (cat meows, dog barks, bird tweets).

Theme Connections

Birds	Dogs
Cats	Numbers
Counting	Sounds of Language

Elastic Exercisers

Cut a 3-foot length of 1" elastic for each child. Sew the ends together to make a circle. Invite the children to stand on their elastic bands and stretch them over their heads. Have them form shapes with the elastic. Create other exercises for bending and stretching.

Theme Connections

Growing Up
Health and Safety
Movement

Elephant and Peanut Match Game

Make 5 to 10 photocopies of the patterns on pages 306-307. Color them, cut them out, write the numerals 1-5 on the saddle of elephants, and laminate them. If you photocopy on gray paper or tagboard, you will have less to color. Have the children feed each elephant the number of peanuts that is indicated on the elephant's saddle.

Theme Connections

Counting
Elephants
Food
Numbers

Feely Boxes

Line two or three empty boxes with fabrics that have a distinct texture. Cut a 2" to 3" hole in the lids of the boxes and tape the lids to the boxes. Encourage the children to put their hands in the box and describe the fabric inside.

Theme Connections

Senses

Find a Friend Game

Take photos of the children. Generally, you can fit three children in each shot. Cut the photos into small squares similar to small-size school pictures. Make two photocopies of the pictures. Glue one set inside a manila folder and laminate. Laminate the second set to be like a set of playing cards. Encourage the children to match the photo cards to the photos inside the folder.

Theme Connections

Friends
Growing Up

Finger Pal Puppets

Draw faces on the fingers of a glove, or glue on pictures of children in your room. Cut the fingers off the glove to make finger puppets.

Theme Connections

Friends
Growing Up

Floaters and Sinkers

Cut a piece of poster board in half to make a chart for the floaters and sinkers. Make a column for each on the poster board, write "float" in one column and "sink" in the other column, illustrate each column, and laminate. Gather items that will float and some that will sink. Invite the children to examine each item and predict whether it will float or sink. Encourage the children to test their predictions by tossing each item

gently into the air. Then have the children drop the items in the water. How many predictions did they get right? What makes some things sink quickly and other things float slowly downward? What causes all things to drop?

Theme Connections

Discovery
Opposites

Floor Mats

Cut a clear vinyl shower curtain liner into four squares. Fold each square in half and use wide vinyl tape to tape two of the sides together to form a pocket. Leave one side open so that photos and posters can be slipped in and out of the vinyl covering. You may want to use Velcro on the opening side to further protect the photos or posters inside the mat. Children will love being able to explore the photos or posters up close.

Theme Connections

Use with any theme

Garages

Collect and wash half-pint milk cartons. Staple the top together on each carton. Cut an opening on one side for a garage door. Cover the carton with contact paper or construction paper. Place these "garages" and some small cars in the block center for dramatic play.

Theme Connections

Transportation

Gel Bags

Put one cup of hair gel into a quart-size resealable plastic bag. Glue or tape the bag shut. Invite children to use their index fingers to trace a design or to write their name in the bag.

Theme Connections

Discovery
Shapes

Go Fishing

Cut out fish from construction paper or tagboard. Place a paper clip on each fish's "nose." Make a fishing pole from the cardboard tube of a coat hanger. Tape a piece of yarn at one end of the pole and attach a magnet to the other end to serve as a hook. The round magnets with a hole in them work well. If you have young children you may prefer to use Velcro instead of the paperclip and magnet. If you make the fish different lengths, you can have the children seriate the fish after they are caught. You can also glue rhyming object pictures on the fish and have the children match them. There really is no end to all the different things you can ask the children to do with their "catch."

Theme Connections

Fish
Rhymes and Rhyming

Green Gobblers

Use green spray paint on a set of tongs with a ball press on the end. Glue on two wiggle eyes (or felt pieces for younger children). It will look like a big mouth frog. Invite the children to use the gobblers to pick up pompoms or other fun items.

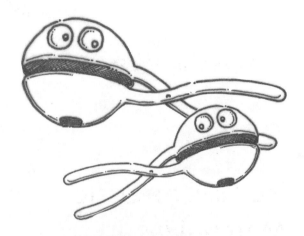

Theme Connections

Colors
Frogs
Movement

Greeting Card Puzzles

Collect greeting cards that have interesting illustrations on the front. Cut the fronts off the cards and cut them into puzzle pieces. This is a great activity for the first day of school. You can make one puzzle for each child and place it in a resealable plastic bag with his or her name on it. Hand it to the children as they arrive and it will occupy them while you take information from families and greet the other children.

Theme Connections

Use with any theme

Heart Stencils/ Lacing Hearts

Draw hearts in the middle of three or four 8" square pieces of poster board. Cut them out with a razor knife (adults only). Use the outside poster board as stencils. Use the heart cutouts to make lacing hearts by punching holes around the perimeter of each cutout heart. Tape a long shoelace on the back of each one.

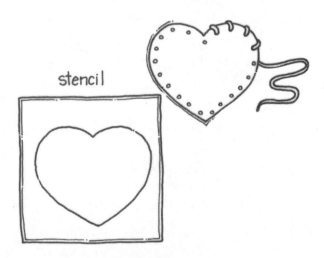

Lace-up card

stencil

Theme Connections

Holidays
Shapes

Homemade Easel

Cut a medium-sized cardboard box (approximately 18" x 24" x 18") diagonally. Turn it over and place it on the table for a tabletop easel. You can use masking tape to hold paper to the easel.

Theme Connections

Use with any theme

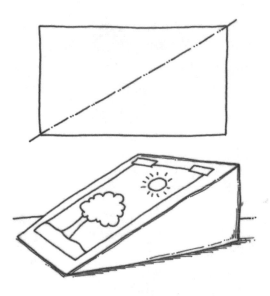

Homemade Thermometer

Use a nail to punch a hole in the lid of a half-liter clear soda bottle. The hole should be large enough to stick a straw through. Fill the bottle with water and a few drops of red food coloring. Replace the lid and stick a clear plastic straw ⅔ of the way into the water. Hold in place with some clay. Move the thermometer to different places in the classroom where the temperature might vary, such as by the windows or by the furnace. Leave the bottle in place for five minutes. Check to see if the water has moved further up or down the straw. The water should move down the straw in cooler places and up the straw in warmer places.

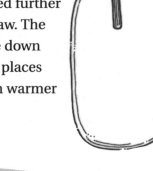

Theme Connections

Discovery
Weather

Ice Cream Cone Match-Ups

Cut out construction paper ice-cream scoops in a variety of colors and some brown construction paper cones. Put colored dots on the cones to match the colors of the ice cream scoops. Encourage the children to match ice-cream scoops to the cones that have the corresponding color dot.

Theme Connections

Colors
Counting
Food
Numbers

ACTIVITIES & PROPS

Indoor Golf

Cut both ends out of several coffee cans (a variety of sizes adds to the fun). Remove or cover all sharp edges. Spray paint the cans (adults only) and number them on the side with stick-on numerals. Place the cans on their sides around the room. Provide Ping-Pong balls and cardboard paper towel tubes. Challenge children to hit the balls through the cans in numeral sequence.

Variation

Play Covered Wagon Golf. Instead of using cans with numerals on them, use pieces of brown construction paper that are taped to the floor to look like the tops of covered wagons.

Theme Connections

Balls
Counting
Movement
Numbers

Kazoos

Give each child a piece of paper (4" x 6") to color. When they are finished, help them glue their art around the outside of an empty toilet paper tube. Secure a piece of wax paper over one end of the tube with a rubber band. Show the children how to blow into the open end of the tube to make music on their "kazoos."

Theme Connections

Humor
Music

Magazine Scavenger Hunt

Make a rebus chart of five or six items that children should try to find in a magazine. Children can play this game in teams of two or three, or individually. The object is to be the first one to find and cut out all the items on the chart.

Theme Connections

Use with any theme

Marble Racers

Fill two clean half-liter bottles, one with water and the other with white corn syrup. Place a marble in each bottle and then glue the lids on securely. Encourage the children

to turn the bottle over and see which marble travels from bottom to top the fastest.

Theme Connections

Discovery

Newspaper Hats

Fold one sheet of newspaper in half to make a rectangle. Place the fold away from your body. Fold down the top  corners so that they meet in the middle of the sheet. The bottom edge of these folded pieces will be about ¼" from the bottom of the original piece. Fold that ¼" section up on both sides and crease them well. Open the hat at the creases.

Theme Connections

Clothing

Number Bags

Use a permanent marker to make a line down the center of five zipper-closure bags.

Write the numerals 1 on the first bag, 2 on the second, and so on. Place one button or washer in the first bag, two in the second, and so on. Show the children how to move the buttons on either side of the line to create set combinations. Encourage the children to use tally marks to indicate how many combinations they find for each number.

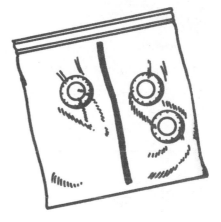

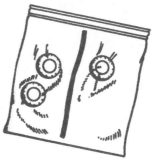

Theme Connections

Counting

Numbers

Observation Bottles

Fill clear half-liter bottles with items that relate to themes. For example, you might make a fall observation bottle by placing acorns, fall leaves, and berries in the bottle. You might make an ocean observation bottle by placing some sand, shells, and plastic sea animals in the bottle. Be sure to glue the lids on securely.

Theme Connections

Oceans and Seas
Seasons

Paper Bag Blocks

Fill paper grocery sacks ¾ full with crumpled newspaper. Fold the tops over to make a square or a rectangle and tape them down with masking or duct tape. Use small or large sacks depending on the size of block you wish to create.

Theme Connections

Shapes

Peg Tubs

Punch several small holes in the top of a margarine tub. Holes should be just big enough to hold colored golf tees or small pegs. Draw a circle around each hole with a permanent marker. The circles should be different colors and match the golf tees or pegs. Store the tees or pegs inside the tub when not in use. Children can place the golf tees or pegs into the holes according to color.

Theme Connections

Colors

Pendulum

Make a duct tape loop on the bottom of an empty mustard or ketchup container (spout type). Fill the container with sand and close the spout. Attach a rope to the loop to allow the container to hang like a pendulum. Place a shower curtain liner or large piece of butcher paper on the floor under the pendulum. Open the spout of the container and invite children to swing it and

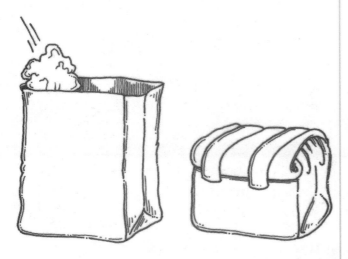

watch the tracks made by the sand. When the container is empty, sweep up the sand in a dust pan, pour it back into the container, and the children can do it again.

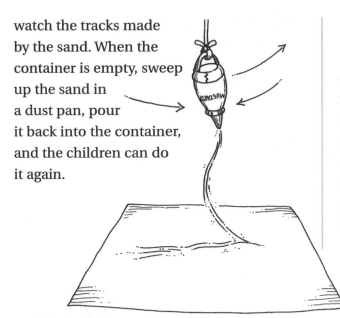

Peter Piper

Photocopy, color, cut out, and laminate the illustrations on pages 308-309. Place them on the wall in random order. Teach the children the following tongue twister:

Peter Piper picked a peck of pickled peppers.
If Peter Piper picked a peck of pickled peppers,
How many peppers did Peter Piper pick?

Have the children point to the appropriate illustration while reciting the rhyme. (It's not as easy as it sounds!)

Theme Connections

Humor
Sounds of Language

Photo Peekers

Glue photos inside a manila folder. Cut small windows (cut only three sides to make a flap) in the top of the folder so children can lift and peek at the photos. You can also glue one large photo inside and let the children try to guess who or what is in the photos by looking through the small windows cut in the top of the folder.

Theme Connections

Discovery

Photo Roll-Overs

Glue photos to empty salt or oatmeal containers. Laminate with clear contact paper. Encourage the children to roll the containers to see the photos on all sides. Young

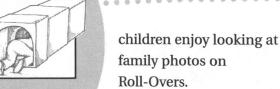

children enjoy looking at family photos on Roll-Overs.

Theme Connections

Families
Growing Up

Pick a Pair of Pears

Cut a treetop shape from green poster board and a trunk from brown poster board. Laminate them and mount them on the wall. Place Velcro circles on the tree. Cut pears from yellow construction paper. Cut pictures from magazines of pairs of items that go together such as a sock and a shoe, or things that rhyme such as a sock and a rock. Glue the pictures on the pears. Laminate the pears and glue the other pieces of the Velcro circle on the back of the pears. Place the pears on the tree and invite the children to pick a pair of pears.

Theme Connections

Food
Growing Things
Nature
Rhymes and Rhyming

Pin the Nose on the Pumpkin

Cut a large pumpkin out of orange butcher paper and add eyes and a mouth. Cut noses out of black construction paper and put a piece of masking tape on the back of it. Invite the children to play Pin the Nose on the Pumpkin just like they would Pin the Tail on the Donkey.

Theme Connections

Holidays
Humor

Plastic Spinning Tops

Use a pushpin tack (adults only) to push a hole through the middle of a small plastic lid (such as a potato chip can lid). Insert a toothpick through the hole to create a top. Invite the children to have a "longest spinning top" contest.

Theme Connections

Discovery
Movement

Prop Boxes

Cover copy paper boxes to create prop storage containers. Below is a list of suggestions for items to go in thematic prop boxes.

Cooking—pots, pans, aprons, rolling pins, salt shakers, tablecloth, egg beater, wooden spoons, basters, funnels, and measuring cups and spoons

Farmer—seeds, shovel, rake, hoe, sun hat, bandana, and coveralls

Firefighter—short hose, spotted stuffed dog, raincoats, boots, and bell

Florist—plastic flowers, vases, ribbon, signs, tape, scissors, order forms, cash register, phone, and wrapping paper

Grocery Store—cash register, play money, pencils, paper sacks, food containers, small scale, berry baskets, plastic fruits and vegetables, and aprons

Hair Salon—hair dryer without a cord, brushes, combs, curlers, mirrors, telephone, hair nets, empty make-up containers, empty shampoo and conditioner containers, empty spray containers, ribbons, play money, and wigs (**Safety Warning:** Make sure all items are kept clean)

Hospital—stethoscope, syringes, towels, scales, small doctor bag, tongue depressors, bandages, blankets, rubber gloves, flashlight, eye chart, Band-Aids, cotton balls, masks, uniforms, and hats

Housekeeping—empty spray bottles, duster, broom, dustpan, whisk broom, sponges, towels, and soap

Mail Carrier—envelopes, stickers to use as stamps, hats, boxes, brown paper, pens, paper, small scale, index card file, stamp pads, and sacks and cartons to hold mail

Mechanic—tools, coveralls, tire pump, rags, flashlight, gloves, funnel, and supply catalog

Police Officer—badges, hats, notepads, horn to use as radar machine, and whistles

Puppets

■ Bag Puppets

Draw a face on a small paper bag.

■ Cup Puppets

Dog—Cut a hole large enough to fit a finger in the side of a paper cup. Lay the cup on its side with the hole on the bottom. Use construction paper scraps and felt-tip markers to add facial features to the cup, making the flat end of the cup the nose of the puppet. Put the puppet on a finger and use it to tell a story or sing a song.

Jack-in-the-Box—Stick a plastic straw into a 2" Styrofoam ball. Pull out the straw, drop some glue into the hole, and then replace the straw. Allow the glue to dry. Poke a hole in the bottom of a paper or Styrofoam cup. Hold the cup upright, and then stick the straw down through the cup and out the hole in the bottom. Decorate the Styrofoam ball with felt and yarn to make a jack-in-the-box face. Say the following rhyme using the puppet as a prop.

Jack-in-the-Box
Jack-in-the-box
Oh, so still.
Won't you come out?
Yes, I will.

You can make other cup puppets by attaching your illustrations to a straw as described in the example on the previous page. For example, "Itsy Bitsy Spider" works great as a cup puppet.

■ Empty Toilet Paper Tube Puppets
Decorate a toilet paper tube with markers, felt, and yarn to make a puppet.

■ Fingertip Puppets
Cut off the fingers of a glove. Use permanent markers to add facial features to each glove fingertip. Glue on yarn hair.

■ Foot Puppets
Draw a face on the bottom of each of your toes. Use your toes for almost any of the counting rhymes that focus on the number five, such as "Five Little Monkeys" or "This Little Piggy."

■ Glove Puppets
Make story characters and attach them to a glove with Velcro.

■ Hand Puppets
Draw a face on each child's hand with a washable marker. Draw eyes, a nose, and a mouth in the creases of the child's palm. Children can create several different expressions by stretching and moving their fingers.

■ Sock Puppets
Add eyes and a nose to an old sock.

■ Stick Puppets
Use tongue depressors to make stick puppets. Cut out story characters and glue them to tongue depressors, attach stickers to the tongue depressors, or use felt and markers to decorate a sponge and attach it to a tongue depressor.

■ Wooden Spoon Puppets
Draw facial features on a small wooden cooking spoon with a permanent marker. Add yarn for hair. For a necklace or collar, cut a circle of fabric or use a coffee filter to go around the neck of the puppet.

Puzzle Box Match-Ups

Trace several small objects such as a block, a crayon, a spoon, and so forth on the lid of a shoebox, then place the objects inside the box. Encourage the children to match the objects to their outlines.

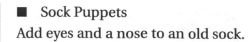
Theme Connections

Shapes

Rhyming Words Musical Chairs

Cut out simple pictures from magazines and glue them on to index cards. Use pictures of words that are easy to ryhme, such as cat, jar, sand, and so on. Place four chairs back to back, making two lines of chairs. Place one of the rhyming word cards on each chair. When the music stops, the children pick up the card in their chair and sit down. Have each child then say a word that rhymes with the picture that is in his or her hand. If the child says a correct word, he or she remains in the game. If the child says an incorrect word, he or she is out of the game. Continue the game until each of the children has had a chance to find a rhyming word for as many cards as possible.

Theme Connections

Humor
Music
Rhymes and Rhyming

Ring Toss

Make a ring-toss game. For stakes, fill two 2-liter soda bottles with water or sand. Secure the lids with glue or tape. Make rings by cutting the centers out of 5-pound coffee-can lids. Invite teams of children to take turns tossing rings onto the bottles.

Theme Connections

Shapes
Movement

Sand Combs

Cut three or four pieces of poster board or cardboard into 3" x 6" strips. Cut teeth in one 6" side of each strip. Cut V-shaped triangular teeth in one and square teeth in another. Cutting scallops in another will give the teeth a circular look. Encourage the children to rake the combs through the sand to create patterns.

Theme Connections

Oceans and Seas
Shapes

Scarf Pull

Tie several scarves together to make one long scarf. Cut a slit in an oatmeal box and stuff the scarf inside, pull one end through the slit, and place the lid on the box. Encourage little ones to pull the scarf through the slit.

Theme Connections

Colors
Discovery

The Complete Book of Activities, Games, Stories, Props, Recipes, and Dances

Scavenger Hunt

Photocopy several copies of the Scavenger Hunt List on page 310. Divide the children into three or four teams and give them a treasure collecting sack. Go over the items on the list to make sure each team recognizes the illustrations and then turn them loose to find the items. The first group to return with all the items wins.

Theme Connections

Discovery
Friends
Nature

Sensory Glove

Fill a latex glove with Gak (see recipe on page 251) or sand. Tie it off at the cuff and encourage the children to explore its weight and texture.

Theme Connections

Discovery
Senses

Shadow Match

Trace around several familiar objects such as a block, a spoon, a crayon, and a bell on black construction paper with white chalk. Cut out each outline and glue it to a sheet of

white construction paper or to the inside of a manila folder. Encourage the children to match the objects to their shadows.

Variation

Trace several small objects such as a block, a crayon, a spoon, and so forth on the lid of a shoebox, and then cut out the outlines. Place the objects inside the box for storage. Encourage the children to sort the objects by pushing the items through the correct cutout outlines.

Theme Connections

Shapes

Slot Drop Game

Cut a 1 ½" slit in the plastic lid of a coffee can. Place large buttons or poker chips in the can. Encourage the children to empty the can and then fill it again by pressing the chips through the slit.

Theme Connections

Counting
Movement
Shapes

Smell Puffs

Collect six powder puffs. Scent pairs of puffs with pleasant-smelling extracts such as peppermint, orange, and vanilla. Challenge the children to match the similarly scented puffs.

Theme Connections

Senses

Sound Canisters

Place paper clips, buttons, washers, pennies, and so forth inside potato chip cans or film canisters. Make two containers with each item and then invite the children to match the containers that make the same sound.

Theme Connections

Senses

Sound Match-Ups

Cut out pictures from magazines of things that make sounds, such as a telephone, a car, a whistle, someone clapping and so forth. Mount the pictures on cards and laminate them. Record the sounds that each item makes on a cassette tape. Encourage the children to listen to the tape and arrange the items in the sequence in which the sounds are heard on the tape.

Theme Connections

Senses

Sundial

Find a sunny spot on the playground. Push a 6' stick in the dirt so that it stands up straight. Draw a circle around the stick. Use a big rock to mark places around the circle where the shadow falls. Go outside and mark

The Complete Book of Activities, Games, Stories, Props, Recipes, and Dances

ACTIVITIES & PROPS

the new location of the shadow every couple of hours with a new rock. Lead the children to understand that the shadow moves with the passing of time. Tell the children that people used sundials before watches and clocks were invented. Show the children a clock and call their attention to how the big hand moves around it just as the shadow moves around the circle.

Theme Connections

Nature
Shapes
Sun, Moon, and Stars
Time of Day

Tactile Box

Cut a hand-size hole in the top or side of a shoebox. Fill the box with two or three items that are easily identified by touching. Invite the children to stick their hand through the hole in the box and identify the objects inside by feeling them.

Theme Connections

Discovery
Senses

Tactile Cylinders

Cover old-fashioned curlers with tactile fabric such as burlap, velvet, fur, satin, art foam, and felt. Use a hot glue gun for best

results (adults only). Encourage the children to match cylinders that feel the same.

Theme Connections

Discovery

Senses

Texture Glove

Glue a different fabric to each finger of a work glove. Use a variety of textures such as burlap, velvet, felt, satin, and so forth to enhance the sensory experience of comparing the textures.

Theme Connections

Senses

Thumb Harp

Stretch five to eight rubber bands of different widths around a Styrofoam meat or vegetable tray. Invite children to play a tune by placing their hands on the outside of the tray and plucking the rubber bands with their thumbs.

Theme Connections

Discovery
Music
Senses

Tic-Tac-Toe

Cut a 9" square of felt and glue it onto a 9" square of cardboard. Glue ribbon on the felt square to make a Tic-Tac-Toe grid. Use two colors of blocks or beads to play a game of Tic-Tac-Toe.

Theme Connections

Colors

Tone Bottles

Fill several glass bottles with varying amounts of water. Start by filling four bottles: one-quarter full, half full, three-quarters full, and completely full. Provide a stick for tapping the bottles. Challenge the children to arrange the bottles according to the pitch of the sound they hear when they tap the bottle. The highest pitch is the bottle with the least water, and the lowest pitch is the bottle with the most water. Now fill additional bottles with water levels in between the levels that you already have. Challenge children to arrange the bottles again by the pitch of the tone. After a little practice, cover the bottles with construction paper so that children are unable to see the water level and try this game again. Are they still able to get the right order?

Theme Connections

Discovery
Music
Senses

Tunnels of Fun

Cut an arch into two sides of three or four boxes Encourage the children to arrange the boxes from largest to smallest, connecting the arches, to make a tunnel. Invite the children to crawl through.

Theme Connections

Movement

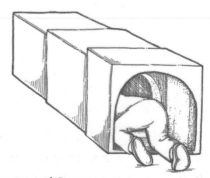

The Complete Book of Activities, Games, Stories, Props, Recipes, and Dances

Twirly Fish

Cut a sheet of copy paper into 1" strips. Fold each strip in half. On both ends of each strip, cut a 1/2" slit about an inch from the end and on opposite sides so that the two ends can slip together. Don't fold the crease. When the children drop their fish from chest height, they will twirl all the way to the floor.

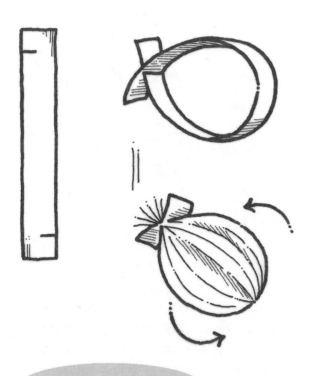

Theme Connections

Fish
Oceans and Seas

Twister

Cut a shower curtain liner in half. Cut out one pair of feet and handprints from yellow, red, and blue contact paper and stick them onto the shower curtain liner. Cover a small milk carton with contact paper. Cut out small matching hands and feet from the contact paper and stick to all six sides of the carton to make a die.

Theme Connections

Colors
Humor
Movement

Water Transfer Fun

Glue an empty pill canister and a sponge to the inside bottom of a Styrofoam meat tray. Fill the canister with water. Invite the children to use an eyedropper to remove the water from the canister and drop it onto the sponge. When all the water has been removed, show them how to squeeze the sponge to release the water into the bottom of the meat tray. They can then use the eyedropper to put the water back into the canister.

Theme Connections

Discovery

Wave Machine

Fill clear plastic bottles one-quarter full with mineral oil or clear vegetable oil. Finish filling with denatured alcohol and a few drops of blue or green food coloring. Glue the lids on securely and invite the children to rotate the bottle to create waves. Individual wave machines can be made using 20-ounce bottles. A 1-liter bottle makes a nice wave machine for the science center.

Theme Connections

Colors
Discovery
Oceans and Seas

Weaving Looms

■ Loom 1

Cut ½" notches in both ends of a Styrofoam meat tray. Cut a yard of yarn. Tape one end of the yarn to the back of the meat tray and wind the other end around the meat tray using the notches to hold it in place. Cut the end of the yarn and tape it to the back of the meat tray. Invite children to weave pipe cleaners, or strips of rickrack, ribbon, or lace through the yarn.

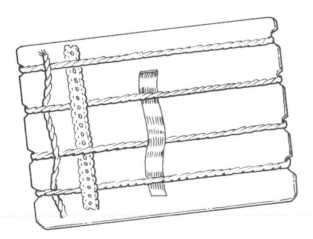

■ Loom 2

Staple 6 to 8 pieces of elastic across a piece of 8" x 11" cardboard. Place tape over the staples to cover sharp edges. Encourage the

children to weave strips of ribbon, lace, and yarn through the elastic.

Theme Connections

Colors
Senses

Wind Chimes

Encourage the children to string buttons on strips of yarn and then tie each strip of yarn to a coat hanger to create wind chimes. Seashells can be used instead of buttons if you have access to shells that have a natural hole in them.

Theme Connections

Music
Oceans and Seas
Senses
Weather

The Complete Book of Activities, Games, Stories, Props, Recipes, and Dances

Wrap-Around Patterns

Children need to learn that not all patterns make continuous horizontal and vertical lines. Cut a piece of felt (or paper) into an 8" x 8" square. Make a grid of 16 2" boxes on the square. Give the children beads, buttons, or color tile with which to make a pattern. If they make an ABC pattern such as red, blue, green, red, blue, green, they will notice that they will have to turn a corner in order to keep the pattern going.

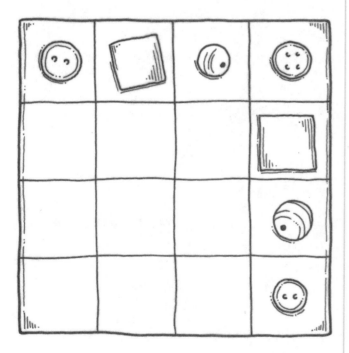

Theme Connections

Alphabet
Colors
Shapes

Yes/No Questions

Glue pictures of animals on sheets of 12" x 18" construction paper. Stack the pictures face down. Have one child draw the top picture and without looking at it, hold it in front of him or her. Then have the child ask the other children questions to determine which animal he or she is holding. The children can only answer "yes" or "no" to questions.

Theme Connections

Animals
Discovery
Friends

Games

The Complete Book of Activities, Games, Stories, Props, Recipes, and Dances

Amazing Mazes

Create a maze with boxes, chairs, sheets, and pillows. Encourage children to navigate the maze.

Theme Connections

Movement

Baby Chicks

Designate one child to be the "hen." The remaining children are the "chickens." The hen and chickens act out the rhyme as they sing or recite it.

The Baby Chicks

Baby chicks are singing "Pío, pío, pío,
Mama we are hungry, Mama we are cold."
Mama looks for wheat, Mama looks for corn,
Mama feeds them dinner, Mama keeps
  them warm.
Under mama's wings sleeping in the hay,
Baby chicks all huddle until the next day.

Spanish Translation

Los Pollitos

Los pollitos dicen, "Pío, pío, pío,
Cuando tienen hambre, cuando tienen
  frío."
La galena busca el maíz y el trigo,
Les da la comida y les presta abrigo.

Theme Connections

Chickens
Families
Farms

Back Thing

Hold an empty paper towel tube against your chest. Encourage the children to chase you around the room. Suddenly, change the game by turning around and holding the empty paper towel tube out toward the children. Say, "Back thing!" This is the signal for the children to turn and run from you. When you catch them start the game over. Hide the tube against your chest and run from the children.

Theme Connections

Humor
Movement

Back-to-Back Building

Invite two children to sit back to back. Give them identical sets of blocks. Encourage one child to build something and describe it to the other child, who then tries to copy it. How similar are the two structures? How could the directions be clearer? As a variation, ask two children to build while you give instructions.

Theme Connections

Movement
Self-Esteem
Work

Back-to-Back Lifts

Invite the children to choose partners. Ask partners to sit back to back on the floor. On the count of three, partners help each other stand, keeping their backs together and pushing against each other.

Theme Connections

Friends
Movement
Self-Esteem

Ball Rolling

Have children sit in a circle on the floor with their legs spread. Have one child begin the game by calling a friend's name and then rolling a ball across the circle to that child. Continue the game until all the children have had a turn.

Theme Connections

Friends
Shapes

Bead in a Bucket

Invite the children to try to drop a bead into a bucket. Place felt or foam in the bottom of the bucket to reduce the noise.

Theme Connections

Colors
Movement
Shapes

Bead Pick Up

Have the children take off their shoes and socks and pick up stringing beads from a box with their toes and drop them into a bucket.

Theme Connections

Humor
Movement
Parts of the Body
Shapes

Beanbag Games

■ **Balance on the Balance Beam**

Encourage the children to walk the balance beam with a blue beanbag on their heads.

Theme Connections

Movement
Parts of the Body

■ **Off or On**

Place a piece of paper in the middle of the floor. Invite children to toss a beanbag to land on the paper. Have them record with tally marks how many times their beanbag lands on the paper and how many times it lands off the paper.

Theme Connections

Counting
Movement
Numbers

■ **Ring the Bell**

Provide beanbags and a service bell. Challenge the children to stand several feet away from the service bell, take aim, and fire the beanbag to ring the bell.

Theme Connections

Movement
Spatial Relationships

■ **Zap the Zone**

Divide a piece of poster board into four areas or zones. Color each zone a different color. Place corresponding colored dots on several index cards. Turn the cards over like a deck of cards. Provide a beanbag and challenge children to draw a card, and then toss the beanbag to land on the corresponding color zone on the poster board.

Theme Connections

Colors

Blanket Fun

Have the children stand around the perimeter of a large blanket or sheet and hold tight to its edges. Instruct them to raise their arms quickly and forcefully over their heads. The force will raise the blanket and the blanket will catch the air. Invite groups of children to run under the blanket. For

example, you might send all the boys under the blanket or all the children who are wearing red. For another game place balls or balloons on top of the blanket and toss them. Try raising and lowering the blanket to music.

Theme Connections

Colors
Movement
Spatial Relationships

Block Busters

Help the children make a set of large, soft blocks by stuffing newspaper into large grocery sacks and sealing them closed with masking tape. Then invite the children to build a tower or a wall with the blocks and take turns knocking it down by tossing a beanbag from about six feet away.

Theme Connections

Humor
Movement
Occupations
Shapes

Broad Jumps

Place a piece of masking tape on the ground. Encourage the children to stand behind the line of tape and jump as far as they can. Mark the length of their jumps with a beanbag or block. Challenge each child to jump a distance that is equal to his or her own height.

Theme Connections

Movement
Spatial Relationships

Cat and Mouse

This is a simple game of chase with you or one child being the Cat and the rest of the children being Mice. The Cat chases the Mice. The Mouse who is tagged becomes the next Cat. You might also use the rhyme, "Old Gray Cat" (see page 79) to play a version of this game.

Theme Connections

Cats
Mice
Movement

Che Che Koolay

Have the children form a large circle around the leader, who stands in the middle of the circle. The leader speaks each line of the following chant, and the children repeat the line in an echo fashion. At the end of the chant, the leader tries to tag one of the children. The children may get up and run when the leader gets up, but not before. The tagged child becomes leader for the next game.

Che-che-koo-lay (leader places hands on head)
Che-che-koo-lay (children copy)

Che-che-ko-fi-sa (leader places hands on shoulders)
Che-che-ko-fi-sa (children copy)

Ko-fi-sa-lan-ga (leader places hands on hips)
Ko-fi-sa-lan-ga (children copy)

Ca-ca-shi-lan-ga (leader falls to the ground)
Ca-ca-shi-lan-ga (children copy)
Koom-ma-dei-day (leader jumps up and tries to tag another child)
Koom-ma-dei-day (children jump up and run)

Theme Connections

Movement
Sounds of Language

Circle Relays

■ **Art Relay:** Divide the children into groups. Give each group a piece of paper, and each child in each group a crayon. Assign each group an object to draw, for example, a house. The first child in each group draws part of the house and then passes it to the

next child to add something to the picture. The group who finishes their drawing first wins.

Theme Connections

Colors
Shapes

■ **Beanbag Relay:** Divide the children into two groups. Give each group a beanbag. Ask the children to cup their hands. Give the beanbag to the first child in each group and have him hold it in his cupped hands. On your command, encourage the children to pass the beanbag by receiving it in their cupped hands and dumping it into the cupped hands of the child next to them.

Theme Connections

Colors
Senses

■ **Movement Relay:** Divide the class into three or four groups. Create a series of movements such as touch your toes, clap your hands, and put your hands on your head. Have one child in each group repeat the pattern and then signal the next child with a tap on the shoulder. See which group can finish the activity first.

Theme Connections

Movement

■ **Stringing Beads Relay:** Divide the children into groups. Give each group a string and each child a bead. Have the first child string his or her bead and then pass the string to the next child. The group that strings all their beads first wins.

Theme Connections

Shapes

Clue

Hide an object and then give clues as to where to find it. This is a great game for helping children learn positional and spatial vocabulary.

Theme Connections

Senses
Spatial Relationships

Cooperative Musical Circle

This game is a variation of Musical Chairs. Make a circle on the floor with masking tape. Play a piece of music. Encourage the children to walk around the circle until the music stops. When the music stops everyone steps into the circle. The idea is to get everyone inside the circle so everyone wins. Continue playing for as long as the children are interested.

Theme Connections

Friends
Movement
Music
Shapes

Copycat

Two children stand face-to-face. One child creates actions and makes faces. The second child mimics the faces and actions.

Theme Connections

Friends
Humor

Creep and Crawl

Use masking tape to make a crooked line across the floor. Have children crawl the length of the line. Have them try to move down the line like a snake (without using hands and feet). Can they do it?

Theme Connections

Movement
Snakes

Dog and Bone

Children sit in a circle. One child, who is IT, walks around the outside of the circle, carrying a paper or plastic bone. Eventually IT drops the bone behind a child. That player picks up the bone and chases IT around the circle. If she taps IT before they get around the circle, IT goes to the "doghouse" (center of the circle). If she doesn't, IT takes her place in the circle. The player with the bone becomes the new IT and the game continues.

Theme Connections

Dogs
Movement

Don't Let the Ball Fall

Have the children stand in a circle. Challenge the children to toss a ball to someone else in the circle without letting the ball fall.

Theme Connections

Friends
Movement
Shapes

Dreidel

Each player puts one token (for example, nuts, raisins, marbles, toothpicks, pennies) in the pot (bowl). One player spins a dreidel. If the dreidel lands on "N," the player receives nothing. If it lands on "G," the player receives all the tokens in the pot. If it lands on "H," the player gets half. If the player lands on "S," the player adds two tokens to the pot. The game continues until one player has won all the tokens. You may sing "My Dreidel" while playing the game. See page 30 for directions for making a dreidel.

My Dreidel
I have a little dreidel,
I made it out of clay;
And when it's dry and ready,
Then dreidel I shall play.

Chorus
Oh dreidel, dreidel, dreidel,
I made it out of clay;

Oh dreidel, dreidel, dreidel,
Now dreidel I shall play.

It has a lovely body,
With legs so short and thin;
And when it is all tired.
It drops and then I win.

Chorus

Theme Connections

Holidays

Drop the Clothespin

Set a coffee can on the floor. Give each child five or six clothespins with a goal of getting three of them into the can. Begin by asking the children to hold the clothespins waist high. As the children get better at hitting their target, challenge them to hold the clothespins chest high. You can change the name and directions of this game to reflect your theme. For example, if you are studying food you can make playdough cookies and provide a mixing bowl to play Drop the Cookie. If the children are studying shapes, you can play Drop the Shape by dropping different shape blocks, such as rectangles, into containers of different shapes, such as cardboard boxes.

Theme Connections

Colors
Food
Movement
Shapes

The Complete Book of Activities, Games, Stories, Props, Recipes, and Dances

Drop the Handkerchief

Choose one child to be IT while the other children sit in a circle facing the center. The child who is IT skips or walks around the outside of the circle and drops the handkerchief casually behind one of the children sitting in the circle. This child picks up the handkerchief and chases IT around the circle. "IT" tries to run around the circle and sit in the second child's spot without being tagged. If IT is not tagged, then he sits in his new spot in the circle and the child with the handkerchief is now IT. If IT is tagged, then he is "IT" for another round.

When studying colors, you can make this game fit into your theme by using the same color handkerchief that matches the color on which you are focusing. For example, on "green" day, use a green handkerchief.

Variation

Use a thematic object, such as a circle for shapes, a yellow handkerchief for teaching the color yellow, and so on, instead of a handkerchief.

Theme Connections

Colors
Humor
Movement
Shapes

Duck, Duck, Goose

Children sit in a circle. One child—IT—walks around the outside of the circle, tapping each player on the head and saying, "Duck." Eventually IT taps a player and says, "Goose" instead. The tapped player gets up and

chases IT around the circle. If the player taps IT before he or she gets around the circle, the player gets to go back to his or her place. If the player doesn't tap IT before he or she gets around the circle, the player becomes the new IT and the game continues. You can change the name of this game to reflect your theme. For example, if you are studying bugs you can call this game Caterpillar, Caterpillar, Butterfly.

Theme Connections

Ducks
Geese
Movement

Eeny, Meeny, Miney, Mo

Use this chant to determine who is going to be the first one to do an activity. Point to a child on each word. The child you are pointing to on the last word ("Mo") is the child selected.

> *Eeny, Meeny, Miney, Mo*
> *Catch a child by the toe.*
> *If she (he) hollers,*
> *Let her (him) go,*
> *Eeny, Meeny, Miney, Mo*

Theme Connections

Rhymes and Rhyming

Eye Winker

Suit actions to words.

> *Eye winker,* (point to eye)
> *Tom tinker,* (touch ears)
> *Nose smeller,* (touch nose)
> *Mouth eater,* (touch mouth)
> *Chin chopper,* (tap chin)
> *Chin chopper,* (tap chin again)
> *Chin chopper chin.* (tap chin three times)

Theme Connections

Movement
Parts of the Body

Eyes Awake, Eyes Asleep

Give the children nine ½" wiggle eyes and a paper plate. Have the children take turns

dropping the eyes onto the plate. After each drop, the children should count the eyes "awake" (facing up) and the eyes "asleep" (eyes facing down). The child who drops the eyes can predict which kind of eyes will have a higher count.

Theme Connections

Counting
Naptime/Sleeping
Parts of the Body

Fact or Fantasy

Make a statement and let children vote on the statement as fact (true) or fantasy (not true). For example, "Dogs wag their tails when they are happy," or "Cows have three ears."

Theme Connections

Friends
Humor
Self-Esteem

Feather Race

Use masking tape to make start and finish lines about 4" apart. Place two feathers on the start line. Provide straws, a paper towel tube, paper plates, and basters to use as pushers. Invite two children to each choose a "pusher" and then attempt to use their "pusher" to move the feather from the start

to the finish line. They cannot touch the feather with their pusher. The first child to get the feather to the finish line is the winner and can then compete against another challenger.

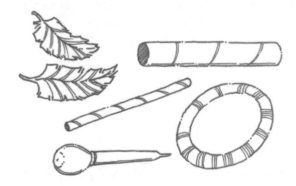

Theme Connections

Birds
Humor
Senses

Fitness Patterns

Perform a pattern of exercises, such as four jumping jacks, two knee bends, four touch-your-toes, and two side bends. Encourage the children to move with you. Invite volunteers to lead other combinations.

Theme Connections

Growing Up
Health and Safety
Movement
Parts of the Body
Self-Esteem

Flashlight Tag

Darken the room. Select one child to be IT and give him or her a flashlight. Players are caught when IT shines a flashlight on them.

Theme Connections

Movement
Senses
Time of Day

Flying Statues

This game requires adult participation. The adult holds hands with a child and then swings that child around in a circle. After a couple of time around, the adult lets go of the child's hand and the child freezes in his or her landing position.

Theme Connections

Humor
Movement

Follow the Leader

Select one child to be the leader. The other children line up behind the first child and copy her movements.

Theme Connections

Humor
Self-Esteem

The Freeze

Play music and have children dance around. When the music stops the children freeze like statues. Stop the music several times.

Theme Connections

Movement
Music
Seasons

Freeze Tag

Play this game with six to eight players. One child is selected to be IT. IT chases the other children. When IT tags a child that child must freeze. When all the children have been tagged, a new IT is selected and the game begins again.

Theme Connections

Movement
Seasons

Fruit Basket Turn Over

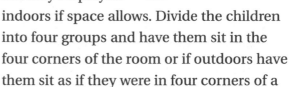

This game is best played outdoors but may be played indoors if space allows. Divide the children into four groups and have them sit in the four corners of the room or if outdoors have them sit as if they were in four corners of a

room. Label the groups: bananas, apples, oranges, and grapes. Give the "apples" a piece of red construction paper to sit on, the "bananas" a yellow sheet, the "oranges" an orange sheet, and the "grapes" a purple sheet. Select a child to be IT. Have IT stand in the center of the groups, close his or her eyes, and then say, "Fruit basket turn over." Each group of children must change the group they are in and become another type of fruit. They must find a seat in the new group. IT tries to catch a child before he or she is able to sit down. If he or she catches another child, that child becomes the new IT. If not, IT is IT again.

Theme Connections

Colors
Food
Humor
Movement

The Complete Book of Activities, Games, Stories, Props, Recipes, and Dances

Go and Stop

Ask the children to say their name as you point to them. Go quickly around the circle and have each child say his or her name. Tell the children that when you say, "Go!" you want them to say their names. Practice a couple of times. Ask the children to say their names repeatedly when you say, "Go!" and then stop saying their names when you say, "Stop!" (Example: Go! "John, John, John, John, John" Stop!) Repeat until the children are following directions well and starting and stopping at the correct time. Compliment the children on their listening abilities when they are able to follow directions.

Variation

Invite children to play the Go and Stop game blindfolded or with their eyes closed. Explain that sometimes we are able to listen better when looking at things around us does not distract us. Choose a child to be IT. Blindfold IT (some children may feel more comfortable just closing and covering their eyes with their hands). Whisper one of the other children's names into ITs ear. Say, "Go!" and have the children chant their own names. Walk IT around the circle to listen for the name that you whispered. Have the blindfolded child stop in front of the child who is chanting the appropriate name. Repeat this activity so as many children as possible can eventually have a turn being IT.

Theme Connections

Opposites
Senses
Sounds of Language

Gossip

Sit children in a circle. Ask a child to select a word or a phrase and whisper it into the ear of the child sitting on her right. That child then whispers what he heard into the ear of the child to his right. Continue around the circle until all the children have heard the word or phrase. Invite the last child to say what he heard out loud. Is it what the first child said? Continue the game for as long as the children show an interest in playing.

Theme Connections

Movement
Senses
Sounds of Language

Guessing Game

Glue animal pictures on some index cards to create Guessing Game playing cards. Invite a child to draw a card and act out the movements and antics of the animal they have drawn. When someone guesses the correct animal, he or she can have the next turn.

Theme Connections

Animals
Movement

Grass Tug of War

Have the children select a partner. Ask each child to pick a blade of grass. One child makes a loop of grass from the blade, and his or her partner threads his or her grass blade through the loop. Children hold their grass blades by the ends, and pull gently until one blade breaks. The player whose blade of grass did not break earns a point (use a counter or make tally marks). Play continues until children tire of the game. The child with the most points wins the game.

Theme Connections

Counting
Nature

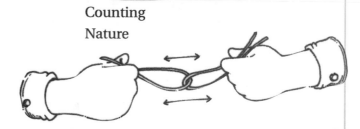

Groundhog

by Jackie Silberg

Have the children sit on the floor in a circle. Tell them the groundhog story. Explain that some people believe that if the groundhog sees its shadow when it comes out of hibernation on February 2, there will be six more weeks of winter. Cut out one sun and one cloud from construction paper for each child. Have the children sit in a circle on the floor. Designate one child to be the "groundhog," who sits in the middle of the circle (in the groundhog hole) with his or her eyes closed. The other children watch the teacher for directions: if the teacher holds up a sun, the children hold up their suns; if the teacher holds up a cloud, the children hold up their clouds. Ask the "groundhog" to open his or her eyes. If the groundhog sees clouds, then he or she chooses a child (a shadow) to be the next groundhog. If the groundhog sees suns, then he or she stays in the groundhog hole (middle of the circle) and hides his or her eyes again. Teach the children the rhyme below and encourage them to say the correct verse as each round of the game is played.

Groundhog, Groundhog
Groundhog, Groundhog come on out and
*   play.*
It's a beautiful, beautiful February day.
The sun is shining and the sky is blue.
Won't you come on out?
I want to play with you.

Groundhog, Groundhog
come on out and play.
It's a gloomy, gloomy
February day.
The air feels chilly and the
sky is gray.
Won't you come on out?
I want to play with you.

Heel to Toe

Challenge the children to walk heel to toe around the playground. How many steps does it take? How long does it take? Try walking around the perimeter with regular steps. How are you going to walk if you are in a hurry?

Theme Connections

Movement
Parts of the Body

Heel to Toe Race

Make two 12' masking tape lines on the floor. Have two children race each other heel to toe down the line.

Theme Connections

Movement
Parts of the Body

Here Sits a Monkey

Ask the children to form a circle around a selected child who sits in a chair or on the floor in the middle of the circle. The children march or skip around the child, singing or chanting the rhyme below. When the words in the rhyme say "rise to your feet," the children stop marching and clap their hands only, while the center child rises and chooses someone from the circle to take his or her place in the chair. The game is repeated. Each new center child chooses a different animal to be, such as a giraffe, zebra, snake, or worm.

Oh, here sits a monkey in the chair, chair, chair,
She (he) lost all the true loves she (he) had last year,
So rise upon your feet and greet the first you meet, the prettiest girl (boy) I know.

Theme Connections

Monkeys
Movement

Hi, Cowboy! Hi, Cowgirl!

Ask the children to sit on the floor in a line. Select one child to be IT, and give him or her a cowboy hat to wear. IT sits at the front of the room with his or her back to all the other children. Point to a child sitting with the group, and have that child stand up and say, "Hi, cowboy!" or "Hi, cowgirl." Can IT identify the speaker?

Theme Connections

Cowboys/Cowgirls
Senses

Hide and Seek

One child is IT. All other players hide while IT counts to a certain number. At the end of the count, IT gives a warning by saying, "Ready or not, here I come!" and then seeks out the hiders.

Theme Connections

Movement
Senses

Hopscotch

Draw a Hopscotch grid on the sidewalk or floor with chalk. It is one square, one square, then two, then one, then two, then one, and finally two. Number the squares 1-10. Provide a chip or a rock. Children play this game one child at a time. The first child tosses the rock onto the first square of the grid, hops over that square, and then follows the pattern of the other squares, hopping on one foot and then jumping on two. At the

end of the grid the child turns around and hops and jumps the patterns back to start (still jumping over the square with the rock.) The next child then takes a turn. When it is the first child's turn again, she tosses the rock or chip onto the square with the "2" written on it and goes through the grid again hopping and jumping but not touching square number 2. The object of the game is to toss the chip onto each square during consecutive turns and execute the jumping and hopping pattern without putting a second foot down on single squares and without stepping in the square where the rock is.

Variation

Make triangles instead of squares for your design.

Theme Connections

Counting
Movement
Numbers
Shapes

The Complete Book of Activities, Games, Stories, Props, Recipes, and Dances

Hot and Cold

Two or more children can play this game. Select a child to be IT. Have IT choose a small object, such as a pinecone or a cookie cutter, for the other children to see. Then have the other children leave the room while IT hides the small object somewhere in the room. When the other children return to the room, they begin to hunt for the object. IT gives hints as to where the object is hidden by saying "cold" when no one is near the object, "warmer" when someone gets closer to the object, and "hot" when someone is very close. The child who finds the object is the next one to become IT.

Variation

Have the children select an item to be hidden. Ask IT to leave the room while the other children hide the item. When IT returns, the children give the "hot" and "cold" clues.

Theme Connections

Opposites
Senses

Hot Potato

Have the children sit in a circle and give them a beanbag. Ask them to pretend they are holding a hot potato. Play lively music as

the children pass the potato quickly around the circle. When you stop the music, the child holding the hot potato is out of the game. Continue until only one child is left.

Theme Connections

Food
Music
Senses

Hula Hoop Hop

Arrange several Hula Hoops in a path on the floor. Encourage the children to jump from the center of one hoop to the center of another.

Theme Connections

Movement
Shapes

Hula Hoop Toss

Suspend a Hula Hoop from the ceiling and challenge the children to toss beanbags through the hoop. You may also lay the Hula

Hoop on the floor and have children toss beanbags into the hoop from behind a line.

Theme Connections

Movement
Shapes

Hummers

Tape wax paper around a comb to make a hummer. Change the paper and let each child have a turn to "hum the hummer."

Theme Connections

Music

I Spy

Gather the children in a group and invite them to find items in the room. Choose easy-to-find things so children can have a high level of success as they first learn to play. Increase the difficulty as children become more familiar with the game.

Theme Connections

Senses

Ice Cubes

On a hot day give each child an ice cube. At a starting signal, challenge the children to

melt their ice cube. The first child to melt his or her ice cube is the winner. Children can blow on the ice, rub it in their hand, rub it on their clothing, crack it, and so forth. You may want to make a rule regarding putting the ice cube in the mouth.

Theme Connections

Senses

In and Out the Windows

Have the children stand in a circle holding hands with arms raised. Choose one child to weave in and out of the circle, walking under the raised arms of friends. Sing the following song.

Go in and out the windows.
Go in and out the windows.
Go in and out the windows.
As we have done before.

You can vary this game by having children crawl, hop, or jump in and out of the circle.

Theme Connections

Houses and Homes
Movement

Inch Worm Relays

Use masking tape to designate a start and a finish line. Demonstrate moving like an inch worm. Get down in a crawling position. Walk your hands out in front of you and then leaving your hands in position, walk your knees up to narrow the gap between hands and knees. Have children choose a partner to race and invite them to race each other moving like inch worms.

Theme Connections

Insects
Movement
Nature

Jack Be Nimble

Place a candlestick (block) in the middle of the play area. Have the children stand in a single file line about 10' from the candlestick. Invite the children to jump over the candlestick one at a time while reciting the verse, "Jack be nimble, Jack be quick, Jack jump over the candlestick." Children who

successfully jump the candlestick remain in the game. Those who don't are out of the game. You can raise the candlestick each round if you would like.

Theme Connections

Movement

Jump Rope Games

Teach the children to jump rope to chants and rhymes. For little ones you will need to play a modified jump rope game where two children hold opposite ends of a rope and swing it back and forth close to the ground instead of swinging it overhead. Here are some favorite chants and rhymes:

■ **Jump Rope Chants**

Tiny Tim
I had a little teddy bear; his name was
Tiny Tim.

*I put him in the bathtub to see if he could
  swim.*
*He drank up all the water; he ate up all
  the soap.*
*I had to call the doctor 'bout the bubble
  in his throat.*
In came the doctor; in came the nurse.
In came the lady with the alligator purse.
"Penicillin!" said the doctor.
"Penicillin!" said the nurse.
*"Penicillin!" said the lady with the
  alligator purse.*
*Out walked the doctor; out walked the
  nurse.*
*Out walked the lady with the alligator
  purse.*

A favorite type of rope-jumping chant ends
with counting numbers until the jumper
stops jumping.

Cinderella
Cinderella dressed in yella,
Went upstairs to kiss a fella.
Made a mistake and kissed a snake.
How many doctors did it take?
1, 2, 3, 4, 5…

Grace
Grace, Grace, dressed in lace,
Went upstairs to powder her face.
How many boxes did she use?
1, 2, 3, 4, 5…

Hen in a Tree
I saw a white hen up in a tree,
And all at once she laid an egg on me.
How many eggs did she lay?
1, 2, 3, 4, 5…

How Many Letters
Every morning at eight o'clock,
You can hear the postman knock.
Up jumps Johnny to open the door,
One letter, two letters, three letters, four,
5, 6, 7, 8, 9…

Mary in the Bathtub
Every night at half past ten,
Mary takes a bath again.
She scrubs her back and soaps her skin.
How many minutes is Mary in?
1, 2, 3, 4, 5…

Mouse in the Meadow
*Down in the meadow on a bright summer
  day,*
I saw a little mouse sneezing in the hay.
How many time did she sneeze?
1, 2, 3, 4, 5…

The Complete Book of Activities, Games, Stories, Props, Recipes, and Dances

Postman

*Postman, postman, do
your duty.
Here comes America's
bathing beauty.
How many letters did she get?
1, 2, 3, 4, 5…*

Some chants are called out in increasing speed. The word that the jumper stumbles on is supposed to be the jumper's future career, type of clothing, or type of house.

Rich Girl/Boy

*Rich girl (or boy), poor girl (or boy),
Beggar man, thief,
Doctor, lawyer, merchant, chief.
Calico, rags, silk, or yarn.
Little house, big house, pigpen, barn.*

These chants direct the jumper to follow certain directions while jumping.

Mrs. Brown

*I went to town to see Mrs. Brown.
She gave me a nickel to buy myself a pickle.
The pickle was sour, so she gave me a flower.
The flower was green, so she gave me some
    cream.
The cream was hard, so she gave me a card.
The card read: HOT PEPPERS!!!* (Twirl
    rope fast until the jumper misses.)

Spanish Dancer

*Spanish dancer, clap your hands low.
Spanish dancer, touch your toe.
Spanish dancer, do high kicks.
Spanish dancer, do the splits.*

Strawberry Shortcake

*Strawberry shortcake, huckleberry pie; I
have to keep jumping until you make a
try.* (Keep jumping until next player
jumps in.)

Teddy Bear

*Teddy bear, teddy bear, turn around.
Teddy bear, teddy bear, touch the ground.
Teddy bear, teddy bear, jump up high.
Teddy bear, teddy bear, wave goodbye.*

These chants direct the player to jump out at the end of the rhyme.

Orange Marmalade

*Orange marmalade and huckleberry jam.
I'm going to marry a Minnesota man.
He'll be sweet and just a little stout.
Anytime we want to, we'll eat dinner
OUT!*

Soda Crackers

*Fresh and salty soda crackers
Fell down in the goo.
Dirty, grimy soda crackers,
OUT goes Y-O-U!*

Teddy Bear

*Teddy bear, teddy bear, do the kangaroo.
Teddy bear, teddy bear, show your shoe.
Teddy bear, teddy bear, count to two.
Teddy bear, teddy bear—OUT, skidoo!*

Three Geese
Wire briar, limber lock;
Three geese flying in a flock.
One flew east; one flew west;
One flew over the cuckoo's nest.
O-U-T spells OUT!

Theme Connections

Counting
Humor
Movement
Numbers
Rhymes and Rhyming

Kagome
(Japan)

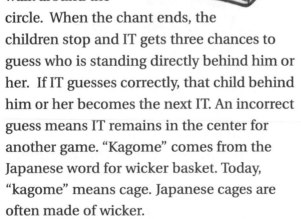

Children stand in a circle, holding hands to form a "cage." One child, who is IT, stands blindfolded in the center of the circle. As the chant is spoken, the children walk around the circle. When the chant ends, the children stop and IT gets three chances to guess who is standing directly behind him or her. If IT guesses correctly, that child behind him or her becomes the next IT. An incorrect guess means IT remains in the center for another game. "Kagome" comes from the Japanese word for wicker basket. Today, "kagome" means cage. Japanese cages are often made of wicker.

Kagome, kagome,
Kago no naka no tori wa,
Itsu Itsu deyaru?
Yoake no nan ni,
Tsuru to Kame to subetta.
Ushirono shomen daare?

Theme Connections

Movement
Senses
Sounds of Language

The Little Ants

This is a follow-the-leader game. You can play it with children in a line and the leader in front or with children in a circle and the leader in the middle.

Little Ants by Pam Schiller
(Tune: This Old Man)

Little ants are marching by,
In a line that's mighty long.
With a hip, hop, happy, hi,
Won't you join my song?
Little ants are marching on.

Little ants are hopping by,
In a line that's mighty long.
With a hip, hop, happy, hi,
Won't you join my song?
Little ants are hopping on.

Little ants are waving by,
In a line that's mighty long.
With a hip, hop, happy, hi,
Won't you join my song?

Spanish Translation

Las hormigas
(Tune: This Old Man)
Las hormigas al marchar,
en una fila sin fin,
van diciendo: ¡hola,
ven aquí a cantar!
y no dejan de marchar

Las hormigas al saltar,
en una fila sin fin,
van diciendo: ¡hola,
ven aquí a cantar!
y no dejan de saltar.

Las hormigas al saludar,
en una fila sin fin,
van diciendo: ¡hola,
vente aquí a cantar!
¡y saludan sin parar!

Theme Connections

Insects
Movement

Leap Frog

Select one child to be the "frog." Have the other children get on the floor on their hands and knees and crouch down. Invite the "frog" to leap over the children by

placing her hands on the back of each child for support while she straddles her legs around their body.

Theme Connections

Frogs
Humor
Movement

Lily Pad Hop

Cut large lily pads out of green vinyl fabric or poster board. Lay them on the floor about a foot apart in a path. Have the children jump from lily pad to lily pad like a frog. You can also draw lily pads on the sidewalk with green chalk and have the children jump from lily pad to lily pad.

Theme Connections

Colors
Frogs
Movement

Log Rollers

Place two 12' lengths of masking tape on the floor, parallel to each other and about 5' apart. Have children lie on the floor between the lines and roll from one end to the other while staying between the lines. It's not easy!

Theme Connections

Humor
Movement

London Bridge Is Falling Down

Choose two children to form the bridge. Between the two of them, they secretly decide which one will represent the gold and the other silver. They face each other, raise their arms above their heads, and join hands. The players form a single file line at one side of the bridge. Together they sing:

London Bridge is falling down,
Falling down, falling down.
London Bridge is falling down,
My fair lady.

While singing, the players march through the arch formed by the bridge players. At the words "My fair lady," the bridge players lower their arms over the player who happens to be standing underneath, taking him or her "prisoner." The bridge players whisper to the prisoner to choose gold or silver and place him or her on the gold or silver side of the bridge according to the choice.

The players march again through the succeeding verses of the song. A player is imprisoned with every "My fair lady."

Take the key and lock her up
Lock her up, lock her up.
Take the key and lock her up
My fair lady.

Build it up with iron bars…
Iron bars will rust away…
Build it up with steel and stone…
Steel and stone will bend and break…

Build it up with gold and silver…
Gold and silver will be stolen away…
Get a man to watch all night…
Suppose the man should fall asleep…

When all the players have been taken prisoner, the two teams (silver and gold) have a tug of war.

London Bridge/Este Puente
Este puente va a caer, a caer, a caer.
Este puente va a caer sobre éste(a).

Theme Connections

Friends
Movement

Marco Polo

Play this game outdoors in an open area. Select one child to be IT. Ask the rest of the children to close their eyes. IT chooses a spot to stand. Start the game by asking the children to call out "Marco" to which IT answers "Polo." Children use their listening skills to try to find IT with their eyes still closed. The first child to locate IT becomes the new IT.

Theme Connections

Movement
Senses

Milk Cap Towers

Collect plastic lids from milk bottles. Give the children the bottle caps and have them stack the lids as high as they can. The child with the highest tower wins the game.

Theme Connections

Humor
Occupations
Shapes

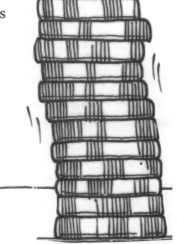

Monkey See, Monkey Do

One child is selected as the Lead Monkey. The Lead Monkey creates an action and the rest of the "monkeys" copy it.

Theme Connections

Humor
Monkeys
Movement

Mother, May I?

Play a teacher-directed game of "Mother, May I?" Call out to children one at a time, asking them to make animal movements (for example, puppy skips, cat jumps, horse gallops, and so on) toward you. Encourage children to make the sounds of the animals as they move.

Theme Connections

Movement
Sounds of Language

Musical Ball

Have the children stand in a circle facing the center. Give one child a ball and instruct that child to toss the ball to another child of his or her choice. Tell the children to keep the ball moving until the music stops. The child who is holding the ball when the music stops is out of the game until the next round.

Theme Connections

Humor
Movement
Music

Musical Chairs

Arrange chairs in two rows, back to back. Use one less chair than there are children playing the game. Start some music and have the children circle the chairs. When you stop the music, the children quickly find a chair and sit down. The child left without a chair is out. Continue the game, removing one or more chairs each round, until there are two children and one chair left. The child who gets the last chair wins.

Theme Connections

Movement
Music

Musical Hide and Seek

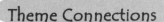

Hide a musical toy just out of sight and see if children can find it.

Theme Connections

Music
Senses

Mystery Voices

Record children's voices (one at a time) all saying the same thing on a cassette tape. Play the tape back and see if children can identify the speaker.

Theme Connections

Senses

Name Game

Challenge children to think of rhyming words that go with their names (nonsense words are okay). During the day try to use the children's names as rhyming riddles. For example, "Will the girl whose name rhymes with 'ham' pick up the blocks?"

Theme Connections

Rhymes and Rhyming

Name Game 2

During the first week of school play a game to help the children remember each other's names. Have the children sit in a circle. Go around the circle and let each child introduce himself or herself. Then let the children name as many friends as they can. Can anyone name everyone?

Theme Connections

Friends
Self-Esteem

Name That Tune

Select a child to be the first hummer. He or she selects a familiar tune and hums the first line. The other children try to guess what tune is being hummed. If one line is not enough, have the hummer hum a second and even a third and fourth line, if necessary. You may want to play this game with yourself as the hummer.

Theme Connections

Music
Senses

Nose Nudging

Place two pieces of masking tape on the floor 12' apart for a starting line and a finish line.

Place two Nerf® balls on the start line. Select two children to race each other. The children must move the ball from the start line to the finish line by nudging it with their nose.

Theme Connections

Humor
Movement
Parts of the Body

Octopus

Make two 20' masking tape or yarn lines about 20' to 25' apart to represent the edges of the ocean. Designate one child to be the "octopus." The rest of the children are fish. When the octopus yells "cross!" the fish attempt to move from one side of the ocean to the other without being tagged by the octopus. Any fish that is caught by the octopus becomes a "tentacle" and helps the octopus catch other fish. The tentacles must stand still and can only use their arms to tag a fish.

Theme Connections

Movement
Octopus
Parts of the Body

Officer, Will You Help Me Find My Child?

Select a child to be the police officer. Give a description of one of the children in the group to the police officer and see if the police officer can identify the child you are describing.

Theme Connections

Growing Up
Health and Safety
Occupations
Senses

Old Gray Cat

Suit actions to words.

The old gray cat is sleeping, sleeping, sleeping.
The old gray cat is sleeping in the house. (one child is Cat and curls up, pretending to sleep)

The little mice are creeping, creeping, creeping.
The little mice are creeping through the house. (other children are Mice creeping around sleeping Cat)

The old gray cat is waking, waking, waking.
The old gray cat is waking through the house. (Cat slowly sits up and stretches)

The old gray cat is chasing, chasing, chasing.
The old gray cat is chasing through the house. (Cat chases Mice)

All the mice are squealing, squealing, squealing.
All the mice are squealing through the house.
(Mice squeal; when Cat catches a Mouse, that Mouse becomes the Cat)

Theme Connections

Cats
Houses and Homes
Mice
Movement
Naptime/Sleeping
Sounds of Language

One Elephant

Children sit in a circle. One child places one arm out in front to make a trunk, and then walks around the circle while the group sings the following song. When the group sings "called for another elephant to come," the first child chooses another to become an "elephant." The first child extends her free hand between her legs to make a tail. The second child extends one arm to make a trunk and grabs hold of the first child's tail. The two walk trunk to tail as the song continues.

One Elephant
One elephant went out to play.
Out on a spider's web one day.

He had such enormous fun,
He called for another ele-
phant to come.

Two elephants…

Spanish Translation

Un Elefante
Un elefante se balanceaba
Sobre la tela de una arraria.
Como veía que resistía
Fue a llamar a otro elefante.

Dos elefantes…

Theme Connections

Counting
Elephants
Friends
Movement
Numbers

Paper Chase

Give each child a sheet of newspaper or tissue paper and ask them to wad up the papers into balls. Challenge children to toss the paper balls into the air and keep them aloft using their hands, head, knees, and other body parts.

Theme Connections

Humor
Movement

Pass the Penny

Ask children to stand or sit in a circle. Pass around a penny to music. When the music stops, whoever is holding the penny gets to keep it. Continue for several rounds. Who has the most pennies?

Theme Connections

Counting
Music
Numbers
Shapes

Pease Porridge Hot

Children clap hands with a partner in rhythm with the chant.

Pease porridge hot.
Pease porridge cold.
Pease porridge in the pot
Nine days old.

Some like it hot.
Some like it cold.
Some like it in the pot
Nine days old.

Theme Connections

Food
Rhymes and Rhyming

Pillowcase Race

Bring old pillowcases from home or get empty feedbags from local feed stores. Mark start and finish lines about 20' apart. Have the children step into a pillowcase, pull it up to the waist, and hop to the finish line.

Theme Connections

Humor
Movement

Ping-Pong Relay

Place two masking tape lines about 20' apart on the floor for start and finish lines. Divide children into two groups. Give each team a Ping-Pong ball and several objects, such as a straw, a baster, a cardboard tissue tube, and a book. Each team may use one of these objects to move the Ping-Pong ball across the finish line without actually touching the ball. For example, children might move the ball toward the finish line by blowing through the straw or by using air from the baster.

Theme Connections

Humor
Shapes

Pretzel Pass

Invite the children to stand or sit in a circle. Give each child a stick (straw, chopstick, or dowel rod). Place a large pretzel on every stick. Challenge the children to pass the pretzels around the circle using only their sticks. You can use any circular snack for this activity. When you finish the game, eat the pretzels!

Theme Connections

Food
Humor
Shapes

Pumpkin Roll Relay

Divide the children into two teams. For each team, have the children face each other in two parallel lines about 10' apart. Give each team a small pumpkin (or a pretend pumpkin, such as a ball). Instruct the first member of each team to roll the pumpkin to

the first team member standing in the opposite line. That person rolls the pumpkin across the distance to the team member standing second in line. Continue until all children on each team have had a turn.

Theme Connections

Holidays
Movement
Shapes

Punchinello

Children form a circle. One child is chosen to be Punchinello. Punchinello skips around the outside of the circle until the children sing the line "What can you do Punchinello, Punchinello?" Then Punchinello makes up an action such as jumping up and down, doing jumping jacks, or clapping his or her hands. The other children copy the action. In the next verse, Punchinello closes his or her eyes and turns in a circle with his or her arm extended with the index finger of the hand in a pointing position. At the end of the song, Punchinello stops turning and the child to whom Punchinello is pointing becomes the new Punchinello.

Punchinello (song or chant)
Here comes Punchinello, Punchinello.
Here comes Punchinello, funny you.
(children walk in a circle)

What can you do, Punchinello, Punchinello?
What can you do, Punchinello, funny

you? (child in the center of the circle initiates a movement)

We can do it, too, Punchinello, Punchinello.
We can do it, too, Punchinello, funny you.
(children in the circle copy the movement)

Who do you choose, Punchinello, Punchinello?
Who do you choose, Punchinello, funny you? (child in the center chooses another child to take her place)

Quarters in a Cup

Provide several quarters and a cup to toss them into. Challenge children to stand back several feet and attempt to toss the quarters into the cup.

Theme Connections

Movement
Spatial Relationships
Shapes

The Quiet Game

Gather the children in a circle and explain that you are going to play The Quiet Game. Explain that everyone must stay totally quiet and still. The first person to talk or to laugh loses the game. Try playing this game in teams. You can also ask one child to be the clown who is trying to make someone laugh.

Theme Connections

Friends
Humor
Senses

Rabbit

Select one child to be the rabbit and another to be the hunter. Divide the rest of the children into groups of three. Within these groups, two children hold hands to form a "rabbit hutch" and the third plays a rabbit inside the hutch. Begin the game by instructing the hunter to start chasing the rabbit without a home. After a little bit of chasing, the rabbit can decide to hide in a hutch by trading places with a rabbit in one of the hutches. The hunter then chases the new rabbit. If the hunter catches the rabbit, they switch roles. There are no losers or winners in this game. Make sure to allow the children who are forming the hutch to have a turn at being a rabbit.

Theme Connections

Movement
Rabbits

Red Light! Green Light!

Choose one child to be the "stoplight." The other children line up side by side about 30' away from and facing the stoplight. When the stoplight turns his back to the other children, she says, "Green light!" and the children may run toward her. When she turns back around and says, "Red light!" all of the children must stop. If the child playing the stoplight sees any of the other children move after she has said, "Red light!" then she says the child's name and he must go back to the beginning. The first child to reach the stoplight is the stoplight in the next game of "Red Light! Green Light!"

Theme Connections

Colors
Movement
Opposites

Rhyme or Reason Game

Sit in a circle with the children. Start the game by giving a word to the child next to you. Let's say the word is *sun*. The child must either provide a rhyming word or a connecting word. A rhyming word for sun might be *bun*. A connecting word for sun might be *moon* because the sun and the moon are both in the sky. The next child in the circle must then provide a rhyming word or connecting word for the word the child next to you has chosen.

Theme Connections

Rhymes and Rhyming
Sounds of Language

Rhyming Riddles

Say, "I am thinking of something that you wear on your foot that rhymes with rock," (sock), or "I am thinking of something that you wear on your head that rhymes with cat" (hat). The children guess the rhyming word.

Theme Connections

Rhymes and Rhyming

Ring Around the Rosie

Children hold hands and walk in a circle. Everyone falls down on the words "all fall down."

Ring around the rosie,
Pocket full of posies,
Ashes, ashes,
All fall down.

Variation

Change the last two lines to "last one down is a red, red rose."

Theme Connections

Movement
Rhymes and Rhyming

Roly Poly Relay Races

Divide the children into two teams. Use masking tape or yarn to create a start and a finish line. Encourage one child from each team to roll from the start to the finish line in relay fashion. The team whose members finish rolling first is the winning team.

Theme Connections

Movement

Round-Up

Choose four or five children to be cowboys and cowgirls. The other children are cattle. Designate a corral and several bases. When the signal is given, the cattle must run from one base to another. If the cowboys/cowgirls tag the cattle they must go to the corral and wait until the game is over. The last four or five children to be tagged become the cowboys/cowgirls for the next game.

Sally Go 'Round the Sun

Have the children join hands to form a circle. Recite or sing the rhyme and move as directed.

> *Sally go 'round the sun,* (walk to the left)
> *Sally go 'round the moon,* (walk to the right)
> *Sally go 'round the sunshine* (walk to the left)
> *Every afternoon,*
> *Boom Boom!* (fall down)

Theme Connections

Movement
Rhymes and Rhyming

Theme Connections

Cowboys/Cowgirls
Cows
Farms

Run, Rabbit, Run

Choose four or five children to be foxes. The other children are rabbits. Designate a base at one end of the playground to represent the brier patch, where the rabbits are safe and one at the other end to serve as a fox den. When the signal "Run, Rabbit, Run" is given, the rabbits must run all over the playground. The foxes try to catch the rabbits and take them to their den. The last four of five rabbits caught become the foxes in the next game.

Theme Connections

Foxes
Movements
Rabbits

Shadow Games

During outdoor playtime invite the children to look for shadows on the playground. Can they find shadows with a pattern? Can they use their own bodies to create shadows? Can they make up a shadow dance? Can they catch their shadow?

Theme Connections

Movement
Nature

Simon Says

Choose one child to be "Simon." All the other children stand side by side in a line facing Simon. The child playing Simon gives the other children orders that they have to carry out, but only when the orders follow the phrase "Simon says…" (e.g., *"Simon says touch your nose"*). If a child follows an order that Simon did not say (e.g., *"Touch your nose"*), then he is out and must sit down. The last child standing becomes the new Simon for the next game of "Simon Says." You can change the name of this game to reflect your theme. For example, you can call it "Mad Hatter Says" or "Goldilocks Says."

Theme Connections
Movement
Parts of the Body

Sound Patterns

Have the children make up rhythm patterns such as clap/clap/snap or clap/snap/clap/snap. Record the patterns and then see if the children can identify their pattern when they hear the patterns played back.

Theme Connections
Music
Senses

Spider Walk

Four children stand back to back in a circle. They hook elbows for support and then attempt to walk using eight legs.

Theme Connections
Humor
Insects
Movement

Straw Structures

Divide the children into two teams (no more than three children to a team). You may have multiple pairs of teams. Provide drinking straws, masking tape, paper clips, yarn and scissors to each team. Ask the teams to build a straw structure using the materials they have been given. Explain that the team with the tallest tower will win the game.

Theme Connections
Friends

Stringing Up

Challenge children to string beads on a string hung from the ceiling. Hang two strings and invite partners to see how many beads they can string before a one-minute egg timer runs down.

Theme Connections

Colors

Shapes

Table Polo

Place a piece of masking tape across the middle of a table and then a strip at each end of the table about 5" from the edge. Choose two children and ask each of them to sit at opposite ends of the table. Place a cotton ball on the middle line. Have the children begin to blow the cotton ball. The first one to get the cotton ball across their opponent's line is the winner. If the cotton ball is blown off the table, put it back on the table in the center.

Theme Connections

Humor

Shapes

Think, Pair, Share

Give the children a question to think about. For example, you might ask the children how they could make the letter "O" with their bodies. Encourage them to point to their heads while they are thinking. Give them a minute to think, and then ask them to discuss the question with a partner. Give the partners a minute to discuss their ideas, and then ask the pairs to share their ideas with the class.

Theme Connections

Friends

Self-Esteem

Shapes

Three-Legged Movements

Invite the children to choose partners and stand side by side. Use a wide, soft cloth to tie the partner's inside legs together. Challenge the partners to walk, skip, skate, crawl, or run.

Theme Connections

Friends

Humor

Movement

Parts of the Body

Tightrope Walking

Place a 12' piece of yarn or tape on the floor in a straight line. Invite the children to walk the line without stepping off. Challenge them to try it with beanbags on their heads.

Theme Connections

Movement
Self-Esteem

Torchlight Relay

Make two torches. Use paper towel tubes for the torches and orange construction paper for the flames. Divide the children into two relay teams. The idea is for each child to run a lap and then pass the torch to the next team member. The first team to finish wins. This game is in honor of the torch that is run in Tel Aviv to begin the Hanukkah season.

Theme Connections

Holidays
Movement

Toss and Rhyme

Teach the children three sets of rhyming words, such as *cat/hat, pan/can,* and *rake/cake.* Arrange the children in two parallel lines. Hand a beanbag to the first child in one of the lines. Ask the child to say one of the rhyming words while tossing the beanbag to the first child standing in the opposite line. The friend who catches the beanbag must complete the rhyming pair by saying the word that rhymes with the first child's word. Continue playing the game, letting every child have a turn.

Theme Connections

Movement
Rhymes and Rhyming

Trail Builders

Start two simple pattern trails out of blocks on one side of the classroom. Divide the children into two three-member teams. Have the two teams race to see which team can extend their trail all the way across the room first.

Theme Connections

Movement

Tug of Peace

Take Hula Hoops® outdoors and encourage the children to play the Tug of Peace Game. It takes cooperative effort. Children sit around the Hula Hoop and grab hold with both hands. By pulling back on the hoop, can everyone stand up together?

Theme Connections

Friends
Movement

Tummy Ticklers

Have the children lie on the floor on their backs with their heads on someone else's tummy. Do something silly to make the children start laughing. Ask the children what is making their heads jiggle.

Hee! Hee!

Walk a Crooked Line

Lay a long piece of rope or yarn in a crazy, looping pattern all around the room. Have the children walk the line individually and then as a group. Vary the game by having the children hop the crooked line or crawl the crooked line.

The Wave

Have the children form a circle. Stand in the center of the circle and perform a movement, such as raising both hands over your head. Have the children copy the movement in turn around the circle. Invite volunteers to take your place in the center.

What's Missing?

Place three items on the floor and ask the children to note the items. Ask the children to cover their eyes, and while their eyes are covered remove one of the items. Have the children open their eyes and tell you which item is missing. As the children get better at this activity, you can increase the number of items used in the game.

GAMES

Where's My Hat?

Have the children sit in a circle. Select one child to be IT. IT sits in the middle with a hat on his or her head and with his or her eyes closed. Select a second child to be Mr. Wind. Mr. Wind removes ITs hat while saying, "Whooo" to imitate the sound of the wind. Mr. Wind returns to his or her place and puts the hat behind his or her back to hide it. All the other children also put their hands behind their backs and say in unison:

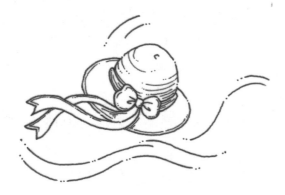

Mr. Wind is such a funny guy,
He blows your hat off in the sky.
Where is it on this windy day?
We know but we will not say.

The child in the center must guess who took his or her hat. After guessing, he or she chooses another child to take his or her place in the center.

Theme Connections

Seasons
Weather

Where, Oh, Where Is Pretty Little Susie?

Designate a place in the classroom or outdoors as home. Divide the class into two groups. Ask group 1 to hide. Have group 2 look for the hidden children. Group 2 sings the first two verses of the following song and begins looking for the hidden children during the second verse. The third verse is sung when all the children are found and the "hunters" bring their found friends back to the place that has been established as home.

Where, oh, where is pretty little Susie?
Where, oh, where is pretty little Susie?
Where, oh, where is pretty little Susie?
Way down yonder in the paw paw patch.

Come on, friends, let's go find her,
Come on, friends, let's go find her,
Come on, friends, let's go find her,
'Way down yonder in the paw paw patch.

Come on, friends, bring her back again,
Come on, friends, bring her back again,
Come on, friends, bring her back again,
Way down yonder in the paw paw patch.

Theme Connections

Friends
Senses

Which Cup Hides the Stone?

Hide a stone under one of three cups turned upside down on a table. Move the cups around and let the children guess which cup hides the stone.

Theme Connections

Humor

Shapes

Who Is Traipsing on My Bridge?

Make a bridge out of blocks. Select one child to be the troll. Have the troll sit with his or her back to the bridge and his or her eyes closed. Select a child to walk across the bridge saying, "Trip, trap, trip, trap" as he or she walks. Have the troll respond with the verse below.

Who is traipsing on my bridge?
Trip, trap, trip, trap! Get off my bridge!
No one should be traipsing there.
Get off! Get off! Don't you dare!

Have the child on the bridge respond with the following lines:

Traipsing, traipsing, is the game
Can you guess my name, name, name?

If the troll guesses correctly, the child on the bridge becomes the next troll. If the troll guesses incorrectly, he or she remains the troll.

Grrr!

Theme Connections

Goats

Movement

Senses

The Complete Book of Activities, Games, Stories, Props, Recipes, and Dances

Who Said That?

Select a child to be IT. Explain that IT must try to identify a speaker by listening to the speaker's voice. Have IT cover his or her eyes or wear a blindfold. Point to a child in the group and ask him or her to start talking. (If the children are unfamiliar with each child's name, have the blindfolded child state whether it is a boy or girl speaking or from which direction the sound is coming.) Give as many children as possible a chance to be IT. Point out that when we listen very carefully, we are able to hear that everyone's voice is uniquely different.

Theme Connections

Senses

Who Took the Cookie From the Cookie Jar?

Pat your thighs and snap in a rhythmic motion as you say the following chant. Continue until everyone has been accused. End with accusing the cookie monster.

Who took the cookie from the cookie jar?
(Name) took the cookie from the cookie jar.
Who, me?
Yes, you.
Couldn't be.
Then who?

(Different child, chosen by first child accused) *stole the cookie from the cookie jar.*
Who, me?
Yes, you.
Couldn't be.
Then who?

Theme Connections

Food
Humor

Who's Got the Button?

Have the children sit in a circle. Choose a child to be IT. Give IT a button. Have children close their eyes. Help IT choose a friend to give the button to. Invite children to open their eyes and try to guess who has the button. The child who guesses correctly becomes the next IT.

Theme Connections

Friends
Senses

Wind-Up Toys

Encourage the children to pretend they are wind-up toys. Invite them to work with a partner—one is the winder and one is the toy. Give the children suggestions for toys to portray such as moving baby dolls, soldiers, dancing chimps, and so forth. Have the children switch roles with their partners.

Theme Connections

Animals
Friends
Monkeys
Toys

Yeah or Yuck

Pose different statements to children and have them respond with their feelings about what you proposed. For example, if you say, "Broccoli is good," they say, "Yeah" if they agree and "Yuck" if they disagree. Children can also use a "thumbs up" and a "thumbs down" when responding.

Theme Connections

Emotions
Self-Esteem

Action Stories

The Calliope

Directions: Make up a story about a trip to the fair or amusement park. Have the children ride a variety of rides. When they ride the merry-go-round, use the following activity.

Divide children into four groups. Assign a sound and movement from the list below to each of the first three groups and have the fourth group hum the circus song, which is the song you most often hear on a merry-go-round.

Sound 1: Um pa pa, um pa pa . . . *(bend up and down from the knees)*
Sound 2: Um tweedli-dee, um tweedli-dee . . .*(sway side to side)*
Sound 3: Um shhh, um shhh, um shhh… *(turn around slowly in a circle)*

Theme Connections

Humor
Movement
Sounds of Language

Candy Land Journey

by Pam Schiller

Let's go on a trip. Who wants to go to Candy Land? *(raise hands)* OK! Let's go! *(sweep arm in forward motion)*

It's just a short trip from here. First, we walk. *(walk in place about 10 steps)* Now we need to get on a plane and fly. *(put arms out to fly for a few seconds)* Look! We're here! *(put arms down and step out of the plane)*

Wow! Here is a sidewalk made of peppermint disks. Let's hop on them and see where they go. *(pretend to jump from disk to disk a few times)* Be careful not to fall off.

What do we have here? It looks like a river made of caramel. Let's try to walk across. *(walk as if stepping in something gooey)*

That was fun! Who likes caramel? *(raise hands)* Let's taste some. *(stoop and scoop up some caramel and pretend to taste it)* Ummm!

Hey, look at the lemon-drop tree. *(point)* Let's pick some lemon drops. *(pick lemon drops)* Let's taste one. *(pretend to chew/crunch)*

Let's go over there into the forest. *(take a few steps)* Here are some licorice laces. Let's play jump rope. *(jump rope)*

It's time to go now. Let's head back to the plane. We have to cross the caramel river again. *(cross river)* Hop across the peppermint disks. *(jump from disk to disk)*

Oh! Look at those great lollipops growing like flowers in a garden. Let's pick one to take home. *(pick a lollipop)*

OK. Let's fly. *(fly)*

Now let's walk back to our classroom. *(walk)*

We're home! Who had a good time? *(raise hands)*

Me, too. I love Candy Land!

Theme Connections

Food
Humor
Movement

The Fall of the Last Leaf

by Pam Schiller

Sam was raking the leaves for his dad. He thought that he would never be able to clear up all the leaves. He looked up to see how many leaves were still hanging on the branches of the large maple tree above him. Wow! There was only one and just as Sam noticed it, it began to fall.

(children become the leaf)

It rocked. *(rock)*

It twisted. *(twist)*

It turned around and around in the hands of the wind. *(turn around)*

Then the wind grew still, and the little leaf floated softly and silently. *(be still and slowly float)*

It rocked. *(rock slowly)*

It turned. *(turn slowly)*

It danced on the wind. *(dance slowly)*

Suddenly, the wind regained its strength.

The little leaf shook. *(shake)*

It zoomed high into the air. *(swoosh arms overhead)*

It rocked. *(rock fast)*

It twisted. *(twist fast)*

It danced in the wind. *(dance fast)*

Then, again, suddenly the wind slowed and released the leaf.

The little leaf twirled. *(twirl around)*

It glided. *(glide)*

It rocked. *(rock slowly)*

And it finally landed on top of a pile of other fallen leaves. *(sit down)*

I wonder if she was happy to see her friends again.

Theme Connections

Movement
Seasons
Weather

Going for a Swim

by Pam Schiller

I love to swim. I love to swim. I love to swim. *(cross arms over chest and hug yourself)*

When we are going to the beach I wake up early, *(yawn)*

I wash my goggles. *(pretend to wash goggles)*

I blow up my float. *(pretend to blow up float—three big breaths)*

I fold my beach towel. *(pretend to fold beach towel)*

I put on my sandals. *(pretend to put on sandals)*

I put on my swimsuit. *(pretend to put on swimsuit)*

I eat my breakfast. *(pretend to eat)*

I know I will need lots of energy for a day at the beach.

Then I help my mom and dad pack the car. *(pretend to gather things and carry to car)*

We will need our cooler, our picnic basket, and our beach chairs.

Then we are off to the beach. *(pretend to be looking out car windows)*

When we arrive, I hop out of the car. *(hop)*

I help mom and dad find a place on the beach. *(shade eyes with hand and look around)*

It is hard to walk in the sand. *(walk as if in sand)*

I stop and listen to the wind on the ocean. *(hand to ear)*

Then I rub on my sunscreen *(rub on lotion)*

Now I can head to the water. *(run in place)*

I love the ocean. *(hands up overhead)*

I love to swim. I love to swim. I love to swim. *(place arms across chest and hug yourself)*

Don't you? *(hands out to side)*

Theme Connections

Emotions
Families
Oceans and Seas
Seasons

Going on a Bear Hunt

We're going on a bear hunt.

Want to come along?

Well, come on then.

Let's go! *(walk in place)*

Look! There's a river.

Can't go over it.

Can't go under it.

Can't go around it.

We'll have to go through it. *(pretend to walk into river, through the water, and onto other bank, then resume walking in place)*

Look! There's a tree.

Can't go under it.

Can't go through it.

We'll have to go over it. *(pretend to climb up and over tree; then resume walking in place)*

Look! There's a wheat field.

Can't go over it.

Can't go under it.

Can't go around it.

We'll have to go through it. *(pretend to walk through field, make swishing sounds with hands against thighs, then resume walking in place)*

Add verses to make the story as long as you want.

Look! There's a cave.

Want to go inside?

Ooh, it's dark in here. *(look around, squinting)*

I see two eyes.

Wonder what it is. *(reach hands to touch)*

It's soft and furry.

It's big.

It's a bear! Let's run! *(retrace steps, running in place, through wheat field, in place, over tree, in place, across river, in place, then stop)*

Home safely. Whew!

Theme Connections

Bears
Movement
Spatial Relationships

Going on a Trail Ride

by Pam Schiller

We're going on a trail ride.

Want to come along?

Well, then, come on.

Let's get ready!

Got to rope and brand the cattle. *(children echo)*

Let's rope. *(children echo)*

Stick on the brand. *(children echo)*

Got to load up the chuck wagon. *(children echo)*

Get the blankets and the food. *(children echo)*

Don't forget the water. *(children echo)*

Got to water our horses. *(children echo)*

Slurp, slurp. *(children echo)*

Ready to go.

Now jump on your horse.

Let's go. (children hold horse reins and clip clop between verses)

Look! There's a river.

Can't go over it. (children echo)

Can't go under it. (children echo)

Can't go around it. (children echo)

We'll have to go through it.

Look! There's a cactus.

Can't go under it. (children echo)

Can't go over it. (children echo)

Can't go through it. (children echo)

We'll have to go around it.

Look! There's a mountain.

Can't go through it. (children echo)

Can't go under it. (children echo)

Can't go around it. (children echo)

We'll have to go over it. (lean back)

Look! There's a wagon train.

Can't go through it, (children echo)

Can't go under it, (children echo)

Can't go over it, (children echo)

We'll have to go around it.

(Optional: Stop here and sing some songs with the people on the wagon train.)

Look! There's the town! (shade eyes as if looking off in the distance)

Just what we are looking for!

Let's hurry! Get along, little doggies! (ride fast)

We're almost there. (continue to ride fast)

Civilization at last!

Theme Connections

Cowboys/Cowgirls
Horses
Movement
Nature
Work

Going on a Whale Watch

by Pam Schiller

We're going on a whale watch.

Want to come along?

Well, come on then.

Let's go! (walk in place)

Look! There's our boat.

Can't go over it.

Can't go under it.

Can't go around it.

We'll need to get on it. (pretend to walk onto boat, and locate a good place to stand. Shade eyes as if watching for a whale and begin tapping fingers as if impatiently waiting)

Look! There's a ship.

Can't go over it.

Can't go under it.

Can't go through it.

We'll have to go around it. *(pretend to steer around the ship and then resume tapping fingers and watching for a whale)*

Look! There's an iceberg.

Can't go over it.

Can't go under it.

Can't go through it.

We'll have to go around it. *(pretend to steer around the iceberg and then resume tapping fingers and looking for a whale)*

Add verses to make the story as long as you want.

Look! There's a spout of water.

Is it a whale?

Ooh, I think it might be. *(look straight ahead, squinting)*

I see a huge head.

Wonder what it is.

I see a tail.

It's big.

It's a whale! We found a whale!

Look out! Here comes a s-p-l-a-s-h!

Too late! We're soaked!

Theme Connections

Boats and Ships
Movement
Oceans and Seas
Spatial Relationships
Whales

Hey, My Name Is Joe!

Hey! My name is Joe!

I have a wife, one kid, and I work in a button factory.

One day, my boss said, "Are you busy, Joe?"

I said, "No."

"Then turn a button with your right hand." *(make a turning gesture with right hand)*

Hello! My name is Joe!

I have a wife, two kids, and I work in a button factory.

One day, my boss said, "Are you busy, Joe?"

I said, "No."

"Then turn a button with your left hand." *(make a turning gesture with left hand as you continue with the right hand)*

(Continue adding number of children and adding right and left feet and head.)

Hello! My name is Joe!

I have a wife, six kids, and I work in a button factory.

One day, my boss said, "Are you busy, Joe?"

I said, "Yes!"

Family
Humor
Numbers
Occupations
Work

I Can, You Can!

by Pam Schiller

(suit actions to words)

I can put my hands up high. Can you?

I can wink my eye. Can you?

I can stick out my tongue. Can you?

I can open my mouth wide. Can you?

I can fold my arms. Can you?

I can cover my ears. Can you?

I can touch my nose. Can you?

I can give myself a great big hug. Can you?

And if I give my hug to you, will you give yours to me?

Theme Connections

Parts of the Body
Self-Esteem

Let's Pretend to Bake a Cake

by Pam Schiller

(Act out the story, encouraging the children to copy your actions.)

Who wants to bake a cake? I need all the bakers to come sit by me. Let's see. We need a mixer, two bowls, measuring cups and spoons, and a cake pan. *(pretend to take items out of shelves and drawers)* Now I think we are ready.

First we put our butter and sugar in our bowl. *(place both into bowl)* Now we need the mixer. *(run it over bowl as you make a humming noise)* That looks nice and smooth. Let's add the eggs. *(count and crack four eggs into bowl)* Let's mix again. *(run mixer and hum)* This looks good.

Now we need to add the flour. *(measure two cups full and dump into bowl)* Just one more ingredient—a teaspoon of vanilla. *(measure in a teaspoon of vanilla)* A final mix *(mix)* and we are ready to pour our batter into our cake pan. *(pour)* Now it's time to put our cake in the oven. *(open oven door as you make a squeaking sound, slide the cake in, and close the door)*

Now our cake is baking. *(tap fingers to act like you are waiting)* I can't wait! Who can smell it cooking? *(sniff)* That smells good! OK! Let's take our cake out of the oven. *(take the cake out and smell it)* Who wants some cake?

Theme Connections

Cooking   Movement
Counting   Numbers
Food

The Little Ants

Over the little hills
And all the little roads,
The line of ants walks on and on.
The line of little ants,
The line of little ants,
The line of little ants walks on and on.

Repeat, replacing "walks on and on" with
one of the following phrases:
   ...walks on tippy-toes
   ...spins on and on
   ...jumps on and on
   ...dances on and on
   ...skates on and on
   ...all wave good-bye

Theme Connections

Insects
Movement

Spanish Translation

Las Hormiguitas
Por los cerritos
y vereditas
van caminando las hormiguitas
Las hormiguitas,
las hormiguitas,
van caminando las hormiguitas.

Repeat, replacing "van caminando with one
of the following phrases
   ...van de punitatas
   ...van dando vueltas

...saltan y saltan
...bailan y bailan
...van patinando
...ya se despiden

Little Caterpillar

by Pam Schiller

(suit actions to words)

The little caterpillar poked her head out of
the egg that had been her home for two
weeks. She looked all around her. She felt
like she was in a forest. Everything was
green. She looked down. All she saw was
green leaves. She looked to the left. All she
saw was green leaves. She looked to the
right. Again, all she saw was green leaves.
She looked up. The bright sun made her turn
her head quickly back toward the ground.
She took a breath of the fresh air and
realized she was extremely hungry. She took
a bite of the leaf where her egg home was
still attached. That was yummy. She took
another bite and then another bite.

She was suddenly face to face with another
caterpillar on a nearby leaf. She nodded and
the other caterpillar nodded back. Then both
caterpillars began to eat again. Soon they
were almost racing. The two caterpillars ate
and ate greedily. Day by day they ate. Night
by night they ate. How could anyone be so
hungry?

Then one day the first little caterpillar felt
suddenly full and sleepy. She stretched out
on a leaf and began to cover herself with a
silk blanket. Soon she was fast asleep. She

slept warm and snug in her cocoon for several days. When she awoke she felt much better. She stretched. She flapped her wings. Her what? Something was different. She burst out of her cocoon. She felt full of energy. She flapped her wings!? Soon she was leaving the only home she had ever known and was zooming through the sky high above the earth.

So, if ever you eat too much and fall asleep under a blanket of silk, don't be surprised if you wake up with a pair wings.

Theme Connections

Growing Up
Insects
Movement
Nature

The Little Spaceman

by Pam Schiller

A flying saucer came whirling down from the sky and landed right in my back yard. I couldn't believe my eyes. I watched as the hatch door to the flying saucer slowly opened. Out hopped a little purple man.

He stretched. *(children reach hands over head to stretch)*

He bent down and touched the ground. *(children bend down to touch their toes)*

He twisted to the left stretching his back. *(twist to left)*

And then he twisted to the right and stretched his back again. *(twist to right)*

He pulled up two antennae; one on the left side of his head and one on the right side of his head. *(pull up antennae)*

He took an oxygen tank off his back. *(pretend to take tank off)*

He took in a deep breath from his nostrils and then let it out through his mouth. *(breathe in through the nose and out through the mouth)*

He jumped up and down several times. *(jump up and down several times)*

I moved a little closer.

He saw me. He jumped back into his ship, pulled the hatch door closed, and off he sailed. *(jump into ship and pull down hatch)*

I've told everyone what I saw. But no one believes me. I wish the little purple man would come back.

Theme Connections

Colors
Outer Space

The Many Faces of Me

by Pam Schiller

My mother says I wear many faces.

When I am happy, I look like this. *(turn around and smile)*

When I am mad, I look like this. *(turn around and look angry)*

When I am sad, I look like this. *(turn around and look sad)*

When I am confused, I look like this. *(turn around and look confused)*

When I daydream, I look like this. *(turn around and look pensive)*

When my grandmother comes to visit, I look like this. *(turn opposite direction and smile)*

When my brother knocks down my sand castle, I look like this. *(turn and look angry)*

When I can't have a second helping of ice cream, I look like this. *(turn and look sad)*

When I can't find my shoes, I look like this. *(turn and look confused)*

When I am thinking about summer vacation, I look like this. *(turn and look pensive)*

How many faces do you have? *(point to another child)*

Invite children to think of other things that cause them to make faces.

Theme Connections

Emotions
Self-Esteem

Marley Markle

Directions: Instruct the children to pat their heads when they hear the words, "good dog" and to shake their finger when they hear the words, "bad dog."

Marley is my dog. He is my best friend. He is a Golden Labrador Retriever. That is a big yellow dog. You may have seen one before. He is a good dog.

Marley sleeps by the foot of my bed. Every morning when I wake up I say, "Good morning, Marley. You are a good dog."

When we go downstairs to breakfast my mother says, "Good morning, Austin. Good morning, Marley. Have you been a good dog?"

Marley eats his breakfast while I eat mine. He sometimes tries to sneak a bite of my sausage. I say, "No, Marley. Bad dog."

My mom says, "No, Marley. Bad dog."

When I go outside Marley goes with me. I throw balls and Marley brings them back. I say, "Good dog" when he puts the ball in my hand.

When Tigger, the neighbor's cat, stops by to play, Marley chases her away. I say, "Bad dog, Marley."

Marley likes to run. He chases everything. Sometimes he is not careful. He knocks over the trash. My dad yells, "Bad dog!"

He runs through mom's garden. She yells, "Bad dog!"

One day when we were not home and Marley was all alone a burglar tried to break into our back door. Marley heard him and started to bark. Our neighbor came to see what all the commotion was about and the burglar ran away. Our neighbor said, "Good dog, Marley."

When we came home my mom said that Marley was a good dog. My dad said, "He sure is." And I said, "Marley, you are the best friend any boy could have. You are a good dog!"

Theme Connections

Insects
Movement

Metamorphosis

I'm an egg. I'm an egg. I'm an egg, egg, egg! *(curl up in fetal position)*

I'm a worm. I'm a worm. I'm a wiggly, humpty worm! *(open up and wiggle on the ground)*

I'm a cocoon. I'm a cocoon. I'm a round and silky cocoon! *(curl up in a fetal position with hands over the face)*

I'm a butterfly. I'm a butterfly. I'm a grand and glorious butterfly! *(stand and fly around using arms for wings)*

I can fly! I can fly! I can fly, fly, fly!   *(After the children have turned into butterflies give them each two colorful plastic plates to use as wings and encourage them to fly around the room to classical music.)*

Theme Connections

Insects
Movement

Mr. Wiggle and Mr. Waggle

This is Mr. Wiggle *(hold up right hand, make a fist but keep the thumb pointing up – wiggle thumb)* and this is Mr. *Waggle (hold up left hand, make a fist but keep the thumb pointing up – wiggle thumb)*. Mr. Wiggle and Mr. Waggle live in houses on top of different hills and three hills apart *(put thumbs inside fists)*.

One day, Mr. Wiggle decided to visit Mr. Waggle. He opened his door *(open right fist)*, pop, stepped outside *(raise thumb)*, pop, and closed his door *(close fist)*, pop. Then he went down the hill and up the hill, and down the hill and up the hill, and down the hill and up the hill (*move right hand up and down in a wave fashion to go with text*).

When he reached Mr. Waggle's house, he knocked on the door—knock, knock, knock (*tap right thumb against left fist*). No one answered. So Mr. Wiggle went down the hill and up the hill, and down the hill and up the hill, and down the hill and up the hill to his house (*use wave motion to follow text*).

When he reached his house, Mr. Wiggle opened the door (*open right fist*), pop, went inside (*place thumb in palm*), pop, and closed the door (close fist), pop.

The next day Mr. Waggle decided to visit Mr. Wiggle. He opened his door (*open left fist*), pop, stepped outside (*raise thumb*), pop, and closed his door (*close fist*), pop. Then he went down the hill and up the hill, and down the hill and up the hill, and down the hill and up the hill (*move left hand up and down in a wave fashion to go with text*).

When he reached Mr. Wiggle's house he knocked on the door—knock, knock, knock (*tap left thumb against right fist*). No one answered. So Mr. Waggle went down the hill and up the hill, and down the hill and up the hill, and down the hill and up the hill to his house (*use wave motion to follow text*). When he reached his house, Mr. Waggle opened the door (*open left fist*), pop, went inside (*place thumb in palm*), pop, and closed the door (*close fist*), pop.

The next day Mr. Wiggle (*shake right fist*) decided to visit Mr. Waggle, and Mr. Waggle (*shake left fist*) decided to visit Mr. Wiggle. So they opened their doors (*open both fists*), pop, stepped outside (*raise thumbs*), and

closed their doors (*close fists*), pop. They each went down the hill and up the hill, and down the hill and up the hill (*wave motion to follow text*), and they met on top of the hill.

Theme Connections

Friends
Parts of the body

Monkey See, Monkey Do

by Pam Schiller

When my friends and I go to the zoo our favorite spot is the monkey house. We love to watch the funny things the monkeys do and I think perhaps the monkeys like to watch us, too. I wonder if they think we are as funny as we think they are. I am never really sure exactly who is watching whom.

Hey, I have an idea. You pretend to be the monkeys and I'll be me. I'll show you what happens at the zoo. Listen carefully because sometimes you will be leading. Remember, you are the monkeys. (*The teacher is the storyteller and the children are the monkeys. Suit actions to words.*)

When we run up to the monkey cages we clap our hands with glee. In no time at all the monkeys are clapping their hands, too.

They jump up and down and so do we.

We make funny faces and so do they.

They turn in circles and so do we.

We swing our arms monkey style *(randomly all around)* and they do the same.

They lift their legs up monkey style *(out to the side and up and down)* and we do the same.

We scratch our heads and they scratch their heads.

They scratch under their arms and we scratch under our arms.

We pull our ears and they pull theirs.

They sit on the ground and count their toes.

We pretend to do the same.

Then they laugh tee-hee-hee, tee-hee-hee.

That makes us roll on the ground with laughter.

Guess what the monkeys do then—

You got it. They roll on the ground with laughter.

Have you ever seen the monkeys at the zoo? You really must go to see them.

When you get there, be sure to play our funny game of Monkey See, Monkey Do.

Theme Connections

Humor
Monkeys
Movement
Parts of the Body

My Body Talks

by Pam Schiller

When I want to say hello, I wave my hand.

When I want to say no, I shake my head from side to side.

When I want to say yes, I nod my head up and down.

When I want to say good job, I stick up my thumb.

When I want to say I disagree, I turn my thumb down.

When I want to celebrate a success, I clap my hands.

When I want to say enough or stop, I hold my hand out.

When I want to say come here, I wave my hand toward me.

When I want to say goodbye, I wave my hand or blow you a kiss.

When I want to say I love you, I wrap my arms around you and squeeze.

Theme Connections

Emotions
Movement
Parts of the Body
Self-Esteem

Spanish Translation

Mi Cuerpo Habla

Cuando yo quiero decir hola, yo agito mi mano.

Cuando yo quiero decir no, yo muevo mi cabeza de un lado para otro.

Cuando yo quiero decir sí, yo muevo mi cabeza de arriba hacia abajo.

Cuando yo quiero decir bien hecho, yo levanto mi dedo pulgar.

Cuando yo quiero decir que no estoy de acuerdo, yo bajo mi dedo pulgar.

Cuando yo quiero celebrar un triunfo, yo aplaudo con mis manos.

Cuando yo quiero decir suficiente o parar, yo levanto la palma de mi mano.

Cuando yo quiero decir venga aquí, yo señalo con mi mano hacia mí.

Cuando yo quiero decir adios, yo agito mi mano, o te envoi un beso.

Cuando yo quiero decir te amo, yo envuelvo mis brazos a tu alrededor y te aprieto.

Okki-Tokki-Unga

Directions: This song and the motions that go with it illustrate a whale search, Eskimo style. Sing or say the words with the following motions:

Okki-tokki-unga, okki-tokki unga *(make paddling motions, as if paddling a canoe)*
Hey Missa Day, Missa Doh, Missa Day.
Okki-tokki-unga, okki-tokki unga *(make paddling motions, as if paddling a canoe)*
Hey Missa Day, Missa Doh, Missa Day.
Hexa-cola-misha-won-i *(shade eyes and pretend to be scanning the sea)*
Hexa-cola-misha-won-i.

The teacher "narrates" the story while the children sing the song and do the above motions.

Teacher:

We are going to look for whales like the Eskimos do. First, we have to put on our boots. *(everyone pretends to pull on boots)* Next, we have to zip up our coats. *(everyone pretends to zip up coats)* Now, let's put our nets and ropes in the canoe. *(pretend to put nets and ropes in canoe)* Okay, get in the canoe. *(pretend to get into canoe)* Let's go!

Everyone:
Okki-tokki-unga, okki-tokki-unga,
Hey Missa Day, Missa Doh, Missa Day.
(pretend to paddle canoe)

Teacher:

Let's look to see if we can find a whale.

The Complete Book of Activities, Games, Stories, Props, Recipes, and Dances

Everyone:

Hexa-cola-misha-won-i,
Hexa-cola-misha-won-i.
(pretend to scan horizon)

Teacher:

I don't see one, do you? Let's keep going.

Repeat the above exchange, and then continue with the story.

Teacher:

Look! There's a whale! Let's paddle over to it! *(sing chorus and paddle very quickly)* Let's throw our nets out and try to catch it. *(pretend to throw nets over whale)* Now, tie the rope around its tail. *(pretend to tie rope)* Now, drag it into the canoe. *(pretend to drag a very heavy whale into canoe)* Let's take it to Seaworld! *(sing chorus and paddle very slowly)*

Teacher:

Can we find Seaworld from here? *(sing verse, pretending to scan horizon; repeat, and then go on)* There's Seaworld! Let's paddle our canoe over to it! *(sing chorus slowly—the canoe is still very heavy)* Let's paddle in and let our whale go into the tank. *(sing chorus and paddle a little faster)*

Teacher:

Untie the rope. *(pretend to untie the rope)* Now, take off the net. *(pretend to take the net off the whale)* Now, let it go! *(pretend to push the whale over the side of the canoe)*

Teacher:

Now, let's go home!

Sing chorus one more time and paddle fast to get home.

Theme Connections

Oceans and Seas
Whales

A Spring Walk

by Pam Schiller

I love to walk in the garden during the spring. Everything is so beautiful and so alive.

I stop and take some deep breaths just to smell the wonderful fragrance of the flowers. *(take two or three deep breaths)*

I squat down and watch the ants carrying small parcels to their homes.

(squat and pretend to watch ants)

Sometimes they carry overhead things that are bigger than they are.

(hold hands overhead, as if carrying something)

When I walk through the wild flowers, I am careful not to step on them.

(walk carefully and pretend to step around flowers)

I stop again and breathe in all the fragrances of spring. *(stop and breathe deeply)*

I feel the warmth of the sun on my arms and face. *(lift face to sun)*

I feel the gentle breeze of the wind. *(wrap arms around self)*

Bees are everywhere, taking the pollen from the flowers. I watch them as they do their waggle dance around the flowers. It is fun to imitate their dance. *(wiggle and dance in a circle)*

The blackberries are just turning from red to black. I stop to pick a few, and then I eat them right on the spot. They are still tart. *(pick berries, eat them, and pucker your lips)*

The flowers are beautiful. There seems to be a flower in every color. I have a great idea. I will pick some flowers for the dinner table. *(pick flowers)*

My mom will be glad to have a little bit of spring on our dinner table.

Theme Connections

Food
Growing Things
Insects
Seasons
Weather

Walk-On Nursery Rhyme

Directions: Cut a piece of butcher paper 15' long. Draw the following items on the paper in this sequence: a pair of feet (trace shoes), a spiral arrow, a pair of walking feet, grass, a pair of walking feet, a door, a pair of walking feet, a bowl, a pair of walking feet, a chair, a pair of walking feet, a bed, a pair of walking feet, a pair of walking feet going off the end of the paper. Laminate the paper. Invite children to say the following rhyme as they walk across the path.

Goldilocks, Goldilocks

Goldilocks, Goldilocks, turn around. (turn around)

Goldilocks, Goldilocks, touch the ground. (touch the ground)

Goldilocks, Goldilocks, knock on the door. (knock with hand)

Goldilocks, Goldilocks, eat some porridge. (pretend to eat porridge)

Goldilocks, Goldilocks, have a seat. (squat)

Goldilocks, Goldilocks, go to sleep. (put head on folded hands)

Goldilocks, Goldilocks, run, run, run. (run off paper and back to beginning)

Theme Connections

Humor
Movement

ACTION STORIES

Weather

by Pam Schiller

The children were excited. They jumped up and down with delight. *(jump up and down)* It was time to go outdoors. They put on their coats. *(pretend to put on a coat)* They put on their mittens. *(pretend to put on mittens)* And then put on their hats. *(pretend to put on a hat)* They opened the door *(pretend to open door)*, and out they ran.

The wind was strong. It blew hard against them. *(pretend to walk against the wind)* The children walked more slowly toward the swings and the slide. They swung awhile. *(pretend to swing)* The wind blew their swings crooked. *(pretend to go crooked)* They decided to try the slide. They climbed up the ladder. *(pretend to climb)* When they went

down the slide, the wind pushed them faster. *(pretend to slide - land on bottom)* Next, some of the children rode on the tricycles. *(pretend to pedal)* while others played ball. *(pretend to catch a ball)*

Soon the children noticed that the wind had died down. They began to feel warm. *(fan yourself)* The children took off their mittens. *(pretend to take off mittens)* Then they went to play in the sand. *(pretend to hold sand in your hand)*

They were still hot. *(fan)* They took off their hats. *(pretend to take off hat)* They took off their coats. *(pretend to take off coat)* They went back to play on the swings *(pretend to swing)* and the slide *(pretend to slide)*.

Just then, they began to feel raindrops. *(hold out hand as if feeling for rain)* The children picked up their mittens, their coats, and their hats and ran inside just in time. When they looked out the window *(shade eyes as if looking)*, they saw a big black cloud and lots and lots of raindrops.

Theme Connections

Clothing
Movement
Seasons
Weather

Flannel Board Stories & Magnetic Board Stories

All of the stories in this section can be used on either a flannel board or a magnetic board. Sometimes, the story is better represented as a magnetic board story. If that is the case, it is mentioned in the directions.

The Bun
(Russia)

Directions: Photocopy the story patterns on pages 311-315. Use a black fine-point permanent marker to trace patterns onto a piece of interfacing. Color them and cut them out.

Once there was an old woman and an old man who lived alone on the edge of the forest.

The old man asked the old woman to bake him a bun.

"What shall I make it from?" she asked. "We have no flour."

"Scrape the bottom of the flour bin and you will have enough," said the old man.

The old woman opened the flour bin and scraped the bottom of the flour bin until she had just enough flour to make one small, round bun. She mixed it with milk and baked it in butter. When she took it out of the oven she placed it on the windowsill to cool. Suddenly, the bun jumped off the bench and onto the floor, and rolled across the floor and out the door. On it rolled across the yard and out the gate and on and on and on.

The bun rolled along the road, and it met a hare.

"Little bun, little bun, let me eat you up!" said the hare.

"Don't eat me! Don't eat me! I will sing you a song." And the bun sang,

"I'm a bun! I'm a bun!
I was scraped from the bin,
I was mixed with milk,
I was baked in butter.
I ran away from Grandpa,
I ran away from Grandma,
And I will run away from you!"

The bun rolled on faster, and the hare was left far behind. The bun rolled on and met a wolf.

"Little bun, little bun, I shall eat you up," said the wolf.

"Don't eat me, gray wolf!" said the bun. "I will sing a song for you." And the bun sang.

"I'm a bun! I'm a bun!
I was scraped from the bin,
I was mixed with milk,
I was baked in butter.
I ran away from Grandpa,
I ran away from Grandma,
I ran away from the hare,
And I will run away from you!"

And the bun rolled faster, and the wolf was left far behind. The bun rolled on and met a bear.

"Little bun, little bun, I shall eat you up," said the bear.

"You'll never eat me, old bowlegged bear!" said the bun, and it sang,

"I'm a bun! I'm a bun!
I was scraped from the bin,
I was mixed with milk,
I was baked in butter.
I ran away from Grandpa,
I ran away from Grandma,
I ran away from the hare,
I ran away from the wolf,
And I will run away from you!"

And again the bun rolled faster, and left the bear far behind.

The bun rolled and rolled and met a fox.

Good day, little bun, how sweet you look," said the fox. And the bun sang,

"I'm a bun! I'm a bun!
I was scraped from the bin,
I was mixed with milk,
I was baked in butter.
I ran away from Grandpa,
I ran away from Grandma,
I ran away from the hare,
I ran away from the wolf,
I ran away from the bear,
And I will run away from you!"

"What a wonderful song," said the fox. "But little bun, I am old, I can't hear you very well. Please sit down on my snout and sing your song again, louder this time."

The bun jumped on the fox's snout and sang,

"I'm a bun! I'm a bun!
I was scraped from the bin,
I was mixed with milk,
I was baked in butter.
I ran away from Grandpa,
I ran away from Grandma,
I ran away from the hare,
I ran away from the wolf,
I ran away from the bear,
And I will run away from you!"

"Thank you, little bun, for your wonderful song. How I would love to hear it again! Come now, sit on my tongue and sing it one last time."

The fox stuck out her tongue. The bun foolishly jumped on it. Snap! The fox ate the little bun in one bite. Yummy!

Theme Connections

Bears
Food
Foxes
Rabbits
Tricksters
Wolves

Caps for Sale

by Esphyr Slobodkina

Directions: Photocopy the story patterns on pages 316-317. Use a black fine-point permanent marker to trace patterns onto a piece of interfacing. Color them and cut them out.

Once upon a time, there was a cap peddler, but he was not an ordinary peddler. He didn't carry his wares on his back or in a cart. He carried them on top of his head.

First, he had on his own checked cap. On top of that he had gray caps and then brown caps, blue caps, and yellow caps. On the very top, he had red caps. He walked very, very slowly up and down the street. He had to walk very straight so that he wouldn't upset his caps. As he walked along, he called, "Caps! Caps for sale! Fifty cents a cap!"

But this morning no one wanted any caps. Not a gray one or a brown one or a blue one or a yellow one. Not even a red one. The peddler was not happy. So he decided to take a walk in the country. He walked very, very slowly so that he wouldn't upset his caps.

After a long time, he came to a big tree. "This looks like a nice place to rest," he said.

He sat down slowly, very, very slowly. He leaned back against the tree slowly, very, very slowly. Then he put his hand up to feel the caps. Were they all there? He touched his own checked cap. He touched the gray caps and then the brown caps, the blue caps, and the yellow caps. On the very top, he touched the red caps. They were all there. He could go to sleep.

He slept a long time. He woke up. He yawned. He stretched slowly, very, very slowly. He didn't want to upset his caps. His caps? Something felt funny. He touched his own checked cap. Then he touched . . . "Where are my caps?" he cried.

He looked here. He looked there. No caps.

He looked left. He looked right. No caps.

He looked down. He looked up. And what did he see?

A tree full of monkeys. And on each monkey there was a cap. Gray caps and brown caps. Blue caps and yellow caps. At the very top of the tree, he saw red caps. The peddler looked at the monkeys. The monkeys looked at the peddler. What was he to do?

"Hey, you monkeys!" he shouted, shaking his finger. "Give me my caps."

"Tsk, tsk, tsk," said the monkeys, shaking their fingers at the peddler.

The peddler got mad.

"Hey, you monkeys!" he shouted, stamping his foot. "Give me my caps."

"Tsk, tsk, tsk," said the monkeys, stamping their feet at the peddler.

The peddler got madder.

"Hey, you monkeys!" he shouted, jumping up and down. "Give me my caps."

"Tsk, tsk, tsk," said the monkeys, jumping up and down.

The peddler got even madder.

"That's it," the peddler said.

He got so mad that he took off his cap and threw it on the ground. Then each monkey took off its cap and threw it down. Caps came floating to the ground, slowly, very, very slowly. Gray caps and brown caps. Blue caps and yellow caps. And from the very top of the tree came red caps. The peddler smiled. He put on his caps. And slowly, very, very slowly, he walked back to town.

"Caps! Caps for sale! Fifty cents a cap!"

Theme Connections

Humor
Monkeys
Work

The Color Song

by Pam Schiller

Directions: Photocopy the story patterns on pages 318-321. Use a black fine-point permanent marker to trace patterns onto a piece of interfacing. Color them and cut them out.

Red is the color for an apple to eat.
Red is the color for cherries, too.
Red is the color for strawberries.
I like red, don't you?

Blue is the color for the big blue sky.
Blue is the color for baby things, too.
Blue is the color of my sister's eyes.
I like blue, don't you?

Yellow is the color for the great big sun.
Yellow is the color for lemonade, too.
Yellow is the color of a baby chick.
I like yellow, don't you?

Green is the color for the leaves on the trees.
Green is the color for green peas, too.
Green is the color of a watermelon.
I like green, don't you?

Orange is the color for oranges.
Orange is the color for carrots, too.
Orange is the color of a jack-o'-lantern.
I like orange, don't you?

Purple is the color for a bunch of grapes.
Purple is the color for grape juice, too.
Purple is the color for a violet.
I like purple, don't you?

Theme Connections

Colors
Nature

Dress-Me Dolls: Mark and Melissa

by Pam Schiller

Directions: Photocopy the story patterns on pages 322-336. Use a black fine-point permanent marker to trace patterns onto a piece of interfacing. Color them and cut them out. Or, photocopy the story patterns, color them, cut them out, laminate them, and place a piece of magnetic tape on the back of each piece to create a magnetic story.

Note: The clothes stay on the characters better when you use the magnetic tape rather than the pelon.

Basic Story

Every morning, Mark and Melissa jump out of bed, brush their teeth, and run to their closets. And every morning they say the same thing, "Hmmm. What will I wear today?"

This morning was just the same.

Mark looks in his closet. "I think I'll wear blue jeans and a purple shirt." He looks at himself in the mirror. "No, I think I'll wear my blue striped shirt and my red overalls."

"Perfect!" he said.

Melissa looks in her closet. "I think I'll wear my pink shirt and green shorts," she says. "Or maybe I'll wear my yellow jumper instead." So she puts on her yellow jumper and looks at herself in the mirror. "This is just right!" she says.

After breakfast, Mark, Melissa, and their mom are ready to go. Mark and Melissa put on their shoes and run to the car. They are ready for another great day at school.

Theme Connections

Clothing
Colors
Families
Self-Esteem

Dress-Me Dolls: Fall

Fall is Melissa's favorite time of year. She loves the colors of the trees and the crispness of the weather. One of her favorite things to do is to watch the falling leaves. She and Mark love playing in the leaves.

When Melissa and Mark want to play in the leaves their mom always says, "Put on your old clothes and be sure to wear a sweatshirt. The weather is getting chilly."

So Mark and Melissa get out their old jeans, the ones with the patches on the knees, and their sweatshirts. They wear thick socks and old tennis shoes. They rake the leaves into big piles and then the jump in the middle of them. Sometimes they see who can build the biggest pile of leaves and sometimes the try to bury each other in the leaves. When the fun is over, Dad says, "Rake the leaves into a pile. We will carry them to the compost."

Mark and Melissa don't care. They know that tomorrow there will be a whole new batch of leaves in which to play.

Clothing
Seasons
Self-Esteem
Weather

Dress-Me Dolls: Winter

Mark and Melissa are not fond of the wintertime weather. They like to play in the snow but they don't like having to wear so many clothes just to keep warm. Melissa worries about keeping up with all her winter clothes at school and Mark always loses a mitten.

Melissa likes to wear tights/leggings under her skirt to keep her legs warm. She has tights in several different colors. Her favorite winter outfit is a plaid pleated skirt and a turtleneck sweater that her cousin gave her. When she leaves for school she puts on her scarf, her coat, her mittens, her hat, and her snow boots.

Mark wears his heavy socks, his corduroy pants, his undershirt and his sweater vest. When he leaves for school he puts on his coat, his neck scarf, his hat, his mittens and his snow boots. He says, "I have to be careful not to lose my mittens. My mom says she is not buying me another pair."

When Mark and Melissa get home from school. They take off their good clothes and put on their snowsuits. Now it is time to build that snow fort.

Clothing
Seasons
Self-Esteem
Weather

Dress-Me Dolls: Spring

Mark loves the springtime. The weather is perfect—not too hot and not too cold. The crispness in the air makes him feel full of energy. He brushes his teeth and combs his hair and then he wakes up Melissa. "Get up you sleepy head. The sun is climbing in the sky. We'll be late to school." Melissa opens her eyes and then pulls the covers up over her head. She is not ready to get up.

Mark hurries off to look in his closet for something to wear. "Let's see," he says, "I already wore a red shirt this week. I think I will wear my purple shirt with the yellow stripes." He pulls the shirt over his head. Then he puts on his favorite jeans. He wishes he could wear shorts but the weather is still a little chilly.

Mark puts on his socks and tennis shoes and goes back to see what Melissa is doing.

She is sitting on the edge of her bed staring at the jeans and shirt she laid out last night. Melissa is good about choosing her clothes at night so she doesn't have to think about it in the morning. However, this morning she is unhappy with her choice.

"What's wrong?" asks Mark.

FLANNEL BOARD / MAGNETIC BOARD STORIES

"I don't want to wear jeans. It feels like a dress kind of day to me today."

Melissa looks through her closet. She passes plaid dresses and polka-dot dresses and dresses with no designs at all. She finally decides on a green dress with daisies on the skirt.

"I will wear this one. It looks just like spring."

The two children finish dressing and hurry downstairs for breakfast. It is a beautiful spring day and both Mark and Melissa are ready to enjoy the weather.

Theme Connections

Clothing
Seasons
Self-Esteem
Weather

Dress-Me Dolls: Summer

Mark and Melissa love the summertime. They enjoy the many activities that are part of summer—baseball games, swimming lessons, picnics, days at the beach, and summer vacation. Mark and Melissa are packing their suitcases to go visit their grandparents for a week. Their grandparents live right on a beautiful lake.

Mark is going to wear his green shorts and a green and white striped T-shirt. Of course, he always wears his favorite sneakers in the summertime.

Melissa is going to wear her yellow sundress and sandals.

Mark is taking his swimming trunks and his baseball cap.

Melissa is taking two swimming suits and her sunglasses.

Mom won't let them get out of the house without their sunscreen. So both Mark and Melissa will be taking plenty of sunscreen along. Can you think of other things Mark and Melissa might need to pack?

Theme Connections

Clothing
Colors
Seasons
Self-Esteem
Weather

The Elf and the Dormouse

by Oliver Herford

Directions: Photocopy the story patterns on pages 337-339. Use a black fine-point permanent marker to trace patterns onto a piece of interfacing. Color them with crayons and cut them out.

Under a toadstool crept a wee elf,
Out of the rain to shelter himself.
Under the toadstool sound asleep,
Sat a big dormouse all in a heap.

Trembled the wee elf, frightened and yet,
Fearing to fly away lest he get wet.
To the next shelter—maybe a mile!
Suddenly the wee elf smiled a wee smile,
Tugged at the toadstool toppled in two.
Holding it over him happily he flew.
Soon he was safe home dry as could be.
Soon woke the dormouse—"Good
  gracious me!
Where is my toadstool?" loudly he
  lamented.
And that's how umbrellas first were
  invented.

Theme Connections

Mice
Opposites
Weather

The Elves and the Shoemaker

by Hans Christian Anderson

Directions: Make two photocopies of the story patterns on pages 340-345. Use a black fine-point marker to trace patterns onto interfacing. Color them with crayons and cut them out.

Once there was a kind and honest shoemaker who worked very hard every day. Even so, the poor man did not earn enough money to feed his wife and himself. Some days he and his wife had only water and a little bread for their supper. Finally, the poor shoemaker was down to his last piece of leather, and there was no money to buy more. Without leather he could make no more shoes.

Sadly, he drew a pattern on the last piece of leather and cut it out. When he was finished, he laid the pieces on his workbench. "In the morning," he said, "I will sew these pieces of leather together to make my last pair of shoes." Then he went upstairs to bed.

The next morning, the shoemaker went downstairs to his shop to stitch together the shoes. On his workbench, in the same spot where he had laid the leather piece the night before, sat a beautiful pair of shoes, all stitched and shined and ready to sell.

The shoemaker could hardly believe his eyes. He looked around his shop for any clue or explanation. Who could have made the shoes? He ran upstairs to his wife. "How did you do it?" he asked.

His wife only looked up at him and asked, "Do what?"

"The shoes! The shoes!" he cried. The wife looked at her husband, and he realized she did not know what he was talking about. The shoemaker pulled his wife up out of her chair and down the stairs to the shop. "Where did they come from? Who could have made them?" she asked as she picked up the shoes. "Look! They are beautiful!" She was still admiring the shoes when a customer came in.

The customer also admired the shoes and paid a very good price for them. The shoemaker was very excited. He took the money and bought enough leather to make two more pairs of shoes. That night, he cut the pieces, laid them on his workbench, and went upstairs. He dreamed about the next morning when he would stitch up the shoes.

The next morning, the shoemaker went down to his shop. There on the workbench were two fine pairs of shoes, stitched and polished and beautiful. Again, the shoemaker went upstairs for his wife and the two of them looked for any sign that might tell them how the shoes came to be.

Soon, more customers came in. Each paid a very good price for the shoes and ordered more. The shoemaker ran out and bought leather to make more shoes. From then on, he cut out the pieces in the evening and found the finished shoes in the morning. His customers were happy, his wife was happy, and the shoemaker was happy.

One night, the wife said to her husband, "I want to know who is sewing the shoes every night. Let's stay in the shop tonight and watch. Maybe we can get a look at whoever it is that comes to help us each night."

So the man and woman crept down the stairs and hid behind the counter and waited. Just about midnight, they saw two little elves come into the shop. They were so small, and so very ragged looking. Their clothes were torn and tattered. Their little toes stuck through the holes in their shoes.

The next day, the shoemaker and his wife thought about how the elves had helped them. They wanted to do something for the elves in return. The shoemaker set about to make the elves new shoes. The wife sewed new pants and a shirt, vest, and jacket for each of them. When the new clothes were ready, the couple laid everything out on the workbench. Then they hid behind the counter and waited.

Just about midnight, the elves came into the shop. When they found their handsome new shoes and beautiful new clothes, they hurried to put them on. They danced and laughed and sang. The happy little elves finally danced themselves out the door. The shoemaker and his wife never saw them again. But the shoe shop continued to do well and the man and woman were very happy. Often they would think about the elves and hope that they were happy, too.

Theme Connections

Clothing
Emotions
Families
Money
Opposites

Fat Cat: A Danish Folktale

Directions: Photocopy the story patterns on pages 346-353. Use a black fine-point marker to trace patterns onto interfacing. Color them with crayons and cut them out.

There was once an old woman who was cooking gruel. She was going to visit a neighbor so she asked the cat if he could look after the gruel while she was gone. "I'll be glad to," said the cat.

But when the old woman had gone, the gruel looked so good that the cat ate it all.

And the pot, too. When the old woman came back, she said to the cat, "Now what has happened to the gruel?"

"Oh," said the cat, "I ate the gruel and I ate the pot, too, and now I am going to also eat you." And he ate the old woman.

He went for a walk and on the way he met Skohottentot. And Skottentot said to him, "What have you been eating, my little cat?

You are so fat."

And the cat said, "I ate the gruel and the pot and the old woman, too. And now I am going to also eat you."

So he ate Skohottentot.

Afterwards he met Skolinkenlot. Skolinkenlot said, "What have you been eating, my little cat? You are so fat."

"I ate the gruel and the pot and the old woman, too, and Skohottentot," said the cat. "And now I am going to also eat you."

So he ate Skolinkenlot.

Next he met five birds in a flock. And they said to him, "What have you been eating, my little cat? You are so fat."

"I ate the gruel and the pot and the old woman, too, and Skohottentot and Skolinkenlot. And now I am going to also eat you."

And he ate the five birds in a flock.

Later he met three girls dancing. And they, too, said to him, "Gracious! What have you been eating, my little cat? You are so fat."

And the cat said, "I ate the gruel and the pot and the old woman, too, and Skohottentot and Skolinkenlot and five birds in a flock. And now I am going to also eat you."

And he ate the three girls dancing.

When he had gone a little farther, he met a lady with a pink parasol. And she, too, said to him,

"Heavens! What have you been eating my little cat? You are so fat."

"I ate the gruel and the pot and the old woman, too, and Skohottentot and Skolinkenlot and five birds in a flock and three girls dancing. And now I am going to also eat you." And he ate the lady with the pink parasol.

A little later he met a parson with a crooked staff. "Dear me! What have you been eating, my little cat? You are so fat."

"Oh," said the cat, "I ate the gruel and the pot and the old woman, too, and Skohottentot and Skolinkenlot and five birds in a flock and three girls dancing and the lady with the pink parasol. And now I am going to also eat you."

And he ate the parson with the crooked staff.

Next he met a woodcutter with an axe. "My! What have you been eating, my little cat! You are so fat."

"I ate the gruel and the pot and the old woman, too, and Skohottentot and Skolinkenlot and five birds in a flock and three girls dancing and the lady with the pink parasol and the parson with the crooked staff. And now I am going to also eat you."

"No. You are wrong, my little cat," said the woodcutter.

He took his axe and cut the cat open.

Out jumped the parson with the crooked staff and the lady with the pink parasol and the three girls dancing and the five birds in a flock and Skolinkenlot and Skohottentot. And the old woman took her pot and her gruel and went home with them.

As for the cat, the woodcutter stitched him up and placed a bandage on his tummy and made him promise to eat only cat food.

Theme Connections

Birds
Food
Opposites
Rhymes and Rhyming

Five Little Chickadees

Directions: Photocopy the story patterns on pages 354-358. Use a black fine-point marker to trace patterns onto interfacing. Color them with crayons and cut them out.

Presentation: Teach the children the following rhyme. Set up the flannel board with the door, sun and tree. Hold up the number five card. Ask a child to put five chickadees in the tree.

Have the class count together: "one, two, three, four, five." Repeat the rhyme. When the words "chickadee fly away" are said, ask the same child to remove one of the birds. Have the class count the chickadees again— "one, two, three, four." At the end of the rhyme, choose another child and repeat the activity.

Five little chickadees peeping at the door,
One flew away, and then there were four.

Chickadee, chickadee, happy and gay,
Chickadee, chickadee, fly away.

Four little chickadees sitting in a tree,
One flew away, and then there were three.

Chickadee, chickadee, happy and gay,
Chickadee, chickadee, fly away.

Three little chickadees looking at you,
One flew away, and then there were two.

Chickadee, chickadee, happy and gay,
Chickadee, chickadee, fly away.

Two little chickadees sitting in the sun,
One flew away, and then there was one.

Chickadee, chickadee, happy and gay,
Chickadee, chickadee, fly away.

One little chickadee left all alone,
It flew away, and then there was none.

Chickadee, chickadee, happy and gay,
Chickadee, chickadee, fly away.

Theme Connections

Birds
Counting
Emotions
Nature
Numbers

Frosty the Snowman

Directions: Photocopy the story patterns on pages 359-361. Use a black fine-point marker to trace patterns onto interfacing. Color them with crayons and cut them out.

Frosty the Snowman was a jolly happy soul,
With a corncob pipe and a button nose and two eyes made out of coal.
Frosty the snowman is a fairy tale they say:
He was made of snow but the children know how he came to life one day.

There must have been some magic in that old silk hat they found.
For when they placed it on his head, he began to dance around.
Oh, Frosty the Snowman was alive as he could be,
And the children say he could laugh and play just the same as you and me.

Frosty the Snowman knew the sun was hot that day,
So he said, "Let's run and we'll have some fun now before I melt away."
Down to the village with a broomstick in his hand,
Running here and there all around the square, sayin', "Catch me if you can."

He led them down the streets of town right to the traffic cop.
And he only paused a moment when he heard him holler, "Stop!"
For Frosty the snowman had to hurry on his way.

*So he waved goodbye, sayin', "Don't you
cry; I'll be back again someday."
Thumpety, thump thump, thumpety
thump thump,
Look at Frosty go;
Thumpety thump thump, thumpety
thump thump,
Over the hill of snow.*

Theme Connections

Emotions
Seasons
Sounds of Language
Weather

The Gingerbread Man

Directions: Photocopy the story patterns on pages 362-366. Use a black fine-point permanent marker to trace patterns onto a piece of interfacing. Color them with crayons and cut them out.

Once upon a time, a little old woman and a little old man lived in a little old house in a little old village. One day the little old woman decided to make a gingerbread man. She cut him out of dough and put him in the oven to bake. After a while, the little old woman said to herself, "That gingerbread man must be ready by now." She went to the oven door and opened it. Up jumped the gingerbread man, and away he ran. As he ran he shouted, "Run, run as fast as you can. You can't catch me. I'm the gingerbread man!"

The little old woman ran after the gingerbread man, but she couldn't catch him.

He ran past the little old man who was working in the garden. "Stop, stop!" called the little old man. But the gingerbread man just called back, "Run, run as fast as you can. You can't catch me. I'm the gingerbread man."

The little old man joined the little old woman and ran as fast as he could after the gingerbread man, but he couldn't catch him. The gingerbread man ran past a dog. "Stop, stop!" said the dog. But the gingerbread man just called back, "Run, run as fast as you can. You can't catch me. I'm the gingerbread man."

The dog joined the little old woman and the little old man and ran as fast as he could after the gingerbread man, but he couldn't catch him. The gingerbread man ran past a cat. "Stop, stop!" said the cat. But the gingerbread man just called back, "Run, run as fast as you can. You can't catch me. I'm the gingerbread man."

The cat joined the little old woman and the little old man and the dog, but she couldn't catch the gingerbread man. Soon the gingerbread man came to a fox lying by the side of a river, and he shouted, "Run, run, as fast as you can. You can't catch me. I'm the gingerbread man! I ran away from the little old woman, the little old man, the dog, and the cat, and I can run away from you, I can."

But the sly old fox just laughed and said, "If you don't get across this river quickly, you will surely get caught. If you hop on my tail I will carry you across." The gingerbread man saw that he had no time to lose, so he quickly hopped onto the fox's tail.

"Oh!" said the fox. "The water is getting deeper. Climb on my back so you won't get wet." And the gingerbread man did.

"Oh!" said the fox. "The water is getting deeper. Climb on my nose so you won't get wet." And the gingerbread man did. Then the fox tossed the gingerbread man into his mouth. And that was the end of the gingerbread man!

Theme Connections

Cats
Dogs
Food
Foxes
Tricksters

Goldilocks and the Three Bears

Directions: Photocopy the story patterns on pages 367-372. Use a black fine-point permanent marker to trace patterns onto a piece of interfacing. Color them with crayons and cut them out.

Once upon a time there were three bears. There was a mama bear, a papa bear, and a little bear. They all lived in the forest. One day, the bears went out for a walk to visit a sick friend.

While they were gone, a little girl named Goldilocks was walking in the woods. Realizing that she had lost her way, she walked till she came to a small cottage. Upon entering the house, she saw three bowls of porridge sitting on a table. She was very hungry. She tasted the porridge in the large bowl. It was too hot. So she tried the porridge in the middle size bowl. It was too cold. She tried the porridge in the small bowl. It was just right, so Goldilocks ate it all up.

After eating, she went over to the three chairs sitting before a fireplace. She found the biggest chair to be too hard. The middle-size chair was too soft. She sat in the third chair because it seemed just right. As she sat in the chair, it wobbled, rattled, and fell apart.

By now the little girl was very tired, so she went into the other room and found three beds. The first bed was very hard. The second bed was too soft. The third bed was just right, so she fell asleep right away.

Meanwhile, the bears came home from their walk. Finding an empty bowl on the table

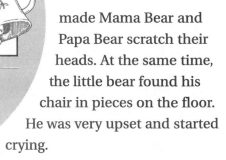

made Mama Bear and Papa Bear scratch their heads. At the same time, the little bear found his chair in pieces on the floor. He was very upset and started crying.

Hearing the noise, Goldilocks came down to find out what was wrong. When she saw the bears, she was very surprised and a little frightened! She explained that she was lost, and that she was sorry she ate up the porridge and broke the chair. The bears were kind bears. They told Goldilocks she was forgiven. Mama ear packed Goldilocks a basket of cookies, and Papa Bear and Baby Bear helped her find her way to the path back home.

Theme Connections

Bears
Emotions
Food
Houses and Homes
Numbers

Spanish Translation

Goldilocks y los Tres Osos

La traviesa Ricitos de Oro se fue al bosque a pasear. Descubrio la mas simpatica casita. Como la puerta estaba abierta, entro. En la sala habia tres sillones. En el comedor, tres sillas. En la mesa, tres platos de sopa. Ricitos de Oro probo los tres sillones.

El mas grande lo encontro muy alto. El mediano lo encontro muy bajo. Y el mas pequeno? Bueno, del mas pequeno solo supo que, cuando ella se sento, se rompio.

Luego probo los tres platos de sopa. La sopa del mayor estaba muy caliente, la del mediano muy fria. Y la del menor? La del plato menor se la tomo toda!

Ricitos de Oro subio al dormitorio. Probo la cama mayor y estaba muy dura.

Probo la cama mediana y estaba muy blanda. Y la menor?

La menor estaba tan rica y tan suave que se durmio en ella.

Cuando los tres osos regresaron a su casita encontraron la puerta abierta.

El papa Oso dijo, rugiendo con voz de trueno:

-¡Alguien se ha sentado en mi sillon y alguien ha probado mi sopa! Entonces la mama Osa, dijo enojada:

-¡Alguien se ha sentado en mi silla y alguien ha probado mi sopa! Por ultimo, el Osito dijo Il orando:

-¡Alguien se ha sentado en mi sillita...y me la ha roto y alguien...se ha tomado toda mi sopa!

Los tres osos entonces subieron al dormitorio. El papa Oso rugio con voz de trueno:

-¡Alguien se ha acostado en mi cama! La mama Osa dijo enojada:

-¡Alguien se ha acostado en mi cama! Y el Osito dijo muy bajito:

-¡Shhh...que alguien se ha acostado en mi cama y esta dormida en ella!

En ese momento Ricitos de Oro se desperto. Al ver a los tres osos se dio un susto terrible.

Entonces se acordo que tenia varios caramelos en el bolsillo de su delantal.

Le convido uno a cada oso. Y desde ese dia se hicieron muy amigos.

The Great Big Pumpkin

by Pam Schiller

Directions: Photocopy the story patterns on pages 373-374. Use a black fine-point permanent marker to trace patterns onto a piece of interfacing. Color them with crayons and cut them out.

One day Little Bear was out looking for honey. She was very hungry. But she couldn't find a single thing to eat. Just as she was about to give up, she spied a very funny something. It was big, very big, and round, very round, and orange, very orange. Little Bear had never seen anything quite like it.

She went to get a closer look.

"I'm going to take you home to my Mama," she said. Little Bear tried to roll the big, round, orange thing. It didn't move. She tried again. It didn't move.

Just then Skunk came along. "Hey, what's that?"

"I don't know," said Little Bear. "I want to take it home to my Mama, but I can't move it."

"Let me help," said Skunk.

Little Bear and Skunk pushed and pushed. The big, round, orange thing didn't move.

Just then Squirrel came along. "Hey, what's that?"

"We don't know," said Little Bear. "I want to take it home to my Mama, but we can't move it."

"Let me help," said Squirrel.

Little Bear and Skunk and Squirrel pushed and pushed and pushed. The big, round, orange thing didn't move.

Just then Mouse came along. "Hey, what's that?"

"I don't know," said Little Bear. "I want to take it home to my Mama, but we can't move it."

"Let me help," said Mouse. Little Bear and Skunk and Squirrel and Mouse pushed and pushed and pushed and pushed.

Slowly, the big, round, orange thing started to move. Then it started to roll. It rolled and rolled and rolled. . . all the way to Little Bear's den. Little Bear's Mama came out to see what was going on. "Where did you find this lovely, big, round, orange pumpkin?" she asked.

The four friends looked at each other and said, "PUMPKIN?"

Little Bear's mama used the big pumpkin to make a great, big pumpkin pie, and it was delicious! Yum!

Theme Connections

Bears
Families
Food
Growing Things
Opposites
Skunks
Squirrels

The Great Big Turnip

by Pam Schiller

Directions: Photocopy the story patterns on pages 374-375. Use a black fine-point permanent marker to trace patterns onto a piece of interfacing. Color them with crayons and cut them out.

Once upon a time an old man planted a turnip. The turnip grew and grew. At last it was ready to be pulled.

The old man tugged at the turnip. He pulled and he tugged. He tugged and he pulled. But the turnip would not come out of the ground.

The old man called the old woman. The old man tugged at the turnip. The old woman tugged at the old man. They pulled and they tugged. They tugged and they pulled. But the turnip would not come out of the ground.

The old woman called the dog.

The old man tugged at the turnip. The old woman tugged at the old man.

The dog tugged at the old woman. They pulled and they tugged. The tugged and they pulled. But the turnip would not come out of the ground.

The dog called the pig.

The old man tugged at the turnip. The old woman tugged at the old man. The dog tugged at the old woman. The pig tugged at the dog. They pulled and they tugged. They tugged and they pulled. But the turnip would not come out of the ground.

The pig called the cat.

The old man tugged at the turnip. The old woman tugged at the old man. The dog tugged at the old woman. The pig tugged at the dog. The cat pulled at the pig. They pulled and they tugged. They tugged and they pulled. But the turnip would not come out of the ground.

The cat called the mouse.

The old man tugged at the turnip. The old woman tugged at the old man. The dog tugged at the old woman. The pig tugged at the dog. The cat pulled at the pig. The mouse tugged at the cat. They pulled and they tugged. They tugged and they pulled-Oh, how they pulled! Oh, how they tugged! And the turnip came out of the ground.

Theme Connections

Cats	Mice
Dogs	Oppsites
Food	Pigs
Growing Things	

The Gunny Wolf
(United States: African–American)

Directions: Photocopy the story patterns on pages 376-377. Use a black fine-point permanent marker to trace patterns onto a piece of interfacing. Color them with crayons and cut them out.

A man and his little daughter lived alone near the edge of the forest. Now, that man knew there were wolves in the forest, so he built a fence around the house, and told his little daughter she must on no account go outside the gate while he was away.

One morning when he had gone away, the little girl was picking flowers. She thought it would do no harm just to peep through the gate to see if there were flowers on the other side. Sure enough, there were beautiful flowers just on the other side of the gate. She stepped outside the gate to pick the flowers and then noticed that there were more flowers just a little further off. She picked those flowers and then continued to walk farther and farther away as she saw flowers just a short distance from the ones she had just picked. As she picked the flowers she sang a song,

Tra-la-la-la
Fa-so-la
Do-re-mi

All of the sudden she heard a noise. She stopped picking flowers, and looked up, and what should she see but a great big gunny wolf. The gunny wolf said, "Sing me that good, sweet song again."

So the little girl sang,

Tra-la-la-la
Fa-so-la
Do-re-mi

And the gunny wolf lay down, and fell asleep.

Zzzzz (make a snoring sound)

The little girl tiptoed away.
But the gunny wolf woke up!

Hunk-a-cha!
Hunk-a-cha!
Hunk-a-cha!

He ran after the little girl, and when he caught her he said, "Sing me that good, sweet song again."

So the little girl sang,

Tra-la-la-la
Fa-so-la
Do-re-mi

And the gunny wolf lay down, and fell asleep.

Zzzzzz (make a snoring sound)

The little girl tiptoed away, and she was almost to the front gate when the gunny wolf woke up!

Hunk-a-cha!
Hunk-a-cha!
Hunk-a-cha!

He ran after the little girl, and when he caught her he said, "Sing me that good, sweet song again." So the little girl sang,

> Tra-la-la-la
> Fa-so-la
> Do-re-mi

And the gunny wolf lay down, and fell asleep.

Zzzzzz *(make a snoring sound)*

The little girl tiptoed all the way home, and she closed the gate, and went inside the house, and locked the door, and after that, she stayed away from the woods where the gunny wolf lived.

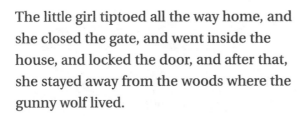

Theme Connections

Families
Flowers
Music
Sounds of Language
Tricksters
Wolves

Henny-Penny

Directions: Photocopy the story patterns on pages 378-379. Use a black fine-point permanent marker to trace patterns onto a piece of interfacing. Color them with crayons and cut them out.

Once upon a time there was a little hen named Henny-Penny. She lived in a barnyard with her friends, Cocky-Locky, Ducky-Lucky, Turkey-Lurkey, and Goosey-Loosey. Everyday the farmer's wife would scatter seeds and grain for Henny-Penny and her friends to eat.

One day while Henny-Penny was peck, peck, pecking the seeds and grains the farmer's wife had scattered, something hit her right on top of her head. "What was that?" said Henny-Penny. She looked up at the sky and, seeing nothing but sky, she began to cluck loudly. "Something just hit me on the head. The sky is falling. I must go quickly and tell the king."

So off Henny-Penny went walking as fast as she could. Soon she met Cocky-Locky. "Where are you going?" said Cocky-Locky. Without even looking back, Henny-Penny answered, "The sky is falling! I'm off to tell the king." Cocky-Locky looked up at the sky. He said, "The sky looks fine to me." "A piece of the sky fell right on my head" said Henny-Penny. "Oh, my!" said Cocky-Locky, and he joined Henny-Penny in her journey.

So on Henny-Penny and Cocky-Locky went walking as fast as they could. Soon they met

Ducky-Lucky. "Where are you going?" said Ducky-Lucky. Without even looking back, Henny-Penny answered, "The sky is falling! We're off to tell the king."

Ducky-Lucky looked up at the sky. She said, "The sky looks fine to me." "A piece of the sky fell right on my head" said Henny-Penny. "Oh, my!" said Ducky-Lucky and she joined Henny-Penny and Cocky-Locky in their journey.

So on Henny-Penny, Cocky-Locky, and Ducky-Lucky went walking as fast as they could. Soon they met Turkey-Lurkey. "Where are you going?" said Turkey-Lurkey.

Without even looking back, Henny-Penny answered, "The sky is falling! We're off to tell the king." Turkey-Lurkey looked up at the sky. He said, "The sky looks fine to me." "A piece of the sky fell right on my head" said Henny-Penny. "Oh, my!" said Turkey-Lurkey and he joined Henny-Penny, Cocky-Locky, and Ducky-Lucky in their journey.

So on Henny-Penny, Cocky-Locky, Ducky-Lucky and Turkey-Lurkey went walking as fast as they could. Soon they met Goosey-Loosey. "Where are you going?" said Goosey-Loosey. Without even looking back, Henny-Penny answered, "The sky is falling! We're off to tell the king." Goosey-Loosey looked up at the sky. She said, "The sky looks fine to me." "A piece of the sky fell right on my head" said Henny-Penny.

"Oh, my!" said Goosey-Loosey and she joined Henny-Penny, Cocky-Locky, Ducky-Lucky and Turkey-Lurkey in their journey.

Soon the five friends met Foxy-Loxy. "Where are you going?" asked Foxy-Loxy.

"The sky is falling. We're off to tell the king." The five answered together. "May I show you the way?" asked Foxy-Loxy. The five friends suddenly realized that they did not know where the king lived. So they said "Oh, thank you, Foxy-Loxy."

Foxy-Loxy took Henny-Penny, Cocky-Locky, Ducky-Lucky, Turkey-Lurkey and Goosey-Loosey straight to his den and they were never seen again. Do you know what happened to them?

Theme Connections

Farms
Foxes
Friends
Kings and Queens
Rhymes and Rhyming
Tricksters

I Like Black

by Pam Schiller

Directions: Photocopy the story patterns on pages 380-381. Use a black fine-point permanent marker to trace patterns onto a piece of interfacing. Color them with crayons and cut them out.

I like black,
Not yellow, red, or blue.
I like black,
I bet you like it, too.
Blackbirds, black flowers,
Tall and shiny black towers.
Tiny black baby kittens,
Warm and wooly black mittens.

FLANNEL BOARD / MAGNETIC BOARD STORIES

Blackberries, black
cherries,
Black socks, black rocks.
I like black,
Not yellow, red, or blue.
I like black
I really, really do!

Theme Connections

Colors

I Like Blue

by Pam Schiller

Directions: Photocopy the story patterns on pages 382-384. Use a black fine-point permanent marker to trace patterns onto a piece of interfacing. Color them with crayons and cut them out.

I like blue,
I really, really do.
I like blue,
Do you like it too?

I like white clouds on blue skies,
I like large ships on blue oceans,
I like the blue color of my sister's eyes
I like blue lotions and notions.

Blue balls, blue cars,
Blue blankets, blue stars,
Blue birds, blue hats,
Do they make blue cats?

Blueberries are yummy,
They tickle my tummy.
Blue suckers are dandy,
My most favorite candy.

I like blue,
I really, really do.
I like blue,
Do you like it too?

Theme Connections

Colors

I Like Green

by Pam Schiller

Directions: Photocopy the story patterns on pages 385-386. Use a black fine-point permanent marker to trace patterns onto a piece of interfacing. Color them with crayons and cut them out.

I like green. I like it a lot.
I like green frogs, believe it or not.
I like green jello. I like green bugs.
I'm a green fellow from blankets to rugs.
Green ribbons are keen. Green clover is neat.
I really love green. It can't be beat.
I like green fish. Oh, can't you see?
Think what you wish. Green's the color for me.

Theme Connections

Colors

I Like Orange

by Pam Schiller

Directions: Photocopy the story patterns on page 387. Use a black fine-point permanent marker to trace patterns onto a piece of interfacing. Color them with crayons and cut them out.

I like orange. I like it a lot.
I like orange. I think it is hot.
Orange candy, orange cats,
Orange balls, and orange bats.
Orange crayons, orange paint,
Isn't orange quaint?
Orange is the color that I like the best.
I say it with zeal; I say it with zest.
You can take away blue, purple, red, yellow, too.
Just don't take away orange whatever you do!

Theme Connections

Colors

I Like Purple

by Pam Schiller

Directions: Photocopy the story patterns on pages 389-390. Use a black fine-point permanent marker to trace patterns onto a piece of interfacing. Color them with crayons and cut them out.

I like purple. Purple, purple, purple.
I like how it looks. I like how it sounds
I like it in books. I like it on clowns.
I like purple every minute of the day.

I like it when I work. I like it when I play.
I like purple, every shade and every hue.
It's purple for me whatever I do.
Purple snow cones, purple drinks,
Purple houses, purple inks,
Purple dogs and purple cats,
Purple snails and purple rats.
Purple monsters, purple dreams,
Purple stars and purple moonbeams.
Give me purple every day.
Let's hear it for purple-hip, hip, hooray!

Theme Connections

Colors

I Like Red

by Pam Schiller

Directions: Photocopy the story patterns on pages 391-392. Use a black fine-point permanent marker to trace patterns onto a piece of interfacing. Color them with crayons and cut them out.

I like red. I like it a bunch.
I like red jam. I like red punch.
I like red flowers. I like red shoes.
Red is the color I always choose.
I like red. Red's the best.
I like red socks. I like red vests.
I like red hair. Oh, can't you see?
Red is the only color for me.

Theme Connections

Colors

I Like White

by Pam Schiller

Directions: Photocopy the story patterns on pages 393-395. Use a black fine-point permanent marker to trace patterns onto a piece of interfacing. Color them with crayons and cut them out.

I like white. I like it day or night.
I like white shoes. I like white socks.
White's the color I choose when I'm picking
    up rocks.
I like white. It never, ever clashes.
It's always just right with ribbons and sashes.
White soft marshmallows, white fluffy
    pillows,
White little birds and white furry cats.
White balls, white flowers, white hats,
White cakes, white clouds, white snow.
It's white, white, white wherever I go.

Theme Connections

Colors

I Like Yellow

by Pam Schiller

Directions: Photocopy the story patterns on pages 396-399. Use a black fine-point permanent marker to trace patterns onto a piece of interfacing. Color them with crayons and cut them out.

I like yellow. Yellow is swell.
I like yellow, I bet you can tell!

Yellow balloons, big yellow bows,
Yellow nail polish on my toes.
Yellow kittens, yellow beach balls,
Yellow mittens, bright yellow walls.
Yellow cake icing on my cake.
Yellow inner tubes on the lake.
Yellow flowers, sweet yellow bees,
Big yellow leaves in yellow trees.
Yellow, yellow, yellow, yellow,
I'm a happy yellow fellow!

Theme Connections

Colors

Issun Boshi

Directions: Photocopy the story patterns on pages 400-405. Use a black fine-point permanent marker to trace patterns onto a piece of pelon. Color them with crayons and cut them out.

Once there was a mother who had a tiny baby boy. He was so tiny; he was only as big as your finger—just one inch long. So his parents called him Issun Boshi. Issun means "one." Boshi means "inch."

Issun Boshi's parents fed him from doll dishes. They dressed him in tiny doll clothes. He slept in a porcelain matchbox. He liked to hide under teacups and paddle around the lily pond on twigs. Issun Boshi was a darling, tiny baby, but he never grew at all. So when he was one year old, he was still one inch tall.

When he was five years old, he was still one inch tall. And when Issun Boshi was twelve, he was still just one inch tall.

But despite his tiny size, Issun Boshi wanted to go out and see the world.

"Mother, Father, " said Issun Boshi. "I am ready to go out into the world."

"No, no. You are much too small," said his mother, "How would you defend yourself?"

"I will take a sword," said Issun Boshi.

"Where will you find a sword small enough for you, Little One Inch?"

Issun Boshi looked around the house. "I will use my mother's sewing needle."

So his mother made him a little belt, and he wore the sewing needle at his waist like a real sword.

"I will need a boat," said Issun Boshi.

"Where would we find a boat small enough for you?" asked his parents.

Issun Boshi looked around the house. "Give me a rice bowl for a boat!"

"Now for my oars," said Issun Boshi.

"But where can we find oars small enough for you?" asked his parents.

Issun Boshi looked around the house. "Just give me a pair of chopsticks!"

Issun Boshi's parents carried his rice bowl boat to the river and set it on the water. They set little Issun Boshi inside the rice bowl and handed him his chopstick oars.

"Goodbye, Mother. Goodbye, Father. When you see me again, I will have made my fortune."

Issun Boshi pushed off from the shore and began to row downstream. He rowed and

rowed. He rowed on one side of the river, and then the other.

At last his little boat reached the city. He rowed his boat to shore and jumped out.

Issun Boshi wandered through the streets, staring up at the grand houses. He had to walk very carefully, right next to a stonewall so that the thousands of feet hurrying by wouldn't trample him.

At last Issun Boshi came to the home of a wealthy prince. He went right up to this house and knocked at the door.

"Issun Boshi has come to offer his services."

A servant opened the door, but little Issun Boshi was standing beside a wooden clog on the step. The servant could see no one. A tiny voice called out, "Issun Boshi has come to offer his services."

The servant looked all around. "Who is speaking?"

"Here I am. Look down," called Little One Inch.

The servant was so frightened by what he saw that he slammed the door shut and ran to call the prince.

The Prince came to the door and spoke to Little One Inch. "Who are you, and what do you want?"

"I am Issun Boshi, and I want to work for you. I want to be your servant."

"My servant?" asked the prince. "No, not my servant, but would you like to be my daughter's playmate?"

So Issun Boshi and the princess became playmates. Everywhere the princess went, Little One Inch went with her—sometimes perched on a flower in her hair, sometimes tucked in her sash.

They liked to play cards-Issun Boshi learned to lay them on the edged of a table and flip them over. The princess taught him origami—he could fold the tiniest paper cranes you've ever seen.

One day, as the princess and Issun Boshi were walking in the forest, a giant leaped out from behind a tree and grabbed the princess.

"Leave my friend alone," Little One Inch shouted. "Let her go or you shall suffer."

This, of course, amused the giant, who couldn't imagine what such a tiny little thing could do to harm him. As tears of laughter streamed down the giant's face, he dropped his magic golden hammer.

"Look," cried Little One Inch. "The giant dropped his magic hammer. Pound the hammer and make a wish quickly."

The giant was so afraid that the princess would wish him dead that he ran off screaming into the forest.

The princess picked up the hammer and looked at Issun Boshi. She looked at the hammer. She looked back at Issun Boshi.

"Do you want to be big?" she asked.

"A little bigger would be nice," he said.

The princess pounded the ground with the hammer. "Make Issun Boshi a little bigger."

Issun Boshi began to grow.

"Still a little bigger would be nice," he said.

The princess pounded the hammer again, and Issun Boshi grew some more. Soon Issun Boshi was as big as the princess.

Issun Boshi was used to being tiny, so he had to learn to be big. It was sometimes inconvenient, but he liked being big. And he certainly enjoyed being the princess's friend for the rest of their lives.

Theme Connections

Boats and Ships
Families
Friends
Opposites

Jack and the Beanstalk

Directions: Photocopy the story patterns on pages 407-410. Use a black fine-point permanent marker to trace patterns onto a piece of interfacing. Color them with crayons and cut them out.

Long ago there was a boy named Jack, who lived with his mother, a poor widow. Jack's father had died of a broken heart when all of his money and his magic goose had been stolen one day. Times had been hard for Jack and his mother. They were very poor. They had sold most of their furniture to buy bread. Their poor little cottage was practically empty. The only thing left of any value was Daisy, their cow. Every morning she gave milk, which Jack took to market and sold. But one sad day Daisy gave no milk, and then things looked bad indeed. "Never mind, mother," said Jack. "We must sell Daisy. Trust me to make a good bargain." And away he went to the market.

As Jack walked down the road toward the market, he met a butcher. "Good morning," said the butcher. "Where are you going?"

"I am going to market to sell the cow." "It's lucky I met you," said the butcher. "You may save yourself the trouble of going so far. I will buy your cow right here."

With this, the butcher put his hand in his pocket and pulled out five curious-looking beans. "I will give you these magic beans in exchange for your cow. If you plant them overnight, they'll grow up and reach the sky by the next morning."

"Done!" cried Jack. He took the beans and ran all the way home to tell his mother how lucky he had been. His mother was horrified. "We could have eaten many meals with the money that cow would have brought, but now all we have are some worthless beans!" she cried. She was so angry that she threw the beans out the window and sent poor Jack to bed.

When Jack woke up the next morning, he ran to the window to see if the beans had grown. There, beside his window, was a giant beanstalk. It stretched up and up as far as Jack could see, into the clouds.

Jack jumped out the window and began to climb the beanstalk. He climbed up and up, into the clouds. When at last the stalk ended, Jack found himself in a new and beautiful country. A little way off there was a great castle.

Jack walked straight to the castle. It was tremendous, much too big for people his size. Jack was very curious. He slipped under the door and went inside. There he saw a great table. On the table were big bags of gold coins. Jack recognized the big bags of gold coins: they used to belong to his father!

All of a sudden, the castle floor began to shake. Footsteps! Then Jack heard a deep, booming voice from down the hall: "Fee, fi, fo, fum, I smell the blood of an Englishman."

Jack was very frightened. He saw a mean, ugly giant coming down the hall. Trembling, he reached up on the table, grabbed one of the moneybags, and ran as fast as he could. He slipped under the door, raced back to the beanstalk, and scurried back to his cottage lickety-split.

Jack and his mother were now quite rich. They had everything they needed and most of what they wanted. But Jack was not satisfied. He kept thinking about the rest of his father's bags of gold coins. So while his mother was away at market, he climbed up the beanstalk until he was at the top again.

Jack ran to the castle and slipped under the door to grab another bag of gold coins. As he sneaked toward the room with the great table, he saw something that shocked him. The giant was sitting at the table talking to the magic goose that had belonged to Jack's father! "Lay!" said the giant, and the goose at once laid a beautiful golden egg. "Lay!" said the giant, and the goose laid another golden egg. "Lay!" said the giant, and the goose laid a third golden egg.

Then the giant stopped. He sniffed the air. He got a mean look on his face and bellowed: "Fee, fi, fo, fum, I smell the blood of an Englishman." With a fearful roar, the giant seized his oak-tree club, and dashed after Jack. Jack ran under the table. When the giant brought down his mighty club, the table smashed to pieces and the goose fell to the floor. At once, Jack scooped up the goose and ran for the door.

The giant chased after Jack, but he was clumsy and tripped over his own big foot. Jack started down the beanstalk lickity-split. Before the giant could stand and run, Jack had reached the ground. Quickly, he took an ax and cut down the beanstalk. The giant could never chase him now.

Jack then skipped into the house to show his mother the magic goose that would lay golden eggs for them. And the three of them—Jack, his mother, and the goose— lived happily ever after.

Theme Connections

Cows
Emotions
Families
Food
Geese
Growing Things
Houses and Homes
Money

The Lazy Fox
(Argentina)

Directions: Photocopy the story patterns on page 411-413. Use a black fine-point permanent marker to trace patterns onto a piece of interfacing. Color them with crayons and cut them out.

A tricky fox had a farm. He was too lazy to work on his farm. No one wanted to work for him. One morning, he said, "I must plant something in my fields, or I will be hungry. What can I do?" He thought and thought. Finally he had an idea. "I will tell my neighbor, who is a silly armadillo, to plant my fields. I will promise to give him a part of the crop. But it will only be a very small part."

The fox went to see the armadillo. "Good day, my friend," the fox called. "I want to help you." "Help me?" asked the armadillo. He could not believe his ears. "Yes. The land on your farm is dry and full of rocks. Why don't you plant on my good land? As payment, you can give me a small part of your crop."

"You are very kind," answered the armadillo. The armadillo knew the fox was very smart. He thought the fox had some trick. "You may plant anything you want," said the fox. "I will take only half of it." "That is fair," the armadillo said slowly. "I have a better idea," said the fox. "I will take only the part that grows under the ground. You may have everything that grows above the ground." "Okay," said the armadillo. The next morning, the armadillo and his family went to the fox's fields. The fox saw them working hard. He was happy with his trick. He did not ask what they were planting.

The plants grew in the rain and the sunshine. Finally it was time to pick the crop. The armadillo and his family picked a big crop of wheat. But the lazy fox got only roots. The fox was very angry and very hungry. He went to the armadillo's house. "You made a terrible mistake," the fox shouted at his neighbor. "I cannot eat these roots! You know the good part of the wheat grows above the ground. Next year, we will work together again. You take the part that grows under the ground. I will take the part that grows above the ground." "That is fair," said the armadillo slowly. "Do you want to choose the crop?" "No, but you must choose it carefully. Just tell me when the food is ready to eat."

The next year, the armadillo planted potatoes. Again the crop was very good. The fox got only the tops of the potato plants. The potatoes grew under the ground. The fox went to his neighbor's farm. "Last year I thought you made a stupid mistake. Now I think you are tricking me. I cannot eat the tops of the potato plants. You never think about me when you plant your crop. See how thin and weak I am."

"You are thin," said the armadillo, "but you look better that way." The fox was angry. "Next year I will take the tops of the plants and the part that grows under the ground. You take the part that grows in the middle. I must have the bigger part next year. I had nothing for two years." The armadillo answered slowly, "That is fair." The fox was happy. He was sure the armadillo could not trick him again.

The next year, the armadillo planted corn. The crop was large, with beautiful fat ears of corn in the middle of the plants. The fox got only the roots and the leaves. The fox ran to the armadillo's house. He and his family were eating some corn. "Come, eat some corn with us," said the armadillo. "Then we can talk about next year's crop." "No!" said the fox. "You tricked me for three years." The armadillo said, "I'm sorry. You asked for a part of the crop. I gave you the part you wanted." The hungry fox looked at the corn. He looked at the armadillo and said to himself, "Why did I call him stupid?"

"Next year, I will plant my own crop," said the fox, "and keep all of it!" He went home sadly. The armadillo took one more ear of corn and laughed so hard that his armor almost cracked.

Theme Connections

Armadillos
Growing Things
Foxes
Tricksters

Little Annie Oakley

by Pam Schiller

Directions: Photocopy the story patterns on pages 414-416. Use a black fine-point permanent marker to trace patterns onto a piece of interfacing. Color them and cut them out.

Annie Oakley lived a long time ago. She was one of the bravest cowgirls in the entire West. Madison loved Annie Oakley. She watched all the Annie Oakley shows on TV. She read all the Annie Oakley books in the library. She had a big poster of Annie Oakley right over her bed. Madison loved how well Annie Oakley rode her horse. She loved how skillful her aim was. She loved the way she wore her cowgirl hat, her cowgirl boots, and her fringed cowgirl vest and skirt. Madison wanted to be just like Annie Oakley when she grew up.

When Madison's daddy gave her an Annie Oakley outfit for her birthday, Madison was happy beyond words. Right on top of the box, it said: The Official Annie Oakley Cowgirl Outfit. When Madison put on the outfit, she was convinced that she had become the real, true, one and only Annie Oakley, Queen of the West.

On Rodeo Day, Madison was excited about wearing her new Annie Oakley outfit to school. She put on the boots. She put on the fringed vest and the skirt. She put on the big cowgirl hat. She looked in the mirror and said, "I am the true, real, one and only Annie Oakley, Queen of the West."

When Madison got to school, she told everyone she was the real, true, one and only Annie Oakley. Her friends laughed and said it wasn't true. Madison said, "Yes, I really am Annie Oakley." Her friends said, " No, you aren't." Madison said, "Yes, I am!"

Her friends told the teacher. Madison didn't care. She still declared, "I am the real, true, one and only Annie Oakley."

Madison's teacher smiled and put her arm around Madison. She said, "When I was a little girl, I wanted to be a famous singer. When I sang for my mom and dad and they applauded I felt like I was a real performer. I think Madison looks every bit like the Annie Oakley I've seen on TV. I'm sure when she grows up she will make a fine cowgirl—she will be just like Annie Oakley."

Madison was so happy that someone took her seriously. She felt 10 feet tall! When she got home from school she told her mom all about what her teacher had said. Then she took off her Annie Oakley outfit, folded it neatly, and put it back in the box. She decided that when she grew up she would create her own special cowgirl outfit.

Theme Connections

Clothing
Cowboys/Cowgirls
Emotions
Growing Up

Little Engine Ninety-Nine

by Pam Schiller

Directions: Photocopy the story patterns on page s 417-422. Use a black fine-point permanent marker to trace patterns onto a piece of interfacing. Color them and cut them out.

Even before the last coat of the shiny black paint on his smokestack was dry little engine ninety-nine knew what kind of a train he wanted to be.

He didn't want to pull tank cars full of chemicals. He didn't want to pull cars full of passengers. He didn't want to pull heavy equipment. He wanted to be a circus train. He wanted to pull cars full of elephants, giraffes, bears, and lions. He loved animals. He had been dreaming of being a circus train ever since the mechanics where tightening the first bolts on his wheels.

Now it was his moment. Soon someone would start his engine and he would begin to work just like the other trains he had watched come and go from the station. He was so excited he wanted to toot his horn but he stood quiet and still, hoping that someone would declare him ready for work.

He stood still all day and all night and all day again. Would anyone ever come for him? He saw a big brown engine coming toward him. He spoke as the engine drew near, "Hey do you know when they will put me to work?"

"When they are ready," huffed the brown engine.

So little engine ninety-nine continued to wait.

Just when he was sure he could wait no longer, a man in striped coverall came aboard. The man started the engine and little engine ninety-nine was overwhelmed with joy. He began to move slowly. Then he picked up speed. Then he was breezing along the tracks. Wow! He loved the way the wind felt on his face.

After a while, the man pulled back on the controls and stopped the engine. He got out and switched the tracks. When the man returned he started the engine again. This time, little engine ninety-nine felt his self being pulled forward then backward then forward and then backward 'til CLINK! He was attached to some cars behind him. Little engine ninety-nine held his breath and looked behind him. The elephants, lions, giraffes, and bears that he had dreamed of hauling were not there. There was something even better. Do you know what it was?

Children—-lots of happy, singing, laughing, children.

Little Engine Ninety-Nine was thrilled.

Little Engine Ninety-Nine was a working engine. And he was even better than the kind of engine he dreamed he would be.

Toot-toot!

Theme Connections

Emotions
Growing Up
Trains
Transportation
Work

The Little Old Woman Who Lived in a Vinegar Bottle

Directions: Photocopy the story patterns on pages 423-428. Use a black fine-point permanent marker to trace patterns onto a piece of interfacing. Color them with crayons and cut them out.

There once was a little old woman who lived in a vinegar bottle. Don't ask me why. It was a common old vinegar bottle but unusually large. Still it did make a very cramped space to live in.

Every day the old woman would sit on her front step and complain about her house.

"Oh, what a pity! What a pity, pity, pity! That I should live in a house such as this.

Why, I should be living in a dear little cottage with a thatched roof and roses growing up the walls."

Just then a fairy happened to be passing by. When she heard the old woman she thought, "Well, if that's what she wants, that's what she'll get."

The fairy spoke to the old woman. She said, "When you go to bed tonight, turn around three times and close your eyes. When you open them in the morning see what you shall see."

Well, the old woman thought the fairy was likely batty, but when she went to bed that night she turned around three times, closed her eyes, and went to sleep.

In the morning when she opened them again, she was in a dear little cottage with a thatched roof and roses growing up the walls.

"It's just what I've always wanted," she said. "How content I'll be living here." But she said not a word of thanks to the fairy.

The fairy went north and the fairy went south. The fairy went east and the fairy went west. She did all the fairy work she had to do.

Then the fairy remembered the old woman. "I wonder how she's getting on in her cottage. She must be very happy indeed. I'll just stop by for a visit."

When the fairy came near, she saw the old woman sitting on her front step...complaining.

"Oh, what a pity! What a pity, pity, pity! That I should live in a cramped little cottage like this. Why I should be living in a fine row house with handsome houses on either side and lace curtains at the window and a brass knocker on the door! That's what I deserve!"

"I can do that," thought the fairy. "If that's what she wants, that's what she'll get."

The fairy spoke to the old woman. She said, "When you go to bed tonight, turn around three times and close your eyes. When you open them in the morning see what you shall see."

The old woman didn't have to be told twice. She went to bed. She turned around three times and closed her eyes and went to sleep.

In the morning when she opened her eyes, she was in a spanking new row house!

With neighbors on either side and lace curtains at the window and a brass knocker on the door!"

"It's just what I always wanted," said the old woman. "I'll be so contented here." But she never said a word of thanks to the fairy.

The fairy went north and the fairy went south. The fairy went east and the fairy went west. She did all the fairy work she had to do.

Then she thought about the old woman. "I wonder how that old woman who used to live in the vinegar bottle is doing these day? I'll just stop by to see."

But when the fairy came to the old woman's fine house, the old woman was sitting in her shiny new rocking chair and rocking and ...complaining.

"Oh, what a pity! What a pity, pity, pity! That I should have to live in a row house like this

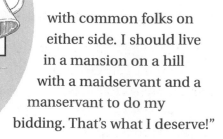

with common folks on either side. I should live in a mansion on a hill with a maidservant and a manservant to do my bidding. That's what I deserve!"

When the fairy heard that she was much amazed. She said, "Well, if that's what she wants, that's what she'll get."

The fairy spoke to the old woman. She said, "When you go to bed tonight turn round three times and close your eyes. When you open them in the morning see what you shall see."

So the old woman hopped into bed. She turned around three times and closed her eyes and went to sleep.

In the morning when she opened her eyes she was in a mansion on a hill with a maidservant and a manservant to do her bidding.

"This is just what I've always wanted," said the old woman. "How contented I will be here." But it never occurred to her to thank the fairy.

The fairy went north and the fairy went south. The fairy went east and the fairy went west. She did all the fairy work she had to do.

Then she remembered the old woman again. "I wonder how that old woman who used to live in a vinegar bottle is getting on now. She must be quite happy in her new mansion."

But when she came near she saw the old woman sitting in her velvet chair... complaining.

"Oh, what a pity! What a pity, pity, pity! That I should have to live all alone in this old

mansion. Why I should be the queen. I should be living in the palace with ladies in waiting for company and musicians to entertain me. That's what I deserve."

"Good heavens," thought the fairy. "Will she never be content? Well, if that is what she wants, that's what she'll get."

The fairy spoke to the old woman. She said, "When you go to bed tonight turn around three times and close your eyes. When you open them in the morning, see what you shall see."

The old woman hurried to bed. She turned around three times and closed her eyes and went to sleep.

In the morning, she was in the palace with ladies in waiting to keep her company and musicians to entertain her."

"This is what I've always wanted," said the old woman. "I will be very contented living here." She never thought to thank the fairy.

The fairy went north and the fairy went south. The fairy went east and the fairy went west. She did all the fairy work she had to do.

Then she thought about the old woman who used to live in a vinegar bottle.

So she stopped at the palace to see.

There sat the old woman on her throne...you guessed it...complaining.

"Oh, what a pity! What a pity, pity, pity! That I should be queen of such a tiny little kingdom. Why I should be the Pope in Rome. The Pope rules the Holy Roman Empire. Then I could rule the minds of everybody in the world! That's what I deserve."

"Well!" said the fairy. "If that's what she wants, that's what she'll NOT get!"

And to the old woman she said, "When you go to bed tonight turn around three times and close your eyes. In the morning see what you shall see."

The old woman went right to bed. She turned around three times and closed her eyes.

In the morning when she opened them...she was right back in her vinegar bottle!

Theme Connections

Emotions
Houses and Homes
Kings and Queens

The Little Red Hen

Directions: Photocopy the story patterns on pages 429-431. Use a black fine-point permanent marker to trace patterns onto a piece of interfacing. Color them with crayons and cut them out.

Once upon a time there was a Little Red Hen who shared her tiny cottage with a pig, a cat, and a dog. The pig was a gossip. She chatted with the neighbors all day long. The cat was vain. She brushed her fur, straightened her whiskers, and polished her claws all day long. The dog was sleepy. He napped on the front porch all day long. The Little Red Hen did all the work. She cooked, she cleaned, and she took out the trash. She mowed, she raked, and she did all the shopping.

One day on her way to market, the Little Red Hen found a few grains of wheat. She put them in her pocket. When she got home she asked her friends, "Who will plant these grains of wheat?"

"Not I," said the pig.
"Not I," said the cat.
"Not I," said the dog.
"Then I will plant them myself," said the Little Red Hen. And she did.

All summer long she cared for the wheat. She made sure that it got enough water, and she hoed the weeds out carefully between each row. And when the wheat was finally ready to harvest, the Little Red Hen asked her friends,

"Who will help me thresh this wheat?"

"Not I," said the pig.
"Not I," said the cat.
"Not I," said the dog.
"Then I will cut and thresh it myself," said the Little Red Hen. And she did.

When the wheat had been cut and threshed, the Little Red Hen scooped the wheat into a wheelbarrow and said, "This wheat must be ground into flour. Who will help me take it to the mill?"

"Not I," said the pig.
"Not I," said the cat.
"Not I," said the dog.
"Then I will do it myself," said the Little Red Hen. And she did.

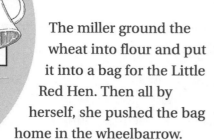

The miller ground the wheat into flour and put it into a bag for the Little Red Hen. Then all by herself, she pushed the bag home in the wheelbarrow.

One cool morning a few weeks later, the Little Red Hen got up early and said, "Today is a perfect day to bake some bread. Who will help me bake it?"

"Not I," said the pig.
"Not I," said the cat.
"Not I," said the dog.
"Then I will bake the bread myself," said the Little Red Hen. And she did.

She mixed the flour with milk and eggs and butter and salt. She kneaded the dough. She shaped the dough into a nice plump loaf. Then she put the loaf in the oven and watched it as it baked.

The smell of the bread soon filled the air. The pig stopped rolling. The cat stopped brushing and the dog woke up. One by one, they came into the kitchen. When the Little Red Hen took the bread from the oven she said, "Who will help me eat this bread?"

"I will," said the pig.
"I will," said the cat.
"I will," said the dog.

"You will?" said the Little Red Hen. "Who planted the wheat and took care of it? Who cut the wheat and threshed it? Who took the wheat to the mill? Who baked the bread? I did it all by myself. Now I am going to eat it all by myself." And she did.

Theme Connections

Cats	Pig
Dogs	Growing Things
Food	Hens
Friends	Work

Little Red Riding Hood

Directions: Photocopy the story patterns on pages 432-435. Use a black fine-point permanent marker to trace patterns onto a piece of interfacing. Color them with crayons and cut them out.

It was a beautiful sunny day. The birds were singing, and the butterflies were darting here and there, collecting nectar from the flowers. Little Red Riding Hood skipped happily through the forest on her way to her grandmother's house. Suddenly in her pathway appeared a huge gray wolf. "Where are you going?" asked the wolf.

"To my grandmother's house," said Little Red Riding Hood. "I am taking her a basket of goodies."

"Where does your grandmother live?" asked the wolf.

"Up the path beside the stream," answered Little Red Riding Hood.

"Be careful," whispered the wolf. "The forest is full of surprises." Then off he ran. The wolf was thinking that Little Red Riding Hood and her grandmother would make a very tasty dinner. He knew a shortcut through the forest. He was sure he could be at grandmother's cottage before Little Red Riding Hood.

When the wolf arrived at the cottage, he knocked on the door. But no one answered. He knocked again. No answer. He opened the door and walked right in. No one was home.

The wolf grabbed grandmother's gown and hopped in her bed. He was hoping to fool Little Red Riding Hood. Soon there was a knock at the door. "Come in," said the wolf, pretending to be Little Red Riding Hood's grandmother.

Little Red Riding Hood walked into the cottage. It was dark inside. She walked all the way to her grandmother's bed before she realized how terrible her grandmother looked.

"Grandmother," she said, "you look terrible."

"I know dear. I've been ill," said the wolf.

"Grandmother, what big eyes you have, " said Little Red Riding Hood.

"All the better to see you with, my dear," whispered the wolf.

"Grandmother, what a black nose you have," said Little Red Riding Hood.

"All the better to smell you with, my dear," answered the sneaky wolf.

"Grandmother, what big teeth you have," she said.

"All the better to eat you with" said the wolf as he jumped from the bed.

Little Red Riding Hood screamed and ran for the door. The wolf tried to chase after her, but he was all tangled up in grandmother's gown. When Little Red Riding Hood opened the door, in ran grandmother with a broom in her hand. She hit the wolf hard on the nose. He yelped. She smacked him again as he jumped across the floor trying to untangle himself. When he was free, he ran for the door. Grandmother whacked him on the backside and swept him right out the door. The wolf ran so far away he was never seen again.

Little Red Riding Hood hugged her grandmother. "Grandmother, I am so glad you came home. Where were you?"

"I was out in the barn sweeping the floor. I heard you scream."

Little Red Riding Hood told her grandmother about meeting the wolf in the forest on the way to her house. Grandmother hugged her

granddaughter, whom she loved more than anything, and then she asked, "Did you learn anything today?"

"Yes," said Little Red Riding Hood. "I learned not to talk to strangers."

"Good job!" said her grandmother.

Theme Connections

Families
Parts of the Body
Tricksters
Wolves

Spanish Translation

Caperucita Roja

Directions: Photocopy the story patterns on pages 432-435. Use a black fine-point permanent marker to trace patterns onto a piece of interfacing. Color them with crayons and cut them out.

Érase una vez una niña muy bonita y muy querida por su abuelita. Su abuelita vivía en una casita de madera de color café detrás de una montaña en el bosque. A su abuelita le agradaba darle muchos regalos. Un regalo muy especial que le llevó mucho tiempo hacerlo fue una preciosa caperusa de lana y de color rojo. Tan preciosa era esta caperusa que todos los vecinos le llamaban Caperucita Roja. Una mañana después de tomar el desayuno su mamá le dijo a Caperucita Roja que un vecino leñador le había informado que su abuelita estaba muy enferma y que sería bueno irla a visitar. Su mamá le dijo que le llevara unos taquitos, pan dulce, y café. Momentos antes de partir, su mamá le recomendó, que no fuera hablar con nadie, mucho menos que se detuviera, o aceptara alguna cosa. Caperucita Roja caminó y caminó. Todos los animales que encontraba en el camino le saludaban a su paso. De pronto escuchó la voz ronca de un enorme y feroz lobo que con una gran sonrisa le preguntaba, -¿A dónde vas Caperucita Roja por estos lugares tan solitarios? La inocente niña le responde, -Voy a casa de mi abuelita. Ella se encuentra muy enferma y necesita de mi.

-Dime, ¿Qué llevas allí?

-Llevo unos taquitos, pan dulce, y café para mi abuelita.

-Que noble corazón tienes. Más interesado, el lobo le pregunta, -Y ¿Donde vive tu abuelita?

-Ella vive detrás de la montaña en una casita de madera de color café.

-Oh, si, yo conozco ese lugar; pero, porque estas caminando por este camino. Hay otro que es mas corto y ademas vas a ver muchos animales y flores tambien.

-Gracias señor. Voy a seguir su consejo," dijo Caperucita, y tomó el camino recomendado por el lobo. Pero, Caperucita no sabía que el lobo feroz le había puesto una trampa. En realidad, el lobo había tomado el camino mas corto para llegar a casa de la abuelita. Inmediatamente que llegó, el lobo llamó a la puerta, ton-toron-ton.

-¿Quien es? preguntó la abuelita desde su cama.

Imitando la voz de Caperucita, el lobo respondió, -Soy yo Caperucita Roja, Abuelita. Te he traído unos taquitos, pan dulce y café también. Ábreme la puerta por favor.

-Empújala está sin candado, respondió la abuelita. El lobo abrió la puerta muy rápido, dió un gran salto donde estaba la abuelita, y se le tragó entera. Después se puso el camisón de la abuelita, se cubrió la cabeza con una gorra verde y se metió a la cama y esperó que Caperucita llegara.

De pronto alguién llamó a la puerta, ton-toron-ton. -¿Quién es?, preguntó el lobo, imitando la voz de la abuelita.

-Soy yo, Abuelita, Caperucita Roja; traigo unos taquitos, pan dulce, y café para tí.

-Pasa adelante mi querida nietecita, respondió el lobo. Caperucita roja entró, y el lobo escondido dentro de la cama de la abuelita le dijo, -Muchas gracias por preocuparte por mi. Pon las cositas sobre la mesa y acercate a mi. Caperucita vino a la cama, e inmediatamente notó lo extraño que su abuelita vestía. -Abuelita, ¡Que orejas tan grandes tienes!

-Si, mi nietecita, es para escucharte mejor.

-Abuelita, ¡Que ojos tan grandes tienes!

-Si, mi nietecita, es para verte mejor.

-Abuelita, ¡Que dientes tan grandes tienes!

-Es para comerte mejor.

Inmediatamente el lobo se lanzó sobre Caperucita y de una gran zarpada se la trago.

Tiempo mas tarde pasaban por allí unos cazadores quienes escucharon grandes ronquidos que salían de la casa de la abuelita. Empujaron la puerta y entraron. Cual va siendo su sorpresa cuando encontraron al lobo placidamente dormido con el camisón y la gorra de la abuelita. Pero ellos notaron que el estómago del lobo se movía alrededor y pensaron que tal vez la abuelita podría estar adentro. Ellos dieron un gran grito que despertó al lobo inmediatamente. Cuando el lobo abrió sus ojos y vió a los cazadores enfrente de él, se puso más miedoso. En ese momento abrió su gran boca y abuelita y nietecita salieron una por una de la boca del lobo. El lobo dió un par de saltos de la cama todavía vistiendo el camison y el gorro de la abuelita, dió otro gran salto hacia la puerta, y corrió tan rápido como pudo hasta desaparecer dentro del bosque. Abuelita, Caperucita Roja y los cazadores se abrazaron y estuvieron muy felices. Ellos disfrutaron los taquitos, el pan dulce y café que Caperucita había traído a la abuelita. Mientras ellos disfrutan de tan rica comida, Caperucita dijo a su abuelita que nunca iría al bosque sola y que jamás hablaría con ningún extraño.

Madison's Day

by Pam Schiller

Directions: Photocopy the story patterns on pages 436-437. Use a black fine-point permanent marker to trace patterns onto a piece of interfacing. Color them with crayons and cut them out.

Let me tell you about my wonderful, terrific, super, great day! But first, I'll introduce you to my family. I'll start with my mom and dad. I have two brothers, Sam and Austin. Sam is the oldest. I have a sister, too. Her name is Gabrielle. Oh, I almost forgot—Madison—that's me. I'm four—almost five! I'm the youngest. Together we're the Markle family, and you'll never guess what happened to me on my wonderful, terrific, super, great day!

Yesterday our family went to the park. When everyone was all ready to go, Sam, Austin, and Gabrielle hurried downstairs and ran out the door. They were already getting into the van by the time I was at the door. "Wait for me!" I yelled, as I ran. Last, again! I am always last, I thought. Just once I would like to be first!

Being the youngest and the littlest is hard. I try so hard to keep up with them. It's always the same old thing…I'm the last one Mom wakes up for school, the last one to get into the bathroom to brush my teeth, the last to get my food at the dinner table, and always, always the last to get in line for anything!

I went to bed that night wishing I could be first, first to do something—anything—just once! The very next morning, Mom came to wake me up. I took my good, old time getting downstairs, but when I got to the kitchen, guess what? I was the first one Mom had gotten out of bed! "Happy Birthday, Madison!" said Dad, smiling.

Wow! I forgot that today was my birthday! Sam, Austin, and Gabrielle came into the kitchen with big smiles and a birthday greeting. Mom had breakfast ready, and set a big plate of pancakes down right in front of me FIRST! After breakfast, I was the first one to brush my teeth, too. My whole day was like that—I got to do everything first! Wow! What a wonderful, terrific, super, great day! What a great birthday present!

Theme Connections

Birthdays
Families
Growing Up
Opposites

Miguel the Fearless

by Pam Schiller

Directions: Photocopy the story patterns on pages 438-440. Use a black fine-point permanent marker to trace patterns onto a piece of interfacing. Color them with crayons and cut them out.

Miguel is the most fearless cowboy in the wild, wild west. He wears a huge ten-gallon hat and a pair of snakeskin boots. He is always on the lookout for trouble. It is nothing for Miguel to jump on his faithful horse, Buck, and ride off in search of someone in need of his help.

Some days he wrestles vicious mountain lions until they fall to the ground, too exhausted to roar. The mountain lions try to stay clear of Miguel the Fearless.

Other days Miguel rides across the prairie to help the pioneers fight off the bandits. When his water gets low, he is thankful to find a riverbed with a trickle of water.

When he finally reaches the wagon train, he quickly rounds up the bad guys.

When night falls, Miguel sleeps out on the prairie all alone. Miguel the Fearless is afraid of nothing.

Theme Connections

Bears
Clothing
Cowboys/Cowgirls
Food
Horses

My First Day of School

Directions: Photocopy the story patterns on pages 441-443. Use a black fine-point permanent marker to trace patterns onto a piece of interfacing. Color them with crayons and cut them out.

Then he helps the pioneers fix their broken wagon wheel.

When Miguel shows up at the jail with the bad guys, no one is surprised. Miguel shows up every day with someone to hand over to the sheriff.

One story all the town's people know is the story of Miguel and the bear. The bear came out of nowhere and jumped on Miguel. Miguel beat the bear singlehandedly. Everyone knows he was lucky to survive.

Miguel seldom thinks of food. He survives on dried beef and a handful of beans.

It was the first day of school. Heather woke up easily. She was excited, but she was also a little bit afraid. Her mother said there was nothing to be afraid of. Her big brother said there was nothing to be afraid of.

But Heather was still just a little bit afraid. She ate her breakfast, dressed up in her new school clothes, and helped her mom pack her lunch. Finally, it was time to go.

Heather's mother drove her to school. Heather was surprised at how big the school looked. She held onto her mother's hand as they walked down the hall and to the floor of Heather's new classroom. Mrs. Marotta met Heather at the door with a big, friendly smile.

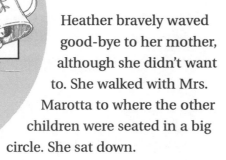

Heather bravely waved good-bye to her mother, although she didn't want to. She walked with Mrs. Marotta to where the other children were seated in a big circle. She sat down.

Mrs. Marotta told the children about all the things they would be doing at school: painting at the easel with brightly colored paints in the art center, playing with playdough in the fine motor center, dressing up in big-people clothes in the dramatic play center, building with blocks in the block center, working puzzles in the game center, and dancing with scarves to happy music during music and movement time. She was even going to listen to a story or two.

Heather began to think that school might be fun. She looked at the other children. They looked happy. When Mrs. Marotta said that everyone could go work in one of the centers, a nice boy named Michael asked Heather to come play with her. Heather and Michael had a great time. They did all the activities that Mrs. Marotta described. When Heather's mother came for her, Heather didn't really want to go. She reluctantly waved goodbye to Michael and said, "I'll see you tomorrow!"

Theme Connections

Emotions
Families
Growing Up
School

My Shadow

by Robert Louis Stevenson

Directions: Photocopy the story patterns on pages 444-447. Use a black fine-point permanent marker to trace patterns onto a piece of interfacing. Color them with crayons and cut them out.

*I have a little shadow that goes in and out
    with me,
And what can be the use of him is more
    than I can see.
He is very, very like me from his heels up
to his head;
And I see him jump before me when I
jump into my bed.*

*The funniest thing about him is the way
he likes to grow-
Not at all like proper children, which is
    always very slow;
For he sometimes shoots up taller like an
    India-rubber ball,
And he sometimes gets so little that there's
    none of him at all.*

*He hasn't got a notion of how children
    ought to play,
And can only make a fool of me in every
    sort of way.
He stays so close beside me, he's a coward
    you can see;
I'd think shame to stick to nursie as that
    shadow sticks to me.*

*One morning, very early, before the sun
    was up,
I rose and found the shining dew on every
    buttercup;*

But my lazy little shadow, like an errant
*   sleepy head,*
Had stayed at home behind me and was
*   fast asleep in bed.*

Theme Connections

Humor
Opposites
Self-Esteem
Time of Day

My Sick Little Donkey

(Mexico)

Directions: Photocopy the story patterns on page 448. Use a black fine-point permanent marker to trace patterns onto a piece of interfacing. Color them and cut them out.

My donkey has a headache.
My donkey cannot play.
The vet will soon deliver a black hat
*   and some hay.*
A black hat and some hay,
And click your little hooves.
Tap, tap, tap, tap. Hooray!

My donkey has a sore throat. My donkey
*   cannot play.*
The vet will soon deliver a white scarf
and some hay.
A white scarf and some hay,
A black hat for the headache
And click your little hooves.
Tap, tap, tap, tap. Hooray!

My donkey's ribs are very sore. My donkey
*   cannot play.*
The vet will soon deliver a yellow coat
*   and hay.*
A yellow coat and some hay,
A white scarf and some hay,
A black hat for the headache
And click your little hooves
Tap, tap, tap, tap. Hooray!

My donkey's heart is aching. My donkey
*   cannot play.*
The vet will soon deliver lemon drops and
*   hay.*
Lemon drops and hay,
A yellow coat and some hay,
A white scarf and some hay,
A black hat for the headache
And click your little hooves
Tap, tap, tap, tap. Hooray!

My donkey is very happy. My donkey can
*   now play,*
The vet will soon deliver green apples and
*   some hay.*
Green apples and some hay,
Lemon drops and hay,

A yellow coat and some hay,
A white scarf and some hay,
A black hat for the headache

And click your little hooves
Tap, tap, tap, tap. Hooray!

Theme Connections

Colors
Donkeys
Emotions
Humor

Spanish Translation

El Burrito Enfermo

A mi burro, a mi burro le duele la cabeza,
y el médico le manda una gorrita negra,
una gorrita negra
y mueve las patiatas
tap, tap, tap, tap.
A mi burro, a mi burro le duelen la gar-
ganta,
y el médico le manda una bufanda blan-
ca,
una bufanda blanca,
una gorrita negra
y mueve las patitas
tap, tap, tap, tap.
A mi burro, a mi burro le duele las costillas,
y el médico le manda chaqueta amarilla,
chaqueta amarilla,
una bufanda blanca,
una gorrita negra
y mueve las patitas
tap, tap, tap, tap.
A mi burro, a mi burro le duele el corazón
y el médico le manda gotitas de limón,
gotitas de limón,

chaqueta amarilla,
una bufanda blanca,
una gorrita negra
y mueve las patitas
tap, tap, tap, tap.
A mi burro, a mi burro ya no le duele
nada,
y el médico le manda trocitos de man-
zana,
trocitos de manzana,
gotitas de limón,
chaqueta amarilla,
una bufanda blanca,
una gorrita negra
y mueve las patitas
tap, tap, tap, tap.

My Very Own Pet

by Pam Schiller

Directions: Photocopy the story patterns on page 449. Use a black fine-point permanent marker to trace patterns onto a piece of interfacing. Color them with crayons and cut them out.

Austin wanted a pet. He had wanted one for a long time. All his friends had pets. Austin dreamed about pets at night. He thought about pets all day. He thought about elephants, and giraffes, and lions, like the ones he saw at the zoo. But he knew his mother would certainly say "No!" to those big animals.

Austin had found a turtle once and brought it home. But his mom said that it needed to go back to its home in the lake, because it wouldn't be happy in Austin's room.

Another time he tried to hide a lizard in his pocket. But it jumped out at the dinner table, and his mom shooed it out the back door.

Once his best friend, Chen, gave him a frog. Austin used a box to make a house for it to live in. He made sure the box had a lid, so it wouldn't jump out. But Austin's mother was not convinced the frog belonged in the house either. She said, "Don't bring any more pets in this house!" Austin was beginning to think he would never have a pet of his very own.

Yesterday was Austin's birthday. He had asked for a pet, but he knew he would probably get a tricycle. As he finished getting dressed, he tried not to think about pets so he wouldn't be disappointed. Just then he heard his mom coming into his room. When Austin turned around, was he ever surprised!

Yep, there it was! Not a tricycle at all. Standing there next to his mom was a puppy just for him. At last, Austin got a pet of his very own.

Theme Connections

Dogs
Emotions
Families

Old MacDonald

Directions: Photocopy the story patterns on pages 450-452. Use a black fine-point permanent marker to trace patterns onto a piece of interfacing. Color them with crayons and cut them out.

Old MacDonald had a farm
E-I-E-I-O.
And on this farm she had a cow
E-I-E-I-O.
With a moo, moo here,
And a moo, moo there,
Here a moo, there a moo,
Everywhere a moo, moo.
Old MacDonald had a farm
E-I-E-I-O!

Additional verses
Pig - oink, oink
Cat - meow, meow
Dog - bow-wow
Horse - neigh, neigh
Duck - quack, quack

Theme Connections

Cats   Horses
Cows   Occupations
Dogs   Pigs
Farms   Work

The Pancake
(Norway)

Directions: Photocopy the story patterns on page 453-456. Use a black fine-point permanent marker to trace patterns onto a piece of interfacing. Color them with crayons and cut them out.

Once upon a time there was a good woman who had seven hungry children. She was frying a pancake for them. It was a sweet-milk pancake. The pancake was sizzling in

the pan, bubbling, and browning, and the seven children were watching and waiting with hungry eyes.

"Oh, give me a bit of pancake, Mother dear," said one of the children.

"Oh, darling Mother," said the second child.

"Oh, darling, good Mother," said the third.

"Oh, darling, good, nice Mother," said the fourth.

"Oh, darling, pretty, good, nice Mother," said the fifth.

"Oh, darling, pretty, good, nice, clever Mother," said the sixth.

"Oh, darling, pretty, good, nice, clever, sweet Mother," said the seventh.

So they all begged for the pancake, the one more sweetly than the other, because they were all so hungry.

"Yes, yes, children," the good woman said. "Just wait a bit till it turns itself."

The pancake was quite surprised to hear her say this.

"Why, I shall turn myself then," it said. The pancake jumped up in the air and landed on its other side, where it sizzled a bit.

Then up it jumped again, so high and so far that it landed on the floor. Then the pancake rolled out the door.

"Whoa, pancake! Stop, pancake!" cried the woman, and she chased after it with the frying pan in one hand and the ladle in the other. She ran as fast as she could, and the seven children ran after her.

"Stop that pancake! Stop that pancake!" they all shouted as they tried to grab hold of it, but the pancake rolled on and on until they could no longer see it.

When it had rolled a bit farther, the pancake met a man.

"Good day, pancake," said the man.

"The same to you, manny-panny," said the pancake.

"Dear pancake, don't roll so fast. Stop awhile and let me take a bite of you."

But the pancake didn't stop, and as it rolled it called out,
"I have rolled away from goody-poody,
And her seven squalling children.
And I shall roll away from you, too, manny-panny!"

Then the pancake rolled on and on until it met a hen.

"Good day, pancake," said the hen.

"The same to you, henny-penny," said the pancake.

"Sweet pancake, don't roll so fast. Please stop awhile and let me have a peck at you."

But the pancake didn't stop, and as it rolled it called out,

"I have rolled away from goody-poody,
And her seven squalling children,
And manny-panny,
And I shall roll away from you, too, henny-penny!"

The pancake rolled down the road like a wheel. Just then it met a duck.

"Good day, pancake," said the duck.

"The same to you, ducky-lucky," said the pancake.

"Pancake, dear, don't roll away so fast. Wait a bit so that I can eat you up."

But the pancake didn't stop, and as it rolled it called out,
"I have rolled away from goody-poody,
And her seven squalling children,
And manny-panny,
And henny-penny,
And I shall roll away from you, too, ducky-lucky!"

And the pancake rolled along faster than ever. Then it met a goose.

"Good day, pancake," said the goose.

"The same to you, goosey-poosey," said the pancake.

"Pancake dear, don't roll so quickly. Wait a minute and I'll eat you up."

But the pancake kept on rolling, and as it rolled it called out,
"I have rolled away from goody-poody,
And her seven squalling children,
And manny-panny,
And henny-penny,
And ducky-lucky,

And I shall roll away from you, too, goosey-poosey!"

When it had rolled a long way farther, the pancake came to the edge of a wood, and there stood a pig.

"Good day, pancake," said the pig.

"The same to you, piggy-wiggy," said the pancake.

"Don't be in such a hurry," said the pig. "The wood is dangerous, and we should walk together."

The pancake thought that might be true, and so it rolled along beside the pig for a bit. But when they had gone a ways, they came to a brook. The pig jumped right into the water and began to swim across.

"What about me? What about me?" cried the pancake.

"Oh, you just sit on my snout," said the pig, "and I'll carry you across."

So the pancake sat on the pig's snout.

The pig tossed the pancake up into the air, and—ouf, ouf, ouf—the pig swallowed the pancake in three bites.

And since the pancake went no further, this story can go no further, either.

Theme Connections

Colors	Hens
Ducks	Pigs
Food	Tricksters
Geese	

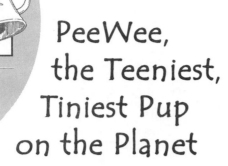

PeeWee, the Teeniest, Tiniest Pup on the Planet

by Pam Schiller

Directions: Photocopy the story patterns on pages 457-459. Use a black fine-point permanent marker to trace patterns onto interfacing. Color them with crayons, and cut them out.

PeeWee was the happiest, teeniest, tiniest dog in the world. He lived on the fairgrounds and was the star attraction at the fair. Everyone loved PeeWee, and every day people would come from miles around just to see him. It was a good thing that so many people loved PeeWee, because he didn't have any family—at least none that he remembered.

PeeWee had always lived at the fair. The pigs had raised him. One night in the middle of a huge thunderstorm, PeeWee had wandered into the pigpen to get out of the rain. The pigs liked him right away. They fed him and kept him warm. When Steve, the owner of the fair, saw PeeWee in the pigpen the next morning, he was shocked. He picked PeeWee up and looked at him closely. He said, "You're not a pig. You are, however, the teeniest, tiniest puppy I have ever seen. You will make a great addition to the fair. You will be my star attraction."

So every day after that, Steve would put a small ruffled collar and a little clown hat on PeeWee and gently place him under a teeny, tiny box. Then he would say, "Come one, come all, to see the teeniest, tiniest pup on the planet!" When Steve lifted the box, everyone would gasp. They couldn't believe their eyes. No one had ever seen a puppy that small before.

Things went on like that for quite a while. One day, however, something awful happened. PeeWee began to grow. He grew, and he grew, and he grew. Soon he was not the teeniest, tiniest puppy on the planet. He wasn't even close. He probably grew because he was so loved and well cared for now, but he was no longer the star attraction at the fair. No one wanted to come see an ordinary dog. PeeWee was very sad. His little collar and hat wouldn't even fit on his foot. The little box that used to cover him wouldn't even hold his dinner.

Days passed, and PeeWee continued to grow not only in size, but also in sadness. He knew he would have to leave the fair and find something else to do.

But then something else happened. PeeWee kept on growing—and very quickly, too. He grew, and he grew, and he grew. He grew so large that he no longer fit in the pigpen. When Steve saw how big PeeWee had become, he laughed out loud. He said, "PeeWee, you will be my star attraction again. Now you are the biggest dog on the entire planet."

He made PeeWee a new collar and hat, and he built a new, very large box to cover him. Then he said, "Come one, come all to see PeeWee, the largest, grandest dog on the planet." People traveled from all around to see PeeWee again. They couldn't believe their eyes. Under the box was the largest, grandest, happiest dog they had ever seen!

The Princess and the Pea

by Hans Christian Anderson

Directions: Photocopy the story patterns on pages 460-463. Use a black fine-point permanent marker to trace patterns onto a piece of interfacing. Color them with crayons and cut them out.

Once upon a time there was prince who wanted to marry a princess. But she had to be real princess in every way. He traveled all over the world, but nowhere could he find what he wanted. Everywhere he went there were women who claimed they were real princesses, but it was difficult to find one he believed was truly a princess in every way. There was always something about each one that was not as it should be. So he came home again and was sad, for marrying a real princess was very important to him.

One evening there was a terrible storm. There was thunder and lightning and the rain poured down in torrents. Suddenly a knocking was heard at the castle gate, and the old king went to open it.

There stood a princess in front of the gate. But good gracious! What a sight the rain and the wind had made of her good looks. The water ran down from her hair and clothes. It ran down into the heels of her shoes and out again at the toes. And yet she said that she was a princess nonetheless.

She was brought into the palace and given dry clothing to wear and food to eat. The prince was quite pleased when he saw how pretty she was. But how could he be sure she was indeed a real princess?

"Well, we'll soon find that out," thought the old queen when she heard what was happening. But she said nothing. Quietly she slipped into the guest room and took 20 mattresses and laid them on the pea, and then 20 feather comforters on top of the mattresses.

On this the princess had to lie all night. In the morning she was asked how she slept.

"Oh, very badly!" she said. "I scarcely closed my eyes all night. Heaven only knows what was in the bed, but I was lying on something so hard that I am black and blue all over my body."

The old queen knew at once that the princess was a real princess because she had felt the pea right through the 20 mattresses and the 20 feather comforters. Nobody but a real princess could be as sensitive as that. So the prince took her for his wife, and the pea was put in the museum, where it may still be seen, if no one has stolen it.

Theme Connections

Emotions   Opposites
Kings and Queens

The Complete Book of Activities, Games, Stories, Props, Recipes, and Dances

The Ram in the Chile Patch

(Mexico)

Directions: Photocopy the story patterns on pages 465-466. Use a black fine-point permanent marker to trace patterns onto a piece of interfacing. Color them with crayons and cut them out.

There was a little boy who had a little patch of chile peppers. He tended it with the greatest care. That was what gave him his livelihood. And then one day a little ram got into it.

So the boy began, "Little ram, little ram, get out of that chile patch."

The ram said, "You unmannerly boy, what are you about? Get out of here or I'll kick you out."

Finally the boy did try to get the little ram out, and the little ram, instead of leaving, gave him a kick and knocked the boy down. He struggled to his feet and went away crying.

He met a cow, and she asked him, "What's the matter, little boy?"

He said, "The little ram knocked me down."

"And why?"

"Because he's in my little chile patch," cried the boy.

"Just wait. I'll go get him out."

The cow went over and said, "Moo, moo, moo! Little ram, little ram, get out of that chile patch."

"You big-horned cow, what are you about? Get out of here or I'll kick you out."

Finally she did try. She tried to hook him with her horns, but the little ram turned around and kicked the cow out.

Then along came a dog, and he said, "I can get him out for sure." And he began to bark. "Bow-wow-wow-wow! Little ram, little ram, get out of that chile patch."

"You shameless dog, what are you about? Get out of here or I'll kick you out."

The dog kept insisting and he got closer and closer, so the little ram kicked him and left him the same as the cow.

Then along came a cock. He began to crow and said, "Little ram, little ram, get out of that chile patch."

"You silly-looking cock, what are you about? Get out of here or I'll kick you out."

Finally the ram kicked the cock and left him there with his legs in the air, and he went away.

The ram kept on eating the little chile patch, and the boy was very sad because his chile patch was being eaten up. A burro came along, and he said, "Don't worry, little boy, I'll go get the ram out." The burro began, "Little ram, little ram, get out of that chile patch."

"You long-eared burro, what are you about? Get out of here or I'll kick you out."

At last the ram came up close. He kicked the burro and threw him out. The boy saw that his little chile patch was almost gone.

When a little ant came along, the boy said, "Little ant, little ant, if you would get the little ram out of my little chile patch for me, I would give you a lot of corn."

"How much will you give me?" asked the ant.

"I'll give you a bushel."

"That's too much," said the ant.

"I'll give you half a bushel."

"That's too much," said the ant.

"I'll give you a handful."

"All right, then," said the ant. So while the boy started grinding the corn, the little ant started to climb, little by little, up one of the ram's little legs. She climbed and climbed until she got to the little ram's behind, and then she stung him. The little ram jumped and leaped and began to yell, "Oh, my dear! Oh, my dear! She has stung me on the rear!

Oh, my dear! Oh, my dear! She has stung me on the rear!"

And that is how they were able to get the little ram out of the chile patch.

Theme Connections

Cows
Dogs
Donkeys
Goats
Growing Things
Humor
Insects
Opposites
Roosters

The Runaway Cookie Parade

Directions: Photocopy the story patterns on pages 467-471. Use a black fine-point permanent marker to trace patterns onto a piece of interfacing. Color them and cut them out.

One day Linda decided to bake some fancy cookies. She was in the mood to be creative. She mixed up her batter and rolled it out on the table. Then she got out her favorite cookie cutters. She cut out a duck, a rabbit, a dog, a cat, and a bear. She baked the cookies until they were nice and brown. When the cookies were cool, Linda was ready for the fun part—the decorating.

She made some icing and then she looked at each cookie with a creative eye.

She decided to make the duck purple with yellow dots. She thought the rabbit would look good with a stripe pattern and the dog with little spiral designs. She gave the bear a lovely plaid pattern and the cat an "x" design. When she had iced and decorated every cookie she stood back and sighed, "These are the prettiest cookies in town."

Linda placed the cookies in the cookie jar. She thought they were too pretty to eat. What Linda didn't know was that the cookie jar was magic. When the cookies were placed inside they came to life. As soon as Linda left the room the cookies pushed off the cookie jar lid and danced right out of the jar.

They danced in a long line just like a parade. They danced onto the table, onto the chairs, onto the floor, and right out the door. Those beautiful cookies must be dancing still because they never returned to the cookie jar.

Theme Connections

Bears
Cats
Color
Cooking
Dogs
Ducks
Food
Horses
Rabbits

Sammy, the Rodeo Seahorse

by Pam Schiller

Directions: Photocopy the story patterns on pages 472-474. Use a black fine-point permanent marker to trace patterns onto a piece of interfacing. Color them with crayons and cut them out.

Sammy is a seahorse. He lives in the ocean. He loves the ocean. It is the only home he has ever known. However, Sammy dreams of being a real horse. He wants to be a rodeo horse.

You might wonder how a little seahorse in the middle of the Atlantic Ocean even knows about rodeo horses. Well, ever since Sammy was a baby seahorse, his daddy has told him rodeo stories. You see, there are lots of rodeos in Texas, and Sammy's daddy once lived in the Sea World aquarium in San Antonio, Texas. Sammy's daddy loved to hear the people talk about rodeos, especially the rodeo horses. Of course, all of that was a long time ago, before the people at Sea World decided to let Sammy's daddy return to the ocean.

Early every morning, Sammy plays in the waves, pretending to be a bucking rodeo horse. Around noontime, he heads home for lunch, pretending to ride herd on a school of fish. He thinks the fish make great cattle. The fish ignore him, but he doesn't care. He heads on down to the bottom of the ocean and nibbles on seaweed pretending all the while that it is a bale of hay.

After lunch, Sammy darts in and out of the coral pretending to be a cutting horse carrying a rider around the barrels. He has gotten really good at moving quickly in and out of tight places. When a school of brightly colored parrotfish comes along, Sammy pretends that they are rodeo clowns. He likes to think that they have come to rescue him from the horns of an angry bull.

Sammy knows he will never get to be in a real rodeo, but that's all right with him. He loves living in the ocean and wouldn't want to leave it. Besides, he has lots of fun just pretending in his world of make-believe.

Theme Connections

Cowboys/Cowgirls
Families
Oceans and Seas
Self-Esteem

Silly Jack

Directions: Photocopy the story patterns on pages 475-479. Use a black fine-point permanent marker to trace patterns onto a piece of interfacing. Color them with crayons and cut them out.

Once upon a time, there was a boy named Jack. Jack lived with his mother in a little, old house. They did not have much money, and Jack's mother earned her living by sewing.

Jack was so lazy that all he did was lay around. In the summer he would lie in the sun on the porch. In the winter he would lie in front of the fire. His mother could not get him to work. Finally, his mother said, "Jack, if you don't work, you won't get anything to eat." Well that got Jack's attention. He loved to eat. So the very next day, Jack went to work for a farmer. At the end of the day, the farmer gave Jack a penny for his work. Because Jack had never had any money before, he didn't know how to take care of it. As he was walking home, he dropped the penny in a stream and lost it.

"Oh, you silly boy!" his mother said. "You should have put it in your pocket."

"I'll do that next time," he said.

The next day, Jack went to work for a cow-keeper. The cow-keeper gave Jack a quart of milk for his pay. Jack remembered what his mother had said and put the milk bottle in his pocket. By the time he got home, the milk had spilled.

"Oh, you silly boy!" said his mother. "You should have carried it on your head."

"I'll do that the next time," he said.

The following day, Jack went to work for another farmer who paid him a pound of butter for his work. Jack remembered what his mother had said and put the butter on his head. By the time he got home, the hot sun had melted the butter. Part of it was running down Jack's neck, and part of it was stuck in his hair.

"Oh, you silly boy!" said his mother. "You should have wrapped it in a cloth and put it in a bucket of ice."

"I'll do that next time," he said.

FLANNEL BOARD / MAGNETIC BOARD STORIES

The next day, Jack worked for a baker. The baker would not give him any bread, but he gave Jack a cat. So Jack very carefully wrapped the cat in a cloth and put it in a bucket of ice. By the time Jack got home, the cat was so mad that he tore through the cloth and scratched Jack all over. Jack had to let the cat go.

"Oh, you silly boy!" said his mother. You should have tied a string around its neck and pulled it along behind you."

"I'll do that next time," he said.

Then Jack went to work for a butcher. The butcher gave Jack a ham for his pay. Jack remembered what his mother had said, and so he tied a string around the ham and pulled it along behind him. When he got home, the ham was ruined.

"Oh, you silly boy!" his mother said. "You should have carried it on your shoulder."

"I'll do that next time," he said.

Once more Jack got a job. He went to work for another cow-keeper who gave him a donkey for his pay. Jack remembered what his mother had said. Although Jack was very strong, he had trouble getting the donkey onto his shoulders. But when he finally did, he began walking home, whistling happily.

As he walked, he passed the King's castle. The king had a daughter who was very sad; she had never laughed in her life. When the King's daughter saw Jack carrying the donkey on his shoulder, she began to laugh. She laughed and laughed and laughed. The King was so happy that his daughter had laughed

that he invited Jack and his mother to live in the castle. Jack and the princess became very best friends, and Jack and his mother lived in the castle happily ever after.

Theme Connections

Families
Food
Growing Things
Humor
Work

Silly Millie

by Pam Schiller

Directions: Photocopy the story patterns on pages 480-483. Use a black fine-point permanent marker to trace patterns onto a piece of interfacing. Color them with crayons and cut them out.

Silly Millie lives in Kalamazoo, Michigan with her mother and her father. She is so silly. She makes everyone laugh. Her daddy says, "Where'd I get this daughter?"

She combs her teeth and brushes her brows.

She uses washcloths instead of towels.

She is so very silly.

She walks her goldfish; lets her cat swim in the bowl.

And eats her hot rolls only after they are cold.

Silly Millie is so very surprisingly silly.

She puts on her socks after her shoes.

And plays a drum while she sings the blues.

Silly Millie is so very surprisingly ridiculously silly.

She walks on her hands wherever she goes.

And wears bright red bows on each of her toes.

Silly Millie is so very surprisingly ridiculously outlandishly silly.

She wears diving gear when she takes a bath.

I bet Silly Millie can make you laugh!

She is so very surprisingly ridiculously outlandishly foolishly silly.

Theme Connections

Families
Humor

Silly Nellie: The Story of One Funny Turkey

by Pam Schiller

Directions: Photocopy the story patterns on pages 484-488. Use a black fine-point permanent marker to trace patterns onto a piece of interfacing. Color them with crayons and cut them out.

Nellie is one of the silliest turkeys you have ever seen. She has two very large turkey feet, a neck longer than a goose's neck, and an assortment of feathers that make her look like she belongs in a parade. Nellie has a mommy who thinks she is truly the most beautiful turkey in the world and a daddy who thinks she hung the moon.

Nellie also has more friends than anyone I know. Her friends like her not because she has big feet, or a long neck, or even because she has strange colored feathers. They like her because she has a big heart. She is always ready to help her friends.

The squirrels are thankful for her long neck because she can reach high up in the trees to pick an acorn that is growing on the end of a branch too fragile for the squirrels to climb on.

The rabbits like her because with her big feet she can run faster than they can hop. When the old barnyard dogs are chasing the rabbits, Nellie puts the rabbits on her back and carries them to safety.

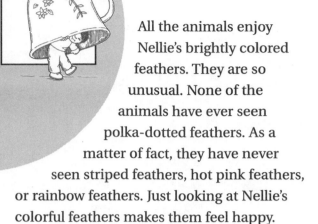

All the animals enjoy Nellie's brightly colored feathers. They are so unusual. None of the animals have ever seen polka-dotted feathers. As a matter of fact, they have never seen striped feathers, hot pink feathers, or rainbow feathers. Just looking at Nellie's colorful feathers makes them feel happy.

There is a secret funny thing about Nellie that only her mommy and daddy, her animal friends, and now you, know. That funny thing is that when Nellie is really happy, like when she is helping her friends, she gets a very silly, very funny grin on her turkey face.

Close your eyes for a minute, and I'll ask Nellie to show you her grin.

OK, now you can look. Here's Nellie!

Theme Connections

Dogs
Families
Friends
Holidays
Rabbits
Self-Esteem
Squirrels
Turkeys

Sing a Song of Opposites

by Pam Schiller

Directions: Photocopy the story patterns on pages 489-491. Use a black fine-point permanent marker to trace patterns onto a piece of interfacing. Color them with crayons and cut them out.

This is big and this is small,
This is big; this is small,
This is big and this is small,
Sing along with me.

Additional verses
This is tall and this is short.
This is up and this is down.
This is in and this is out.
This is happy and this is sad.
This is soft and this is hard.
This is fast and this is slow.

Theme Connections

Opposites
Spatial Relationships

Spanish Translation

Un Cuento de Opuestos
Éste es grande y éste es pequeño,
Éste es grande; éste es pequeño,
Éste es grande y éste es pequeño,
Canta conmigo.

Otros Versos
Éste es alto y éste es bajo.
Éste es largo y éste es corto.
Éste es izquierda y éste es derecha.

Smart Cookie's Best Friend, Gabby Graham

by Pam Schiller

Directions: Photocopy the story patterns on pages 492-493. Use a black fine-point permanent marker to trace patterns onto a piece of interfacing. Color them with crayons and cut them out.

Smart Cookie is a wonderful, round, perfect chocolate chip cookie. Gabby Graham is a fine, square, graham cracker. Smart Cookie and Gabby Graham are best friends. They can't wait to get to school each day so they can play together. Their favorite activity is building in the block center. They make roads and highways, barns and farms, tall skyscrapers and cozy cottages.

Smart Cookie always finds a square block that matches Gabby's graham cracker-shaped body and says with a laugh, "Hey, this block is the same shape you are." Gabby finds two half-circle arches, puts them together, and says with a laugh, "Hey, these blocks are the same shape you are." Both cookies laugh.

Next to playing with the blocks the cookies both love story time. They like all the Dr. Seuss stories but, of course, *If You Give a Mouse a Cookie* is their favorite story. Do you know why?

The cookies like drawing and painting. They love to play outdoors. They enjoy playing games with the other children and they both sing loudly during Morning Circle. The cookies love everything about school but there is no doubt that their favorite thing about school is the opportunity to spend time together. They are best friends. Do you have a best friend?

Theme Connections

Friends
School
Shapes

Smart Cookie's Clever Idea

by Pam Schiller

Directions: Photocopy the story patterns on pages 494-495. Use a black fine-point permanent marker to trace patterns onto a piece of interfacing. Color them with crayons and cut them out.

Smart Cookie was helping her mother bake animal cookies one day. It was her job to take the cookies off the cookie sheet when they came out of the oven and arrange them on the cookie platter. She really liked her job because she liked all the different animal shapes.

Smart Cookie was putting all the elephant cookies on one platter and the giraffe cookies on another, just like her mother had told her. She was really proud of the nice, even rows she was making. She was paying close attention to her work. She wanted her mother to be proud of her.

Suddenly Smart Cookie thought about her math lesson at school that morning. It was about making patterns. Maybe with that idea, she could make her platters look even better.

Smart Cookie rearranged the cookies. She made a row of elephant cookies, giraffe cookies, elephant cookies, giraffe cookies, and so on across the platter. This was so much more interesting. She couldn't wait to show her mother.

Smart Cookie finished arranging the cookies on the platter, and then she took it to show her mother. Her mother grinned from ear to ear. She was so proud. The tray looked beautiful. She hugged Smart Cookie and said, "You are one Smart Cookie!"

Theme Connections

Families
Food
Growing Up
Self-Esteem

The Snow Child

Directions: Photocopy the story patterns on pages 496-498. Use a black fine-point permanent marker to trace patterns onto a piece of interfacing. Color them with crayons and cut them out.

Once upon a time, an old man and woman lived on a farm in the far north. The winters were long and cold. The winter winds blew,

and the snow piled higher and higher. No one could travel or visit during the winter. The old man and woman were lonely. Every day, the old man would go to the barn and feed the cow and horse. Every day, the old woman would cook the potatoes, cabbages, and other vegetables they had grown in the summer. There were many jobs to be done.

Still they were lonely. Sometimes in the evenings, they would sit by the fire and tell stories. One story they liked to tell was of the child they would like to have. She would be beautiful! Her laugh would tinkle like the ice crystals that fell from the roof in the wind. Her eyes would twinkle like the sun sparkling on the white snow.

One morning, the old man and woman had an idea. They decided to make a child of snow. They put on their heavy clothes and boots. It was very cold outside, but the sun was shining brightly. First, they made the snow child's body. Then they made a small ball for the head. Carefully, they drew twinkling eyes and a smiling mouth. They were nearly done, and what a wonderful snow child she was! The old man and woman stepped back to take a good look at their snow child. Quickly, they rubbed their eyes. What was happening? Was the snow child moving? Yes! Yes!

They could hardly believe their eyes: their snow child was coming alive! She stepped forward, and they hugged her. Now at last, they had a child of their own. Every day, the old man and woman loved their snow child more and more. She helped her father care for the animals in the barn. She helped her mother cook. More than anything else, she loved to play in the snow. She would dance and twirl in the falling snowflakes and the

Child began to smile. The old woman smiled, too, and they all began to plan what they would do when the snow came again next winter.

One day, the boys and girls planned a picnic to celebrate spring. Everyone went to the forest. In a clearing, they built a small fire to dance around. The snow child joined hands with the other children. But as she passed close to the fire, she turned into a puddle of water. When the boys and girls looked for her, they could not find her anywhere.

The old man and the old woman were very sad, but they knew that it would not be long before they would have their sweet child again. They gathered the puddle of water and took it home to wait for winter. They knew that the same magic that brought them their snow child last winter would come again next winter.

whirling, cold wind. Then one morning, winter began to end. The piles of snow started to melt. Birds began to sing. The wind was not as strong and cold.

Spring was a happy time for the old man and woman. At last, they could visit their neighbors. They could get ready to plant their potatoes and cabbages. The horse and cow could come out of the barn. But the snow child seemed sad. Boys and girls came to play with her, but she was very quiet. She only wanted to sit near the melting piles of snow. The old man and the old woman asked her why she was sad. She told them that the warm weather was making her feel tired. She longed for the cold, icy winds of winter. The old woman and the old man suddenly realized that the warm weather would cause their sweet child to melt away. The old woman began to think of what she could do. "There is no way to stop the summer," she cried to her husband. "We can't stop the summer, but we also know that winter will return next year." The Snow

Theme Connections

Emotions
Families
Farms
Seasons

The Sun and the Moon

Directions: Photocopy the story patterns on pages 499-500. Use a black fine-point permanent marker to trace patterns onto a piece of interfacing. Color them with crayons and cut them out.

The Sun and the Moon lived in a cave. No light of the Sun or Moon came out of the cave. Only the stars shone in the sky.

The Sun and the Moon got tired of living in the cave together. It was too crowded. The Sun said to the Moon, "I am the father of all life. It is not right for me to be together with you in a cave. Go away and leave this cave for me."

"Where can I go?" asked the Moon. "I have no other home," she said.

"Go into the sky," answered the Sun. "There is plenty of space for you in the big, blue sky."

The moon was sad, but she left the cave. She was scared to be in the big, blue sky. She was only a thin, silver moon. She hid behind the clouds. Later she wasn't so scared. Little by little, she showed her whole face. Everyone said it was beautiful.

The Sun saw the Moon in the beautiful, blue sky and got angry. The little Moon was in a better place than he was! He ran out of the cave and jumped into the sky. When she saw the Sun coming, the Moon got scared and ran away. She kept looking back at the Sun. Soon nobody saw the Moon.

Now the Sun had the whole sky to live in. He sent his wonderful light in all directions. He warmed the cold Earth. Green plants and beautiful flowers began to grow. People danced and played in the sunshine. But the Sun was lonely. No one came near him. He had no one to talk to. The Sun wanted to find the Moon. The Sun went to look for her. The Moon was hiding in the old cave. When the Sun came near the cave, the Moon ran out.

"Oh, Moon," shouted the Sun. "Where are you going? Why do you leave when I come near? Dear Moon, do not go away again!"

The Moon did not wait for the Sun. She went quickly into the sky. When the Sun came into the sky, the Moon left.

To this day, the Sun cannot catch up with the Moon. Sometimes the Moon turns her cold face toward the Sun for a short time. Sometimes she turns her back on the Sun and passes quietly in front of him. Now the Sun and the Moon take turns sleeping in the cave. Each day, they travel separately through the sky.

Theme Connections

Nature
Outer Space
Sun, Moon, Stars
Time of Day

This Old Man Is Rockin' On
(Tune: This Old Man)

by Pam Schiller and Tracy Moncure

Directions: Photocopy the story patterns on pages 501-502. Use a black fine-point permanent marker to trace patterns onto a piece of interfacing. Color them with crayons and cut them out.

This Old Man, he played drums
With his fingers and his thumbs.

Chorus:
With a knick-knack paddy whack give a
dog a bone
This Old Man is rockin' on.

This Old Man, he played flute,
Made it hum and made it toot.

Chorus

This Old Man, he played strings,
Twangs and twops and zips and zings.

Chorus

This Old Man, he played bass,
With a big grin on his face.

Chorus

This Old Man, he played gong
At the end of every song.

Chorus

This Old Man, he could dance.
He could strut and he could prance.

Chorus

This Old Man was a band,
Very best band in the land.

Chorus

Theme Connections

Humor
Movement
Music

The Three Billy Goats Gruff

Directions: Photocopy the story patterns on pages 503–506. Use a black fine-point permanent marker to trace patterns onto a piece of interfacing. Color them with crayons and cut them out.

Once upon a time, there were three billy goats called Gruff. In the winter, they lived in a barn in the valley. When spring came, they longed to travel up to the mountains to eat the lush, sweet grass.

On their way to the mountains, the three Billy Goats Gruff had to cross a rushing river. But there was only one bridge across it, made of wooden planks. And underneath the bridge, there lived a terrible, ugly troll. Nobody was allowed to cross the bridge without the troll's permission, and nobody ever got permission. He always ate them up.

The smallest Billy Goat Gruff was first to reach the bridge. Trippity-trop, trippity-trop went his little hooves as he trotted over the wooden planks. Ting-tang, ting-tang went the little bell round his neck.

"Who's that trotting over my bridge?" growled the troll from under the planks.

"Billy Goat Gruff," squeaked the smallest goat in his little voice. "I'm only going up to the mountain to eat the sweet spring grass."

"Oh, no, you're not!" said the troll. "I'm going to eat you for breakfast!"

"Oh, no, please, Mr. Troll," pleaded the goat. "I'm only the smallest Billy Goat Gruff. I'm much too tiny for you to eat, and I wouldn't taste very good. Why don't you wait for my brother, the second Billy Goat Gruff? He's much bigger than I am and would be much more tasty."

The troll did not want to waste his time on a little goat if there was a bigger and better one to eat. "All right, you can cross my bridge," he grunted. "Go and get fatter on the mountain, and I'll eat you on your way back!"

So the smallest Billy Goat Gruff skipped across to the other side.

The troll did not have to wait long for the second Billy Goat Gruff. Clip-clop, clip-clop went his hooves as he clattered over the wooden planks. Ding-dong, ding-dong went the bell around his neck.

"Who's that clattering across my bridge?" screamed the troll, suddenly appearing from under the planks. "Billy Goat Gruff," said the second goat in his middle-sized voice. "I'm going up to the mountain to eat the lovely spring grass."

"Oh, no you're not!" said the troll. "I'm going to eat you for breakfast."

"Oh, no, please," said the second goat. "I may be bigger than the first Billy Goat Gruff, but I'm much smaller than my brother, the third Billy Goat Gruff. Why don't you wait for him? He would be much more of a meal than I would."

The troll was getting very hungry, but he did not want to waste his appetite on a middle-sized goat if there was an even bigger one to come. "All right, you can cross my bridge," he rumbled. "Go and get fatter on the mountain, and I'll eat you on your way back!" So the middle-sized Billy Goat Gruff scampered across to the other side.

The troll did not have to wait long for the third Billy Goat Gruff. Tromp-tramp, tromp-tramp went his hooves as he stomped across the wooden planks. Bong-bang, bong-bang went the big bell round his neck.

"Who's that stomping over my bridge?" roared the troll, resting his chin on his hands. "Billy Goat Gruff," said the third goat in a deep voice. "I'm going up to the mountain to eat the lush spring grass."

"Oh, no, you're not," said the troll as he clambered up on to the bridge. "I'm going to eat you for breakfast!"

"That's what you think," said the biggest Billy Goat Gruff. Then he lowered his horns, galloped along the bridge and butted the ugly troll. Up, up, up, went the troll into the air... then down, down, down into the rushing river below. He disappeared below the swirling waters.

"So much for his breakfast," thought the biggest Billy Goat Gruff. "Now what about mine?" And he walked in triumph over the bridge to join his two brothers on the mountain pastures. From then on anyone could cross the bridge whenever they liked, thanks to the three Billy Goats Gruff.

Variation

Use an overhead projector to tell this as a "shadow" story. Photocopy the story patterns on page 503-506. Use the patterns to cut shapes from black construction paper. Place the cutouts on the overhead projector as you tell the story.

Theme Connections

Goats
Numbers
Opposites
Spatial Relationships
Tricksters

The Three Little Pigs

Directions: Photocopy the story patterns on pages 507-512. Use a black fine-point permanent marker to trace patterns onto a piece of interfacing. Color them with crayons and cut them out.

Once upon a time, there were three little pigs that left their mother and father to find their places in the world. All summer long, they roamed through the woods and over the plains, playing games and having fun. No one was happier than the three little pigs, and they easily made friends with everyone. Wherever they went, they were given a warm welcome. But as summer drew to a close, they realized that folks were returning to their usual jobs and preparing for winter.

Autumn came, and it began to grow cold and to rain. The three little pigs decided they needed real a home of their own. Sadly they knew that the fun was over. Now they must set to work like the others, or they'd be left in the cold and rain with no roof over their heads. They talked about what kind of a home they should build.

The first little pig said they should build a house made from straw.

"It will only take a day," he said.

"It's too fragile," his brothers said. But the first pig didn't care. He was anxious to get

back to playing, so he built a home for himself out of straw.

Not quite so lazy, the second little pig went in search of planks of seasoned wood.

"Clunk! Clunk! Clunk!" It took him two days to nail them together.

The third little pig did not like the wooden house.

"That's not the way to build a house!" he said. "It takes time, patience and hard work

to build a house that is strong enough to stand up to the wind and, rain, and snow, and most of all, to protect us from the wolf!"

The days went by, and the wisest little pig's house took shape, brick by brick. From time to time, his brothers visited him, saying with a chuckle:

"Why are you working so hard? Why don't you come and play?"

"No" said the last little pig. He diligently continued his work. Soon his work was done and just in time.

One autumn day when no one expected it, along came the big bad wolf, scowling fiercely at the first pig's straw house.

"Little pig, little pig, let me in, let me in!" ordered the wolf, his mouth watering.

"Not by the hair of my chinny, chin, chin!" replied the little pig in a tiny voice.

"Then I'll huff and I'll puff and I'll blow your house down!" growled the wolf angrily.

The wolf puffed out his chest, and he huffed, and he puffed, and he blew the first little pig's house of straw right down.

Excited by his own cleverness, the wolf did not notice that the little pig had slithered out from underneath the heap of straw and was dashing towards his brother's wooden house.

When he realized that the little pig was escaping, the wolf grew wild with rage.

"Come back!" he roared, trying to catch the pig as he ran into the wooden house. The second little pig greeted his brother, shaking like a leaf.

"Open up! Open up! I only want to speak to you!" growled the hungry wolf.

"Go away, cried the two little pigs. So the angry wolf puffed out his chest, and he huffed, and he puffed, and he blew the wooden house clean away.

Luckily, the wisest little pig had been watching the scene from the window of his own brick house, and he quickly opened the door to his fleeing brothers. And not a moment too soon, for the wolf was already hammering furiously on the door. This time, the wolf wasted no time talking. He puffed out his chest, and he huffed, and he puffed, and he blew and blew and blew, but the little brick house wouldn't budge. The wolf tried again. He puffed out his chest, and he huffed, and he puffed, but still the little house stood strong.

The three little pigs watched him, and their fear began to fade. Quite exhausted by his efforts, the wolf decided to try one of his tricks. He scrambled up a nearby ladder, onto the roof to have a look at the chimney. However, the now wiser little pigs knew exactly what the wolf was up to.

"Quick! Light the fire! He is coming down the chimney."

The big bad wolf began to crawl down the chimney. It wasn't long before he felt something very hot on his tail. "Ouch!" he exclaimed. His tail was on fire. He jumped out of the chimney and tried to put the out the flames on his tail. Then he ran away as fast as he could.

The three happy little pigs, dancing round and round the yard, began to sing: "Tra-la-la! Tra-la-la! The big bad wolf will never come back!" And he never did!

Theme Connections

Numbers
Pigs
Seasons
Wolves
Work

Three Wishes
(Puerto Rico)

Directions: Photocopy the story patterns on pages 513-514. Use a black fine-point permanent marker to trace patterns onto a piece of interfacing. Color them with crayons and cut them out.

Once upon a time, a woodsman and his wife lived in a little house in the forest. They were poor but very happy. They loved each other very much. They were always ready to share everything they had with anyone who came to their door.

One day the woodsman was working in the forest. His wife was working at home. An old man came to their little house. He said he was very hungry. The woman had only a little food, but she shared it with him. The old man ate. Then he said, "You and your husband share everything you have with everyone. Because you have been so kind, I have a special gift for you."

"What is the gift?" asked the woman. The old man answered, "You and your husband can make any three wishes and they will come true." The woman was very happy. She said, "I wish my husband could be here to hear you!" In a minute, her husband was there. Her first wish came true.

"What happened?" asked the woodsman. "I was in the forest. Why am I here now?" His wife kissed him and explained. The woodsman listened to her story. Then he became angry. He shouted at his wife for the first time. "You wasted one of our wishes. Now we have only two wishes left. You are so foolish! I wish you had donkey ears!" His wife's ears began to grow. They changed into big donkey ears. The woman touched her

long ears and cried. Her husband felt very bad about what he said.

The old man said, "You never shouted at each other before. Now you are different. You know you can have power and be rich. You have only one wish left. Do you want to be rich? Do you want to have beautiful clothes?" The woodsman said, "We only want to be happy again, like before."

The donkey ears disappeared. The woodsman and his wife thanked God. They were happy again. The old man said, "Poor people can be very happy, and rich people can be very unhappy. Soon you will have the biggest happiness a married couple can have." A few months later, the woodsman and his wife had a baby, and the family lived happily ever after.

Theme Connections

Emotions
Families
Humor

Tortoise Wins a Race
(Brazil)

Directions: Photocopy the story patterns on pages 515-517. Use a fine-point permanent marker to trace patterns onto a piece of interfacing material. Color them and cut them out.

A tortoise named Jabotí lived in the Amazon jungle. He played a flute. All the other animals wanted his instrument, but he never gave it to anybody. One day Jabotí was walking and playing his flute. He saw Suasú, the deer.

"Hello, Jabotí," said the deer. "Where are you going?"

"Good morning," said Jabotí. "I'm going to visit my cousin."

"Where did you get that flute?" asked the deer.

"I killed a jaguar and made the flute from his bone."

"You killed a jaguar? I don't believe it!" said the deer. "You couldn't kill a fly. Everyone in the jungle knows that."

"You think that I am weak, but you are wrong," said Jabotí. "Tell me something. What can you do best of all?"

"I can run," answered Suasú.

"All right. Then let's have a race!" said Jabotí.

Suasú laughed and laughed. "Do you really think you can race with me?" she asked.

"I can race with you," said Jabotí.

"Okay, let's begin right now," said the deer.

"I'm busy today," said Jabotí. "We can race tomorrow. You can run in this clearing. I know you can't run in the jungle. It is full of vines. I'll run near the edge of the jungle. When you want to know where I am, just call out and I'll answer you. Okay?"

"That is fair," answered the deer. "I have an idea, too. The winner of the race gets your flute."

Jabotí was scared. What if he lost his flute?

But he couldn't say no now.

"Okay," said Jabotí. He sounded brave, but he was scared. That night, Jabotí asked his family and friends to come to a meeting.

"Friends and relatives, this is a very important meeting," said Jabotí. "Tomorrow I am running a race with Suasú, the deer. I must win this race."

"That's foolish!" shouted the tortoises. "Jabotí is crazy. He can't run a race with a deer! We must do something, or he will get all of us in trouble!"

Jabotí said, "Just a minute, everybody. Let me finish." He quietly told them his plan. They all listened. The next day, Suasú came to the clearing. She was surprised to hear Jabotí's voice in the jungle.

"Good morning, my friend Suasú. Here I am, ready to go. Are you ready?"

"Ready," answered the deer.

"One...two...three...go!" shouted the tortoise.

Suasú thought that she would win the race easily. She walked a little way. Then she looked back and called, "Jabotí!" The answer came from the jungle—ahead of her!

"Here I am. You must hurry, or I will win!"

The deer was very surprised. "How did he get ahead of me?" she asked herself. Suasú began to run. A little later, she called again. Again a voice answered from ahead of her:

"Here I am, Suasú."

Suasú ran faster. But when she called again, she heard a voice in the jungle ahead of her:

"Here I am, Suasú."

So the race continued. The deer ran as fast as she could. The tortoise's voice always came from the jungle ahead of her. Finally, Suasú couldn't run anymore. She was too tired. Jabotí found her lying on the ground. Her tongue was hanging out.

"Well," said Jabotí. "A tortoise can win a race against a deer! You thought that you could get my flute. But look at you! You are too tired to move."

Jabotí was very happy. His plan worked. His friends and family helped him. Each tortoise took a place in the jungle, near the clearing. When Suasú called Jabotí, the tortoise ahead of her answered. Jabotí took his flute and went away. He walked and played a happy song for everyone to hear.

Theme Connections

Deer   Tortoises
Emotions   Tricksters
Friends

The Traveling Musicians

Directions: Photocopy the story patterns on pages 518-523. Use a black fine-point permanent marker to trace patterns onto a piece of interfacing. Color them with crayons and cut them out.

Once upon a time, an old, gray donkey stood under a tree thinking, "The farmer has been good to me. I have plenty of food to eat. I have a nice, warm barn to sleep in. I don't have to work hard. I have a pretty good life as a pet, yet I'm tired of this life. I want to do something more exciting. I really want to be a singer and go to the city." So the donkey ran back to the barn, grabbed his tambourine and his sequined headband, and trotted off down the road to the city.

Soon he spied a big, red dog sitting on a fence playing her guitar. "Well, howdy, dog!" the donkey said. "You play a mean guitar!" The dog replied, "Thank you, kind sir. I do my best. Would you care to join me in singing a song?" "Why, sure!" said the donkey. They found several songs, which they both knew. Their favorite was "Old MacDonald Had a Farm," which they sang over and over.

As the donkey and the dog were singing "Old MacDonald" for the fourth time, a cat with his keyboard and a duck with her saxophone joined them. Because "Old MacDonald" was the only song they all knew, they kept singing and playing it throughout the day.

Around sunset, the animals were interrupted by a strange thumping sound. They looked all around until they saw a little, white rabbit dancing merrily on his drum. The rabbit suddenly realized the others were watching him and became embarrassed. He stopped dancing and began to run away. "Wait!" called the duck, "Come back. We love your dancing. We're tired of being pets, so we're going to have a band and go to the city to play. Would you like to come with us?"

The rabbit peeked out from behind a bush. "Do you really like my dancing?"

"Of course we like it. You're wonderful. Can you do the moonwalk?" asked the duck.

"Just watch this," said the rabbit, as he hopped up on his drum and did the moonwalk. He even managed to add a twirl and a split. Everyone clapped and cheered, and soon they were all singing and dancing and playing as the sun set.

Now you're probably wondering, "Didn't those crazy animals ever get tired or hungry?" Well, sure they did. In fact, at about this time, their growling stomachs were louder than their singing and playing. "I'm starving and tired and wish I were home," said the duck. "I'm starving and tired and wish I were home, too," said the dog and the cat at the same time. "We can't go home," said the donkey. "We've said that we want to do something more exciting. We can't quit. We have to go on."

So the animals decided to go on to the city and get something to eat and a place to sleep. They walked and walked and walked. Finally they saw an old house at the top of a hill. "There's a light on at that house," said the cat. "Let's see whether we can find something to eat. Maybe the owner will let us sleep in the barn."

When the hungry, tired animals got to the house, the donkey, who was the tallest, trotted up to a window and peeked in. "What do you see?" asked the dog. The donkey answered, "I see a table covered with food, and around the table there are ugly robbers laughing and acting silly."

"Oh, I'm so hungry and tired," said the cat.

"Oh, I'm so hungry and tired," said the rabbit. "This would be a good place for us to stay," said the duck, "if only we could think of a way to get ourselves in and the robbers out."

The animals thought and thought and finally came up with a plan. The donkey stood on his hind legs near the window and held his tambourine between his front legs. The dog grabbed her guitar and climbed onto the donkey's shoulders. The cat hung his keyboard around his neck and scrambled up the dog's back. The rabbit took his drum and hopped onto the cat's back, and the duck with her saxophone flew up and sat on the rabbit's head. Then all together, the animals began to play and sing "Old MacDonald." Suddenly, they lost their balance and crashed through the window into the room with the robbers. Terrified, the robbers ran screaming out of the house and down the

road. Once the robbers were gone, the animals sat down at the table and ate like they hadn't eaten in a month. Then they turned out the lights and went to sleep.

After a while, the robbers stopped running and realized that they weren't so frightened anymore. In fact, they decided that they had been silly to leave in such a great hurry. They returned to the house and, when it was dark, one robber sneaked in. As he tiptoed around the kitchen, the robber accidentally stepped on the cat's tail. The angry cat leaped up, scratching the robber. This, of course, frightened the robber so much that he tripped over the dog. The dog bit him in the leg. The screeching and hollering awakened the other animals, which began attacking the robber, and the robber ran screaming from the house.

Exhausted, the animals slumped to the floor. "You know," said the donkey, "Life has been exciting since I left home, but I miss being a pet. I'm not very good at being a traveling musician, and I don't like fighting robbers. I like having food and a place to sleep at the farm." "I miss being a pet and swimming in my pond," said the duck. The cat began to cry, "I miss my little boy, and I want to go home!" "Let's go home," said the rabbit. "I'll race you to the road," called the dog as she ran out of the house. So, the animals went home and lived happily ever after as pets. If you listen carefully on a quiet night, you might hear the animals singing to each other.

Theme Connections

Cats	Ducks	Friends
Dogs	Emotions	Music
Donkeys	Farms	Rabbits

Valerie Valentine

by Pam Schiller

Directions: Photocopy the story patterns on page 525. Use a black fine-point permanent marker to trace patterns onto a piece of interfacing. Color them with crayons and cut them out.

It was almost Valentine's Day. Valerie couldn't wait. She had been looking forward to finally being old enough to be a store valentine. Her brothers, Victor and Vance, had left home last year, and now it was her turn. She wanted to look vibrant. She put on her Victorian lace trim. She thought it was her very best outfit.

She found a good spot on the shelf at Victoria's Card shop. She put on her best smile and waited. The first day came and went and no one bought Valerie. She was very sad. She didn't want to sound vain but she really thought she looked better than any other card. Valerie decided to put on her black hat with the lace veil. That should do it.

The next day was the same. People came and went and never even picked her up. When the school van came loaded with children and no one even noticed her she was devastated.

That night Valerie gathered a honeysuckle vine and wrapped it around her middle. Then she picked a vacant spot on the shelf where she would be right in view of the door. Surely this will work she thought.

But the next day was the same. When the store closed, Valerie started to cry. She was too sad to even think of another idea. Then suddenly, she heard a voice beside her. It was Valentino, the Beanie Baby Bear. He said he knew a secret that would be just the right thing to make Valerie the most special Valentine on the shelf. He whispered it into her ear. Do you know what it was?

It was a special verse. Valerie wrote it right across her face with a violet crayon. It said:

> *"Roses are red,*
> *Violets are blue,*
> *Sugar is sweet*
> *And so are you!"*

And at last, Valerie was victorious. She was the first valentine to be bought the next morning.

Theme Connections

Celebrations
Emotions
Holidays
Self-Esteem

What's in the Box?

by Pam Schiller

Directions: Photocopy the story patterns on pages 526-529. Use a black fine-point permanent marker to trace patterns onto interfacing. Color them with crayons and cut them out.

Look at this wonderful box. It's all wrapped up. It has pretty paper and a pretty bow. It's a present. I wonder what's inside. Do you wonder what's inside?

What do you think is in the box? Maybe it's a ball. Maybe it's a doll. Maybe it's a rattle for baby.

If we could pick up the box, we'd know if it was heavy or light. If we could shake the box, we might hear something inside. We'd know if the thing inside makes a hard sound or a soft sound. But we can't shake this box so we just have to guess.

Maybe it's a book. Maybe it's a toy car. Maybe it's a jack-in-the-box. Let's find out.

First we take off the bow. We'll put it right here. It's so pretty. Maybe we can use it again. Now let's take off the paper. If we are gentle and don't tear it, we can use the paper again, too.

OK! Are you ready to see what's inside? Look! It's a top!

Theme Connections

Birthdays
Emotions
Holidays

The Zebra on the Zyder Zee

by Pam Schiller

Directions: Photocopy the story patterns on pages 530-536. Use a black fine-point permanent marker to trace patterns onto interfacing. Color them with crayons and cut them out.

The Zebra on the Zyder Zee
Wanted to sail across the sea,
He called to his friends 1, 2, 3,
"Come along and sail with me."

The Zebra on the Zyder Zee
Said, "I am lonesome, don't you see.
I want to sail across the sea,
But I simply must have company."

The first to come on the Zyder Zee
Was the Zebra's friend Sir Ronnee Ree.
He said, "I'll be your company
I'm dying to sail across the sea."

The next to come to the Zyder Zee
Was Elizabeth Holleque de Dundee
She brought her little urchins three
And said, "Let's sail across the sea."

The Zebra on the Zyder Zee
Was just as happy as he could be.
He was going to sail across the sea.
And the Zyder Zee had company.

He hoisted the sails 1, 2, 3,
And the friends were off to see the sea.
Day and night and day times three,
The jolly mates sailed across the sea.

The little ship rocked on the sea
The jolly mates ate bread and brie,
The little ones sipped cinnamon tea
And the Zebra sailed the Zyder Zee.

Day by day Ronnee studied the sea,
While Elizabeth read her poetry.
The urchins played tic-tac-three
And the Zebra sailed the Zyder Zee.

*When nighttime fell
across the sea
    Elizabeth sang to the
    urchins three
    And her new friend Sir
    Ronnee Ree
    Hummed along in harmony.*

*At last, the journey across the sea
Came to an end at half past three.
The Zebra and his company
Had finally sailed across the sea.*

*The little ones and Ms. Dundee
Took the hand of Ronnee Ree
And left the deck of the Zyder Zee,
Saying good-bye to the deep blue sea.*

*The Zebra cleaned the Zyder Zee
Lowered the sails, 1, 2, 3.
Polished the decks merrily,
And dreamed of sailing back to sea.*

Theme Connections

Boats and Ships
Emotions
Friends
Numbers
Time of Day
Zebras

Listening Stories

The Ant and the Dove
(Aesop)

An ant went to the bank of a river to quench his thirst. He was carried away by the rush of the stream and was on the point of drowning. A dove sitting on a tree overhanging the water plucked a leaf and let it fall into the stream close to the ant. The ant climbed onto the leaf and floated safely to the bank. Shortly afterwards a bird catcher came and stood under the tree where the dove was sitting, and laid his lime-twigs (trap) for the dove. The ant realized what the bird catcher was going to do. He stung the bird catcher in the foot. The bird catcher screamed in pain and threw down the twigs. The noise made the dove fly away and he was saved.

Moral

One good turn deserves another!

Variation

The Dove and the Ant (Aesop)

An ant, going to the river to drink, fell in the water and was carried along in the stream. A dove perched in a near by tree felt sorry for the ant and threw into the river a small bough. This bough enabled the ant to float to the shore. Afterward, the ant saw a man with a gun aimed at the dove. She stung the man on the foot sharply, and made him miss his aim, and so saved the dove's life.

Theme Connections

Birds
Friends
Insects

The Boy Who Cried Wolf
(Aesop)

Once upon a time, there was a little boy who liked to tell lies. He thought it was great fun to make people believe a thing was true when it wasn't. Of course, this made his family unhappy, and it made his friends unhappy, and it got the little boy into trouble.

To help his father, the little boy sometimes went to the fields to watch the sheep. It was his job as a shepherd to keep the wolf away from the sheep. If he saw a wolf, he was supposed to yell as loud as he could, "Wolf! Wolf!" Then anyone who could hear him would help him chase the wolf away.

One sunny afternoon, the little boy was bored, so he decided to have some fun. What do you think he did? He cried, "Wolf! Wolf!" as loud as he could. His father and his brothers and sisters and the neighbors all grabbed big sticks and went running to chase away the wolf. When they found the little boy and the sheep, the little boy was rolling around on the ground laughing. He thought it was so funny to see all those

neighbors sneaked out to the field where the boy was watching the sheep, and they hid behind some bushes. The brother in the wolf suit crept out from behind a bush and growled. The little boy looked around. His brother, the "wolf," growled again and began creeping slowly toward the little boy and his sheep. The little boy screamed, "Wolf! Wolf! Wolf!"

The wolf crept closer and closer. The little boy screamed again, "Wolf! Wolf!" He kept screaming, but no one came to help him. As the wolf got closer, the little boy became more frightened. He was sure the wolf would eat him and all his sheep.

The little boy took off running back to the house, all the time telling himself, "I'll never tell a lie again. I'll never tell a lie again." And he didn't.

people leave their work and come running to help him. No one else thought it was funny.

The next afternoon, the little boy was bored again, so what do you think he did? He cried, "Wolf! Wolf!" as loud as he could. His father and his brothers and his sisters and the neighbors all grabbed big sticks and went running to chase away the wolf. When they found the little boy and the sheep, the little boy was rolling on the ground laughing. This time, the people got very angry, and his father told him, "Lying is not right. One day the wolf will come, and you will really need help, but no one will believe you because you've lied so many times." The little boy just laughed.

When the father and the brothers and the neighbors were back at the farmer's house, they talked about the little boy and his lying. They decided to teach him a lesson before the wolf hurt him. What do you think they did? A few days later, one of the brothers dressed up like a wolf. Then the boy's father and his brothers and his sisters and the

Theme Connections

Families
Growing Up
Wolves
Work

The Cat and the Mouse

Food was becoming scarce in the small village, so Ramón, the village cat, decided to go to another village. He walked and walked for several days until finally he arrived in a little town that looked good to him. All the mice in that town cried, "A big cat has just arrived in the village!" "Meow, Meow, Meoooww..." said the cat, and the mice responded, "We know that you are out there waiting to eat us, but we are never going to come out of our houses."

Hours and days passed, and the same conversation continued. "Meow, Meow, Meoooww..." said the cat; the mice responded, "We know that you are out there waiting to eat us, but we are never going to come out of our houses." After some time had passed, the mice heard the barking of a dog, "Bow, wow, bow, wow." The mice immediately thought the cat had been chased away by the dog. "Now we can go out of our houses," they said to each other. They stepped outside, but to their surprise, they did not see a dog. Instead, they saw the very same cat that had been meowing earlier, only now it was barking like a dog. The cat had tricked the mice! In a very frightened voice, one of them asked the cat, "What happened to the barking that we heard? We believed that there was a dog outside our houses and thought that it had scared you away. Were you making the sound of the dog?" With great satisfaction, the cat responded, "Indeed it was I who made the sound of the barking dog. I have learned that those who speak at least two languages have many opportunities to succeed in life."

Theme Connections

Cats
Dogs
Mice
Sounds of Language
Tricksters

Spanish Translation

El Gato y los Ratones

El alimento día a día escaseaba en la pequeña ciudad. De allí que el gato Ramón había decidido mudarse a otra ciudad. Caminó y caminó por varios días hasta que finalmente llegó a la ciudad deseada por el. La voz no se hizo esperar por todo el vecindario porque todos los ratones ya habían avisado de que un enorme gato había llegado a la ciudad.

-Miau, miau, miauuu...- maullaba el gato. Los ratones le respondían, -Sabemos que estas ahí gato sin misericordia, y jamás vamos a salir de nuestras casas-. Las horas y los días pasaron, miau, miau, miauuu... continuaba maullando el gato y los ratones le respondían, sabemos que segues ahí gato sin misericordia, y jamás vamos a salir de nuestras casas. Tiempo más tarde los ratones escucharon el ladrar de un perro -Guau, guau, rrr-guau, guau, guau, rr-guau-. Los ratones inmediatamente pensaron que el gato se había marchado debido a la presencia del perro.

-Ya podemos salir-se dijeron entre sí. En efecto salieron, pero cual va siendo su sorpresa cuando ven que el mismo gato que antes maullaba ahora con ladridos de perro los había atrapado. Uno de ellos temerosamente le pregunta al gato -¿Qué pasó con los ladridos que habíamos escuchado? ¡Pensamos que era un perro y que el perro te había asustado y tú te habías marchado! ¿Acaso fuistes tú? El gato con tremenda satisfacción les responde -En efecto fuí yo. ¡La vida nos enseña día a día que en estos tiempos el que habla por lo menos dos idiomas tiene más oportunidades para triunfar en la vida!

The Crow and the Fox
(Aesop)

High in the branches of a tree, a crow was eating a delicious cheese. Meanwhile, because of the smell of the cheese, a very clever fox was prowling around the crow under the tree branches. The fox started to flatter the crow to get the cheese. "Good morning, Mr. Crow, what beautiful feathers you have, what a beauty never seen. With those shiny and silky feathers, who can resist so much beauty?" The crow unable to resist so much flattery could not stay quiet, and he responded, "Thanks, Mr. Fox. Good morning to you." But, when he opened his beak to give thanks, the delicious cheese fell, and the fox ate it.

Moral

Do not believe everything you hear because you can lose what is already yours.

Theme Connections

Birds
Food
Foxes
Tricksters

Dog: A Mayan Legend

Long ago, Dog was the only creature that could speak. He told all the secrets of creation. Deciding that Dog could not keep the secrets to himself, Shaper and Creator took Dog's short tail and put it in Dog's mouth. Then Shaper and Creator put Dog's long, loose tongue where his tail had been. That is why now, when Dog wants to tell you something, he wags his tail.

Theme Connections

Dogs
Humor

The Donkey in the Lion's Skin
(Aesop)

A donkey put on a lion costume and roamed about in the forest amusing himself by frightening all the animals he met. He frightened birds, rabbits, squirrels, and deer. Eventually he came upon a fox. He tried to frighten him too, but the fox only laughed. "I might possibly have been frightened myself, if I had not heard your bray."

Moral

Clothes may disguise a fool but his words will give him away.

Theme Connections

Donkeys
Foxes
Lions
Tricksters

The Duel

by Eugene Field

The gingham dog and the
    calico cat
Side by side on the table sat.
'Twas half-past twelve, and (what do you
    think!)
Not one or the other had slept a wink!
The old Dutch clock and the Chinese plate
Appeared to know as sure as fate

There was going to be a terrible spat.
I wasn't there; I simply state what was
    told to me by the Chinese plate!

The gingham dog said "Bow-wow-wow!"
And the calico cat replied, "Mee-ow!"
The air was littered, an hour or so,
With bits of gingham and calico,
While the old Dutch clock in the chimney-
    place
Held up its hands before its face,
For it always dreaded a family row!
Now mind: I'm only telling you what the
old Dutch clock declares is true!

The Chinese plate looked very blue,
And wailed, "Oh dear! What shall we do?"
But the gingham dog and the calico cat
Wallowed this way and tumbled that,
Employing every tooth and claw
In the awfullest way you ever saw-
And, oh! How the gingham and calico
    flew!
Don't fancy I exaggerate-I got my news
    from the Chinese plate!

Next morning, where the two had sat
They found no trace of dog or cat.
And some folks think unto this day
That burglars stole the pair away!
But the truth about the cat and pup
Is this: they ate each other up!
Now what do you really think of that?
The old Dutch clock, it told me so, and
    that is how I came to know.

Theme Connections

Cats
Dogs
Humor
Rhymes and Rhyming
Sounds of Language

The Eagle and the Snake
(Aesop)

An eagle swooped down upon a snake and
seized it in his talons with the intention of
carrying it off and devouring it. But the
snake was too quick for him and had its coils
around him in a moment; and then a
struggle began between the two. A man, who
was a witness to the encounter, came to the
assistance of the eagle, and succeeded in

freeing him from the snake and enabling him to escape. In revenge, the snake spat some of his poison into the man's drinking-horn. Heated from his exertions, the man was about to slake his thirst with a draught from the horn, when the eagle knocked it out of his hand and spilled its contents upon the ground.

Moral

One good deed deserves another.

Theme Connections

Eagles
Emotions
Friends
Snakes

The Evil King

Once there was an evil king who was mean and hateful to everyone he met. He went from town to town stealing the people's money and possessions. When he was feeling especially wicked, he put the people in jail and laughed at them until he became bored.

Everyone was afraid of the evil king. Even the biggest, strongest soldiers were afraid. To his face they called him Good King, but behind his back they called him evil.

One day, the Evil King went to rob the people in one of the nearby towns. When he got to the town, he saw that he had already taken everything they had. He went on to the next village. He had already robbed the people there too. From town to town he traveled, only to find that he had already taken everything the people had.

Well, the Evil King was perplexed. What was he to do? Who could he steal from now? What would he do? Suddenly, an idea came to him. "I will take over the skies!" he said. "I will rule the world from above!"

The Evil King ordered his servants and soldiers to build him an airship. When it was completed, it looked like a ship attached to a giant balloon. One hundred eagles waited to lift the airship up into the clouds.

The Evil King was very excited! He climbed into his airship and ordered the eagles to lift him to the sky. "I shall rule the world!" he cried. I shall rule the universe! Even the sun and the moon will bow down to me!"

Just then, a tiny mosquito buzzed into the king's ear and bit him. The king jumped. He slapped at his ear with his hands. He jumped again. He rolled on the floor of his mighty airship. Still the pain did not go away. The king jumped and rolled and slapped and jumped and rolled and slapped. The soldiers, the servants, and even the eagles began to giggle. Then they began to laugh. They laughed so hard they shook the airship.

When the Evil King saw that all the people were laughing at him, he was embarrassed and ashamed. After all, he thought he was the mightiest, meanest king of all, but a tiny mosquito had beaten him. The king was so embarrassed that he ran away and never

came back to his kingdom. The people took back all their money and possessions and were never afraid again.

Theme Connections

Birds
Emotions
Insects
Kings and Queens
Opposites

Fish Games

by Pam Schiller

Many small and beautiful fish live, swim, and play in the big, blue sea. Freddie and Frankie are fish friends. They live in the coral reef. Freddie is an angelfish and Frankie is a rainbow fish. They play together everyday.

Freddie and Frankie love to swim in the coral reef. They believe they have the best playground anywhere in the whole ocean. They love to play Fish Tag. In and out, in and out, in and out of the coral reef they race.

Freddie and Frankie have many fish friends. Their friends often join in the games that Freddie and Frankie play. The fish play Musical Shells like we play Musical Chairs. They use the sounds of the waves as their music. Freddie always wins this game.

They play Jump Seaweed like we play jump rope. Here is one of the chants they use when jumping the chains of seaweed.

Little fishes in the ocean blue,
Little fishes swimming two by two.
Little fishes, if you make a wish
How many wishes will come true?
One, two, three...

Frankie and Freddie play Hide and Seek in an old boat that sunk to the bottom of the sea many years ago. There is a trunk inside the boat and it is full of necklaces and jewels that the fish love to wear when they play dress-up with their friends.

At school, the fish play Salmon Says. Can you think of which of our games that game might be like?

Theme Connections

Fish
Friends
Oceans and Seas

The Fox Who Lost His Dinner

Once upon a time there was a barnyard full of fine, fat, feathered fowls happily pecking for food and chatting. "Cluck, cluck," said the hens. "Quack, quack," said the ducks. "Honk, honk," said the geese. "Gobble, gobble," said the turkeys. "Cock-a-doodle-doo," said the rooster.

But along came a sly fox that thought to himself, "Ah-ha! Tonight I shall have my dinner from this barnyard full of fine, feathered fowls."

"Hello my fine, fat, feathered fowls," said the sly fox. "I am going to eat you for my dinner tonight."

"Oh, please, do not eat us," said the hens.

"Let us return to our home in the barn," said the ducks.

"Indeed I will not let you go," said the sly fox. "I will eat you all up, one at a time."

"Oh me, oh my! Oh me, oh my!" said the geese.

"It is very hard for us to die this way," said the turkeys. "Would you let us do just one thing before you eat us all up?"

"Yes," said the rooster. "Let us have just one wish, then we will stand in a row and let you eat us all up, one at a time."

"What is this wish?" asked the sly fox.

"Please let us pray before you eat us," said the hens.

"Oh yes, please do," said the ducks.

"Very well," said the sly fox. "I will grant you just this one wish, but make it quick. I'm getting very hungry."

So all the fine, fat, feathered fowls gathered 'round and began to pray.

"You are making too much noise," said the sly fox. "Pray more quietly." But the fine, fat, feathered fowls prayed still louder.

"I said quieter, not louder," shouted the sly fox, who was beginning to lose his patience. But the hens, ducks, geese, turkeys, and rooster prayed in their very loudest voices.

The praying was so loud that the farmer rushed out to see what was the matter. When he saw the sly fox he grabbed his gun and ran to the barnyard to protect his flock, firing as he ran. The sly fox disappeared into the field, running even faster than the bullets.

Moral

If you work together you can fool even the sly fox.

Theme Connections

Chickens
Ducks
Farms
Food
Foxes
Geese
Tricksters

A Home for Francesca

by Pam Schiller

Richele was so excited. "Guess what I found at the pond?" she called as she opened the back door.

"If it's alive, don't bring it in the house," said her mother.

Richele pulled something small and green from her pocket. "Oh, Mom, it's only a little green frog. Isn't it cute? I'm going to name her Francesca."

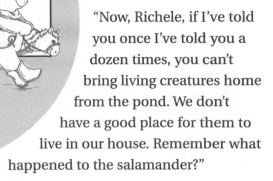

"Now, Richele, if I've told you once I've told you a dozen times, you can't bring living creatures home from the pond. We don't have a good place for them to live in our house. Remember what happened to the salamander?"

"Yes, but I'll be careful and put a cover over the top of the jar so Francesca can't get out. I'll put in some rocks for her to climb on and I'll catch flies for her to eat."

While Richele was talking to her mother, she took a large jar out of the cupboard. She put some water in it and dropped Francesca in. She swam around in a circle. Then she hung in the water with her eyes peering out.

"Do you think Francesca will like being in that jar?" asked Richele's mother.

"I'd like it if I were a frog," said Richele.

"I bet you would," answered her mother.

"Would you like it if someone came to our house, picked you up, and put you in a tiny room? You might have a bed and a chair, but no toys, no friends, no telephone, and nothing fun to do. You could never go out of the house. Someone might drop in some vegetables for you to eat."

"I like hamburgers better than vegetables," said Richele.

"Well, you'd have to eat whatever someone else chose for you. Think about it, Richele."

With a sigh, Richele looked at Francesca sitting in the jar of water. She was such a beautiful frog. It would be so nice to have her for a pet. But the pond was Francesca's home. Richele thought she probably liked to

hop around on the wet mud and catch her own flies. She could imagine her swimming deep under the lily pads, then popping up with only her eyes showing.

"Have you decided what to do?" asked her mother.

"Yes," said Richele.

What do you think Richele will do? What would you do?

Theme Connections

Emotions
Families
Frogs

How the Camel Got His Hump

Once upon a time, long, long ago, when the world was new and all the animals were just beginning to work for Man, the Camel lived alone in the middle of the Howling Desert because he was lazy and grumpy and did not want to work. When people spoke to him, he just said, "Humph!"

One Monday morning, Horse came to him all saddled and said, "Camel come out and trot like the rest of us." Camel just said, "Humph!" So, Horse went away and told Man that Camel did not want to work.

Next morning, Dog came along with a stick in his mouth and said, "Camel come out and fetch like the rest of us." But Camel just said, "Humph!" So, Dog went away and told Man that Camel did not want to work.

On Wednesday morning, Ox came along with a yoke on his neck and said, "Camel, come out and plow like the rest of us." Camel just said, "Humph!" So, Ox went away and told Man that Camel wouldn't work.

At the end of the day man called Horse, Dog, and Ox together and said, "With the world so new and all, the three of you will have to do twice as much work because Camel will not do anything; he just says, "Humph!" This made Horse, Dog, and Ox very angry.

While they were grumbling a Genie came along. They asked him if it was right for Camel to be so lazy since the world was so new and all. "Camel won't trot," said Horse. "And he won't fetch," said Dog. "And he won't plow," said Ox.

"What does Camel have to say about this?" asked Genie.

They replied, "He just says 'humph'."

So, Genie went into the Howling Desert to find Camel. When he found Camel he said,

"With the world so new and all, why haven't you been doing any work?" Camel just said, "Humph!"

"You have caused the other animals to work extra because you are so lazy. I want you to work too." Camel just said, "Humph!"

"I wouldn't say that again if I were you. You might say it once too often." But once again, Camel just said, "Humph!"

As soon as he said it, he saw his back, that he was so proud of, began to puff up into a great big hump!

"Do you see that?" said the Genie? "That's your very own hump you have brought upon yourself because you would not work. "Now come out of this Howling Desert and get to work with the other animals."

"But how can I, with this hump on my back?" moaned Camel.

"Since you have not worked for three days you will have to work three days in a row without stopping. That hump you've got will store enough food and water to last. Now behave yourself and work like the rest of the animals," said the Genie.

So, Camel went off the next morning, hump and all, and joined Horse, Dog, and Ox as they helped man with his work. And even to this day Camel still has his hump. He is still three days behind in his work, is still lazy and grumpy, and he still says, "Humph!"

Theme Connections

Camel	Oxen
Dogs	Sounds of Language
Horses	Work

The Complete Book of Activities, Games, Stories, Props, Recipes, and Dances

I Like School

by Pam Schiller

Directions: Photocopy the story patterns on page 441-443. Use a black fine-point permanent marker to trace patterns onto a piece of interfacing. Color them with crayons and cut them out.

I like school,
I like it a lot.
It's my favorite place,
Believe it or not.
I love blowing bubbles.
I love all the toys.
I love the quiet,
And I love the noise.
I love painting with feathers
And building with blocks.
Reading good books
And dancing in socks.
My teacher loves me.
I know that it's true.
She smiles and laughs
The whole day through.
I'm a (insert the name of your school) kid,

It's plain to see,
'Cause I'm just as happy
As a kid can be.

Theme Connections

School

Jack and Ol' Mossyfoot

One day, when Jack was about 10 years old, he got bored playing in his own yard. He thought he was old enough to do a little exploring, so down the road he went. Jack was having a fine time seeing many new things in the world. But soon he got tired and went to sleep under a tree.

He slept for a long time and when he woke up, the sun was starting to set. It was getting dark as Jack walked along and the road was leading into some big woods.

To keep warm, Jack built a nice warm fire. As he was sitting enjoying the fire, all of a sudden he heard something coming: whoomity whop, whoomity whop.

Jack knew right away that it was Ol' Mossyfoot and he was plenty scared! He grabbed a chunk of wood from the fire and threw it toward the sound. It landed with a splash of sparks and off the critter ran, back into the woods. Jack was wondering if he should leave when he heard that sound coming back: whoomity whop, whoomity whop.

He grabbed another chunk of wood and waited 'til Ol' Mossyfoot got so close he could feel the heat from his scary eyes. Then he threw the chunk of wood as hard as he could. It landed right in the pile of slimy moss at the monster's feet, making a steamy, sizzling sound. Off the critter ran, back into the woods.

Jack knew he'd better leave. But before he could get going, he heard that whoomity whop, whoomity whop.

He started running as fast as he could go with that monster's gigantic squishing steps close behind. The first chance he got, Jack climbed up a tall hickory tree. The monster was so slimy that it couldn't climb up after him. It kept slipping back.

Then Jack heard an awful chomp, chomp, chomp sound. The monster was gnawing away at the hickory tree! Pretty soon the tree began to lean a little, then a little more, and a little more. Finally, there was a loud snap and the tree, with Jack in it, was heading down, down, down, right toward Ol' Mossyfoot.

Jack knew he was a goner. Just before the tree hit the ground . . . Jack woke up!

Theme Connections

Emotions
Holidays
Naptime/Sleeping
Time of Day

Jack and the Tale Without End

A long time ago there was a King who had a beautiful daughter. Now this King just loved stories. So he sent word around his kingdom that if any man could tell him a tale that would never end, he would give his beautiful daughter to that man to marry. Someday this girl would be the Queen and the lucky story-teller would be the new King. But there was a hitch! If the story-telling stopped for any reason at all, the man would have his head chopped off!

Even so, lots of young men went on and tried to tell the King a tale without end. But before long each one got tired out, tongue-tied and nervous, or couldn't think of how to go on. So, lots of young men had their heads chopped off!

Well, there was a boy named Jack that lived way up in the hills of that kingdom. He loved to tell tall tales hour after hour. The reason was, if he kept on telling stories he could avoid doing chores. Finally the news of the story-telling contest got to Jack.

He thought, "Shoot, ain't nuthin' t'thet. Reckon I'll jist head on down the holler n'tell the King a tale without end. I got jist the one." So, off he went to find the palace. When he told the man at the door what he had come for, the man just shook his head and looked sad. But he let Jack in, and after the King got comfortable in his favorite chair, here is what Jack told him.

"Once there was this king who fetched up all the wheat that the farmin' folk in his

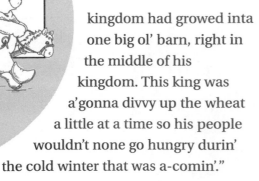

LISTENING STORIES

kingdom had growed inta one big ol' barn, right in the middle of his kingdom. This king was a'gonna divvy up the wheat a little at a time so his people wouldn't none go hungry durin' the cold winter that was a-comin'."

"When this barn was jist 'bout overflowin' with wheat, a lit'le ol' mouse gnawed hisself a lit'le ol' hole in a corner of thet great big barn. The barn was so big and thet mouse was so lit'le, why din't nobody see'm. Well, he squozed on in and got hisself one grain a'wheat, turned 'round and took it back t'his family in the field."

"Next day the mouse—- went back t'the barn, squozed on in, got hisself one more grain a-wheat, turned 'round, and took it back t'his family in the field."

"Next day the mouse—- went back t'the barn, squozed on in, got hisself one more grain a-wheat, turned 'round, and took it back t'his family in the field."

"Next day the mouse—- went back t'the barn, squozed on in, got. . .'"

Jack kept telling about the mouse all day long and past supper too. Finally, the King couldn't stand it any more.

"Stop!" he commanded in a loud voice. "Is that all you are going to tell, the same thing over and over?"

"Shore am, 'cause that's all the mouse done; took one grain a'wheat after t'other back t'his fam'ly in the field. Now kin I carry on?"

"No, no, stop!" said the King. "I've heard enough. I can't stand any more. You can marry my beautiful daughter."

So Jack married the King's beautiful daughter and one day she did become the new Queen. Then, Jack didn't have to tell stories to keep from working, ever again. And as far as we know, the mouse never did finish carrying out the wheat.

Theme Connections

Food
Humor
Kings and Queens
Mice
Tricksters
Work

Johnny Appleseed

Johnny Appleseed lived a long time ago—almost 150 years ago. Even though he lived a long time ago, the fruits of his work—the apple tree—are still with us today. He is famous for planting apple trees all over the country.

Johnny Appleseed's real name is John Chapman. People just call him Johnny

Appleseed because of how much he loved apple trees.

Johnny was a simple man who spent most of his time alone and out under the stars and trees he loved so much. He was a friend to everyone he met and to every creature he encountered. People say that the animals would walk right up to Johnny. They weren't afraid of him at all.

Here are some fun things to know about Johnny Appleseed.

He went barefoot most of the time even when the weather was cold. Shoes were hard to come by back in the days when Johnny was alive and as much as he walked, he would have surely worn out many a pair of shoes.

Johnny wore a cooking pot on his head instead of a hat. Can you imagine that? The truth is he probably tied it to his back for most of his journey.

He was a small man and people often show pictures of him in clothing that looks like it is two sizes too big.

Johnny Appleseed preferred to walk instead of ride. He walked along planting apple seeds everywhere he went. Some people say we would not have the abundance of apples we have today if it hadn't been for the work he did one hundred and fifty years ago.

Johnny loved all people but the people he loved best were children. He would tell them stories and read to them by firelight at night after dinner. People say he was a little sad that he had no children of his own.

Next time you take a bite of an apple you might want to say a quiet thank you to Johnny Appleseed.

Theme Connections

Apples
Emotions
Food
Growing Things

The Kid and the Wolf
(Aesop)

A kid (baby goat), returning without protection from the pasture, was pursued by a wolf. Seeing he could not escape, he turned around and said: "I know, friend wolf, that I must be your prey, but before I die I would ask of you one favor. Will you play me a tune to which I may dance?" The wolf took out his flute and played a dance tune. While he was piping and the kid was dancing, some hounds heard the sound and began chasing the wolf. Turning to the kid, the wolf said, "This is just what I deserve; for I should not have turned piper to please you."

Moral: In time of dire need, clever thinking is key to outwit your enemy to save your skin.

Theme Connections

Food   Tricksters
Goats   Wolves
Music

Little Buckaroo

by Pam Schiller

Mama says that I'm her "little buckaroo." I love to watch western movies and to read western books. I love to dress in western clothes. I always wear my boots. I wish I could sleep in them.

My teacher asked us to write a story about what we want to be when we grow up. This is what my story says:

"I will be a rodeo rider. I will ride bucking bulls. I will be the best bull rider in all of Texas. I will be a great roper. I will be able to rope a steer a hundred feet away. I will wave my big, black hat when the crowd begins to cheer. I will have some fancy boots with silver spurs and a special saddle for my horse. My horse's name will be Dusty. Do you know why? He will always be covered in rodeo dust, just like me! When I grow up, I will be famous. I will never get married. My wife would be too lonely, because I would be riding bulls everywhere, everyday, all of the time. The end!"

Theme Connections

Bulls
Cowboys/Cowgirls
Families
Horses

The Lion and the Mouse
(Aesop)

A lion awakened from sleep by a mouse running over his face. Rising up angrily, he caught the mouse by his tail and was about to kill him, when the mouse very pitifully said, "If you would only spare my life, I would surely repay your kindness someday."

The lion roared with laughter. "How could a small little creature like you ever repay a mighty lion?" The lion roared another laugh and let the mouse go. He settled back down to finish his nap. "Thank you, mighty lion. You won't be sorry," said the mouse. It happened shortly thereafter that hunters trapped the mighty lion. The hunters caught him in a net made of ropes. The lion roared in anguish. The little mouse was not far away. He recognized the lion's roar and he came quickly and gnawed the ropes away to free the lion. The lion was very grateful and quite surprised to see the mouse, and even more surprised that such a small creature was able to save his life. The mouse said, "You ridiculed the idea that I might ever be able to repay you for your help. I hope you know now that it is possible for even a small mouse to help a mighty lion." The lion and the mouse were friends from that moment on.

Theme Connections

Friends
Lions
Mice
Opposites

Spanish Translation

El León y el Ratón Agradecido

En medio de una gran selva dormía plácidamente un emorme león. De pronto un pequeño ratón que por alli jugaba se resbala de lo alto de un árbol y cae sobre el enorme león. Este se despierta malhumorado y atrapa al pequeño ratón. A punto de comérselo está cuando el ratón le dice, que por piedad no se lo coma y le suplica que lo deje en libertad y que algún día el favor le retornará. El enorme león al ver al pobre ratón implorándo compasión se rié y decide dejarlo en libertad. Sucedió que tiempo después el enorme león fué desesperado. El ratón que oyó sus lamentos, acudió al sitio donde estaba fuertemente amarrado el fuerte león y royó la enorme cuerda y liberó al enorme león.

Antes te reías de mí le dijo el noble ratón, porque no esperabas por mi parte te fuera algún día a salvar tu vida. Ahora has aprendido que entre los ratones también existe gratitud.

The Magic Pot

There was once a little girl who lived with her mother at the edge of the forest. They were so poor that they had nothing to eat. One day, the little girl was so hungry that she went into the forest to look for food. There she met an old woman. The old woman liked the kind little girl and she didn't want her to be hungry. The old woman gave the little girl a pot.

"Whenever you want porridge, say 'Cook, little pot, cook,' and the pot will cook good sweet porridge," the old woman told the girl. "When you want the pot to stop cooking you must say 'Stop, little pot, stop' and the pot will stop."

The child took the pot home to her mother, and they were no longer hungry. They ate good sweet porridge whenever they wished.

One day the little girl went out to play in the forest. Her mother was hungry so she said, "Cook, little pot, cook" and the pot began to cook. When the little girl's mother was full she wanted to stop the pot from cooking, but guess what? She forgot the words to use. The pot kept on cooking and cooking and the porridge bubbled over the sides of the pot. It cooked until the kitchen was full of porridge, and the whole house was full of porridge. It cooked until the yard and then the town close by was covered in porridge.

Finally, the little girl came home. She could barely find her house with the porridge covering everything. She said the magic words. Do you remember what they are? "Stop, little pot, stop." At last the pot stopped. It took a very long time for the little girl and her mother and the people in the nearby town to eat all that porridge.

Theme Connections

Cooking
Food
Families
Humor

Mercury and the Woodsman
(Aesop)

A woodsman was cutting down a tree on the bank of a river, when his axe flew out of his hands and fell into the water. As he stood by the water's edge lamenting his loss, Mercury appeared and asked him why he was so sad. When Mercury heard the story, he dove into the river and brought up a golden axe. "Is this the one you lost?" asked Mercury?

The Woodman replied that it was not, and Mercury then dove a second time and, brought up a silver axe. "Is this the one that you lost?" asked Mercury.

"No, that is not mine either," said the woodsman.

Once more Mercury dove into the river, and this time brought up the missing axe. The woodsman was very happy to have his axe, and he thanked Mercury warmly. Mercury was so pleased with the woodsman's honesty that he made him a present of the other two axes.

When the woodsman told the story to his friends, one of them was envious of the woodsman's good fortune. He decided to try his luck. He went to the river and began to chop down a tree at the edge of the river. He let his axe drop into the water. Mercury appeared as before, and, on learning that the man's axe had fallen in the water, he dove in and brought up a golden axe, as he had done for the woodman.

Without waiting to be asked whether it was his or not, the fellow cried, "That's mine, that's mine," and stretched out his hand eagerly for the golden axe.

Mercury was so disgusted at the man's dishonesty that he not only did not give him the golden axe, but also refused to recover the one that had fallen into the stream.

Moral

Honesty is the best policy!

Theme Connections

Emotions
Work

My Father Picks Oranges

by Pam Schiller

Every day my father wakes very early. He dresses, eats his breakfast, kisses me good-bye while I am still tucked snugly in my bed, and walks out to the road to wait for the big truck to come and pick him up. The truck takes him to the orange grove where he will pick oranges all day. He puts on his gloves, gathers a basket and a short ladder, and off he goes to the field of oranges.

My father picks each orange carefully. He examines it to be sure it is ripe enough and to be sure that no bugs have found the orange first. Then my father places the oranges carefully in a basket. The hot sun makes sweat tickle down my father's back, but still he carefully picks the oranges. His legs grow weary from standing on the ladder, but still he carefully picks the oranges.

At lunchtime, my father sits in the shade of a large tree and eats his lunch that my mother made for him. He laughs and jokes with the other orange pickers for a while and then he returns to the grove to pick more oranges. At the end of the day the man who owns the orange grove will count the baskets my father has picked and he will say, "Very good, Miguel." My father will smile because he is happy to know that his oranges will soon go to the big store where people will buy them and take them home to their families.

When my father comes home I jump in his arms. He smells of the sweet juice of the orange. He takes a gift from his pocket and hands it to me. It is an orange from the orange grove. My father says it is the juiciest orange he saw all day. When I eat the orange I think of my father. I am happy to know that my father helps bring delicious oranges to people all over the country.

Theme Connections

Emotions
Families
Food
Work

My Grandmother's Garden

by Pam Schiller

Directions: Have the children say, "Ah-h-h!" each time they hear the word "roses" spoken in the story.

My grandmother's garden is one of the most beautiful places I know. She has every kind of flower you can think of: chrysanthemums, violets, lilies, daisies, sunflowers, tulips, daffodils, morning glories, petunias, and pansies. And that's naming only some of them. If I named them all, we would be here all day. I must tell you about one more flower, though, because it is my grandmother's favorite. It is her roses. *(ah-h-h!)* When she bends down to smell her roses she always says, "Ah-h-h." *(ah-h-h!)*

My grandmother lets me help take care of the flowers in her garden. We water them. We pull the weeds. We trim back the flowers that have grown too big. We fertilize some of the flowers to make them grow bigger, and we dust them with bug powder to keep the bugs away. We always trim back her roses, *(ah-h-h!)* dust them for bugs, and of course, we always take a minute to enjoy their beauty. My grandmother says there are no flowers that smell as good as her roses. *(ah-h-h!)*

Sometimes I just sit in my grandmother's garden and watch all the birds, bees, and butterflies that live there. My grandmother loves the animals, too. She says that insects, like ladybugs, bees, and butterflies, are good for her flowers. Ladybugs eat the aphids that destroy the leaves on the flowers. The bees and the butterflies help pollinate the flowers so new flowers will grow. One time I caught a ladybug. It was on my grandmother's favorite flowers, the roses. *(ah-h-h!)* My grandmother let me keep the ladybug all day. But at the end of the day, my grandmother said I had to let the ladybug go back to nature so it could do its job. I put it back on the roses. *(ah-h-h!)*

When company is coming to dinner, we always pick some flowers from the garden to put on the table. We cut yellow flowers, purple flowers, orange flowers, and we always cut red roses. *(ah-h-h!)* My grandmother says the color red makes people feel extra hungry, and the smell of the roses *(ah-h-h!)* helps people feel calm and relaxed. She wants people to enjoy her dinners.

If you ever come to Texas, you must stop by to see my grandmother's garden. You will surely say it is beautiful. If you stay for dinner, you can help me pick the flowers. You can cut the roses. *(ah-h-h!)* And when you leave to go back home, my grandmother will give you a few of her roses. *(ah-h-h!)* Then you can have some roses *(ah-h-h!)* at your house, too.

Theme Connections

Colors
Emotions
Families
Growing Things
Insects
Seasons

One More Child

Once upon a time there was a very rich woman. She had beautiful clothes and a big house. She had no children, so she was very sad.

She asked a friend, "How can I get a child?"

Her friend told her, "Go to your poor neighbor. She has twelve children. She and her husband do not have enough money to feed all their children. Maybe she will give you one of her children. You are rich. You can feed the children much better than she can."

The rich woman asked her friend, "Do you think she will give away a child?"

Her friend answered, "Why not? Give her a bag of gold. I know she will give you a child."

The next day the rich woman took a bag of gold to the poor woman's little house. The poor woman was surprised to see her. She said, "Come in and sit down."

The children came to their mother and cried, "Please give us food. We are hungry."

The mother brought rice soup for the children. The poor family had no bowls. She put the soup in twelve holes in the floor. The children ate. Then the hungry mother ate the rice water they left in the holes.

The mother looked up and said, "Oh, God! Please give me one more child. Then I will have one more hole of rice water to eat from."

The rich woman watched quietly. She was surprised to hear the poor woman wish for one more child. She thought, "This woman will never give away any of her children."

She put the bag of gold in the poor woman's hand and left the little house. She was sad because she had no child. Now she understood a mother's love for her children.

Theme Connections

Families
Food
Money

The Owl and the Pussy-Cat

by Edward Lear

The Owl and the Pussy-Cat went to sea
In a beautiful pea-green boat.
They took some honey, and plenty of
*   money,*
Wrapped in a five-pound note.

The Owl looked up to the stars above,
And sang to a small guitar,
"O lovely Pussy! O Pussy, my love,
What a beautiful Pussy you are,
You Are!
What a beautiful Pussy you are."

Pussy said to the Owl, "You elegant fowl!
How charmingly sweet you sing!
O let us be married! Too long we have
*   tarried:*
But what shall we do for a ring?"

They sailed away for a year and a day,
To the land where the Bong-tree grows,
And there in a wood a Piggy-wig stood,
With a ring in the end of his nose.

His nose,
With a ring in the end of
his nose.

"Dear Pig, are you willing to
sell for one shilling
Your ring?" Said the Piggy, "I will."
So they took it away, and were married
next day
By the Turkey who lives on the hill.

They dined on mince, and slices of quince,
Which they ate with a runcible spoon;
And hand in hand, on the edge of
the sand,
They danced by the light of the moon.

Theme Connections

Birds
Cats
Emotions
Food
Oceans and Seas
Pigs
Sun, Moon, Stars

Pam and Sam

by Pam Schiller

Pam and Sam are best friends. They are so much alike. Pam and Sam both love to be outdoors. Pam and Sam both like peanut butter and jelly sandwiches better than any other food. They both love to swim and love to dance. They love to watch movies, and they love to blow bubbles. They hate rainy days. They love puppy dogs, ice cream, sunshine, baseball, trips to Mexico, bicycle

riding, and nature hikes. There is even something about their names that is the same. Do you know what it is?

As much as Sam and Pam are alike, they are also very different. In many ways they are opposites. Sam is tall, but Pam is short. Sam has short hair, but Pam's hair is long. Sam has brown eyes, but Pam's eyes are blue. Sam hates to work puzzles, but Pam enjoys working puzzles. Sam likes to ride his bike fast, but Pam prefers to ride slowly. Sam likes the weather when it is hot, but Pam likes the weather better when it is cold.

Now it is easy to see that, as much as Pam and Sam are alike, they are still very different. There is something else different about Pam and Sam. Do you know what it is? *(If necessary, give the children hints to help them determine that Sam is a boy and Pam is a girl.)*

Theme Connections

Friends

The Quangle Wangle's Hat

by Edward Lear

On the top of the Crumpetty Tree
The Quangle sat,
But his face you could not see,
On account of his Beaver Hat,
For his Hat was a hundred and two feet
wide,
With ribbons and bibbons on every side,
And bells and buttons and loops and lace,

So nobody ever could see the face
Of the Quangle Wangle Quee.

The Quangle Wangle said
To himself on the Crumpetty Tree,
"Jam and jelly and bread
Are the best food for me!
But the longer I live on this Crumpetty
    Tree,
The plainer than ever it seems to me
That very few people come this way,
And that life on the whole is far from gay!"

But there came to the Crumpetty Tree,
Mr. and Mrs. Canary;
And they said, "Did ever you see
Any spot so charmingly airy?
May we build a nest on your lovely Hat?
Mr. Quangle Wangle, grant us that!
O please let us come and build a nest
Of whatever material suits you best,
Mr. Quangle Wangle Quee!"

And beside, to the Crumpetty Tree
Came the Stork and the Duck and the Owl:
The snail and the Bumble-Bee,
The Frog and the Fimble Fowl;
(The Fimble Fowl, with a Corkscrew leg);
And all of them said, "We humbly beg,
May we build our home on your lovely Hat
Mr. Quangle Wangle, grant us that!
Mr. Quangle Wangle Quee!"

And the Golden Grouse came there,
And the Pobble who has no toes,
And the small Olympian bear,
And the Dong with the luminous nose.
And the Blue Baboon, who played the flute,
And the Orient Calf from the Land of Tute,
And the Attery Squash, and the Bisky Bat,

All came and built on the lovely Hat
Of the Quangle Wangle Quee.

And the Quangle Wangle said
To himself on the Crumpetty Tree,
"When all these creatures move
What a wonderful noise there'll be!"
And at night by the light of the Mulberry
    moon
They danced to the Flute of the Blue
    Baboon,
On the broad green leaves of the
    Crumpetty Tree,
And all were as happy as happy could be
With the Quangle Wangle Quee.

Theme Connections

Birds
Ducks
Houses and Homes
Humor
Insects

Quilla Bung

One day, a man and his wife had nothing to eat for dinner. The man took his gun and went out to shoot something for dinner. As he was going along, he heard a song.

Quilla, quilla, bung, bung, bung
(Tune: London Bridge)
Quilla, quilla, bung, bung, bung
Bung, bung, bung
Bung, bung, bung
Quilla, quilla, bung, bung, bung
Bung, bung, quilla

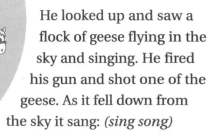

He looked up and saw a flock of geese flying in the sky and singing. He fired his gun and shot one of the geese. As it fell down from the sky it sang: *(sing song)*

He took the goose home for his wife to cook. She laid it down, and began to pluck it. But every feather that she plucked flew out of her hand and floated out the window. And all the time, the goose kept singing. *(sing song)*

She finished at last and put the goose in the oven to cook. But all the time it was cooking, she could hear it singing from inside the oven. *(sing song)*

The man and wife sat down to dinner. She put the goose on the table between them. The man picked up the carving knife to carve it, but all the time it kept singing. *(sing song)*

As he held up the carving fork ready to stick into the goose, there came a tremendous noise. In through the window flew the whole flock of geese and they were all singing as loud as could be. *(sing song)* Each goose took out a feather and stuck it into the goose and then all together, they lifted that goose right out of the dish. Up it flew and followed them round and round and out the window.

The man and his wife sat there with empty plates and open mouths. All they got for dinner that night was a song. *(sing song)*.

Theme Connections

Animals
Food
Geese
Humor
Music

Rabbit: A Mayan Legend

At the beginning of creation, Rabbit had great antlers. Deer, though, had none. He was so jealous and so very offended that he planned to get his own magnificent antlers. Deer told Rabbit how wonderfully majestic he looked and asked Rabbit if he might borrow Rabbit's antlers just to try them on and see how they looked. Flattered, Rabbit agreed as long as it would be for just for a moment. Rabbit placed them on top of Deer's head and Deer immediately pranced and jumped, walking around asking how they looked on him. He walked further away until he was out of sight. Rabbit grew worried, finally realizing that Deer was not going to return his antlers. Rabbit angrily complained to Shaper and Creator, asking for another pair of antlers. Shaper and Creator told him that what had been done by

Rabbit's own hands could not be undone. Rabbit must live without his antlers. Rabbit then asked to be made larger to show his importance to the other animals. Shaper and Creator refused, but Rabbit begged and whined so much, that Shaper and Creator leaned over, grabbed Rabbit's ears and pulled, stretching them out long. That is how Rabbit shows his importance to this day, with his long ears.

Theme Connections

Deer
Emotions
Rabbits
Tricksters

Three Little Kittens

Three little kittens lost their mittens;
And they began to cry,

"Oh, mother dear, we very much fear
Our mittens we have lost."
"What! Lost your mittens, you naughty
*   kittens!*
Then you shall have no pie."
"Mee-ow, mee-ow, mee-ow, mee-ow."
"No, you shall have no pie."

The three little kittens they found their
*   mittens;*
And they began to cry,
"Oh, Mother dear, see here, see here!
Our mittens we have found."
"What! found your mittens! You good
*   little kittens,*
Now you shall have some pie."
"Purr, purr, purr, purr,
Purr, purr, purr."

Theme Connections

Cats
Emotions
Food
Sounds of Language

The Tortoise and the Hare
(Greece)

One day a hare was making fun of a tortoise. "You are a slowpoke," he said. "You couldn't run if you tried."

"Don't laugh at me," said the tortoise. "I bet that I could beat you in a race."

"Couldn't," replied the hare.

"Could," replied the tortoise.

"All right," said the hare. "I'll race you. But I'll win, even with my eyes shut."

They asked a passing fox to set them off.

"Ready, set, go!" said the fox.

The hare went off at a great pace. He got so far ahead, he decided he might as well stop for a rest. Soon he fell fast asleep.

The tortoise came plodding along, never stopping for a moment.

When the hare woke up, he ran as fast as he could to the finish line. But he was too late—the tortoise had already won the race!

Theme Connections

Animals
Opposites

Uncle Rabbit and Uncle Coyote

It had been a long time since Uncle Coyote had seen Uncle Rabbit. The last time they met, Uncle Rabbit had promised Uncle Coyote that he would bring his nieces over for Uncle Coyote to make into a delicious rabbit stew. But this never happened.

Ever since then, Uncle Coyote had wanted to catch Uncle Rabbit by surprise and force him to keep his promise.

One day, Uncle Coyote saw Uncle Rabbit leaning against a big rock enjoying the canyons that separated the forest from the dense jungle. Uncle Coyote snuck up on him and said, "This time you won't escape, Uncle Rabbit."

"Why do you say that?" asked Uncle Rabbit.

"Because the last time I saw you, you promised to bring me your nieces to make into a nice rabbit stew."

"But I did bring them," said Uncle Rabbit, "I left you to go get them, but when I returned with them, you were gone. I can bring them here right now if you like, but you will have to help me first."

"Help you in what way?" asked Uncle Coyote.

Uncle Rabbit replied, "I have been here for several days holding this rock. If I drop it, the world will come to an end. In addition, as you can see, I have not been able to eat, so I am becoming weaker and weaker."

"Go ahead," said Uncle Coyote. "Get something to eat, and then bring your nieces to me. I will wait here holding the big rock for you."

"Thank you very much," responded Uncle Rabbit. "Now, come stand right beside me, Uncle Coyote, and lean against this big rock. Little by little, I will inch away, and you can take my place holding the rock exactly the way I am holding it now." Uncle Coyote did just as Uncle Rabbit suggested. "I feel like I have the rock now," said Uncle Coyote. "Very good," said Uncle Rabbit, "I will be back." Hours passed, then days went by until finally Uncle Coyote could not hold up his arms any longer, and he let them go. To his surprise, nothing happened; the world did not fall down. He thought to himself, "One more time I have been fooled by this clever rabbit, but the next time he won't trick me."

Theme Connections

Coyotes
Food
Humor
Rabbits
Tricksters

Spanish Translation

Tío Conejo y Tío Coyote

Hacía mucho tiempo que tío coyote no veía a tío conejo. La última vez que se vieron, tío conejo había prometido a tió coyote que iría a traer a sus sobrinos para que él se los comiera en estofado. Pero esto nunca pasó. Esta vez, tío coyote había sorprendido a tío conejo quien estaba de pié cerca de una gran peña contemplando el gran barranco que separaba el bosque de la gran selva. -Esta vez no te me va a escapar le había dicho a tío conejo. -¿Porque dice así? le dijo tío conejo.

-Porque la última vez que te ví me dijiste que me traerías a tus sobrinos para que me los comiera en estofado.

Por supuesto que los traje dijo tío conejo. Pero cuando regresamos ya usted se había marchado. Si quiere los voy a traer ahorita, pero tendrá que ayudarme primero, continuó tío conejo. Ayudarle en que forma replico tío coyote, Como puede ver, estoy deteniendo esta gran peña porque si no lo hago se acabará el mundo le dijo muy preocupado. Como dice, le preguntó de nuevo tío coyote, le digo que llevo ya varios días aquí deteniendo esta gran peña porque si no lo hago se caerá el mundo. Además no he comido y ya mis fuerzas se están terminando. Vaya pues a traer a sus sobrinos y a comer algo le respondió tío coyote, yo me quedaré deteniendo la peña. Muchas gracias respondió tío conejo. Ahora venga al lado mío y poco a poco trate de detenerla exactamente como lo hago yo. Tío coyote poco a poco fue tomando el lugar de tío conejo hasta que le dijo, ya siento que tengo bien sujetada la peña. Muy bién dijo tío conejo. Ya regreso. Pasaron horas y días hasta que finalmente tío coyote cansado ya no pudo más y soltó sus brazos cual va siendo su sorpresa ¡que la gran peña siguió igual! Otra vez me ha engañado ese conejo bandido, pero la próxima vez no va a jugar conmigo.

The Wind and the Sun

The Wind and the Sun were arguing which one of them was stronger. Suddenly they saw a traveler coming down the road, and the Sun said, "I see a way to decide our dispute. Whichever of us can cause that traveler to take off his coat shall be regarded as the stronger one. You begin." So the Sun retired behind a cloud, and the Wind began to blow as hard as it could upon the traveler. But the harder he blew the more closely the traveler wrapped his coat around him. At last the Wind had to give up in despair. Then the Sun

came out and shone in all his glory upon the traveler, who soon found it too hot to walk with his coat on.

Theme Connections

Opposites
Sun, Moon, Stars
Weather

Spanish Translation

El Viento y El Sol

El viento y el sol discutían sobre cuál de los dos era más fuerte.

-Sin duda soy mucho más fuerte -afirmaba el viento-. Puedo tumbar un árbol, puedo derribar una casa, puedo...

-Puedes ser muy presumido, querido amigo -añadió el sol-. Si de verdad eres tan poderoso, demuéstralo en esta prueba. ¿Ves a aquel hombre que avanza por el camino? Quien consiga que vaya sin abrigo sera el vencedor.

-Me parece bien -contestó el viento-. Yo empezaré. El sol se ocultó entonces tras una nube y el viento comenzó a soplar, pero el hombre se envolvía tenazmente en su abrigo.

-Un gran trabajo, querido amigo; sospecho que ese individuo no tiene intención de perder su abrigo -dijo el sol.

-Espera un poco -contestó el viento antes de tomar aire para soplar contodas sus fuerzas. El viento sopló y sopló, pero el hombre se sujetaba el abrigo con tanto empeño que fue imposible arrebatárselo.

-Me rindo, este tipo es demasiado duro -dijo el viento-. Ahora enviable tus mejores rayos. El sol se asomó por detrás de la nube y brilló con todo su poder. El caminante sintió el calor y enseguida se quitó el abrigo. La delicadeza es más poderosa que la fuerza.

Prop Stories

Egbert the Egg

Directions: Decorate a large plastic egg like a puppet. Glue on yarn hair and wiggle eyes. Cut a mouth from felt and use ribbons for legs and arms.

Make up a story about Egbert's first day of school. Gather a few props for your story such as a favorite book, a favorite-colored crayon, a few blocks, a drawing, and so forth. Tell your own version of Egbert's favorite parts of his school day.

Theme Connections

Growing Up

Ellie's Party

by Pam Schiller

Directions: Make photocopies of the patterns on pages 537-541. Make 2 or 3 copies of each animal. Make one copy of Arnie and one copy of the keys (use real keys if you have them). Color the patterns, cut them out, and glue them to 6" x 8" strips of poster board. Attach yarn to the poster board to create necklaces.

Select children to play the roles of the animals and the zookeeper. Have them act out the story as you narrate.

Lots and lots of animals live at the zoo. Animals of all kinds—elephants, gorillas, snakes, turtles, lions, bears, and ostriches, too! They all live at the zoo but in separate houses. Each morning the animals all say good morning to each other—the lions roar a mighty roar, the gorillas proudly pound their chest, the elephants trumpet a loud tune, the snakes quietly hiss, the ostriches let out a jolly laugh, the bears growl, and the shy little turtles poke their tiny head in and out of their shells.

The animals all wish they could get together and really enjoy each other's company. They want to get out of their houses and visit.

One day Ellie Elephant has an idea. She decides that when Arnie the zookeeper comes to her cage to feed her she will borrow his keys. After all, she is the last one to get fed so Arnie probably wouldn't miss his keys until the next morning. That night when Arnie is leaving her cage she reaches her trunk into his pocket and takes the keys.

After all the children and other visitors went home and the zoo was silent, Ellie Elephant

used Arnie's keys to let herself and all the other animals out of their cages. She opened the door for the snakes. They hissed with delight. She opened the door for the gorillas. They pounded their chests with joy.

When Ellie Elephant opened the door for the lions, they roared with happiness. Lisa Lion said, "Give me the keys. I will let the others out. You go get things ready for a party."

So Ellie gave the keys to Lisa and she opened the door for the ostriches. They laughed a jolly laugh. Lisa opened the door for the turtles. The turtles stuck their heads in and out of their shells in excitement. Last but not least, Lisa opened the door for the bears. The bears danced and growled with the pleasure of freedom.

At last all animals were free and ready to party. They all marched to Ellie's house. What a feast they had! They all ate, laughed, danced, and had a great time! They ate and danced so much that they got v-e-r-y tired. In fact, they got so tired that they all fell sound asleep in Ellie's house. There were all the animals, asleep in a heap on the ground with great big smiles on their faces.

The next morning when Arnie arrived at the zoo, all the animal homes were empty except for one—Ellie Elephant's house. He was surprised to find all the animals there, asleep in a big pile! Arnie woke up the animals. Now he had to figure out how he would get all the animals back to their own houses. The zoo would be opening any minute, and visitors would begin arriving! How could he make sure that he got all the animals back into the right houses? How would he group the animals? Suddenly Arnie had an idea!

What do you think he did? How would you group the animals?

Theme Connections

Bears
Elephants
Gorillas
Lions
Movement
Occupations
Ostriches
Snakes
Sounds of Language

Ginny's Things

Directions: Decorate a box or use a small jewelry box and place the items mentioned in the story in the box. You can braid yarn for hair if none is available. Take the items out of the box as they are mentioned in the story. If there are items you don't have access to, simply change the item in the story to something more readily available.

Ginny has a treasure chest, in which she keeps her things,

All the things that she likes best from photographs to rings.

A picture of her nana, two rocks, a golden frame,

A letter she wrote to Santa and forgot to sign her name.

A picture she drew for mother, marbles— yellow, green, and blue,

A feather from her brother, and two pennies, shiny new.

She has a braid of her own hair, a wrapper from a candy bar,

A ribbon from the county fair, a heart, a tooth, a tiny star.

All these things go together, all the things that Ginny likes best.

She keeps all these special things—inside her treasure chest.

Theme Connections

Emotions
Growing Up

The Little Red Hen

Directions: Photocopy the character masks on pages 542-545. Color and decorate the mask with the children. Invite the children to dramatize the story. You will need to narrate.

Once upon a time there was a Little Red Hen who shared her tiny cottage with a goose, a cat, and a dog. The goose was a gossip. She chatted with the neighbors all day long. The cat was vain. She brushed her fur, straightened her whiskers, and polished her claws all day long. The dog was sleepy. He napped on the front porch all day long. The Little Red Hen did all the work. She cooked, she cleaned, and she took out the trash. She mowed, she raked, and she did all the shopping.

One day on her way to market, the Little Red Hen found a few grains of wheat. She put them in her pocket. When she got home she asked her friends, "Who will plant these grains of wheat?"

"Not I," said the goose.
"Not I," said the cat.
"Not I," said the dog.
"Then I will plant it myself," said the Little Red Hen. And she did.

All summer long she cared for the wheat. She made sure that it got enough water,

and she hoed the weeds out carefully between each row. And when the wheat was finally ready to harvest, the Little Red Hen asked her friends,

"Who will help me thresh this wheat?"

"Not I," said the goose.
"Not I," said the cat.
"Not I," said the dog.
"Then I will cut and thresh it myself," said the Little Red Hen. And she did.

When the wheat had been cut and threshed, the Little Red Hen scooped the wheat into a wheelbarrow and said, "This wheat must be ground into flour. Who will help me take it to the mill?"

"Not I," said the goose.
"Not I," said the cat.
"Not I," said the dog.
"Then I will do it myself," said the Little Red Hen. And she did.

The miller ground the wheat into flour and put it into a bag for the Little Red Hen. Then all by herself, she pushed the bag home in the wheelbarrow.

One cool morning a few weeks later the Little Red Hen got up early and said, "Today is a perfect day to bake some bread. Who will help me bake it?"

"Not I," said the goose.
"Not I," said the cat.
"Not I," said the dog.
"Then I will bake the bread myself," said the Little Red Hen. And she did.

She mixed the flour with milk and eggs and butter and salt. She kneaded the dough. She shaped the dough into a nice plump loaf. Then she put the loaf in the oven and watched it as it baked.

The smell of the bread soon filled the air. The goose stopped chatting. The cat stopped brushing and the dog woke up. One by one, they came into the kitchen. When the Little Red Hen took the bread from the oven she said, "Who will help me eat this bread?"

"I will," said the goose.
"I will," said the cat
"I will," said the dog

"You will?" said the Little Red Hen. "Who planted the wheat and took care of it? Who cut the wheat and threshed it? Who took the wheat to the mill? Who baked the bread? I did it all by myself. Now I am going to eat it all by myself." And she did.

Theme Connections

Emotions   Friends
Food   Work

Magazine Picture Stories

Cut 5 or 6 pictures from a magazine. Encourage the children to use the pictures to make up a story.

Theme Connections
Use with any theme

Perky Pumpkin's Open House

Directions: You will need a piece of 12" x 18" orange construction paper and a pair of scissors. Follow the cutting directions in the story.

Once upon a time there was a little man named Perky. Perky liked pumpkins so much he even looked like a pumpkin. He was jolly and round. People called him Perky Pumpkin.

Perky's best friend was a cat named Kate. Everywhere that Perky went, Kate went too. They played together, they slept together, they went to school together—they did everything together.

Perky didn't live in a house. He lived in a field among the pumpkin vines. He had been thinking a lot about how nice it would be to have a nice, warm, snug house that he could call his very own. He mentioned it to Kate and they decided to find a house together.

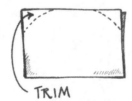

One crisp, fall morning they set out. In front of a school, they found a large piece of orange paper. "My favorite color," said Perky, "It's just what we need." Kate agreed.

With Kate's help. Perky tugged and pushed and pulled until he put the paper together like this:

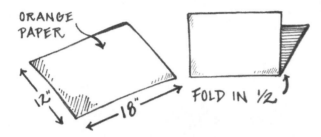

ORANGE PAPER

12" 18" FOLD IN ½

With a pair of scissors, Perky carefully and slowly rounded off the corners, so the paper looked like this:

TRIM

"Meow," said Kate. "Let's set it up and take a look at our work." And for a time, they just smiled in admiration.

But then Perky remembered he would need a door. He cut out a tall one, like this:

A DOOR

"I think I'll add a window, too," he said. And he did, like this:

A WINDOW

Perky was pleased with himself. But not Kate—she was curious to know where she came in. "Meow...Meow." She grumbled.

Perky laughed. He quickly added another door—a teeny, tiny one that was just the right size for a rather thin cat. "This will always be open so you can come in and out as you like," Perky said. Kate purred her thanks.

A TINY DOOR

On Halloween night, Perky and Kate invited all their Mother Goose and storybook friends to an open-house party. And when they opened the house to their friends, everyone was surprised and delighted—including Perky and Kate. For this is what they saw:

Just what Halloween needs—a nice round Jack-o-Lantern.

Theme Connections

Cats
Friends
Holidays
Houses and Homes

PROP STORIES

Rhyming Story in a Can

Place several rhyming objects or photos of objects, such as a rock, a sock, and a lock, in a can. Have the children remove the items one at a time and create a story using the items as part of their story. The teacher should facilitate this group activity.

Theme Connections

Rhymes and Rhyming

A Special Surprise

Directions: You will need chalk and a chalkboard or a pen and a flip chart, a bag of apples, and a knife.

Once there was a little old lady, named Annie, who lived in the mountains in a little house right here. *(draw the stem and the top right part of the apple)*

One day Annie decided to go down the mountain to town, so she left her house and started down the road like this. *(draw one half of the left side of an apple)*

On the way she met Abraham, and he asked, "Where are you going on such a fine day?" "I'm going down to town," replied Annie.

"What are you going to get?" asked Abraham.

"You'll just have to wait and see," said Annie.

On she walked *(draw more of the left side of the apple-illustration)* until she met Ashley and the other boys and girls. They all asked her, "Where are you going on such a fine day?"

"I'm going down to town," she replied.

"What are you going to get?" they asked.

"You'll just have to wait and see," Annie told them.

Annie finally reached town. *(continue drawing the left side of the apple; stop at the center of the bottom of the apple)* She went in the store and she came out with a big bag. *(hold up the paper bag)*

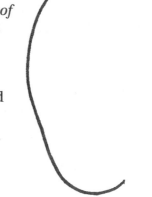

She started back up the mountain like this. *(begin drawing the right side of apple from the bottom to the midpoint-illustration)* All the boys and girls came running up to her. "What did you get? What's in your bag?" they all begged.

"I've got some stars," Annie answered.

"Walk home with me, and I'll give you each one."

So the little old lady and all the boys and girls continued up the mountain like this. *(complete the drawing of the apple)* They finally reached Annie's house.

Annie sat down and opened her bag. She pulled out an apple. *(take an apple from the bag)*

"But where are the stars?" asked the children.

Then Annie smiled and took out her knife. She cut the apple in half, and showed the children a beautiful star inside the apple. *(cut apple in half horizontally and show the children the star)* Then she cut all the apples in half and gave all the children a star of their very own.

Theme Connections

Apples
Food
Spatial Relationships

The Strange Visitor

Directions: Cut out two large shoes; two skinny, long legs; a pair of shorts; a shirt; two long, skinny arms; two large gloved hands; and a jack-o-lantern head from construction paper or art foam. Lay each piece in front of you on the floor as it enters the old woman's cottage.

A little old woman lived all alone in a little old house in the woods.
One Halloween she sat in the chimney corner, and as she sat, she spun.
Still she sat and
Still she spun and
Still she wished for company.

Then she saw her door open a little way, and in came
A pair of broad, broad feet, *(a pair of big shoes)*
And sat down by the fireside.
"That is strange," thought the little old woman, but—
Still she sat and
Still she spun and
Still she wished for company.

Then in came
A pair of long, long legs, *(a pair of long skinny legs)*
And sat down on the broad, broad feet;
"Now this is strange," thought the little old woman, but—
Still she sat and
Still she spun and
Still she wished for company.

Then in came
A wee, wee waist, *(pair of shorts)*
And sat down on the long, long legs.
"Now this is strange," thought the little old woman, but—
Still she sat and
Still she spun and
Still she wished for company.

Then in came
A pair of broad, broad shoulders, *(a shirt)*
And sat down on the wee, wee, waist.
"Now this is strange," thought the little old woman, but—
Still she sat and
Still she spun and
Still she wished for company.

Then in through the door came
A pair of long, long arms, *(a pair of long, skinny arms)*
And sat down on the broad, broad shoulders.
"Now that is strange," thought the little old woman, but—
Still she sat and
Still she spun and
Still she wished for company.

Then in came
A pair of fat, fat hands, *(a pair of large gloved hands)*
And sat down on the long, long arms.
"Now this is strange," thought the little old woman, but—
Still she sat and
Still she spun and
Still she wished for company.

Then in came
A round, round head, *(big jack-o-lantern head)*
And sat down on top of all
That sat by the fireside.

The little old woman stopped her spinning and asked,
"Where did you get such big, big feet?"
"By much tramping, by much tramping," said Somebody.
"Where did you get such long, long legs?"
"By much running, by much running," said Somebody.
"Where did you get such a wee, wee waist?"
"Nobody knows, nobody knows," said Somebody.
"Where did you get such long, long arms?"
"Swinging the scythe, swinging the scythe," said Somebody.
"Where did you get such fat, fat hands?"
"From threshing, from threshing," said Somebody.
"How did you get such a huge, huge head?"
"Of a pumpkin I made it," said Somebody.
Then said the little old woman, "What did you come for?"
"YOU!"

(If you are concerned that the end of the story might frighten young children, change it. Simply add "to keep you company, to keep you company.")

Theme Connections

Holidays
Humor
Parts of the Body

Tillie Triangle

Directions: Follow the directions in the story to draw Tillie with chalk.

Once there was a triangle called Tillie. *(draw a triangle and add stick arms and legs and a round head)*

Tillie was usually a very happy little triangle, but lately she had been feeling sad.

Tillie was unhappy with her shape. She didn't like just having three sides to her shape. She admired all the other shapes. The lovely square with four neat sides, the circle, all smooth and full.

Tillie decided to eat more food so she could grow another side. She ate and ate and ate. She ate candy, and cookies and ice cream and wonderful cream puffs. Tillie ate for three days. On the fourth day when she woke up and looked in the mirror she had another side. She was a square.

(erase triangle shaped body and draw a square)

"Oh, boy," yelled Tillie. It worked.

But now Tillie thought, if I keep on eating I will change again. So she kept right on eating all the sweet things she could find. Sure enough after just two more days Tillie woke up, looked in the mirror and saw that she had become a circle.

(erase square body and make a circle body)

Tillie was so happy... at least for a while.

None of Tillie's friends recognized her. She had to tell them who she was. And worst of all Tillie couldn't stop eating. The more she ate the bigger she got.

(erase circle body and make it bigger)

Tillie called the Doctor. He told her if she didn't stop eating she would pop. So Tillie made herself stop. She didn't eat anything.

In two days she was not so big.

(erase circle and make it smaller)

But Tillie was still lonesome for her old self.

In two more days Tillie was a square again.

(erase circle and make a square)

Tillie was happy but she still wanted to be her old self again. After two more days it finally happened. Tillie woke up to find things back to normal.

(erase square and draw triangle body)

Tillie was so happy. She said, " I will never do such a silly thing again!"

Theme Connections

Self-Esteem
Shapes

A Yarn Tale

Directions: Unravel the end of a yarn ball and hand the end to one of the children. That child begins a story and then hands the ball of yarn to the next child, who then continues the story. The second child continues the story and holds onto the yarn. Then the second child passes the ball of yarn onto the third child, while still holding onto his or her piece of yarn. Continue the process until everyone has had a turn or until the story comes to a natural end.

Discuss the adage, "spinning a yarn." Help the children see the connection between this activity and the adage.

Theme Connections

Self-Esteem

Puppet Stories

The Complete Book of Activities, Games, Stories, Props, Recipes, and Dances

Five Dancing Dolphins

By Pam Schiller

Directions: Photocopy the patterns on pages 546-548. Color them, cut them out, and laminate them. Attach them to tongue depressors, and use them to help tell the story.

One dancing dolphin on a sea of blue,
She called her sister,
Then there were two.
Two dancing dolphins swimming in the sea,
They called for Mother,
Then there were three.
Three dancing dolphins swimming close
   to shore,
They called for Daddy,
Then there were four.
Four dancing dolphins in a graceful dive,
They called for baby,
Then there were five.
Five dancing dolphins on a sea of blue.

Theme Connections

Dolphins
Oceans and Seas

Five Little Chickens

Directions: Photocopy the patterns on page 549. Color them, cut them out, and laminate them. Glue a piece of Velcro on the back of each pattern. Glue the matching piece of Velcro to a clean work glove. Place the five chickens on the five fingers of the glove. Put them on the side that when bent touches the thumb. Place the items the chickens are looking for on the opposite side (nail side) of the glove, upside down. Be sure to match the chicken and the thing it is looking for on the same finger. Use Velcro to attach the mother hen to the topside of the hand of the glove.

Said the first little chicken (wiggle finger
that has the first chicken on it)
With an odd little squirm,
"I wish I could find
A fat little worm." (bend the finger down
to reveal worm)

Said the second little chicken (wiggle
finger that has the second chicken on it)
With an odd little shrug,
"I wish I could find
A fat little bug." (bend the finger down to
reveal bug)

Said the third little chicken (wiggle finger
that has the third chicken on it)
with an odd little tug,
"I wish I could find
A fat little slug." (bend finger down to
reveal slug)

Said the fourth little chicken (wiggle
finger that has the fourth chicken on it)
with an odd little nod,
"I wish I could find

A butterbean pod." (bend finger down to reveal butterbean pod)

Said the fifth little chicken (wiggle finger that has the fifth chicken on it)
with an odd little sigh,
"I wish I could find
A fat little fly." (bend finger down to fly)

Said the old mother hen (turn hand around to reveal the hen)
From the green garden-patch,
"If you want any breakfast
Just come here and scratch!"

Theme Connections

Chickens
Farms
Food

Frog Went a-Courtin'

Directions: Photocopy the patterns on pages 550-553. Color them, cut them out, and laminate them. Attach them to tongue depressors, and use them to help tell the story.

Frog went a-courtin' and he did ride.
Uh-huh, uh-huh.
Frog went a-courtin' and he did ride
With a sword and scabbard by his side.
Uh-huh, uh-huh.

He rode up to Miss Mousie's den.
Uh-huh, uh-huh.
He rode up to Miss Mousie's den,
Said "Please, Miss Mousie, won't you let me in?"
Uh-huh, uh-huh.

"First, I must ask my Uncle Rat.
Uh-huh, uh-huh.
"First I must ask my Uncle Rat
And see what he will say to that."
Uh-huh, uh-huh.

"Miss Mousie, won't you marry me?"
Uh-huh, uh-huh.
"Miss Mousie, won't you marry me
way down under the apple tree?"
Uh-huh, uh-huh.

"Where will the wedding supper be?"
Uh-huh, uh-huh.
"Where will the wedding supper be?"
"Under the same old apple tree."
Uh-huh, uh-huh.

"What will the wedding supper be?"
Uh-huh, uh-huh.
"What will the wedding supper be?"
"Hominy grits and black-eyed peas."
Uh-huh, uh-huh.

The first to come in was a bumblebee.
Uh-huh, uh-huh.
The first to come in was a bumblebee
With a big bass fiddle on his knee.
Uh-huh, uh-huh.

The last to come in was a mockingbird.
Uh-huh, uh-huh.
The last to come in was a mockingbird

*Who said, "This marriage
is absurd."
Uh-huh, uh-huh.*

Theme Connections

Birds
Frogs
Humor
Insects
Mice

Fuzzy Caterpillar

Directions: Use a brown or black sock, or dye a white sock brown or black to create this puppet. Turn the sock inside out and stitch two small scarves (or silky fabric) to the middle of it to simulate butterfly wings or, as an alternative, glue on felt wings. Glue two wiggle eyes or pieces of felt to the toe of the sock. Turn the sock right side out and glue another two wiggle eyes to the toe. Use felt scraps to create details like antennae and legs.

When used with the song, simply turn the sock wrong side out when the caterpillar becomes a butterfly. When used with the chant, start with the sock balled up like an egg, stretch it out when it becomes a worm, ball it up again as you turn it wrong side out to represent a cocoon, and then turn it completely wrong side out when the caterpillar becomes a butterfly.

Song

*A fuzzy caterpillar went out for a walk.
His back went up and down.
He crawled and he crawled
And he crawled and he crawled
'til he crawled all over town.
He wasn't disappointed
Not a bit to be a worm.
Not a tear was in his eye.
Because he knew what he'd become
A very, very pretty butterfly.*

Chant

I'm an egg. I'm an egg. I'm an egg, egg, egg!
    (ball sock)
*I'm a worm. I'm a worm. I'm a wiggly,
    humpty worm!* (open up and wiggle)
*I'm a cocoon. I'm a cocoon. I'm a round
    and silky cocoon!* (ball up sock as you
    turn the sock wrong side out)
*I'm a butterfly. I'm a butterfly. I'm a grand
    and glorious butterfly!* (open the sock
    to the wrong side)
I can fly! I can fly! I can fly, fly, fly! (fly the
    puppet around.)

Theme Connections

Insects

The Lion's Haircut

by Pam Schiller

Directions: Photocopy the lion face on page 554. Color, cut it out, and laminate (optional). Glue it to the center of a 10" Styrofoam plate. Punch small holes all around the edges of the plate. Cut several 8" pieces of yarn. Tie a knot in one end of the yarn. Use a crochet hook to pull the other end of the yarn through the plate, leaving only an inch of yarn exposed on the face side of the puppet. Glue the lion face to a tongue depressor if desired. You will pull the yarn through the plate during the story. You will need to replace the yarn each time you use the puppet.

Leo was a lively baby lion. He loved to frolic and graze in the green grass. He loved to chase butterflies. He loved to splash in the water of the nearby pond. But most of all he loved to look at his reflection in the pond and see how big he was growing.

Leo wanted to be just like his dad. He would look at his paws and then search for his dad's paw prints close by to compare to his own. He would look at his nose and ears and try to remember how much bigger his dad's looked when they were wrestling in the grass. He would look for his mane and simply sigh in sadness as he could tell without any measuring or remembering that it was nothing like his dad's. Leo would say to his mom, "When will my mane grow?" His mom would give him a lick and simply say, "In its own good time."

All through the spring, Leo watched his mane. It didn't grow an inch. All through the summer, Leo watched his mane. It grew only a little *(pull mane through plate a little)*.

All through the fall, Leo watched his mane. It grew only a little more *(pull mane through plate a little)*. All through the winter, Leo watched his mane. It grew only a little more *(pull mane through plate a little)*.

Then when spring came again, something happened. Leo's mane began to grow *(pull mane)*. And it grew and it grew and it grew until he had a full mane just like his dad's *(pull until the mane is very long)*. Leo was so happy he felt like a million dollars, or in lion talk, a million butterflies.

Leo frolicked in the green grass. He chased butterflies. He splashed in the pond. He stopped to take a look at his lovely, long mane and when the water had calmed down and he could see himself, he shrieked. His mane was a tangled and matted mess.

He ran home to his mom in tears. His mom gave him a lick and simply said, "It's time for a haircut." She took out a pair of scissors and began to snip *(cut mane to approximately two inches)*. When she was through the tangles were gone and Leo still had a beautiful mane. It was just the right size for a lively little lion.

Theme Connections

Growing Up
Families
Self-Esteem

Ms. Bumblebee Gathers Honey

by Pam Schiller

Directions: Photocopy patterns from pages 555-556. Color them, cut them out, laminate them, and glue to tongue depressors to create stick puppets. Move puppets as directed in the story.

Ms. Bumblebee spends her day gathering honey. Every morning she gets out of bed, walks to the edge of the beehive, and looks out at the beautiful spring flowers. Most days, she starts with the red flowers because red is her favorite color. She swoops down from the hive, circles around, and lands right on the biggest red flower she can find. *(Hold the bee puppet in one hand and a red flower in the other. Move the bee slowly toward the flower, moving her in small circles as she approaches the flower.)* She drinks nectar from the flower and then carries it back to the hive to make honey. *(Move bee back to hive. Continue to move bee as directed above.)*

Next Ms. Bumblebee tries the nectar of the blue flowers. Again she swoops from the hive and dances toward the flower. She drinks the nectar and then returns to the hive.

She continues to the yellow flowers, which are the queen bee's favorite flowers. She drinks the nectar and returns to the hive. A bee's work is very hard, but Ms. Bumblebee thinks it is also a lot of fun. . . and very tasty.

The last flowers Ms. Bumblebee visits are the orange zinnias. She likes them because they have lots of petals that make a big place for her to land. She takes a minute to look over the field of flowers *(move puppet as if it is looking all around)* before drinking and retuning to the hive.

Ms. Bumblebee is tired. She is glad this is the last nectar for the day. Wait! What's this? Oh, it's that bear again. He wants to take the honey from the hive. Ms. Bumblebee is buzzing mad. She flies out and stings the bear right on the nose. The bear cries out, grabs his nose, and runs away. Ms. Bumblebee puts away her last bit of nectar and falls fast asleep.

Theme Connections

Bears
Insects
Seasons

The Old Woman and Her Pig

Directions: Photocopy patterns from pages 557-561. Color them, cut them out, laminate them, and glue to tongue depressors to create stick puppets. Move puppets as directed in the story.

Once upon a time an old woman found a sixpence while she was sweeping her house. She was so excited that she sang a happy song. With the sixpence, the old woman rushed off to the market to buy a little pig. On their way home they came to a stile, but the pig would not go over the stile. The old woman was upset. So, she said, "Pig, Pig, cross stile or I shan't get home tonight." But the pig would not, so she ran off to seek help.

As she ran along she came to a dog, so she said, "Dog, Dog, bite Pig. Pig won't go over stile and I shan't get home tonight." But the Dog would not, so she ran on to seek help.

As she ran along she found a stick, and so she said, "Stick, Stick, beat Dog. Dog won't bite Pig. Pig won't go over stile and I shan't get home tonight." But the stick would not, so she ran on to seek help.

As she ran along she found a fire, so she said, "Fire, Fire, burn Stick. Stick won't beat Dog. Dog won't bite Pig. Pig won't go over stile and I shan't get home tonight."

But the fire would not, so she ran on to seek some help.

As she ran along she found some water, so she said, "Water, Water, quench Fire. Fire won't burn Stick. Stick won't beat Dog. Dog won't bite Pig. Pig won't go over stile and I shan't get home tonight." But the water would not, so she ran on to seek help.

As she ran along she met a Horse, so she said, "Horse, Horse, drink Water. Water won't quench Fire. Fire won't burn Stick. Stick won't beat Dog. Dog won't bite Pig. Pig won't go over stile and I shan't get home tonight." But the Horse would not, so she ran on to seek help.

As she ran along she met a mouse, so she said, "Mouse, Mouse, scare Horse. Horse won't drink Water. Water won't quench Fire. Fire won't burn Stick. Stick won't beat Dog. Dog won't bite Pig. Pig won't go over stile and I shan't get home tonight." But the mouse would not, so she ran on to seek help.

As she ran along she met a cat, so she said, "Cat, Cat chase Mouse. Mouse won't scare Horse. Horse won't drink Water. Water won't quench Fire. Fire won't burn Stick. Stick won't beat Dog. Dog won't bite Pig. Pig won't go over stile and I shan't get home tonight."

But the cat said, "If you will go to Cow and get me a saucer of milk, I will chase Mouse."

So away went the old woman to find Cow. When she asked for the milk, Cow said to her, "If you will get me an armful of hay from the barn I will give you a saucer of milk." So the old woman went to the barn, got the hay and took it to Cow.

When Cow had eaten the hay she gave milk to the old woman, who took it in a saucer to Cat.

When she drank the milk, Cat began to chase Mouse.

Mouse began to scare Horse.

Horse began to drink Water.

Water began to quench Fire.

Fire began to burn Stick.

Stick began to beat Dog.

Dog began to bite Pig.

Pig was so frightened that it jumped over stile.

So the old woman got home that night.

Theme Connections

Cats
Cows
Dogs
Humor
Mice
Pigs

The Parade

by Pam Schiller

Directions: Photocopy the finger puppets on pages 562-566. Color them, cut them out and laminate them. You may want to reinforce the backside of the leg openings with masking tape prior to laminating. Use the puppets as they are introduced in the story. Feel free to add more description to each parade participant. You might want to have an empty toilet paper tube to use as a microphone like Kathy and Dorothy use in the story.

Kathy lives in New York City. She lives in a tall skyscraper that is right on 42nd Street. Kathy thinks she has the best home ever. She can look right out her window and see the famous Macy's Thanksgiving Parade. She always invites her cousin Dorothy from Texas to spend Thanksgiving at her house. They have been watching the parade together from Kathy's window since they were little girls. Sometimes when the weather is not too cold, they go downstairs and watch the parade from the sidewalk right in front of Kathy's apartment.

Today is the big day and Kathy has decided that this year she and Dorothy will pretend to be announcers. After all they have had plenty of experience watching this parade.

Kathy begins the narration. "Leading the parade this year is the Radio City Rockettes. They are the highest kicking ladies in the world. Listen to the crowd acknowledging these outstanding dancers."

Dorothy takes the toilet paper tube microphone from Kathy's hand and continues the broadcast. "Just look at the brightly colored costumes of the Ringling Brother's Circus clowns. Aren't they phenomenal? It makes you laugh just looking at them. Look at the clown with the green hair walking backwards on his hands. What's coming up next Kathy?"

"Well, Dorothy, here come the dancing bears. They are always a favorite. This year they even have a baby bear. You know it takes a lot of patience to train these bears to dance like that."

Dorothy and Kathy stop for a while to run to the kitchen for a snack. They laugh with delight at how well their imaginary announcing is going. They both agree that they could easily be the real announcers. The girls are so amazed by the beautiful floats that they forget to do the announcing again until the parade is nearly over. Dorothy picks up their pretend microphone and says, "Here comes a marching band from my hometown. It is the Jesse H. Jones Marching Band. Give them a hand. Just listen to those drums."

Just then both girls notice that the parade has come to an end because they see the final float. Do you know who is on that float? That's right—it is the same man every year. It's Santa Claus! After the parade is over, Dorothy and Kathy put away their microphones and head to the kitchen to check on the status of the turkey.

Theme Connections

Holidays
Friends

Photo Puppet Stories

Take a photo of the children and then make a photocopy of the photo to attach to a tongue depressor. Have the children make up stories about themselves. This is a great activity for the first week of school. It helps the children get to know each other.

Theme Connections

Friends
Parts of the Body
Self-Esteem

There Was an Old Woman Who Swallowed a Fly

Directions: Photocopy the story and puppet patterns on pages 567-569. Glue the old lady's face to the bottom of a medium size grocery sack with the chin pointed toward the open edge of the bag. Cut a 2" slit in the crease of the fold on the bottom of the bag. This slit will become the old lady's mouth. As you tell the story, slip the various things she eats down her throat. Cut a small square out of the front of the bag and tape a piece of clear acetate over it. This will allow the children to see the items in the old lady's stomach. Staple the bottom of the bag closed. Cut a 3" slit in the back of the bag so you can retrieve the pieces to use again. Glue or staple the arms and legs to the body. To decorate (optional): Add yarn to the old lady's hair. Cover the eyes on her face with wiggle eyes. Cut a piece of wallpaper to make the old lady a dress. Add fringe across the bottom.

Color and laminate the items that the old lady eats.

> *There was an old woman who swallowed a fly.*
> *I don't know why she swallowed a fly.*
> *Perhaps she'll die.*
>
> *There was an old woman who swallowed a spider*
> *That wiggled and wriggled and jiggled inside her.*

She swallowed the spider
to catch the fly.
   I don't know why she
   swallowed a fly.
   Perhaps she'll die.

There was an old woman who
   swallowed a bird.
My, how absurd to swallow a bird!
She swallowed the bird to catch the spider
That wiggled and wriggled and jiggled
   inside her.
She swallowed the spider to catch the fly.
I don't know why she swallowed a fly.
Perhaps she'll die.

There was an old woman who swallowed
   a cat.
Imagine that, she swallowed a cat!
She swallowed the cat to catch the bird.
She swallowed the bird to catch the spider
That wiggled and wriggled and jiggled
   inside her.
She swallowed the spider to catch the fly.
I don't know why she swallowed a fly.
Perhaps she'll die.

There was an old woman who swallowed
   a dog.
Oh, what a hog to swallow a dog!
She swallowed the dog to catch the cat.
She swallowed the cat to catch the bird.
She swallowed the bird to catch the spider
That wiggled and wriggled and jiggled
   inside her.
She swallowed the spider to catch the fly.
I don't know why she swallowed a fly.
Perhaps she'll die.

There was an old woman who swallowed
   a cow.
I don't know how she swallowed a cow.
She swallowed a cow to catch the dog.
She swallowed the dog to catch the cat.
She swallowed the cat to catch the bird.
She swallowed the bird to catch the spider
That wiggled and wriggled and jiggled
   inside her.
She swallowed the spider to catch the fly.
I don't know why she swallowed a fly.
Perhaps she'll die.

There was an old woman who swallowed
   a horse.
She died, of course!

Theme Connections

Birds
Cats
Cows
Dogs
Horses
Humor
Insects

The Three Bears Rap

Directions: Photocopy the puppet patterns on pages 570-573. Glue bears to tongue depressors. Color story props, cut them out, laminate them, and attach them to tongue depressors. Hold up the appropriate bear or prop as it is mentioned in the rap.

Shh, shh, shh, shh, shh, shh, shh, shh, shh, shh.
Out in the forest in a wee little cottage lived the three bears.
Shh, shh, shh, shh, shh, shh, shh, shh, shh, shh.
One was the Mama Bear, one was the Papa Bear, and one was the wee bear.
Shh, shh, shh, shh, shh, shh, shh, shh, shh, shh.
Out of the forest came a walking, stalking, pretty little Goldilocks
And upon the door she was a-knockin'.
Clack, clack, clack.
But no one was there, unh-unh, no one was there.
So she walked right in and had herself a bowl.
She didn't care, unh-unh, she didn't care.
Home, home, home came the three bears.
"Someone's been eating my porridge," said the Mama Bear.
"Someone's been eating my porridge," said the Papa Bear.
"Baa-baa Barebear," said the little Wee Bear.
"Someone's broken my chair."
Crash!
Just then Goldilocks woke up.
She broke up the party and she beat it out of there.
"Good-bye, good-bye, good-bye," said the Mama Bear.
"Good-bye, good-bye, good-bye," said the Papa Bear.
"Baa-baa Barebear," said the little Wee Bear.
That's the story of the three little bears—yeah!

Theme Connections

Bears
Families
Food
Houses and Homes
Numbers
Sounds of Language

The Three Little Pigs
(England)

Directions: Make photocopies of the patterns on pages 574-575. Color them, cut them out, and laminate them. Glue them to tongue depressor to make stick puppets.

This is a different version of the story than the one included in the flannel board stories. In this version, the wolf eats the first two pigs and the third pig boils the wolf for dinner.

You can use either story with the puppets patterns.

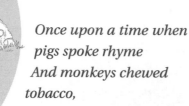

Once upon a time when pigs spoke rhyme
And monkeys chewed tobacco,
And hens took snuff to make them cough,
And ducks went quack, quack, quack, O!

There was an old sow with three little pigs, and as she had not enough to keep them, she sent them out to seek their fortune. The first that went off met a man with a bundle of straw, and said to him, "Please, man, give me that straw to build a house," which the man did, and the little pig build a house with it.

Along came a wolf, and knocked at the door, and said, "Little pig, little pig, let me come in."

To which the pig answered, "No, no, not by the hair of my chinny chin chin."

The wolf then answered to that, "Then I'll huff, and I'll puff, and I'll blow your house in."

So he huffed, and he puffed, and he blew his house in and ate up the little pig.

The second little pig met a man with a bundle of sticks and said, "Please man, give me those sticks to build a house," which the man did, and the pig built his house.

Along came a wolf, and knocked at the door, and said, "Little pig, little pig, let me come in."

To which the pig answered, "No, no, not by the hair of my chinny chin chin."

The wolf then answered to that, "Then I'll huff, and I'll puff, and I'll blow your house in."

So he huffed, and he puffed, and he blew his house in and ate up the little pig.

The third little pig met a man with a load of bricks, and said, "Please, man, give me those bricks to build a house with." So the man gave him the bricks, and he built his house with them. Then the wolf came, as he did to the other little pigs, and said, "Little pig, little pig, let me come in." To which the pig answered, "No, no, not by the hair of my chinny chin chin."

The wolf then answered to that, "Then I'll huff, and I'll puff, and I'll blow your house in."

Well he huffed, and he puffed, and he huffed and he puffed, and he puffed and huffed. But he could not get the house down.

When he found that he could not, with all his huffing and puffing, blow the house down, he said, "Little pig, I know where there is a nice field of turnips."

"Where?" said the little pig.

"Oh, Mr. Smith's field, and if you will be ready tomorrow morning I will call for you, and we will go together and get some for dinner."

"Very well," said the little pig, "I will be ready. What time do you mean to go?"

"Oh, at six o'clock."

Well, the little pig got up at five and got the turnips before the wolf came at six and said, "Little pig, are you ready?" The little pig said, "Ready! I have gone and come back again, and got a nice pot full of turnips for dinner."

The wolf felt very angry at this, but thought that he would get the better of the little pig somehow or other, so he said, "Little pig, I know where there is a nice apple tree."

"Where?" said the pig.

"Down at Merry Garden," replied the wolf, "and if you will not deceive me I will come for you at five o'clock tomorrow and we will get some apples."

Well, the little pig bustled up the next morning at four o'clock, and went off for the apples, hoping to get back before the wolf came. But he had farther to go, and had to climb the tree, so that just as he was coming down from it, he saw the wolf coming, which, as you may suppose, frightened him very much.

When the wolf came up he said, "Little pig....WHAT! Are you here before me! Are they nice apples?"

"Yes, very," said the little pig. "I will throw you down one."

And he threw it so far that while the wolf was gone to pick it up, the little pig jumped down and ran home.

The next day the wolf came again and said to the little pig, "Little pig, there is a fair at Shanklin this afternoon. Will you go?"

"Oh, yes," said the pig. "I will go. What time will you be ready?"

"At three," said the wolf.

So the little pig went off early, as usual, and got to the fair, and bought a butter churn, which he was going home with when he saw the wolf coming. Then he did not know what to do. So he got into the churn to hide and turned it over, and rolled down the hill

inside the churn. This frightened the wolf so much that he ran home without going to the fair. He went to the little pig's house and told him how frightened he had been by the great round thing that came down the hill past him.

Then the little pig said, "Hah! I frightened you, then, I had been to the fair and brought a butter churn, and when I saw you, I got into it and rolled down the hill."

Then the wolf was very angry indeed, and declared he would eat up the little pig, and that he would get down the chimney after him.

When the little pig saw what the wolf was doing, he hung a pot full of water in the fireplace and made up a blazing fire. When the wolf came down the chimney, he fell into the pot. The little pig quickly put the cover on the pot and boiled the wolf and ate him for supper. The third little pig lived happily ever after.

Theme Connections

Families
Numbers
Pigs
Tricksters
Wolves

Rebus Stories

REBUS STORIES

The Boy Who Tried to Fool His Father

(Zaire)

Directions: Make two photocopies of the story patterns on pages 576-579. Color them and cut them out. Read the first part of the story, showing the children the boy and animals as they are mentioned. Write the last part of the story (the spot is indicated in the story) on sentence strips, leaving a blank space for the picture items that will be placed in the story. You will need double copies of the story patterns because the last sentences of the story are interlocking. Challenge the children to remember which item is inside of which item.

One day, a boy said to his father, "I am going to hide and you won't be able to find me."

"Hide wherever you like," said his father, "I will find you." Then he went into the house to rest.

The boy saw a peanut lying on the ground, and he wished he could hide inside it. No sooner said than done; the boy found himself inside the peanut shell. He waited for his father to look for him.

Cock-a-doodle-doo—a rooster found the peanut and gobbled it up.

Rrrrrrr—a wild bush cat came into the yard, swallowed the rooster, and ran off into the thick brush.

Ruff! Ruff!—a dog ran after the bush cat and swallowed it. Then the dog was thirsty, and went to the river for a drink.

Sssssssss—a python crept up from behind, and swallowed the dog. The python fell in the river, and was caught in a fishnet

Meanwhile, the boy's father had searched and searched for his son, but he couldn't find him. It was getting dark, and he had to check his fishnets at the river. When the father pulled his fish net up onto the bank, he found a python with a huge, swollen belly.

(start rebus here)

Inside the python, he found a dog.

Inside the dog, he found a bush cat.

Inside the bush cat, he found a rooster.

Inside the rooster, he found a peanut.

He broke the peanut and out jumped his son.

That boy never tried to fool his father again!

Theme Connections

Dogs
Families
Humor
Roosters
Snakes

Burp!

The House That Jack Built

(England)

Directions: Photocopy the story patterns on pages 581-584. Color them and cut them out. Write the story on sentence strips, leaving a blank space for the picture items that will be placed in the story.

This is the house that Jack built.

This is the grain that lay in the house that Jack built.

This is the rat that ate the grain that lay in the house that Jack built.

This is the cat that chased the rat that lay in the house that Jack built.

This is the dog that worried the cat that chased the rat that lay in the house that Jack built.

This is the cow with the crumpled horn that tossed the dog

that worried the cat that chased the rat that lay in the house that Jack built.

This is the maid all forlorn that milked the cow with the crumpled horn

that tossed the dog that worried the cat that chased the rat that lay in the house that Jack built.

This is the man all tattered and torn that kissed the maid all–forlorn that milked the cow with the crumpled horn that tossed the dog that worried the cat that chased the rat that lay in the house that Jack built.

This is the priest all shaven and shorn that married the man all tattered and torn that kissed the maid all forlorn that milked the cow with the crumpled horn that tossed the dog that worried the cat that chased the rat that lay in the house that Jack built.

This is the cock that crowed in the morn that waked the priest all shaven and shorn that married the man all tattered and torn that kissed the maid all forlorn that milked the cow with the crumpled horn that tossed the dog that worried the cat that chased the rat that lay in the house that Jack built.

Theme Connections

Birds
Cats
Cows
Dogs
Farms
Work

Hush, Little Baby

Directions: Make two photocopies of the story patterns on pages 585-587. Color them and cut them out. Write the story on sentence strips leaving a blank space for the picture items that will be placed in the story.

Hush, little baby, don't say a word.
Mama's gonna buy you a mockingbird.
If that mockingbird won't sing,
Mama's gonna buy you a diamond ring.
If that diamond ring turns brass,
Mama's gonna buy you a looking glass.
If that looking glass gets broke,

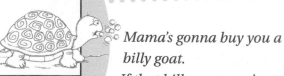

Mama's gonna buy you a
billy goat.
If that billy goat won't
pull,
Mama's gonna buy you a
cart and bull.
If that cart and bull turn over,
Mama's gonna buy you a dog named
Rover.
If that dog named Rover won't bark,
Mama's gonna buy you a horse and cart.
If that horse and cart fall down,
You'll still be the sweetest little baby in town.

Theme Connections

Birds
Bulls
Dogs
Families
Goats
Horses
Naptime/Sleeping
Rhymes and Rhyming

Spanish Translation

Sh, Mi Bébé

Sh, mi bebé, no digas ni una palabra.
Mamá te va enseñar un pajarito.
Que tal si no canta bonito.
Mamá te va enseñar un anillo de
diamantes.
Que tal si se vuelve deslumbrante.
Mamá te va enseñar un vidrio.
Que tal si se converte en cirio.
Mamá te va enseñar un chivo barbón.
Que tal si el chivo barbón me da un
empujón.

Mamá te va enseñar un carretón y un
toro.
Que tal si se voltean y me quedo solo.
Mamá te va a traer un perro llamado
Chico.
Que tal si no ladra el perro y se convierte
en perico.
Mamá te va a traer un caballo y una
carreta.
Que tal si ponemos en ella una veleta.
Tú seguiras siendo el bebé más dulce de
toda la tierra.

Miss Mary Mack

Directions: Photocopy the story patterns on pages 588-593. Color them and cut them out. Write the story on sentence strips, leaving a blank space for the picture items that will be placed in the story.

Miss Mary Mack, Mack, Mack
All dressed in black, black, black
With silver buttons, buttons, buttons
All down her back, back, back.

She asked her mother, mother, mother
For fifteen cents, cents, cents
To see the elephants, elephants, elephants
Jump the fence, fence, fence.

They jumped so high, high, high
They touched the sky, sky, sky
And they didn't come back, back, back
Till the Fourth of July, ly, ly.

July can walk, walk, walk;
July can talk, talk, talk;
July can eat, eat, eat,
With a knife and fork, fork, fork!

Theme Connections

Holidays
Humor
Rhymes and Rhyming

The Months

by Sara Coleridge

Directions: Photocopy the story patterns and month word cards on pages 594-598. Color them and cut them out. Write the story on sentence strips, leaving a blank space for the month's names and the picture items that will be placed in the story. Use the pictures where the name of the month appears.

January brings the snow,
Makes our feet and fingers glow.

February brings the rain,
Thaws the frozen lake again.

March brings breezes loud and shrill,
Stirs the dancing daffodil.

April brings the primrose sweet,
Scatters daisies at our feet.

May brings flocks of pretty lambs,
Skipping by their fleecy dams.

June brings tulips, lilies, roses,
Fills the children's hands with posies.

Hot July brings cooling showers,
Apricots and gillyflowers.

August brings the sheaves of corn,
Then the harvest home is borne.

Warm September brings the fruit,
Sportsmen then begin to shoot.

Fresh October brings the pheasant
Then to gather nuts is pleasant.

Dull November brings the blast,
Then the leaves are whirling fast.

Chill December brings the sleet,
Blazing fire, and Christmas treat.

Theme Connections

Months of the Year
Seasons
Weather

The Complete Book of Activities, Games, Stories, Props, Recipes, and Dances

On Top of a Hillside

(Tune: On Top of Old Smokey)

by Pam Schiller

Directions: Photocopy the story patterns on pages 599-603. Color them and cut them out. Be sure you color the socks lavender. Write the story/song on sentence strips leaving a blank space for the picture items that will be placed in the sentence.

On top of a hillside,
All covered with rocks,
There lives an iguana,
With lavender socks.

She bathes in the sunshine
And cools in the lake.
She dines on tamales
And fly-covered cake.

When she is happy,
She plays her guitar,
And all the iguanas
Think she's a rock star.

They dance on the hillside
And over the rocks.
They dance with the iguana
In lavender socks.

I love that iguana,
She's totally cool.
I wish that iguana
Would dance to my school.

Theme Connections

Colors
Humor
Friends

Santa's Workshop

Directions: Photocopy the story patterns on pages 604-609. Color them and cut them out. Write the story on sentence strips, leaving a blank space for the picture items that will be placed in the story.

In Santa's workshop far away,
Ten little elves work night and day.
This little elf makes candy canes;
This little elf builds choo-choo trains;
This little elf paints dolls for girls;
This little elf puts in their curls;
This little elf dips chocolate drops;
This little elf makes lollipops;
This little elf packs each jack-in-the-box;
This little elf sews dolly socks;
This little elf wraps books for boys;
This little elf checks off the toys;
As Santa packs them in his sleigh
Ready for you on Christmas Day!

Theme Connections

Holidays
Toys
Work

Susie Moriar

(adapted by Pam Schiller)

Directions: Photocopy the story patterns on pages 610-611. Color them and cut them out. Write the story on sentence strips, leaving a blank space for the picture items that will be placed in the story.

This is the story of Susie Moriar
It started one night as Susie sat by the
       _____ (fire).
The fire was so hot
Susie jumped in a _____ (pot).
The pot was so tall
Susie dropped in a _____ (ball).
The ball was so red
Susie fell in the _____ (bed).
The bed was so long,
Susie sang a _____ (song).
The song was so sweet,
Susie ran down the _____ (street).
The street was so big,
Susie picked up a _____ (pig).
The pig jumped so high,
He touched the _____ (sky).
And he couldn't touch higher.
But oh! What a ride
Had Susie _____ (Moriar).

Theme Connections

Humor
Pigs
Rhymes and Rhyming

Tiny Tim

Directions: Photocopy the story patterns on pages 612-615. You will need doubles of some of the patterns such as the doctor and nurse. Color them and cut them out. Write the story on sentence strips, leaving a blank space for the picture items that will be placed in the story.

I had a little turtle,
His name was Tiny Tim,
I put him in the bathtub,
To teach him how to swim.

He drank up all the water,
He ate up all the soap,

Tiny Tim was choking,
On the bubbles in his throat.

In came the doctor,
In came the nurse,
In came the lady,
With the alligator purse.

They pumped out all the water,
They pumped out all the soap,
They popped the airy bubbles,
As the floated from his throat.

The Complete Book of Activities, Games, Stories, Props, Recipes, and Dances

Out went the doctor,
Out went the nurse,
Out went the lady,
With the alligator purse.

Theme Connections

Humor
Rhymes and Rhyming

The money on the bus goes clink, clink,
clink...
The driver on the bus says, "Move on
back"...

Theme Connections

Sounds of Language
Transportation

The Wheels on the Bus

Directions: Make two photocopies of each of the story patterns on pages 616-618. Color them, cut them out, and laminate them. Write the first two lines of the song on sentence strips leaving a blank space for the picture items that will be placed in the sentence. As you sing each new verse, remove the previous item and place the new item in its spot.

> *The wheels on the bus go round and*
> *round, round and round, round and*
> *round.*
> *The wheels on the bus go round and*
> *round, all around the town.*

Continue the story substituting the following verses:

> *The wipers on the bus go swish, swish,*
> *swish...*
> *The baby on the bus goes, "Wah, wah,*
> *wah"...*
> *The people on the bus go up and down...*
> *The horn on the bus goes beep, beep,*
> *beep...*

Arts & Crafts
Recipes

Baker's Clay

1 cup white flour
1 cup salt
Water

Mix flour and salt in a bowl and add water, a little bit at a time, until the mixture becomes a soft clay. Knead until smooth. If the clay is too wet, add more flour. If the clay is too dry, add more water.

After the children create their designs (pendants, charms, sculptures) you can either bake them in the microwave or a conventional oven. In the microwave, heat for 30 seconds at a time, checking for hardness. In the conventional oven, bake at 225°, checking every 15 minutes for hardness. Baking time will vary depending on denseness of the item. Turn the item over halfway through baking time. Paint with poster paint when cool.

Bubble Painting

Mix prepared bubble soap or homemade bubble soap (see recipes below) in a bowl with powdered paint. Test the color strength by blowing bubbles on a paper to see the bubble prints. Add more paint if necessary.

Bubble Soap #1

1 teaspoon glycerin
½ cup liquid detergent
½ cup water

Mix all ingredients gently. For best results, let the mixture sit overnight.

Bubble Soap #2

10 cups water
1 cup Joy® or Dawn® dishwashing soap
3-4 tablespoons glycerin

For best results, make recipe a day ahead.

Buttermilk Chalk

Place about a tablespoon of buttermilk on paper and let each child use chalk or powdered tempera to make designs. The buttermilk breaks down the chalk and the result is similar to fingerpaint but easier to control.

Clay

1 cup salt
1 cup flour
½ cup water
Powdered tempera paint

Mix salt, flour, and water together in a bowl, adding more flour if necessary to give the mixture a doughy consistency. Add powdered tempera as desired and mix well. Objects made with the clay will air dry in about 48 hours.

Cloud Dough

1 cup oil
6 cups flour
1 cup water

Use just enough water to bind the mixture. Start with the quantity called for in the recipe and then add 1 tablespoon at a time as needed. Knead the mixture. Cloud dough is very oily, but provides a different tactile experience.

Colored Glue

Add tempera paint to glue to make various colors. Let children squeeze their pictures instead of painting.

Colored Rock Salt

Dye rock salt by placing food coloring in alcohol and letting the salt sit in the mixture for about 10 minutes. Drain on a paper towel. Use for collage materials or let the children pick the crystals up with a pair of tweezers.

Colored Salt Paste

2 parts salt
1 part flour
Powdered paint
Water

Mix salt and flour. Add powdered paint. Gradually stir in enough water to make a smooth heavy paste. This mixture can be used the same as regular paste. Store in an airtight container.

Colored Sand

Place 2 tablespoons of sand (or salt) on a paper plate. Rub a piece of colored chalk over the sand and it will gradually turn the same color as the chalk.

Cornstarch Dough

1 part cornstarch
2 parts salt
1 part water

Heat the water and salt for a few minutes, and then slowly add the cornstarch, stirring until well mixed. Knead the dough and add more water if necessary.

ARTS & CRAFTS RECIPES

Cornstarch Paint

1 cup water
2 tablespoons cornstarch
Food coloring

Mix the water, cornstarch, and several drops of food coloring together in a saucepan. Heat and stir the mixture until it thickens, about 5 minutes. Let it cool and store in a covered container. Use the paint for fingerpainting or as an almost dripless easel paint. If the mixture becomes too thick, add water until it reaches the desired consistency. Tongue depressors are good to use for mixing. Putting the mixture into a squeeze bottle makes it easy to use.

Craft Clay

1 cup cornstarch
2 cups baking soda (1-pound box)
1¼ cups water

Combine cornstarch and baking soda in a pan and add water, gradually stirring until smooth. Cook over medium heat, stirring constantly. Put mixture out on a cutting board to cool. Knead well. Cover with a damp cloth or keep in a plastic bag. Use for sculptures, beads, or other creations. Paint with poster paint when dry.

Crepe Paper Paste

½ tablespoon flour
½ tablespoon salt
2 tablespoons thinly cut crepe paper
Water

Combine dry ingredients and crepe paper. Add enough water to make a paste. Stir and mash the mixture until it is as smooth as possible. Store in an airtight container.

Crystal Garden

Lay 6 charcoal briquettes and 6 clay shards in a pie tin. Mix 4 tablespoons of each of the following ingredients: non-iodized salt, liquid bluing, and water. Add 1 tablespoon of ammonia. With adult supervision, invite the children to drizzle the liquid mixture over the charcoal and clay. The crystals will begin to grow immediately and will last for three to four days.

Epsom Salt Solution

1 cup hot water
4 tablespoons Epsom salt

Mix the water with the Epsom salt. When this mixture dries it creates a glazed appearance.

Face Paint

2 tablespoons cold cream
½ teaspoon glycerin
1 teaspoon cornstarch
1 teaspoon powdered tempera

Stir ingredients together until well mixed.

Fingerpaint Recipe #1

Pour a tablespoon of liquid starch onto paper or directly onto the tabletop. Sprinkle on a little powdered tempera. Encourage the children to mix the starch and the tempera together.

Fingerpaint Recipe #2

⅓ cup cornstarch dissolved in ¾ cup
    cold water
1 envelope Knox gelatin dissolved in ¼
    cup cold water
½ cups Ivory soap flakes (or Ivory Snow)
2 cups hot water

Add hot water to the cornstarch mixture and cook on a stove top (adults only). Stir until the mixture is clear. Add the gelatin mixture and stir to blend. Add Ivory Flakes or Ivory Snow. Divide into containers. Add desired color of powdered tempera to each container.

Fingerpaint Recipe #3

1½ cups laundry starch
1 quart boiling water
1½ cups soap flakes
½ cup talcum

Mix starch and cold water into a creamy paste. Add boiling water (adults only) and cook until mixture becomes transparent or glossy looking. Stir continually. Add talcum and allow mixture to cool. Add soap flakes and stir until they are evenly distributed.

Pour into containers and add powdered tempera to color.

Gak

2 cups glue
1½ cups tap water
2 teaspoons Borax
1 cup hot water
food coloring

Combine glue, tap water, and food coloring in a bowl. In a larger bowl, dissolve Borax in hot water. Slowly add the glue mixture to the Borax. It will thicken quickly and be difficult to mix. Mix well and drain off excess water. Let stand for a few minutes, then pour into a shallow tray. Let dry for 10 minutes. Store in zipper-closure plastic bags (will keep for 2-3 weeks).

Goop #1

2 cups salt
1 cup water
1 cup cornstarch

Cook salt and ½ cup water 4-5 minutes. Remove from heat. Add cornstarch and ½ cup water. Return to heat. Stir until mixture thickens. Store in a zipper-closure plastic bag or covered container.

Goop #2

3 cups cornstarch
2 cups warm water

Gradually add water to cornstarch. Mix ingredients together with hands. Goop is done when the mass goes from a lumpy to satiny texture.

Goop hardens in the air and turns to liquid when held. It resists punching, but a light touch causes a finger to sink in.

Homemade Gas

1 tablespoon baking soda
2 tablespoons vinegar

Combine baking soda and vinegar to make a carbon dioxide gas.

Homemade Paint

½ teaspoon vinegar
½ teaspoon cornstarch
10 drops foodcoloring

Put all ingredients in a jar. Shake well.

Icing Paint

1 cup powdered tempera paint
2 tablespoons wallpaper paste
¼ to ½ cup liquid starch

Mix the ingredients together until thick enough to spread like frosting. Use Popsicle sticks to spread the mixture onto cardboard.

Kool-Aid Playdough

1 package Kool-Aid
1 cup water
1 tablespoon baby oil
1 cup flour
½ cup salt
2 teaspoons of cream of tartar

Mix Kool-Aid and water on the stove at medium heat until steam rises (adults only). Add baby oil and stir. Mix together remaining dry ingredients. Gradually add to heated liquids and stir until a mashed potato consistency is achieved. Remove from stove. Place playdough on wax paper and knead until smooth. Allow to cool.

Microwave Playdough

1 cup flour
½ cup salt
1 teaspoon cream of tartar
1 tablespoon cooking oil
1 cup water
1 package unsweetened Kool-Aid® or food coloring

Add the food coloring or Kool-Aid to the water. Add all the ingredients into a microwave bowl. Microwave on high for 3-5 minutes. Stir every minute until it forms a ball. Let it cool and store in a zipper-closure plastic bag in the refrigerator.

Natural Dyes

Green	broccoli
Yellow	tea
Blue	blueberries
Purple	beets
Magenta	cranberries

Boil any of the above fruits, vegetables, and herbs. Add 1 teaspoon of salt to each pint of liquid.

No-Dust Chalk

3 parts water
1 part sugar
Colored chalk

Mix water and sugar until sugar is dissolved. Soak a piece of colored chalk in the solution for 30 minutes. When the chalk dries, it can be used without smudging or smearing.

Oatmeal Dough

1 part flour
2 parts oatmeal
1 part water

Add water a little at a time to bind the mixture. Cornmeal can be used instead of oatmeal to vary the mixture. This is a great tactile experience.

Paints

To one pint of tempera add the following ingredients to change paint consistency:

Slimy Paint	Add 2 tablespoons Karo syrup
Gritty Paint	Add 1/2 teaspoon sand
Slippery Paint	Add 1 teaspoon glycerin
Lumpy Paint	Add 1 tablespoon flour
Rough Paint	Add 1 tablespoon sawdust (go to any lumber company)
Shiny Paint	Add 1/2 cup sugar
Sparkly Paint	Add 1/2 cup salt (use immediately)
Creamy Paint	Add 1/4 cup liquid starch
Transparent Paint	Add 2 tablespoons hair gel
Thick Paint	Mix 3 parts powder to 1 part water

Helpful Hints:

Add liquid soap to all paints to make it easier to wash out of clothes.

Add 1 teaspoon of alcohol to paint to keep it from souring.

Papier-Mâché Paste

2 cups wheat paste (see below)
2½ cups of water

Mix the wheat paste and water together.

To make wheat paste:

Prepare 1 cup of very hot water. Make a thin mixture of 3 tablespoons of wheat flour and cold water. Pour the cold mixture slowly into the hot water while stirring constantly. Bring to a boil. When it thickens, allow to cool. Smear on like any other glue. For slightly better strength, add 1 tablespoon of sugar after the glue is thickened. After using a portion, reheat the remaining in a covered jar or container to sterilize it for storage or keep refrigerated. If wheat flour is not available, other flours will work.

To papier-mâché:

Mix wheat flour and water in a large bowl (2 cups of each is a good amount to begin with) until it makes a smooth paste. Dip in the newspaper strips, one at a time, remove the excess paste from your fingers and lay the coated newspaper on the form to be papier-mâchéd. Smooth out the wrinkles and continue to place coated newspaper over the surface until completely covered. When the surface has totally dried, paint your own design using acrylic or poster paint.

Paste (that will keep)

2 tablespoons flour
½ teaspoon alum
Oil of wintergreen (optional)
Food coloring (optional)

Mix flour with a small amount of water to form a paste. Pour 2 cups of boiling water into paste mixture. Boil for 3 minutes in a double boiler. Add alum. Add oil of wintergreen and food coloring, if desired.

Plaster Mix

2 cups patch plaster or plaster of Paris
1¼ cups water

Mix until it is the consistency of pea soup. It will thicken in 3 to 4 minutes and will dry in 20 minutes.

Playdough #1

3 cups flour
1½ cups salt
3 tablespoons oil
2 tablespoons cream of tartar
3 cups water

Combine all ingredients. Cook over very low heat until mixture is no longer sticky to the touch. Store in an airtight container. This is nice, springy dough, close in texture to purchased playdough.

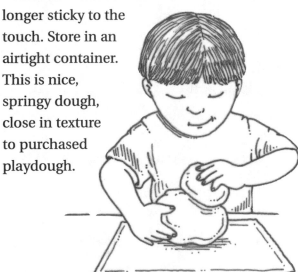

Variation

Scented Playdough

Add 1 teaspoon scented extract (peppermint, lemon, and so on) to basic playdough recipe. You can use massage oils in place of extract, if desired.

Playdough #2

6 cups flour
3 cups salt
2 cups water
½ cup oil
Food coloring

Mix and knead all ingredients. Store in an airtight container.

Playdough #3

2 cups baking soda
1 cup cornstarch
1½ cups cold water
Flour

Combine ingredients and cook over medium heat until soft dough forms (it will stick to spoon). Refrigerate at least 30 minutes. Knead for 4 minutes. Roll on floured paper. Store in an airtight container.

Pud

2 boxes cornstarch
Water

Pour cornstarch into a bowl and slowly add water. Work them together with your hands until desired consistency is reached. Encourage the children to squeeze the mixture. They will be surprised what happens. You can slap the mixture in water and it doesn't splash. Hold it in your hands and it turns to liquid. This is a fascinating mixture. Be sure to cover the floor well. When the mixture dries it vacuums up easily.

Puff Paint

⅓ cup white glue
2 tablespoons tempera paint
2 cups shaving cream

Mix and use as fingerpaint.

Salt Paint #1

Mix 1 teaspoon of salt into fingerpaint and let children enjoy a tactile fingerpainting experience.

Salt Paint #2

Flour
Salt
Water
Tempera paint

Mix equal parts of flour, salt, and water to a creamy consistency. Mix in the paint. Make several different colors. Pour into plastic squeeze bottles with a squirt top. Invite the children to experiment with the paints on cardboard or construction paper. Let the pictures dry. They will sparkle because of the salt.

Sawdust Dough

5 cups sawdust (you can find this free at any lumber company)
1 cup wheat paste (see page 257)
4 cups water

Mix and store in a sealed can in the refrigerator. This dough will dry hard when left in the open air.

Scratch and Sniff Paint

Mix flavored gelatin as directed but using only half the amount of water called for. Use the mixture for paint. When it dries, children can scratch and sniff.

Snow Dough

1 cup flour

½ cup salt

1 cup water

2 tablespoons vegetable oil

1 tablespoon cream of tartar

⅓ cup silver or clear glitter

¼ cup white powdered tempera paint

Mix all the ingredients together. Cook over medium heat, stirring until a ball is formed. Let cool just a bit and then knead dough until cool.

Soap Crayons

1 cup soap flakes (Ivory Flakes)

⅛ cup water

3 drops food coloring

Grease plastic ice cube tray or Popsicle molds with shortening or non-stick canola cooking spray. Mix ingredients together in a bowl. Pour into tray or molds. Allow time for them to harden and pop out.

Soap Paint

1 cup Ivory Snow

Water

Mix soap and enough water to form the consistency of whipping cream. Beat with a mixer until the mixture looks like shaving cream. Add food coloring, if desired. Use like fingerpaint.

Soapsuds Clay

¾ cup soap powder

1 tablespoon warm water

Mix soap powder and water in a bowl. Beat with an electric mixer until it has the consistency of clay.

Soft, Homemade Plasticine

1½ cups flour
1 cup salt
2 tablespoons warm water
1½ cups vegetable oil

Mix all the ingredients together and form into balls. Store the dough at room temperature. It does not have to be kept in a covered container.

Squeeze Paint

Pour glue in a bowl. Add powdered paint and water. Thin to consistency appropriate to use in a squeeze bottle.

Wheat Paste

1 cup hot water
3 tablespoons wheat flour
Cold water

Prepare 1 cup of very hot water. Make a thin mixture of 3 tablespoons of wheat flour and cold water. Pour the cold mixture slowly into the hot water while stirring constantly. Bring to a boil. When it thickens, allow to cool. Smear on like any other glue. For slightly better strength, add 1 tablespoon of sugar after the glue is thickened. After using a portion, reheat the remaining in a covered jar or container to sterilize it for storage or keep refrigerated. If wheat flour is not available, other flours will work.

Food Recipes

Ants on a Log

Peanut butter
Celery
Raisins
Plastic knife

Invite the children to spread peanut butter on a strip of celery and then place raisins on top of the peanut butter to represent ants.

Apple Cider

32 ounces apple juice
1 teaspoon cinnamon
¼ cup lemon juice
2 tablespoons honey

Mix apple juice, cinnamon, lemon juice, and honey. Heat. Cool to room temperature and serve at a special cider party. Do the children like the apple cider?

Apple Rounds
(Allergy Warning)

8 apples
½ cup crunchy peanut butter
¼ cup wheat germ
¼ cup dry milk
2 tablespoons honey

Wash and core apples. Combine the remaining ingredients and stuff into the

center of the apples. Slice into 1" rounds. Serves 12-18.

Baggie Ice Cream

One serving:

½ cup milk
1 tablespoon sugar
¼ teaspoon vanilla
small zipper-closure plastic bag
large zipper-closure plastic bag
3 tablespoons rock salt

Place the milk, sugar, and vanilla in the small bag and seal it. Place the small bag, the rock salt, and ice cubes in the large bag and seal. Shake.

Banana Crunches

Bananas

Milk

Honey

Toasted wheat germ

Zipper-closure plastic bag

Cut bananas into 1" slices. Dip bananas into a mixture of half milk and half honey. Drop bananas into a plastic bag filled with wheat germ and shake until well coated. Cut into slices. Serve on a tray with toothpicks.

Banana Wheels

Bananas (1 for every 2 children)

1 teaspoon dry gelatin (any color and flavor)

Zipper-closure plastic bag

Give the children plastic knives to slice bananas. Place 1 teaspoon of dry gelatin in a zipper-closure bag. Encourage children to put 3 or 4 banana slices in the bag and shake. Remove the Banana Wheels with toothpicks and eat.

Bear Paw Apple Turnovers

(oven or toaster oven required)

Refrigerator biscuits

Apple pie filling

Give each child two refrigerator biscuits and ask them to press them together to make a 6" circle. Have the children put 2 tablespoons of apple pie filling in the middle

of their dough circle. Show them how to fold the circle in half and pinch the edges together. Cut three lines in each turnover to make it look more like a "paw." Bake at 375° for 12 minutes.

Blender Drinks

(blender required)

Banana Milk Shake

2 fully ripe bananas

1 cup chilled milk

1 tablespoon sugar

¼ teaspoon vanilla

Peel and smash bananas. Put into blender. Slowly add milk, sugar, and vanilla. Makes 4 small shakes.

Fruit Smoothie

2 cups fruit juice (orange, pineapple, or grape)

½ cup powdered milk

1 drop vanilla

Combine ingredients in a blender. Add crushed ice. Serves 4 to 6.

FOOD RECIPES

Milkanilla

4 ounces milk

½ teaspoon sugar

⅛ teaspoon vanilla

1 drop food coloring

Mix and enjoy!

Purple Cow Shakes

1 small scoop vanilla ice cream

2 tablespoons grape juice concentrate

2 tablespoons milk

Place ingredients in a baby food jar. Close the lid and shake, shake, shake. Enjoy! For added fun, read the following poem:

The Purple Cow
by Gelett Burgess
I never saw a purple cow,
I never hope to see one!
But I can tell you, anyhow
I'd rather see than be one.

Buckaroo Cookies

½ cup raisins

½ cup chopped dates

2 tablespoons honey

graham crackers

zipper-closure bag

Pour raisins, dates, and honey into mixing bowl. Put several graham crackers in a zipper-closure bag and crush them with a rolling pin. Add crushed crackers to the other mixture until it's dry enough to roll into balls.

Can Ice Cream

2 cups milk

4 tablespoon sugar

1 teaspoon vanilla

rock salt

Place the milk, sugar, and vanilla in a small coffee can and close the lid. Place the small can, the rock salt, and ice cubes in a larger coffee can and close the lid. Have the children roll the can back and forth across the floor for about 15 minutes. Serves 6.

Carousels

Apples
Peanut butter [Check for allergies]
Animal crackers

Core an apple and cut it into round slices. Spread with peanut butter and stand animal crackers in the peanut butter around the perimeter.

Carrot Salad

Carrots
Raisins
Salad dressing (optional)

Grate the carrots. Combine the carrots and raisins to make a salad. You can add a couple of tablespoons of salad dressing if desired. Chill before eating. Eat the salad and enjoy the combination of fruit and vegetable. Combining foods gives young children a chance to experience taste in a different way. Let the children eat a carrot stick and talk about it together and then a raisin and talk about it. How does combining the two items change the taste?

Celery Man

Celery
Raisins
Carrot slices
Toothpicks
Lettuce leaves
Peanut butter

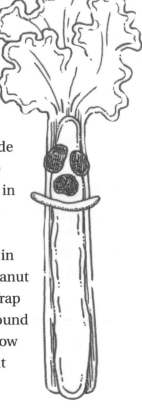

Fill a stalk of celery with peanut butter (be sure to check for allergies). Using the wide end of the celery as the head, place two raisins in the peanut butter for eyes; then add a raisin nose. Cut a carrot slice in half and set it in the peanut butter as the mouth. Wrap a lettuce leaf "cape" around the celery stalk just below the mouth and secure it with a toothpick.

Cheese Crispies
(oven or toaster oven required)

2 cups grated cheddar cheese
½ cup (1 stick) softened butter
1 cup sifted flour
¼ teaspoon salt

Invite the children to mix all the ingredients thoroughly in a mixing bowl with their hands. Roll into small balls and place an inch apart on a cookie sheet. Bake at 375° for 12 minutes.

Cinnamon Snakes
(oven or toaster oven required)

Refrigerator dough biscuits, one for each child
Cinnamon-sugar mixture

Give each child a refrigerator dough biscuit and encourage him or her to roll the dough into a snake and the shape it to look like a moving snake (wavy). Provide a mixture of cinnamon and sugar to sprinkle on the top of their snakes and bake at 375° for 8 to 10 minutes.

Colorful and Tasty Corn
(popcorn maker or stove required)

Pop popcorn in the regular way. Provide a variety of colors of sugar and seasonings for the children to use on their corn. You can color the sugar by adding a drop of food coloring to a small amount of sugar. You can try seasoning like Parmesan cheese, seasoned salt, and a mixture of sugar and cinnamon.

Crazy Chips

Spruce up a bowl of potato chips by adding grapes and raisins.

Cream Cheese Delights

2 tablespoons cherry juice
½ cup cream cheese

Add the cherry juice to the cream cheese and mix well. Let the children spread the mixture on bread or crackers.

Make Cream Hearts by cutting the bread into heart shapes and providing cherry halves to decorate the hearts.

Crispy Hearts
(oven or toaster oven required)

Refrigerator dough biscuits, one for each child
Butter
Cinnamon-sugar mixture

Give each child a refrigerator can biscuit. Show them how to shape the biscuit into a thin heart. Encourage them to brush the heart with butter and then sprinkle it with a cinnamon and sugar mixture. Bake as directed on the package.

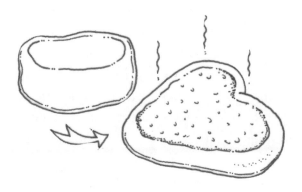

Dessert Salad
(refrigerator required)

- 1 small package cool whip
- 1 small package gelatin (any flavor)
- 1 small carton cottage cheese
- 1 small can fruit cocktail
- 1 cup miniature marshmallows

Mix cool whip, dry flavored gelatin, and cottage cheese together. Drain fruit cocktail and add to other ingredients. Add marshmallows. Chill for 2 hours. Serve in cupcake holders.

Donuts
(deep fryer required)

Invite the children to cut holes into refrigerator biscuits, using a small, round cookie cutter. Drop the biscuits into a deep fryer and fry them until they are golden brown and floating on the top of the grease (adults only). Remove from the oil and let drain. Invite the children to dust their donut with powdered sugar.

Edible Chanukah Menorah (Chanukiah)

- Celery stalks
- Peanut butter
- Cheddar cheese (mild)
- Pretzel sticks

Cut celery stalks into lengthwise strips. Spread peanut butter on the celery strips and put them on a plate. The celery

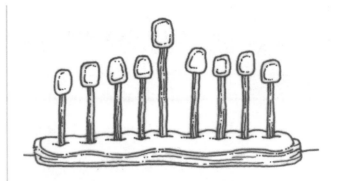

becomes the candleholder (called a "Chanukiah" for Chanukah.) Cut cheese into small cubes, which will become flames. Give the children small pretzel sticks (candlesticks) and show them how to spear a pretzel stick into a cheese cube (flame). Have the children insert the pretzel sticks with the cheese cubes into the peanut butter in the celery. The middle candle (called the shammash or leader) should be placed in first with four more added to each side of it. The middle candle should be a little taller than the others.

Firefighter Treats/ Dalmatian Cookies
(oven or toaster oven required)

- Refrigerated sugar cookie dough
- Chocolate chips

Give the children refrigerator sugar cookie dough and let them shape cookies. Provide some chocolate chips for the children to push into their cookies to make Dalmatian spots. Bake as directed. Take the cookies as a gift to firefighters when you visit the fire station.

A Flavorful Rainbow
(refrigerator required)

Gelatin, 3 or 4 different flavors

Select three or four flavored gelatins. Prepare the gelatins one at a time, as directed on the package. Pour each flavor into a glass bowl and let it cool and set before adding the next flavor. Sing the song "Somewhere over the Rainbow" and eat your lovely rainbow.

French Toast
(electric skillet or stove required)

  2 eggs
  ¼ cup milk
  ⅛ teaspoon salt
  ½ teaspoon vanilla
  1 teaspoon grated orange or lemon rind
    (optional)
  1 tablespoon butter
  4 slices bread
  Syrup or powdered sugar

Beat eggs, milk, salt, vanilla, and rind together and pour into a shallow bowl. Heat butter in electric skillet. Cut bread in half, soak in mixture, and brown on both sides. Serve with syrup or powdered sugar.

Friendship Salad

Have the children bring a piece of fruit to school. Let them help peel and cut the fruit to make a salad. Use whipped cream or

yogurt to mix the salad. Encourage the children to find a friend to sit with while they eat their salad.

Frozen Banana Pops
(freezer required)

  Bananas
  Popsicle sticks
  Chocolate sauce, optional

Peel a banana and cut the banana in half using a plastic knife. Put the banana half on a Popsicle stick. Freeze the banana pop. You can dip the banana in a chocolate sauce before putting into the freezer, if desired.

Frozen Yogurt

  Yogurt, any flavor
  Large coffee can
  Ice
  Rock salt

Place a container of yogurt inside a coffee can. Fill the can with ice and rock salt. Invite children to roll the can back and forth for about 15 minutes. When you take the yogurt out it will be frozen.

Fruit Dip

8 ounces nonfat plain yogurt
2 tablespoons honey
½ orange peel, grated
Fruit, assorted varieties

Mix yogurt, honey and the grated orange peel. Cut fruit (adult only) into chunks. Dip pieces of fruit into the dip. Yum!

Fruit Kabobs

Cut two or three kinds of fruit into chunks (adults only). Invite children to thread chunks of fruit onto a skewer.

Fruit Tree Salad

Lettuce
1 slice pineapple
Banana
1 small can fruit cocktail

Spread lettuce on a salad dish. Place the pineapple slice on top of the lettuce. Cut banana in half (adults only) and stick it upright in the center of the pineapple. Drain fruit cocktail. Put the fruit on toothpicks and then put the toothpicks in the banana to make a fruit tree.

Fruity Yogurt Pops
(freezer required)

4 cups plain yogurt
1 cup fresh fruit (strawberries, bananas, peaches, or pineapple)
Honey (optional)

Crush or finely chop the fruit (adults only). Blend with yogurt. Honey can be added if the fruit is tart. Pour in 3-ounce paper cups. Place a Popsicle stick in the center of each cup and freeze. Serves 15.

Variation

Substitute 1 12 oz. can frozen orange juice concentrate for chopped fruit.

Garden Worms

Chocolate cookies, crumbled
Gummy worms

Invite the children to crumble chocolate cookies (dirt) over gummy worms for snack.

Gelatin Jigglers
(refrigerator required)

Mix flavored gelatin with half the amount of water suggested on the box. Let congeal. Cut into heart shapes or use a cookie cutter to cut. For added fun, read the following poem:

Gelatin Jigglers
Gelatin Jigglers on my tray.
They make me laugh and
want to play.
Wiggle, giggle, smooth and
cool.
What a treat to eat at school.

Gingerbread House

Graham crackers
Gumdrops
M&Ms
Peppermint disks
¼ teaspoon milk
2 tablespoons powdered sugar

Help each child mix 2 tablespoons of powdered sugar with ¼ teaspoon of milk to make an icing that can be used as glue. Give each child a small paper plate to use as a base for the house. Help them construct a house by "gluing" graham crackers together. Encourage them to decorate their houses with the candies using the icing as glue.

Gingerbread People

(oven or toaster oven required)

½ tablespoon butter
½ tablespoon molasses

Flour Mixture:
1 ½ cup whole wheat flour
½ teaspoon ginger
¼ teaspoon cinnamon
⅛ teaspoon nutmeg
¾ teaspoon water
Raisins

Help the children individually mix the ingredients for their gingerbread person. Mix the butter and the molasses. Add 3 tablespoons of the flour mixture. Stir all ingredients and add ¾ teaspoon water (only as much as is needed). Roll the dough on floured wax paper and cut out the gingerbread person. Decorate with raisins. Bake at 325° for 6 to 8 minutes on a greased cookie sheet. (individual portion)

Glittery Sugar Mallows

1 package marshmallows
Light cream or canned milk
½ cup sugar
Food coloring

Mix 5 or 6 drops of food coloring with sugar to make colored sugar. Place colored sugar in a resealable plastic bag. Dunk marshmallows a few at a time in a shallow bowl of milk, and then drop into sugar mixture. Shake vigorously.

Goodnight Bears

Use a cookie cutter to cut out a bear from a slice of cheese. Lay the bear on a slice of bread. Cut a second slice of bread in half and lay it on the bottom half of the bear to make it look like a bear lying in bed with the covers pulled halfway up.

Graham Crackers
(oven or toaster oven required)

½ cup butter
½ half cup brown sugar
2 ¾ cup graham flour
½ teaspoon salt
½ baking powder
¼ teaspoon ground cinnamon
½ cup water

Preheat oven to 350°. Cream butter and sugar well. Mix remaining ingredients and add to creamed mixture, alternating with ½ cup water. Mix well and let stand 30 minutes. Roll out dough on floured board to ⅛" thickness. Cut into 2" squares and place on greased cookie sheet. Bake for 20 minutes. Makes about 3 dozen.

Green Eggs
(electric skillet or stove required)

Eggs
Milk
Green food coloring

Place a few drops of green food coloring in raw eggs before scrambling with milk, and cooking.

Happy Face Pancakes
(electric skillet or stove required)

Pancake batter

On a hot pan or griddle, pour 2 drops of pancake batter for eyes and a half-moon of batter for a mouth. Let cook 1 minute, and then pour enough batter over it to make a regular-sized pancake. Finish cooking. Eyes and mouth will be browner than the rest of the pancake.

Healthy Treats

(freezer required)

12-ounce can of cranberry
juice concentrate
2 cups plain yogurt
1 teaspoon vanilla

Mix ingredients. Pour into small paper cups and put plastic spoons in the cups for handles.

Place in the freezer for two hours.

Homemade Applesauce

(electric skillet or stove required)

6 apples
½ cup water
1 teaspoon lemon juice
¼ cup sugar
Cinnamon
colander

Peel, core, and cut up 6 apples into a large saucepan. Add 1/2 cup water, 1 teaspoon lemon juice, and 1/4 cup of sugar. Cook until tender. Add a pinch of cinnamon. Press through a colander and serve.

Homemade Butter

1 pint heavy whipping cream
¼ teaspoon salt
Yellow food coloring (optional)

Pour whipping cream into baby food jars. Shake until a soft ball forms. Pour off any residue.

Add salt. Spread on crackers or bread to sample.

Homemade Peanut Butter

(check for allergies)
(blender required)

1½ tablespoon vegetable oil
1 cup roasted peanuts
½ teaspoon salt

Put ingredients into an electric blender. Blend to desired smoothness (adults only). Add a little more oil, if needed.

Peanut Butter Ideas
(Check for allergies)

- Blend peanut butter and jelly together before spreading on bread or crackers.

- Try using honey instead of jelly.

- Top peanut butter with apples or banana slices for an extra special yummy treat.

- Peanut butter is easier to spread on bread that is slightly frozen.

Homemade Toothpaste

1 tablespoon baking soda
peppermint extract, 2 or 3 drops

Mix baking soda with the peppermint extract. Stir in a small amount of water to make a paste.

Honey Butter Spread

Two parts honey
One part butter
Dash of cinnamon (optional)

Mix together. Serve on biscuits or crackers.

Honey Custard

(stove and oven required)

3 eggs
⅓ cup honey
2 cups scalded milk
1 teaspoon vanilla
Nutmeg

Preheat oven to 325°. Crack eggs into a mixing bowl and beat well. Mix in all remaining ingredients except nutmeg. Place in a baking dish holding ½" hot water. Bake for 35 minutes or until a knife inserted in the center comes out clean. Cool and sprinkle with nutmeg. Refrigerate. Serves 6-8.

Hot Chocolate

(stove required)

1 tablespoon chocolate syrup
8 ounces milk
Marshmallows

Mix 1 tablespoon of chocolate syrup with 8 ounces of milk and heat. Be sure to add a marshmallow.

Makes 1 serving

Humpty Dumpty Eggs (Deviled Eggs)

(stove required)

Eggs
Sweet relish
Mayonnaise

Make Humpty Dumpty Eggs as you would deviled eggs. Boil eggs and invite the children help peel the hard-boiled eggs. Show them how to slice the eggs and how to remove the yolks and smash them. Add sweet relish and mayonnaise and let the children help stuff the Humpty Dumpty Eggs. Serve for snack.

Ice Cream Clown Faces

Place a scoop of ice cream on a small plate. Have the children stick an ice cream cone on the scoop of ice cream like a hat. Provide chocolate chips for eyes, cherry halves for a nose, and vanilla wafers cut into moon-shapes for mouths.

Latkes
(electric skillet or stove required)

1 grated onion

1 teaspoon salt

1 egg

6 medium potatoes (washed, pared and grated)

3 tablespoons flour

½ teaspoon baking powder

Cooking oil

Mix the onion, salt, and egg with the potatoes. Add flour and baking powder. Drop by spoonfuls into a hot oiled frying pan (adults only). Brown on both sides. Drain on paper towels. Serve with applesauce.

Letter Pretzels
(oven or toaster oven required)

1 ½ sticks margarine, at room temperature

½ cups sugar

1 teaspoon vanilla

1 ¼ cups enriched all-purpose flour

2 tablespoons milk

Beat margarine and sugar until blended. Add the flour and milk. Chill. Divide dough into four parts. Divide each of the four parts into 8 pieces. Roll each piece into an 8" strand. Twist into a letter shape. Bake at 375° for 8–10 minutes.

Lumberjack Pancakes
(electric skillet or stove required)

1 ¼ cups sifted flour

1 ½ teaspoons baking powder

2 tablespoons sugar

¾ teaspoon salt

1 egg

1 ¼ cups milk

3 tablespoons oil

Maple syrup

Sift flour, baking powder, sugar and salt into a large mixing bowl. In a smaller bowl, beat the egg, and then add the milk and oil. Stir liquid into flour mixture until dry ingredients are wet. Cook on griddle or frying pan (adults only).

Mini Bagel Man

    4 mini bagels
    Soft cream cheese
    Wax paper
    Raisins or berries

Slice a bagel and spread both halves with soft cream cheese. Slice the remaining bagels. Place 3 halves on a piece of waxed paper for the body of bagel man. Cut the remaining bagel half into two pieces for arms. Add raisins to make the face. You can also use fresh or dried berries (raspberries, cranberries, and so forth) for facial features.

Miss Muffet's Curds and Whey (Cottage Cheese)

(stove required)
    1 quart milk
    2 tablespoons vinegar
    Salt
    Sour cream (optional)
    Fruit

Heat milk until bubbles begin to form (adults only). Remove from heat and stir in vinegar. Continue to stir while mixtures cools and curds form. Hold a strainer over a glass bowl and pour the mixture through to separate the curds from the liquid (whey). Gently press the curds with a wooden spoon to further squeeze whey. Add salt to taste and a little sour cream for smoothness. Serve with fresh fruit.

No-Cook Candy

Any of these candies can be given as a gift to parents. A plastic egg carton cut in half makes an excellent container when covered with clear plastic wrap

Candy Mints

    2 tablespoons margarine
    2 tablespoons shortening
    3 tablespoons warm water
    5 cups powdered sugar
    Food coloring and flavoring

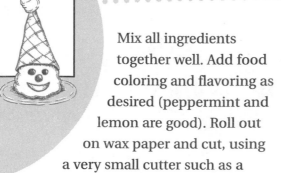

Mix all ingredients together well. Add food coloring and flavoring as desired (peppermint and lemon are good). Roll out on wax paper and cut, using a very small cutter such as a bottle cap.

Easy Fudge
2 cups powdered sugar
⅓ cup cocoa
½ cup peanut butter
3 tablespoons milk

Mix all ingredients together. Moisten hands and roll into balls. Keep refrigerated.

Serves 24.

Haystacks (stove or microwave required)
1 small package butterscotch chips
1 small package chocolate chips
1 can chow mien noodles

Combine butterscotch and chocolate chips in a saucepan. Melt over low heat or in a microwave. Stir in chow mien noodles. When cool enough to touch, shape into haystacks. Let set.

Makes 36 haystacks.

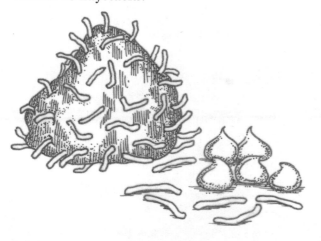

Pat-a-Mints
Oil of peppermint
1 egg
1 tablespoon milk
1 box powdered sugar

Break egg into bowl. Add 2 drops of oil of peppermint, 1 tablespoon of milk, 1 cup of powdered sugar. Mix this together. Add another ½ cup sugar and mix again. Keep adding sugar and mixing. When the mixture is too stiff to mix with a spoon, mix with your hands. When the dough is very stiff roll into small balls. Put on wax paper and pat down. Teach the children this rhyme to say as they pat the mints.

Pat-a-mint, Pat-a-mint
Baker's man–
Roll em', roll em', roll em'
Smash them with your hand.

Peanut Butter Balls
½ cup peanut butter
½ cup honey
1 cup nonfat powdered milk

Mix ingredients well. Squeeze and pull until shiny and soft. Roll into balls and chill before eating. Makes 24 balls.

Soda Cracker Candy Bars
Soda crackers
Peanut butter (crunchy is good)
Canned vanilla frosting

Spread crackers with peanut butter and top with frosting. Delicious. Tastes like a candy bar.

No-Cook Cookies

Chocolate Peanut Butter Oatmeal Cookies

⅓ cup butter
½ cup powdered sugar
¼ cup cocoa
1-½ cup oatmeal (uncooked)
3 teaspoons cold coffee

Blend butter, sugar, cocoa, and coffee. Add oatmeal. Roll into 1" balls and dust with powdered sugar.

Krispie Cookies

½ cup light corn syrup
½ cup peanut butter
3 cups Rice Krispies cereal

Mix all ingredients together and shape into balls. Moisten hands first to eliminate sticking. Makes 24 cookies.

No-Bake Fruit Cookies

½ cup raisins
½ cup chopped dates
2 tablespoon honey
12 graham crackers

Pour raisins, dates, and honey into mixing bowl. Put graham crackers in a resealable plastic bag and crush them with a rolling pin. Add crushed crackers to the other mixture until it's dry enough to roll into balls. Makes 24 balls.

Orange Ball Cookies

35 vanilla wafers
¼ cup orange juice
2 tablespoon sugar
Powdered sugar

Crush vanilla wafers. Add orange juice and sugar. Mix well. Roll into balls with moistened hands. Roll balls in powdered sugar. Makes 24 balls.

Peanut Butter Cookies (stove required)

1 cup Karo syrup (white)
1 cup sugar
12-ounce jar peanut butter
6 cups crushed frosted corn flakes

Combine sugar and syrup, boil until bubbly. Add peanut butter and blend. Stir in flakes. Drop by teaspoon onto wax paper. Cool.

Ocean Blue Ice Cream
(freezer required)

Allow a gallon of vanilla ice cream to soften. Stir in 2 teaspoons of blue cake icing coloring or 2 tablespoons of blue food coloring. Refreeze the ice cream.

One-Cup Salad

(refrigerator required)

1 cup diced bananas

1 cup fruit cocktail

1 cup miniature marshmallows

1 cup crushed pineapple

1 cup sour cream

Mix the ingredients and chill. Serve in small cups.

Makes about 36 servings.

Painted Cookies

(oven or toaster oven required)

2½ cups all-purpose flour

1 teaspoon baking soda

1 teaspoon cream of tartar

1 cup of margarine

1 ½ cups sifted powdered sugar

1 egg

¼ teaspoon orange extract

Sift dry ingredients together. Cream margarine and sugar in large mixing bowl. Stir in egg and extract. Blend in dry ingredients. Cover and chill 2-3 hours. Divide in half. Roll to ¼" thickness on a lightly floured board. Cut into shapes. Place on an ungreased cookie sheet. Decorate with Cookie Paint. Bake at 375° for 8–10 minutes. Makes about 3 dozen cookies.

Cookie Paint

Place small amounts of evaporated milk into separate custard cups. Tint the milk with food coloring. Paint on cookies with small brush.

Peanut Butter Playdough/Balls

(Check for allergies)

½ cup peanut butter

½ cup honey

1 cup nonfat powdered milk

Mix ingredients well. Squeeze and pull until shiny and soft.

Pigs in a Blanket

(oven or toaster oven)

Crescent dough

Small link sausages

Give each child a section of crescent dough and a small link sausage. Show the children how to roll the dough around the sausage. Bake in a toaster oven until brown.

Pita Faces

Pita bread

Tuna salad

Carrots

Celery

Cheese slices

Cream cheese, softened

Fruit and vegetable chunks

Cut off an edge at the end of pita bread. Open it to form a pocket. Fill the pocket with tuna or egg salad. Make a face on the front of the bread with cut-up fruits and vegetables using the cream cheese as the glue. Stick the carrots and celery in the salad to look like hair.

Pizza Faces

(oven or toaster oven required)

English muffins, ½ for each child
Pizza sauce
Grated cheese
Olives, pepperoni, and other toppings

Give each child half of an English muffin. Provide pizza sauce, grated cheese, olives, pepperoni, and other toppings that the children can use to make a face on their pizzas. Toast the pizza faces for 8 minutes in a toaster oven (adults only).

Pumpkin Custard

2 tablespoons pumpkin pie filling
1 tablespoon marshmallow crème
1 tablespoon whipped topping
Cinnamon

For each custard cup, mix together 2 tablespoons of pumpkin pie filling, 1 tablespoon of marshmallow crème, and 1 tablespoon of whipped topping. Sprinkle a little cinnamon on top.

Makes 1 serving.

Quick Breads

Recipe #1

(electric fry pan required)
2 cups sifted whole wheat pastry flour
3¾ teaspoons baking powder
1 teaspoon salt
⅓ cup oil
¾ cup milk

Allow the children to measure the dry ingredients. Gradually stir in the liquids and mix lightly. Place a small amount of flour on the tabletop and invite the children to knead and roll out dough about ¼" thick. Encourage the children to cut the dough into any desired size and shape. Cook in a lightly greased electric fry pan on low heat. Let the biscuits brown and rise. Turn and cook on the other side. Makes about 20 biscuits.

Recipe #2

(oven required)
3¾ cups whole wheat flour
¼ cup wheat germ
1 cup molasses
2 cups buttermilk or plain yogurt
2 teaspoons soda
Pinch of salt
Raisins and chopped dates (optional)

Preheat oven to 375°. Mix all ingredients together. Bake in one large or several small greased loaf pans for 30-40 minutes.

FOOD RECIPES

Rice Cake Bunnies

Miniature rice cakes
Raisins or currants
Sliced almonds
Thinly sliced carrots
Green grapes
Cream cheese

Encourage the children to spread cream cheese on a rice cake. Show them how to use almonds for ears, currants for eyes, vegetables for whiskers, and grape halves for tails.

Or let the children prepare their own animals.

Sea Foam Soda

Ocean Blue Ice Cream (see page X)
2-3 drops green food coloring
Lemon-lime beverage

Put a scoop of Ocean Blue Ice Cream into a clear plastic glass. Add two or three drops of green food coloring to your favorite lemon-lime beverage. Pour over the ice cream.

Shake-a-Pudding

1 tablespoon dry instant pudding
¼ cup milk

Pour into baby food jar and shake until thick.

Makes 1 serving.

Soup with a Face

½ cup of applesauce
½ cup of vanilla yogurt
Raisins

Stir applesauce and yogurt together. Cover the bottom of a bowl with this combination.

Use raisins on top for eyes and a mouth.

Sprouts

Alfalfa seeds, mung beans, or soybeans
Large glass jar
Cheesecloth

Soak approximately 1 teaspoon of alfalfa seeds or a small handful of soy or mung beans overnight in a jar of warm water. Drain. Cover the top of jar with cheesecloth and secure with a rubber band. Put the jar on its side in a dark place or inside an open paper bag. Rinse and drain well 3 times a day for 3 days. On the fourth day, place the jar in direct sunlight to develop chlorophyll. The sprouts will turn green. (Mung beans and soybeans will take 2 or 3 days longer to sprout.) Wash and serve with sandwiches or salads.

Sprout Salad

1 apple
2 small carrots
4 cups mixed sprouts (mung, soy, alfalfa)
½ cup sunflower seeds
½ cup raisins
½ cup plain yogurt
1 tablespoon honey
Juice of ½ lemon

Peel and core the apple. Shred both apple and carrots. Mix sprouts, carrots, apple, sunflower seeds, and raisins in a salad bowl. Mix yogurt, honey, and lemon juice together. Toss with salad. Serves 12.

Strawberry Yogurt

1 cup strawberries
⅓ cup powdered milk
1 cup yogurt

Mash strawberries. Stir in powdered milk and add yogurt. Makes 6 servings.

Stuffed Celery

(Check for allergies)

1 stalk celery
1 cup crunchy peanut butter

¼ cup coconut
½ cup Grape Nuts
¼ cup wheat germ
Dash nutmeg (optional)

Trim and wash celery. Combine remaining ingredients, mix well, and stuff the celery. Cut into bite-size pieces.

Serves 10–12.

Sunshine Sandwiches

(toaster or toaster oven required)

¼ cup undiluted frozen orange juice
½ cup peanut butter
8 slices of bread

Mix orange juice and peanut butter. Spread on toasted bread. Cut into small pieces.

Three Bears Porridge

(stove or microwave required)

Follow the directions on the package to have the children make instant oatmeal. Provide raisins and sunflower seeds for the children to add to their porridge if desired. Discuss the temperature of the oatmeal as they eat it. Is it cooler as they get to the bottom of their bowl?

Toasted Pumpkin Seeds

(oven or toaster oven required)

Wash the pumpkin seeds and dry them. Spread them on a cookie sheet and bake at 350° until brown.

Trail Mix

Recipe #1 (oven or toaster oven required)

½ cup margarine

1 envelope salad dressing mix

2 cups bite-size shredded wheat

2 cups pretzel sticks

2 cups salted peanuts

Mix margarine in a saucepan. Pour in dressing mix. Mix well. Measure the dry ingredients into a large baking pan. Pour margarine mixture over the dry ingredients in the baking pan. Stir with fork until all is coated. Bake at 300° for 30 minutes. Stir every 10 minutes.

Recipe #2

Pretzels

Peanuts

Rice Chex

Wheat Chex

Raisins

Miniature marshmallows

Place each item in separate bowl. Allow the children to serve themselves a teaspoon of each item and mix in a small paper cup or plastic bag.

Tuna Boats

Cut tuna fish sandwiches diagonally into quarter sections. Slice an apple into ¼" thick, round slices. Place a tuna sandwich quarter on the top of each apple slice, like a sail.

Tutti-Fruitti Ice Sparkle

(freezer required)

Mix one package of lime-flavored drink powder with ⅔ cup of sugar and 4 cups of water. Pour the mixture into ice trays. Do the same with one package each of orange and cherry drink powder. Chill until frozen. In tall, clear glasses, put one ice cube of each flavor. Then fill with chilled carbonated lemon-lime drink. Add half a slice of orange and serve. This looks great with a red-and-white striped straw.

Two-Tone Fruit Juice

Poor each child's glass half-full of concentrated Hawaiian Punch, and then fill it with orange juice. The Hawaiian Punch is thicker and will stay on the bottom, creating a two-toned effect.

Wagon Wheel Cookies
(oven or toaster oven required)

Give each child a small piece of refrigerator peanut butter cookie dough. Have them shape it into a circle and then use a craft stick to make indentations for the spokes of the wheel. Bake as directed on the package.

Walk-About Snacks

Apples (one per child)
Miniature marshmallows
Raisins
2 bananas
Grapes
Pecans (optional)

Core the apples and slice the banana. Place each ingredient in a bowl on the table, give each child an apple, and invite them stuff their apple with the ingredients of their choice.

Warm Fruit Punch
(stove required)

1 quart of apple cider
1 cup orange juice
½ cup lemon juice
½ cup pineapple juice
1 cinnamon stick
½ teaspoon ground cloves
1 teaspoon honey (optional)

Combine all ingredients in a pot. Heat thoroughly and simmer for a few minutes (adults only). Serve warm.

Watermelon on a Stick
(freezer required)

1 cup seedless watermelon pieces
1 cup orange juice
1 cup water
Paper cups
Craft sticks
Clear plastic wrap

Combine seedless watermelon pieces, orange juice, and water. Pour the mixture in small paper cups, and set them in the freezer. Insert craft sticks when the mixture is partially frozen. A piece of clear plastic wrap placed over the cup will hold the craft stick in place. Finish freezing.

Whale Spout Cupcakes

Cupcakes, one for each child
Licorice or cherry candy "laces"

Bake and ice cupcakes or purchase cupcakes. Purchase licorice or cherry candy "laces," and cut them into 4" lengths. Have the children decorate their own cupcakes by poking the candy laces into the center of the cupcakes to make a whale spout.

Yankee Doodle Punch

1 gallon pineapple sherbet
1 quart ginger ale
Strawberries or blueberries

Mix pineapple sherbet and ginger ale in a punch bowl. Add strawberries or blueberries.

Dances

Blue Bird, Blue Bird

Directions: Select one child to be the blue bird. Have the remaining children stand in a circle holding hands and then hold their hands up to make arches. Invite the blue bird to go in and out the circle by threading his or her way through the arches.

Blue bird, blue bird,
Fly through my window.
Blue bird, blue bird,
Fly through my window.
Blue bird, blue bird,
Fly through my window,
And buy molasses candy.

Chorus

Go through my window, my sugar lump,
(blue bird chooses another child to be
the new blue bird)
Go through my window, my sugar lump,
And buy molasses candy.

Blue bird, blue bird,
Fly through my window.
Blue bird, blue bird.
Fly through my window.
Blue bird, blue bird,
Fly through my window,
And buy molasses candy.

Continue until as many children as possible have had a turn to be the blue bird.

Theme Connections

Birds
Colors
Houses and Homes
Movement

Bunny Hop

Directions: Children stand in line with their hands on the waist of the child in front them. Everyone moves around the room to music, hopping in unison.

Theme Connections

Friends
Humor
Movement
Rabbits

The Chicken

You will need the music "The Chicken" for this dance.

Directions: Have the children stand in a circle. Hold hands overhead and open and shut fingers and thumbs on each hand as if demonstrating talking. Do this four times. Place hands under armpits and flap arms like a bird four times. Keep hands under armpits and shake bottom side to side for four counts. Clap four times. Join hands with the dancers on each side and move in a circle to the right for eight counts, then change direction and move to the left until the music indicates the dance moves are starting again.

Theme Connections

Chickens
Counting
Friends
Humor
Movement

Circle 'Round the Zero

Directions: Sing the song. IT walks around the circle until the line "Find your lovin' zero." Then IT stops and stands back-to-back with the nearest child. IT moves to the side and front as directed by the lyrics, then taps the chosen child's shoulder. That child is the next IT.

Circle 'round the zero.
Find your lovin' zero.
Back, back, zero.
Side, side, zero.
Front, front, zero.
Tap your lovin' zero.

Theme Connections

Friends
Numbers
Spatial Relationships

Dance, Thumbkin, Dance
(A Finger Dance)

Directions: Follow the directions indicated.

Dance, Thumbkin, dance: *(dance thumb around, moving and bending)*
Dance, ye merrymen, everyone. *(dance all fingers)*
For Thumbkin, he can dance alone,
Thumbkin he can dance alone.

Dance, Foreman, dance: *(dance index finger around, moving and bending)*
Dance, ye merrymen, everyone. *(dance all fingers)*
For Foreman, he can dance alone,
Foreman, he can dance alone.

Dance, Longman, dance: *(dance middle finger around, moving and bending)*
Dance, ye merrymen, everyone. *(dance all fingers)*

For Longman, he can
dance alone,
Longman, he can dance
alone.

Dance, Ringman, dance:
(dance ring finger
around—he won't bend alone)
Dance, ye merrymen, everyone. (dance all
fingers)
For Ringman, he cannot dance alone,
Ringman, he cannot dance alone.

Dance, Littleman, dance: (dance little finger
around, moving and bending)
Dance, ye merrymen, everyone. (dance all
fingers)
For Littleman, he can dance alone,
Littleman, he can dance alone.

Theme Connections

Movement
Parts of the Body

The Farmer in the Dell

Directions: Choose one child to be the
Farmer. Other children walk in a circle
around the Farmer. Sing the song together.

The farmer in the dell, the farmer in the dell.
Heigh-ho the derry-o, the farmer in the dell.

The farmer takes a wife/husband/friend.
(farmer brings a second child into the
circle)

The farmer takes a wife/husband/friend.
Heigh-ho the derry-o, the farmer takes a
wife/husband/friend.

The wife/husband/friend takes a child…
(wife chooses a third child to join in the
circle)
The child takes a dog…
The dog takes a cat…
The cat takes a rat. . .
The rat takes the cheese…

The cheese stands alone… (everyone except
Cheese leaves the center of the circle)

The Giant's Stomp

by Pam Schiller

Directions: Say the chant and do the actions.

Fee, Fi, Fo, Fum, growled the grumbling
giant. (stomp, stomp)
Fee, Fi, Fo, Fum, roared the restless giant.
(stomp, stomp)
Fee, Fi, Fo, Fum, grumbled the gigantic
giant. (stomp, stomp)
Fee, Fi, Fo, Fum! Fee, Fi, Fo, Fum! (stomp,
stomp)

I smell the feet of an Englishman! *(sniff, sniff) (Repeat 2 times.)*
Screamed the big, humongous giant. *(sniff, sniff)*

Be he here or be he there. *(shrug shoulders) (Repeat 2 times.)*
I'll find him anywhere! *(stomp, stomp)*

Theme Connections

Humor
Sounds of Language

Go In and Out the Windows

Directions: Have the children make a circle and hold hands over their heads to create arches. Follow the directions, as indicated.

Go in and out the windows. *(IT walks around circle, weaving in and out between children)*
Go in and out the windows,
Go in and out the windows,
As we have done before.

Stand and face your partner… *(IT chooses a partner)*
Now follow her/him to London… *(IT and partner weave through circle)*
Bow before you leave her/him… *(IT leaves partner [new IT] and joins circle)*

Theme Connections

Houses and Homes
Movement

Hansel and Gretel: A Dance of Opposites

by Pam Schiller

Directions: Have the children select a partner. Have one child take the part of Hansel in the chant and the other child take the role of Gretel.

Hansel takes two steps forward and turns around.
Gretel takes two steps backwards and touches the ground.
Hansel dances with his eyes closed ever so tight.
Gretel's eyes are open, keeping Hansel in her sight.
Hansel sticks his tongue out and wiggles it like this.
Gretel keeps her tongue in and blows Hansel a kiss.
Hansel dances his hands up to his nose.
Gretel dances hers down to touch her toes.
   (No, no, Gretel! Not up; down to your toes! That's right. Now you've got it.)
Hansel glides to the left and bows.
Gretel hops to the right and bows.
Hansel and Gretel twist down to the ground,
And then they twist back up and turn around.

DANCES

(No, no Hansel. Twist up, and then turn
around! That's right. Now you've got it!)
Hansel points his toe to the front, then back,
And then he does a jumping jack.
Come on, Gretel, you can do it.
Point your toe to the back, then front
Now do your own silly stunt.
Hansel and Gretel will happily dance the night thru
Because dancing is one of their favorite things to do.

Theme Connections

Friends
Movement
Opposites
Parts of the Body

Helicopter Ride

Directions: Teach the children the following rhyme and let them move like flying helicopters to any music with a moderate tempo.

Tip-toe up, tip-toe down. *(raise up on toes and then lower heels down)*
Start the motor and turn around. *(pretend to turn a key and then turn around)*
Spread your arms to the side *(spread arms)*
And twist and twist for a helicopter ride. *(twist side to side)*

Encourage the children to fly around the room.

Theme Connections

Parts of the Body
Transportation

Hokey Pokey

Directions: Suit actions to words.

You put your right hand in *(form a circle and act out the words)*
You take your right hand out.
You put your right hand in
And you shake it all about.
You do the Hokey Pokey *(hold hands in the air and shake them)*
And you turn yourself around.
That's what it's all about.

Repeat verses, using other body parts.

Theme Connections

Opposites
Parts of the Body

It's a Simple Dance to Do

Directions: Suit the actions to the words of the chant.

Come on and do a dance with me.
It's just a little step or two.
I'll teach you how.
We'll start right now.
It's a simple dance to do.

First you clap your hands. *(clap three times)*
Then stomp your feet. *(stomp three times)*
It's a simple dance to do.

Wait! I forgot to tell you
There's another little step or two:
Turn around *(turn around)*
And touch your toes. *(touch your toes)*
It's a simple dance to do.

Clap your hands, *(clap three times)*
Stomp your feet, *(stomp three times)*
Turn around *(turn around)*
And touch your toes. *(touch your toes)*
It's a simple dance to do

Wait! I forgot to tell you
There's another little step or two:
Pull your ears *(pull your ears)*
And flap your arms. *(flap your arms)*
It's a simple dance to do.

Clap your hands,
Stomp your feet,
Turn around
And touch your toes,
Pull your ears

And flap your arms.
It's a simple dance to do.

Wait I forgot to tell you
There's another step and then we're through
Stretch up high *(stretch up high)*
All fall down *(fall down)*
It's a simple dance to do.

Clap your hands,
Stomp your feet,
Turn around
And touch your toes,
Pull your ears
And flap your arms.
Now stretch up high,
All fall down
It's a simple dance to do.

Theme Connections

Movement
Opposites
Parts of the Body

Jim Along Josie

Directions: This is a simple dance/song that is based on an old minstrel song. In some versions, Josie appears to the dance itself. Suit the actions to the words.

Hey Jim along, Jim along Josie, *(children stand in a circle and clap their hands while they sing)*
Hey Jim along, Jim along Jo.

Hey Jim along, Jim along Josie,
Hey Jim along, Jim along Jo.

Walk Jim along, Jim along Josie, *(children*
walk in a circle, singing and clapping)
Walk Jim along, Jim along Jo. *(Repeat)*

Hop Jim along, Jim along Josie, *(children hop*
around in a circle)
Hop Jim along, Jim along Jo. *(Repeat)*

Jump Jim along, Jim along Josie, *(children*
jump around in a circle)
Jump Jim along, Jim along Josie. *(Repeat)*

Hold my mule while I dance Josie, *(children*
make up their own unique dance)
Hold my mule while I dance Josie.

Other actions: tiptoe, crawl, swing, and roll.

Variations

"Hey Jim along" is also sung "Hey get along,"
"Hi come along," "Hey jam along," "Come-a-
get along," and "Come-a-high, Jim along."

Theme Connection

Movement

The Macarena

Directions: Play the song "The Macarena."
Model the following movements for the
children to follow.

Put your right arm straight out in front of
you, palm down.
Put your left arm straight out in front of you,
palm down.
Put your right arm straight out in front of
you, palm up.
Put your left arm straight out in front of you,
palm up.
Grasps the inside of the left arm with right
hand at the elbow.
Grasps the inside of the right arm with left
hand at the elbow.
Place the right hand behind the right side of
the back of the neck.
Place left hand behind the left side of the
back of the neck.
Place right hand on the left front pants
pocket.
Place left hand on the right front pants
pocket.
Place right hand on the right back pants
pocket.

Place left hand on the left back pants pocket.
Move your bottom to the left.
Move your bottom to the right.
Move your bottom to the left.
Clap hands and turn 90 degrees to the right.

Repeat

The Mulberry Bush

Directions: Have the children form a circle. Improvise the actions in each verse to match the words of the song.

Here we go 'round the mulberry bush, *(hold hands and walk in circle)*
The mulberry bush, the mulberry bush.
Here we go 'round the mulberry bush
So early in the morning.

This is the way we wash our clothes, *(suit actions to words)*
Wash our clothes, wash our clothes.
This is the way we wash our clothes
So early Monday morning.

This is the way we iron our clothes…
Tuesday morning.
This is the way we scrub the floors…
Wednesday morning.
This is the way we sew our clothes…
Thursday morning.
This is the way we sweep the house…

Friday morning.
This is the way we bake our bread…
Saturday morning.
This is the way we go to church…
Sunday morning.

Musical Freeze

Directions: Invite the children to dance or move in a circle while a favorite song plays. When you stop the music, they stop moving. When you start the music again, they start moving.

Naranja dulce

Directions: Children form two parallel lines facing each other. They walk toward the center and bow to their partners standing opposite them. Then they walk back to their original lines. They walk to the center once again and hug their partners. Then they walk back to their original lines and wave good-bye to their partners.

Naranja Dulce
Naranja dulce. Limón partido
dame un abrazo que yo te pido.
Si fuera falso tu juramento,
en un momento te olvidaré.

DANCES

Toca la marcha, mi pecho llora,
adiós señora, que ya me voy.
Si acaso muero en la batalla,
tened cuidado de no llorar.
Porque su llanto puede ser tanto
que hasta pudiera resucitar.

English Translation

Sweet Orange
Sweet orange, sliced lemon,
Give me a hug, not a persimmon.
Tell me the truth; I won't forget you
But if you leave me, I'll cry for you.
I see you leaving, so I am crying.
Goodbye my friend, we now are smiling.
If I don't see you for some time
I will remember you in my mind.
Sweet orange, sliced lemon
Give me a hug, not a persimmon.

Theme Connections

Colors
Emotions
Food

Old Brass Wagon

Directions: This is an old American folk dance. Have the children form a circle and join hands. Follow the directions indicated below.

Circle to the left, the old brass wagon
> *(children circle around to the left)*

Circle to the left, the old brass wagon
Circle to the left, the old brass wagon
You're the one, my darling. *(children shake the hand of the child to their left)*

Circle to the right, the old brass wagon
> *(children circle around to the right)*
Circle to the right, the old brass wagon
Circle to the right, the old brass wagon
You're the one, my darling. *(children shake the hand of the child to their right)*

Everyone in the old brass wagon,
> *(children continue holding hands and walk into the middle of the circle)*
Everyone in the old brass wagon,
> *(children bow to the center of the circle)*
Everyone in the old brass wagon,
> *(children raise their joined hands)*
You're the one, my darling. *(children hug child to their left)*

Everybody out of the old brass wagon,
> *(children hold hands and move back out to original circle)*
Everybody out of the old brass wagon,
> *(children bow toward center)*
Everybody out of the old brass wagon,
> *(children drop hands and turn around)*
You're the one, my darling. *(children hug child to their right)*

Old Joe Clarke/ Round and Round

Directions: Old Joe Clarke is a well-known square-dance tune. This song lends itself to free rhythmic play and improvisation. The dancing can be fast or slow, the children can jump, hop, walk on tip-toes, or do any other appropriate movements.

Round and round, old Joe Clarke,
Round and round, I say,
Round and round, old Joe Clarke,
I haven't got long to stay.

Old Joe Clarke he had a house,
Sixteen stories high,
Ev'ry story in that house
Was full of chicken pie.

Rock-a-rock, old Joe Clarke,
Rock-a-rock, I'm gone;
Rock-a-rock, old Joe Clarke,
And goodbye, Susan Brown.

I went down to old Joe's house
Never been there before,
He slept on the feather bed
And I slept on the floor.

Fly around, old Joe Clarke,
Fly around, I'm gone;

Fly around, old Joe Clarke,
With the golden slippers on.

Old Joe Clark he had a dog
As blind as he could be,
Chased a redbug 'round a stump
And a coon up a hollow tree.

Row around, old Joe Clarke,
Sail away and gone;
Row around, old Joe Clarke,
With golden slippers on.

If you see that girl of mine
Tell her if you can
Before she goes to make up bread
To wash those dirty hands.

Roll, roll, old Joe Clarke,
Roll, roll, I say;
Roll, roll, old Joe Clarke,
You'd better be getting' away.

When I was a little boy
I used to play in ashes
Now I am a great big boy
Wearing Dad's mustaches.

Variation

Children have always been fond of turning around and around until they are dizzy, then falling down. Try letting them turn to this refrain.

Round and round and round, I turn,
Round and round, I say,
Round and round and round I turn

And . . . now fall down!
(spoken)
And . . . now get up again!
And . . .

Round and round, old Joe
Clarke,
Round and round the other way,
Round and round, old Joe Clarke,
I ain't got long to stay.

Other verses:
Hop on one foot, Old Joe Clarke…
Fly like a bird, Old Joe Clarke…
Wiggle like a snake, Old Joe Clarke…
Play the fiddle, Old Joe Clarke…

Theme Connections

Friends
Houses and Homes
Humor
Movement

Put Your Little Foot

Directions: Have children select a partner and then get into a circle. Have partners hold hands across the front of their bodies—left hand to left hand and right hand to right hand. Instruct the children to step to the right on the first two lines of the song and then step to the right and point their right toe on the third line of the song. Repeat these steps for the next three lines of the song. During the second verse, the children take three steps and then turn under each other's arms and then repeat. On the last verse the children repeat the steps of the first verse, only moving left instead of right.

Put your little foot
Put your little foot,
Put your little foot right there.
Put your little foot,
Put your little foot,
Put your little foot right there.

Walk and walk and walk
And walk and turn.
Walk and walk and walk
And walk and turn.

Theme Connections

Friends
Movement
Parts of the Body

Sally the Camel

Directions: Children stand in a circle. One each line they rock back and forth. On the line that says, "So ride, Sally, ride" the children wiggle hips, bumping the hips of the children on each side.

Sally the camel has five humps *(rock back and forth on heels and toes and hold up 5 fingers)*
Sally the camel has five humps *(repeat movement)*
Sally the camel has five humps *(repeat movement)*
So ride Sally, ride. *(wiggle down to the floor and then back up again)*
Boom, boom, boom, boom. *(wiggle hips bumping the hips of the child on the left and their right)*

Repeat, count down to no humps. End the song with:
"Sally is a horse, of course!" *(hold hands out to side as if not surprised)*

Theme Connections

Camels   Movement
Counting   Numbers
Horses

Scarf Dancing

Give the children colorful scarves and encourage them to dance freely to several different tempos of music. Try some classical, popular, bluegrass, and polka music. Ask the children to describe how their movements change with the different types of music.

Theme Connections

Colors
Music

Shape Dancing

Cut out circles, squares, rectangles, and triangles from construction paper and laminate them. Use masking tape to make a large circle, square, rectangle, and triangle on the floor. Give the children a shape cutout and ask them to find the corresponding shape on the floor. Play music and have the children march around the shape outlines they are standing on. After a while, stop the music and have the children exchange their shape cutouts. Repeat the activity.

Theme Connections

Movement
Shapes

Shoo, Fly!

Directions: Have the children form a circle. Follow directions indicated.

Shoo, fly, don't bother me, *(walk in a circle to   the left)*
Shoo, fly, don't bother me, *(walk in a circle to the right)*
Shoo, fly, don't bother me, *(walk in a circle to the left)*
For I don't want to play. *(place hands on hips and shake head no)*

Flies in the buttermilk *(walk around shooing flies)*
Shoo, fly, shoo.
Flies in the buttermilk
Shoo, fly, shoo.
Flies in the buttermilk
Shoo, fly, shoo,
Please just go away. *(place hands on hips and shake head no)*

Shoo, fly, don't bother me, *(walk to the left in a circle)*
Shoo, fly, don't bother me. *(walk to the right in a circle)*

Shoo, fly, don't bother me, *(walk to the left in a circle)*
Come back another day. *(wave good-bye)*

Theme Connections

Insects
Movement

Skip to My Lou

Directions: "Skip to My Lou" can be played in many ways. The following is one of the simplest: The children form a circle with a child in the center. The children in the circle clap and sing (words below) while the child in the center skips around. At the refrain "Lou, Lou," the child in the center chooses a child from the circle to skip with him or her. At the end of the refrain the first child returns to the circle and the second child repeats the game pattern while a new verse is sung.

The phrase "skip to my Lou" has numerous variants, such as "skip to ma lou," "skip to my lula," "skip come a lou," "shoo li loo," and "shoo la lay."

Lou, Lou, skip-to my Lou,
Lou, Lou, skip-to my Lou,
Lou, Lou, skip-to my Lou,
Skip-to my Lou, my darlin'.
Or

Skip, skip, skip to my Lou,
Skip, skip, skip to my Lou,
Skip, skip, skip to my Lou,
Skip to my Lou, my darlin'.

Flies in the buttermilk, shoo, fly, shoo
Flies in the buttermilk, shoo, fly, shoo

Flies in the buttermilk, shoo, fly, shoo
Skip to my Lou, my darlin'.

Chorus

Lost my partner, what'll I do?
Lost my partner, what'll I do?
Lost my partner, what'll I do?
Skip to my Lou, my darlin.'

Chorus

Additional Verses
  I'll get another one prettier than you…
  Skip a little faster, that won't do…
  Going to Texas, come along too…
  Catch that red bird, skip-a to my Lou…
  If you can't get a red bird, take a blue…
  If you can't get a blue bird, black bird'll do….

  There's a little red wagon, paint it blue…

Verses about animals
  Pig in the parlor, what'll I do? …
  Cat in the buttermilk, lapping up cream…
  Rats in the bread tray, how they chew…
  Chickens in the garden, shoo shoo shoo…
  Rabbit in the cornfield, big as a mule…
  Cow in the kitchen, moo cow moo…
  Hogs in the potato patch, rooting up corn…

Verses about going to market
  Going to market two by two…
  Dad's old hat and Mama's old shoe…
  Back from market, what did you do?…
  Had a glass of buttermilk, one and two…

Theme Connections

Friends
Movement

Sock Skating

Invite the children to remove their shoes and "skate" on a hard-surface floor in their socks. Play some ice skating music and challenge the children to create a skating dance. **Safety Warning:** Make sure the floor isn't too slippery.

Theme Connections

Movement
Seasons
Weather

Square Dance

Have the children choose a partner. Arrange them in a square. You may want to make a masking tape square on the floor for the children to use. Invite them to follow these simple steps:

Bow to your partner. *(bow)*
Swing your partner. *(lock arms and spin around twice)*
Do-si-do. *(fold arms across chest and "back" around your partner)*
Promenade. *(partners hold hands, right and left hands together and walk around the square)*

Theme Connections

Friends
Movement
Shapes

Streamer Dancing

Cut 2' streamers from red, blue, yellow, and green crepe paper. Place 12" strips of red, yellow, blue, and green plastic tape and place them on the floor. Give each child a streamer. Play music and encourage the

children to dance with their streamers. When the music stops, have the children move to the line of tape that is the same color as their streamer. Start the music and let the children mingle again. Next time the music stops, let the children exchange streamers with a friend. Repeat the activity.

Theme Connections

Colors
Movement

Streamer Dancing
(Snake Along)

Cut 2' streamers from brown and green crepe paper. Have the children wiggle their streamers like a snake as they dance creatively to some "snaky music" such as Charlie Pride's, "The Snakes Crawl at Night" (on *The Best of Charlie Pride*) or "Boa Constrictor" by Peter, Paul, and Mary (on *Peter, Paul, and Mommy*).

Theme Connections

Movement
Snakes

The Stroll

Have the children stand in two parallel lines facing each other. Show them how to step first to the right and dip and pause and then to the left with a dip and a pause. Instruct the two children at the head of the line to stroll through the parallel lines. They can do any step they would like as they pass through the middle. Play "The Stroll" or any similar type of music.

If the children are able to handle a more complicated step, they can step to the right then to the right again with their left foot going behind, and then repeat this step to the left. This is called the vine step.

Theme Connections

Movement

The Swim

Have the children step side-to-side and forward and backward while moving their arms as if swimming. Play almost any rock music from the 1960s and this dance will be perfect.

Theme Connections

> Humor
> Movement
> Oceans and Seas

Thelma Thumb

Directions: Move thumb as directed.

Thelma Thumb is up and Thelma Thumb is down.

Thelma Thumb is dancing all around the town.

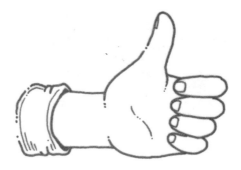

Dance her on your shoulders, dance her on your head.

Dance her on your knees and tuck her into bed.

Name other fingers (Phillip Pointer, Terry Tall, Richie Ring, Baby Finger, and Finger Family) *and dance them on other body parts.*

Theme Connections

> Movement
> Parts of the Body

The Twist

Have the children stand with their feet shoulder width apart and twist their hips. Show them how to twist their arms in the opposite direction. Play "The Twist" by Chubby Checker for a real twisting party.

Theme Connections

> Humor
> Movement

Tooty-Ta

Directions: Chant the words and suit actions to words.

Tooty ta, Tooty ta, Tooty ta, ta.
Thumbs up!
Tooty ta, Tooty ta, Tooty ta, ta.
Elbows back!
Tooty ta, Tooty ta, Tooty ta, ta.
Feet apart!
Tooty ta, Tooty ta, Tooty ta, ta.
Knees together!
Tooty ta, Tooty ta, Tooty ta, ta.
Lean forward!
Tooty ta, Tooty ta, Tooty ta, ta.
Tongue out!
Tooty ta, Tooty ta, Tooty ta, ta.
Eyes shut!
Tooty ta, Tooty ta, Tooty ta, ta.
Turn around!

Theme Connections

Movement
Parts of the Body

Top Hat Tappers

Invite children to tape a washer to the bottom of their shoes and tap on a cement or hard floor. Provide top hats for the full effect.

Theme Connections

Movement

Turn, Cinnamon, Turn

Directions: Ask the children to stand in a circle. Select one child to start the dance. Follow directions as indicated.

All up and down, my honey, *(the appointed child walks around the outside of the circle clapping and singing the song)*
All up and down we go.
All up and down, my honey,
All up and down we go

That lady's a rockin' her sugar lump, *(child selects a partner to be the "sugar lump")*
That lady's a rockin' her sugar lump. *(partners face each other, hold hands, and swing arms back and forth.)*
That lady's a rockin' her sugar lump, *(partners continue swinging their arms)*
Oh, turn, Cinnamon, turn. *(partners turn under each other's arms)*

Partners continue to hold hands and walk around in a circle. Sing the song again, but this time the "sugar lump" chooses a new partner and repeats the dance. The teacher also chooses a new partner and repeats the dance.

Repeat the song until all the children are dancing.

Theme Connections

Movement
Opposites

Waggle Dance

Tell the children that bees do the Waggle Dance to communicate with each other. The direction they fly when they return to the hive lets the other bees know where pollen has been located. Bees also will circle around an area where food has been located. They wiggle their bottoms and circle the area. This is the Waggle Dance we will do.

Directions: Place a flower or a replica of a flower on the floor. Invite the children to spread their wings (arms) and circle the flower while wiggling their bottoms. After a few minutes, change the location of the flower and invite the "bees" (children) to follow. Music adds to the fun.

Theme Connections

Insects
Movement
Nature

Walk Along, John

Directions: Sing or chant the following words. Have the children form two parallel lines. Make up a verse about one of the children at the head of the line and have him or her pass through the lines as you say the chant.

Come on, boys, and hush your talking,
  (children chant the words as they stand in two parallel lines)
All join hands and let's go walking.

Chorus
Walk along, John, with your blue shirt on,
  (John strolls through the parallel lines)
Walk along, John, with your blue shirt on.

Come on, Bill, and hush your talking,
  (children chant the words as they stand in two parallel lines)
Let's join hands and go a-walking,

Walk along, Bill, with your blue pants on,
  (Bill walks through the parallel lines)
Walk along, Bill, with your blue pants on.

Other verse suggestions
Walk *(or come)* along, Judy, with one shoe on,
Walk along, Janet, with your hair falling down,
Walk along, Mike, with your dad's old hat,

Theme Connections

Clothing
Movement

DANCES

Where, Oh, Where Is Pretty Little Susie?

Directions: Have the children form two parallel lines facing each other. Follow directions as indicated.

Where, oh, where is pretty little Susie? *(children sway side to side as front two children walk through the center of the lines)*
Where, oh, where is pretty little Susie?
Where, oh, where is pretty little Susie?
Way down yonder in the paw paw patch. *(point finger off to distance and shake it)*

Come on, friends, let's go find her, *(Have the children skip toward the front of the line, take the hand of the child across from them and skip through the center of the lines and back up to form parallel lines again)*
Come on, friends, let's go find her,
Come on, friends, let's go find her,
'Way down yonder in the paw paw patch.

Theme Connection

Friends
Movement

Whose Dog Art Thou?

Directions: Have the children stand in a circle facing a partner. Follow directions indicated.

Bow, wow, wow. *(face a partner and stomp 3 times)*
Whose dog art thou? *(point index finger on left and right hand at partner)*
Little Tommy Tucker's dog. *(hold hands out to side)*
Bow, wow, wow. *(face partner and stomp 3 times)*

Theme Connections

Dogs
Movement

Appendix

Dog and Bone Match Game

Dog and Bone Match Game

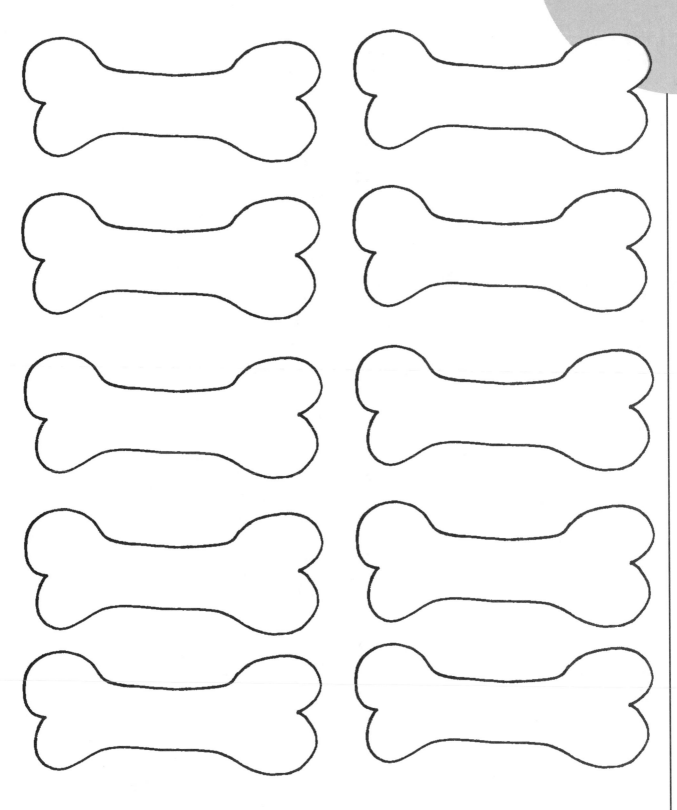

Elephant and Peanut Match Game

Elephant and Peanut Match Game

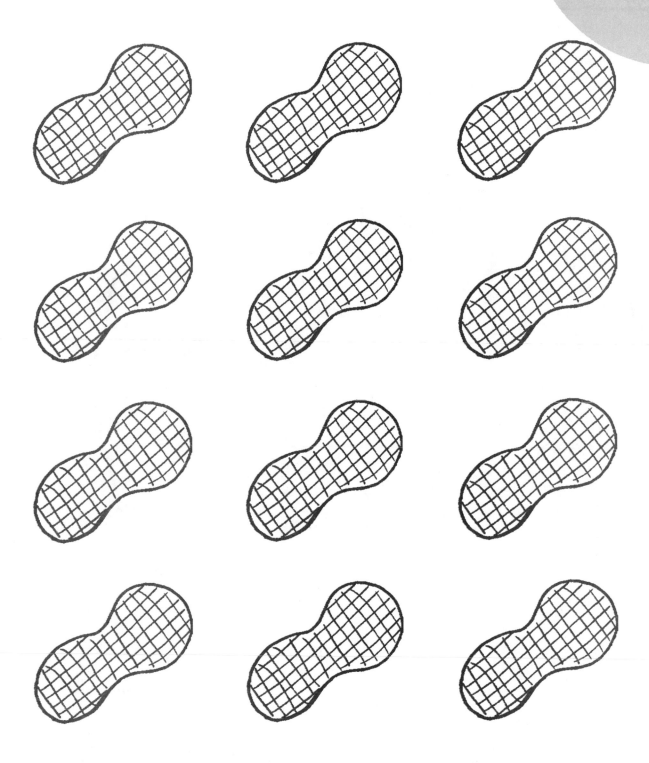

The Complete Book of Activities, Games, Stories, Props, Recipes, and Dances

ACTIVITY PATTERNS

Peter Piper

Peter Piper

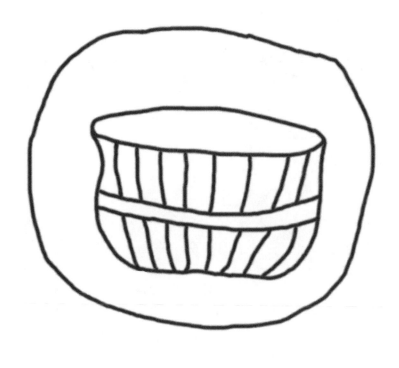

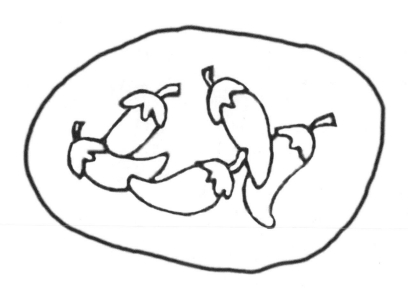

APPENDIX

ACTIVITY PATTERNS

Scavenger Hunt List

The Bun

The Complete Book of Activities, Games, Stories, Props, Recipes, and Dances

STORY PATTERNS: FLANNEL BOARD

The Bun

The Bun

The Complete Book of Activities, Games, Stories, Props, Recipes, and Dances

The Bun

The Bun

The Complete Book of Activities, Games, Stories, Props, Recipes, and Dances

Caps for Sale

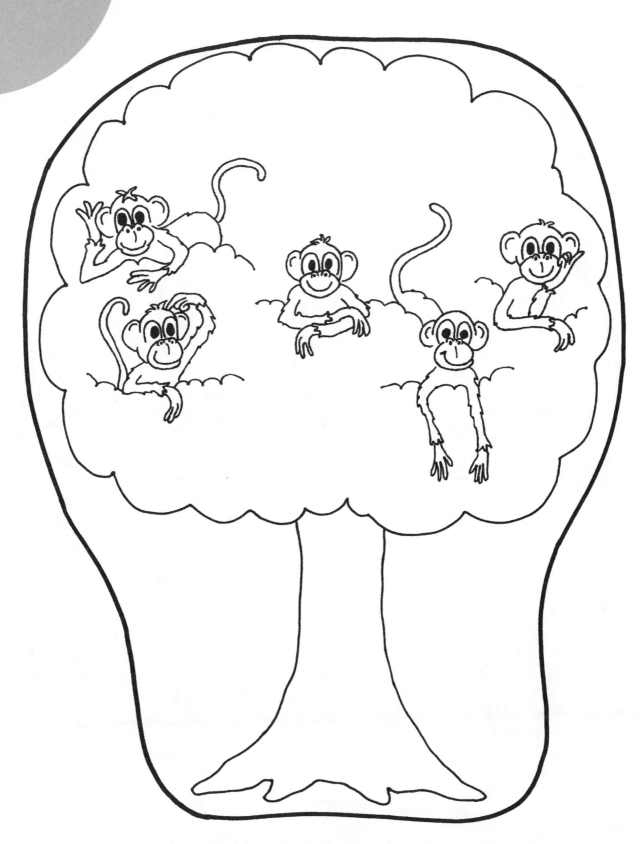

Caps for Sale

The Complete Book of Activities, Games, Stories, Props, Recipes, and Dances

STORY PATTERNS: FLANNEL BOARD

The Color Song

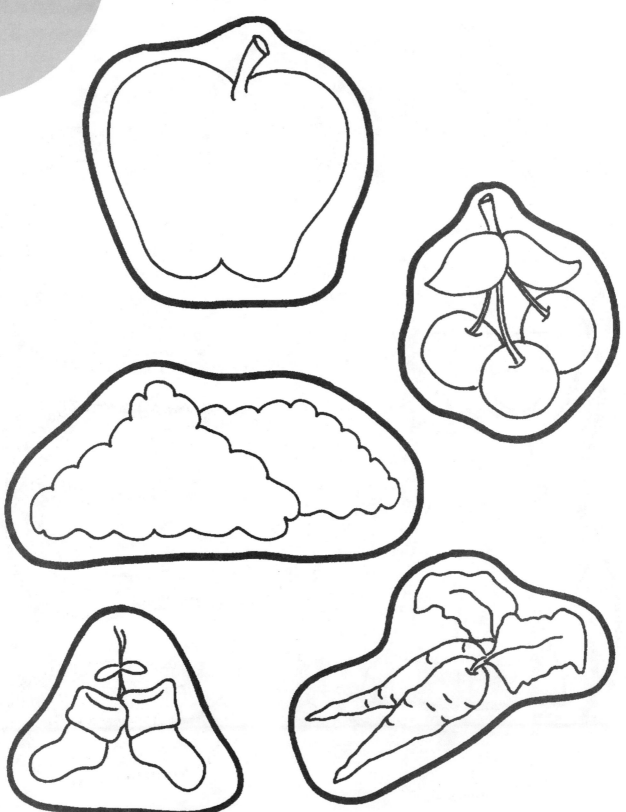

The Color Song

The Complete Book of Activities, Games, Stories, Props, Recipes, and Dances

STORY PATTERNS: FLANNEL BOARD

The Color Song

The Color Song

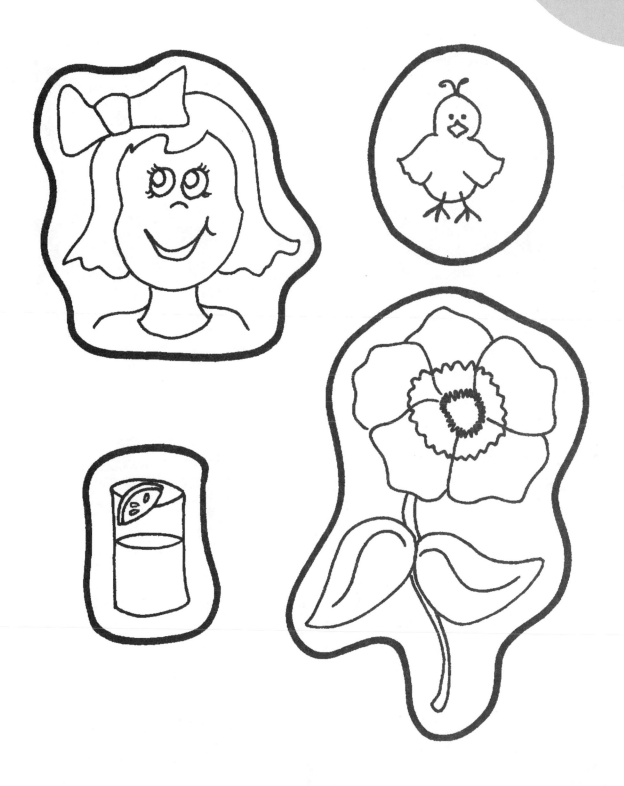

APPENDIX

STORY PATTERNS: FLANNEL BOARD

Dress-Me Dolls: Mark and Melissa

Basic Story

Dress-Me Dolls: Mark and Melissa
Basic Story

The Complete Book of Activities, Games, Stories, Props, Recipes, and Dances

Dress-Me Dolls: Mark and Melissa

Basic Story

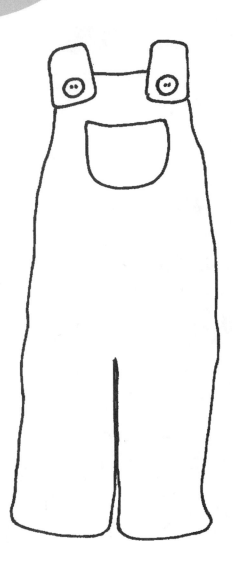

Dress-Me Dolls: Fall

STORY PATTERNS: FLANNEL BOARD

Dress-Me Dolls: Fall

Dress-Me Dolls: Fall

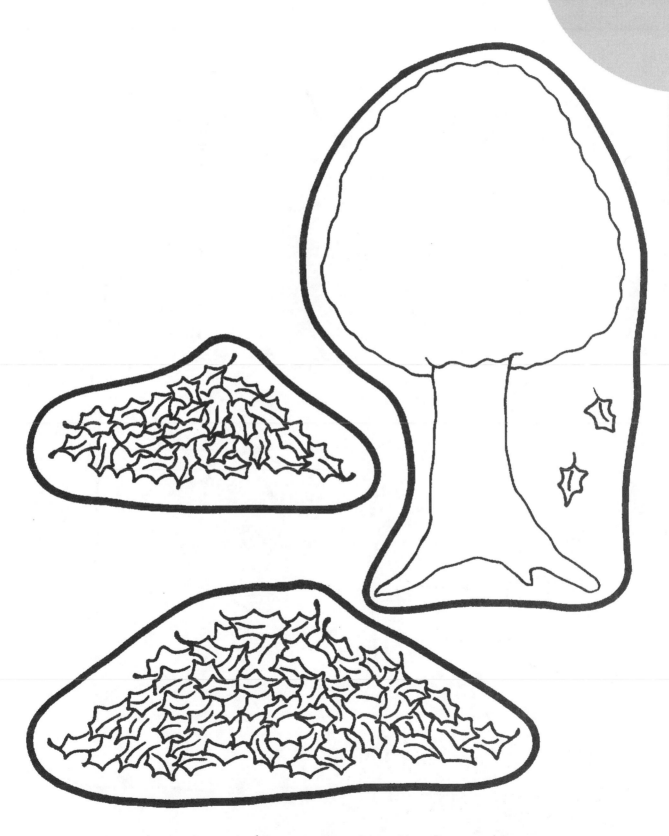

The Complete Book of Activities, Games, Stories, Props, Recipes, and Dances

Dress-Me Dolls: Winter

Dress-Me Dolls: Winter

Dress-Me Dolls: Winter

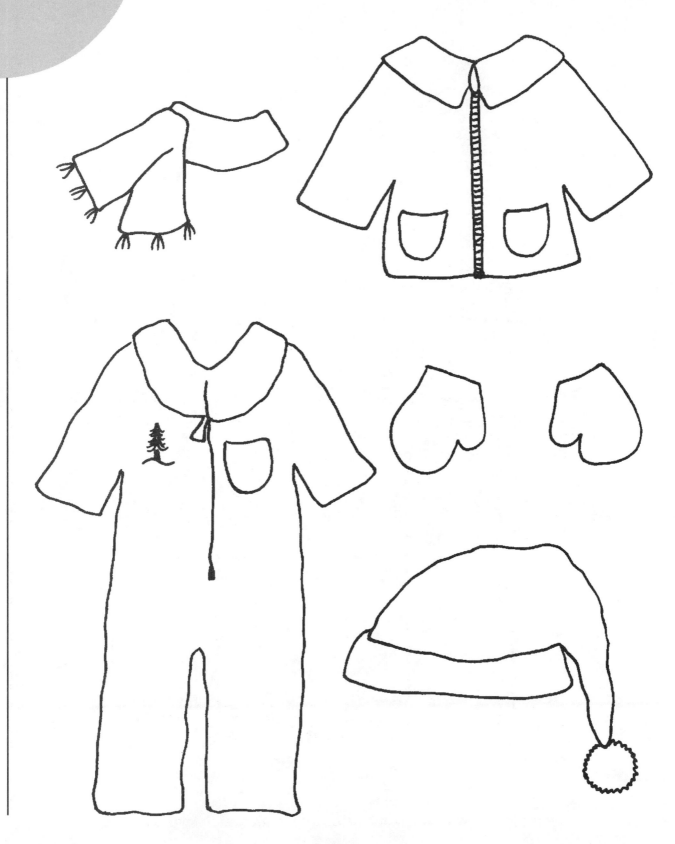

Dress-Me Dolls: Winter

The Complete Book of Activities, Games, Stories, Props, Recipes, and Dances

STORY PATTERNS: FLANNEL BOARD

Dress-Me Dolls: Spring

Dress-Me Dolls: Spring

The Complete Book of Activities, Games, Stories, Props, Recipes, and Dances

STORY PATTERNS: FLANNEL BOARD

Dress-Me Dolls: Spring

Dress-Me Dolls: Summer

The Complete Book of Activities, Games, Stories, Props, Recipes, and Dances

APPENDIX

STORY PATTERNS: FLANNEL BOARD

Dress-Me Dolls: Summer

The Elf and the Dormouse

The Elf and the Dormouse

The Elf and the Dormouse

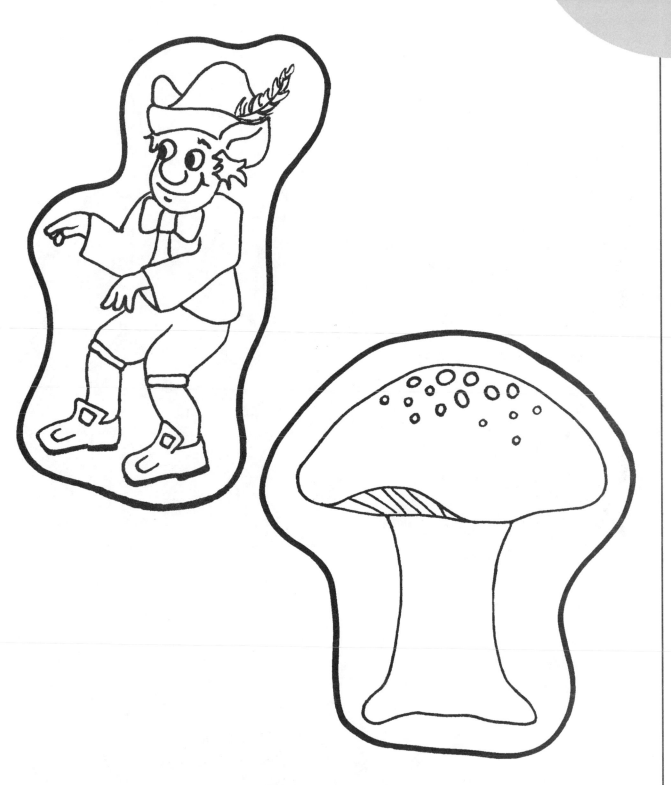

STORY PATTERNS: FLANNEL BOARD

The Elves and the Shoemaker

The Elves and the Shoemaker

The Complete Book of Activities, Games, Stories, Props, Recipes, and Dances

STORY PATTERNS: FLANNEL BOARD

The Elves and the Shoemaker

The Elves and the Shoemaker

The Elves and the Shoemaker

The Elves and the Shoemaker

The Complete Book of Activities, Games, Stories, Props, Recipes, and Dances

STORY PATTERNS: FLANNEL BOARD

Fat Cat: A Danish Folktale

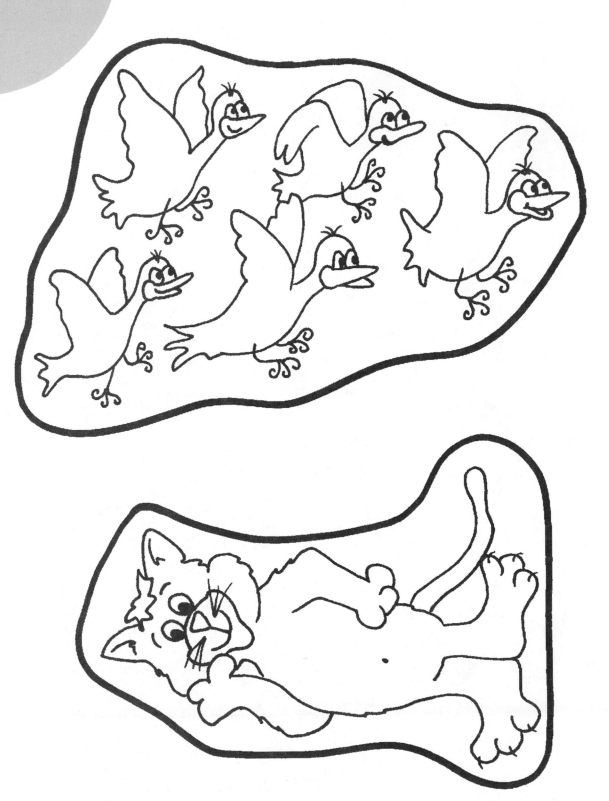

Fat Cat: A Danish Folktale

APPENDIX

STORY PATTERNS: FLANNEL BOARD

Fat Cat: A Danish Folktale

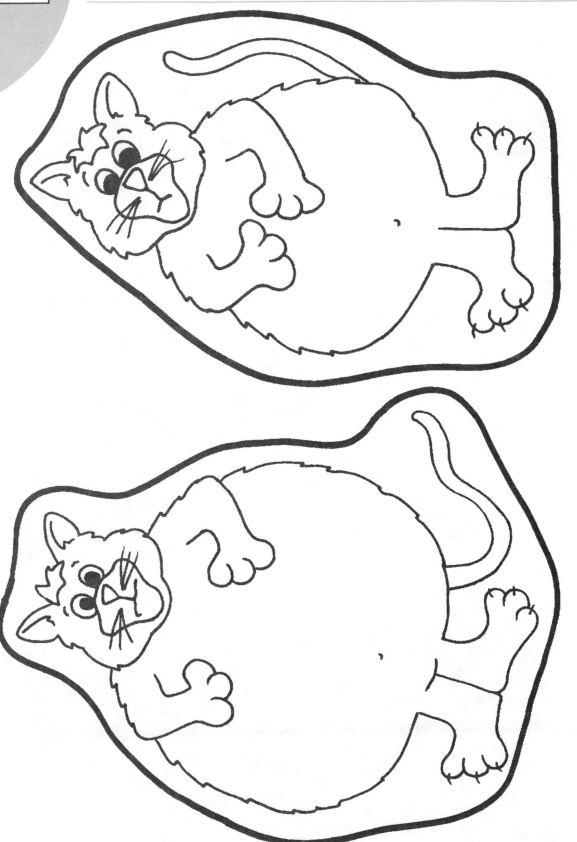

Fat Cat: A Danish Folktale

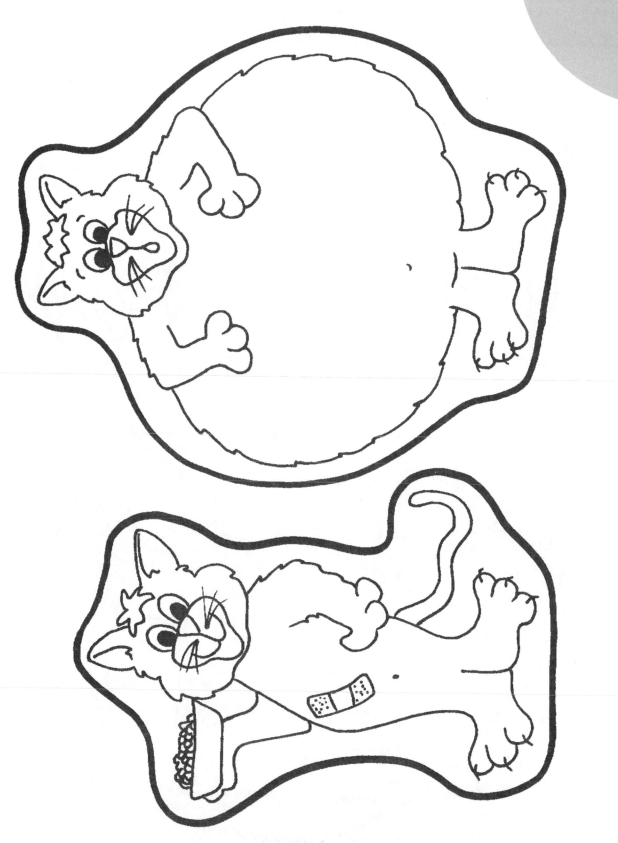

The Complete Book of Activities, Games, Stories, Props, Recipes, and Dances

Fat Cat: A Danish Folktale

Fat Cat: A Danish Folktale

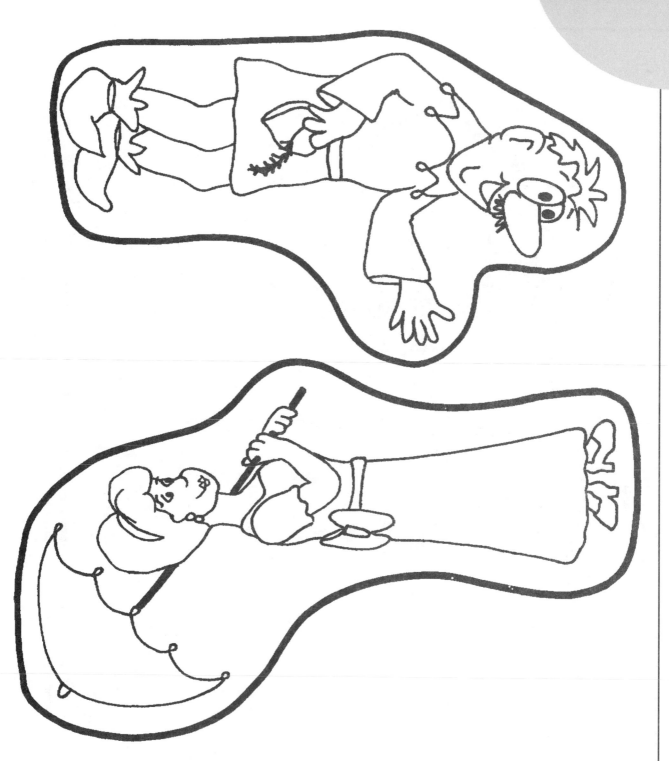

The Complete Book of Activities, Games, Stories, Props, Recipes, and Dances

Fat Cat: A Danish Folktale

STORY PATTERNS: FLANNEL BOARD

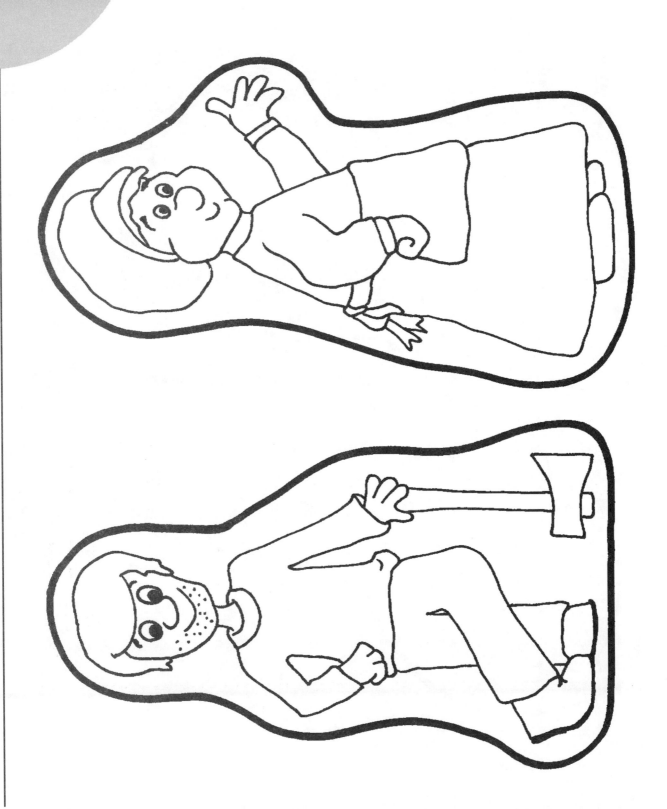

Fat Cat: A Danish Folktale

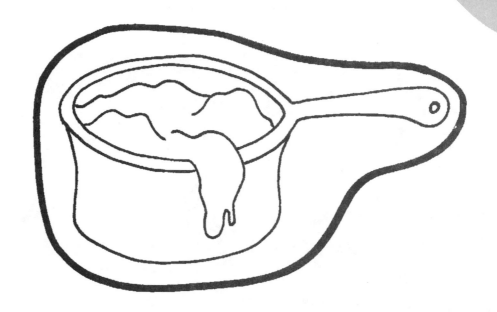

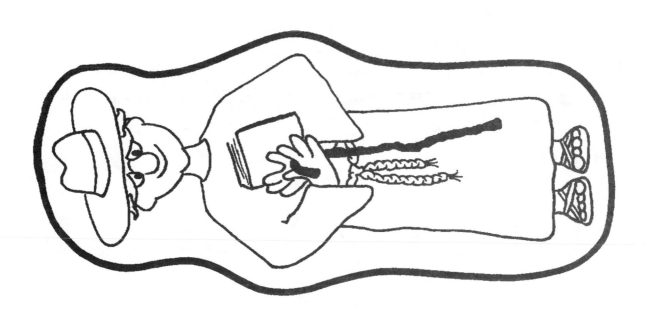

The Complete Book of Activities, Games, Stories, Props, Recipes, and Dances

STORY PATTERNS: FLANNEL BOARD

Five Little Chickadees

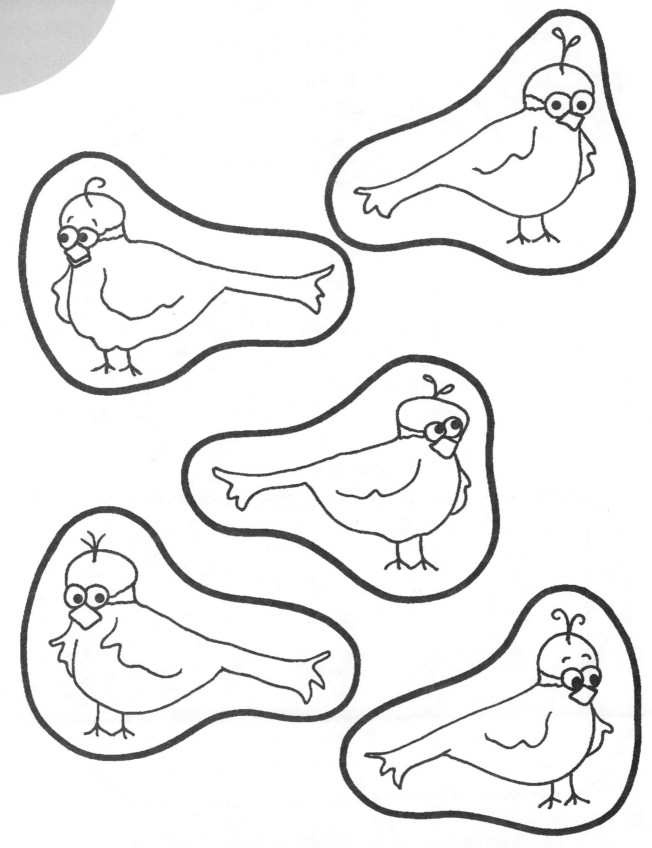

Five Little Chickadees

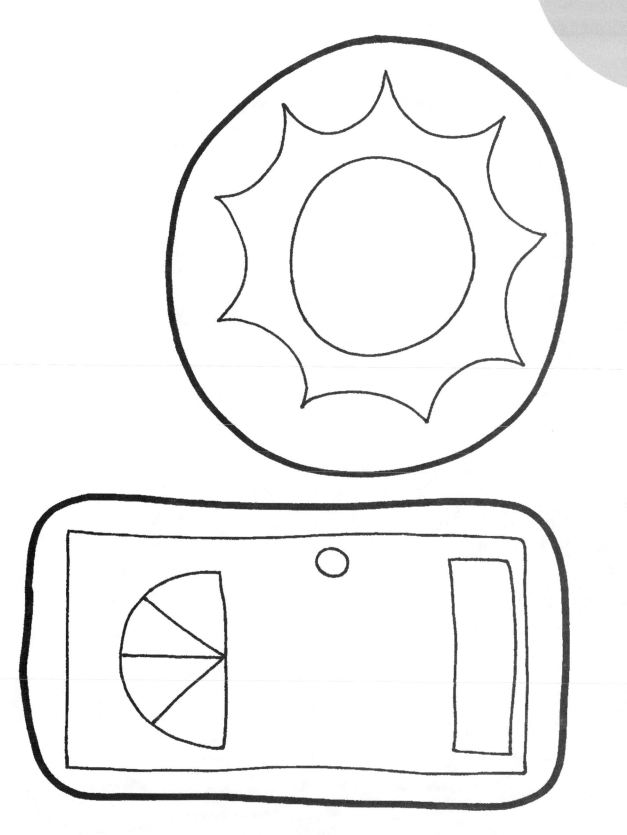

The Complete Book of Activities, Games, Stories, Props, Recipes, and Dances

Five Little Chickadees

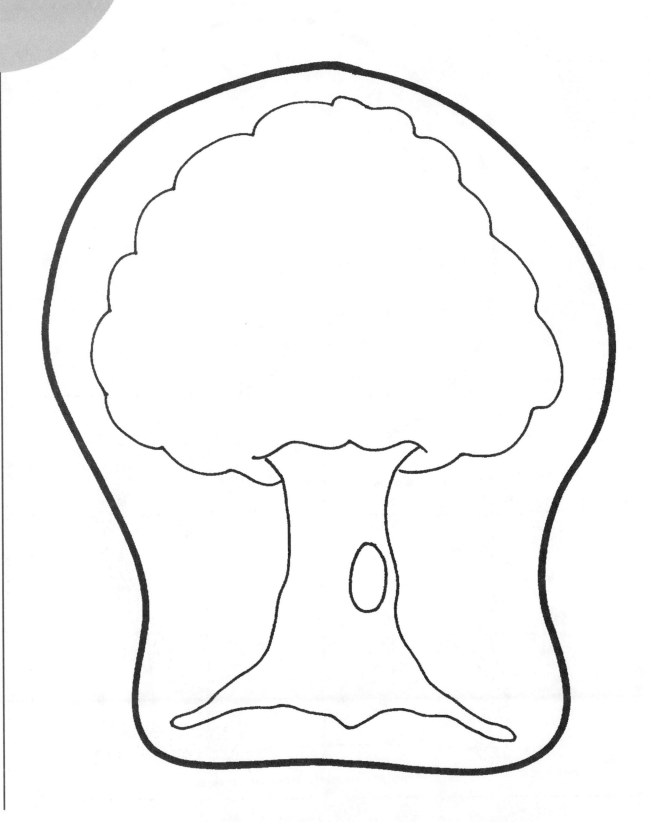

Five Little Chickadees

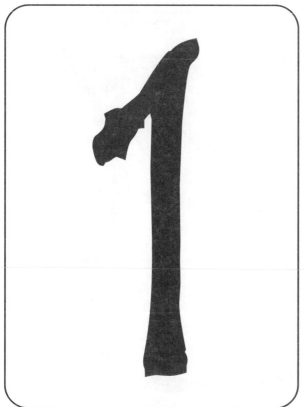

Five Little Chickadees

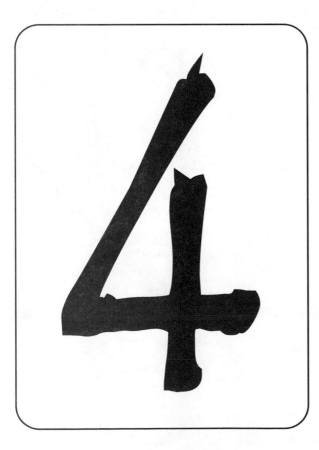

Frosty the Snowman

Stop

Frosty the Snowman

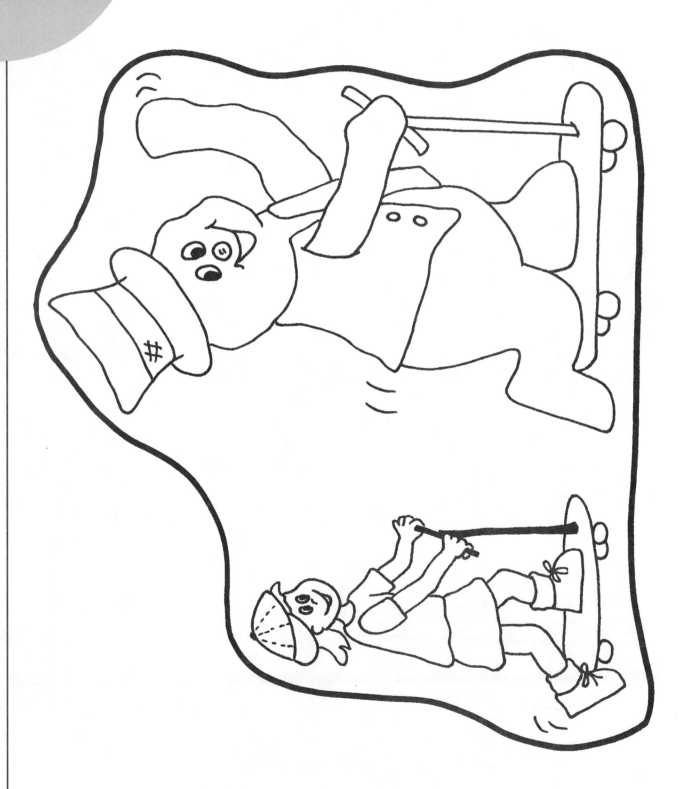

Frosty the Snowman

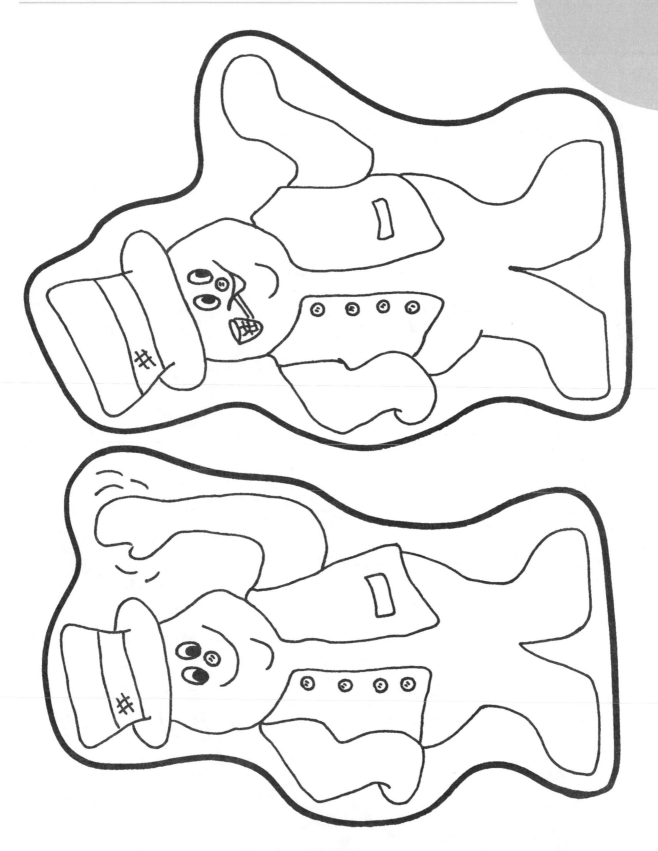

The Complete Book of Activities, Games, Stories, Props, Recipes, and Dances

The Gingerbread Man

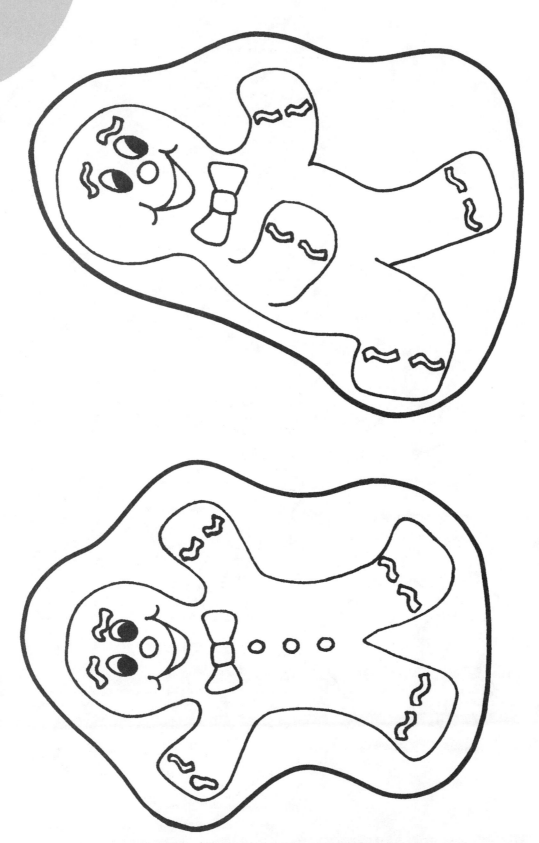

The Gingerbread Man

The Complete Book of Activities, Games, Stories, Props, Recipes, and Dances

The Gingerbread Man

STORY PATTERNS: FLANNEL BOARD

The Gingerbread Man

The Complete Book of Activities, Games, Stories, Props, Recipes, and Dances

The Gingerbread Man

Goldilocks and the Three Bears
Goldilocks y los Tres Osos

The Complete Book of Activities, Games, Stories, Props, Recipes, and Dances

Goldilocks and the Three Bears
Goldilocks y los Tres Osos

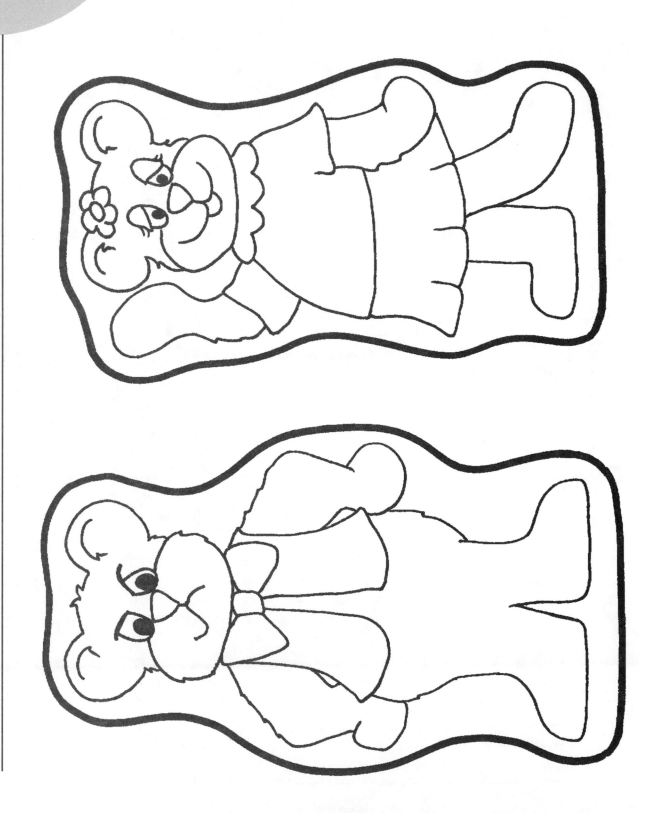

Goldilocks and the Three Bears
Goldilocks y los Tres Osos

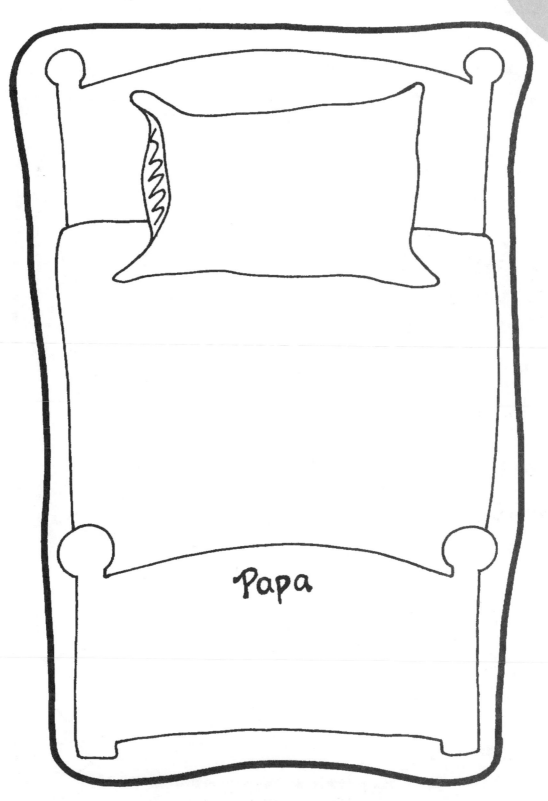

Papa

The Complete Book of Activities, Games, Stories, Props, Recipes, and Dances

Goldilocks and the Three Bears
Goldilocks y los Tres Osos

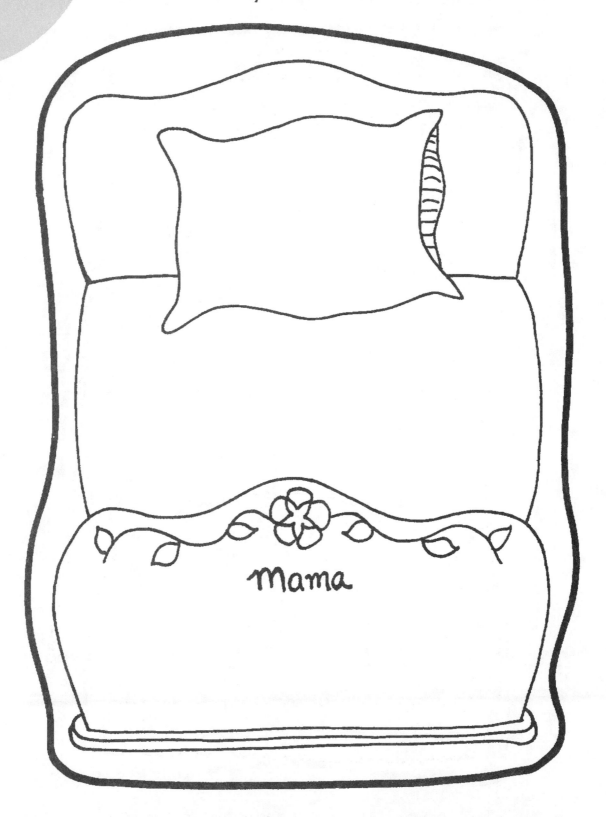

Mama

Goldilocks and the Three Bears
Goldilocks y los Tres Osos

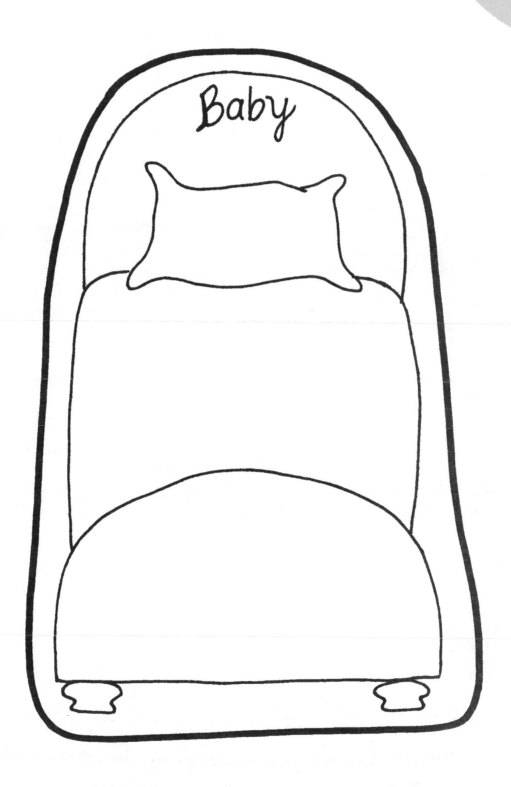

The Complete Book of Activities, Games, Stories, Props, Recipes, and Dances

STORY PATTERNS: FLANNEL BOARD

Goldilocks and the Three Bears
Goldilocks y los Tres Osos

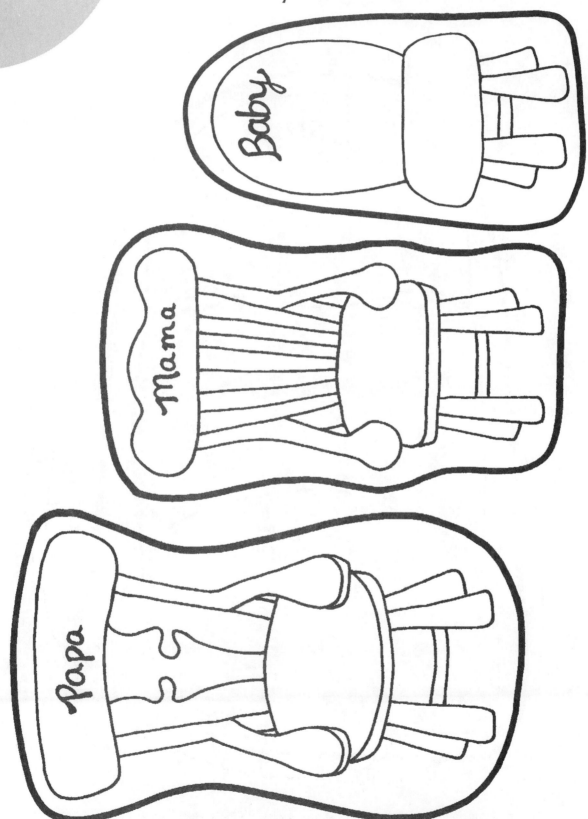

The Great Big Pumpkin

The Complete Book of Activities, Games, Stories, Props, Recipes, and Dances

The Great Big Pumpkin

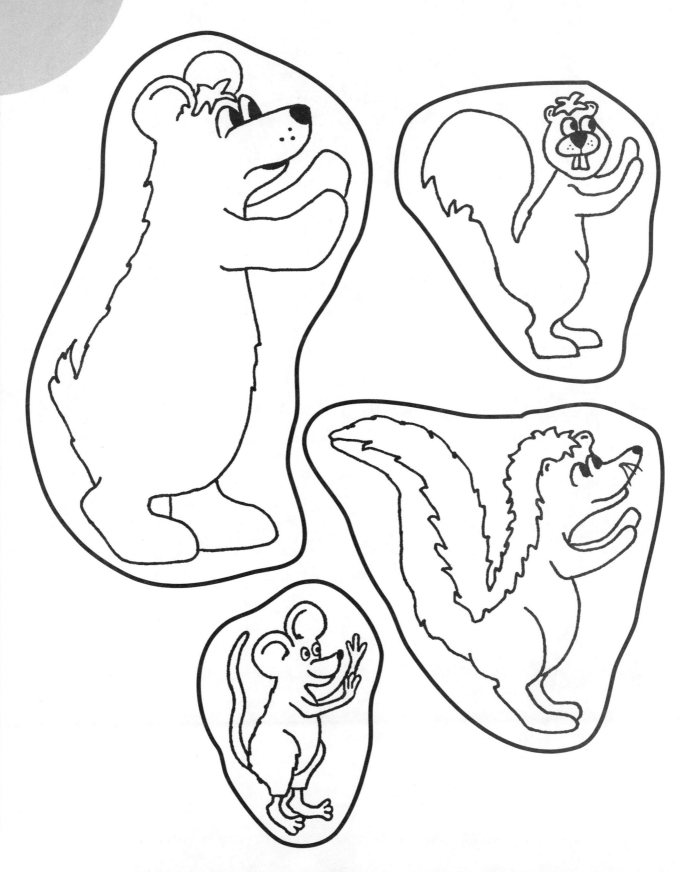

The Great Big Turnip

Also use patterns on pages 374 and 314.

The Gunny Wolf

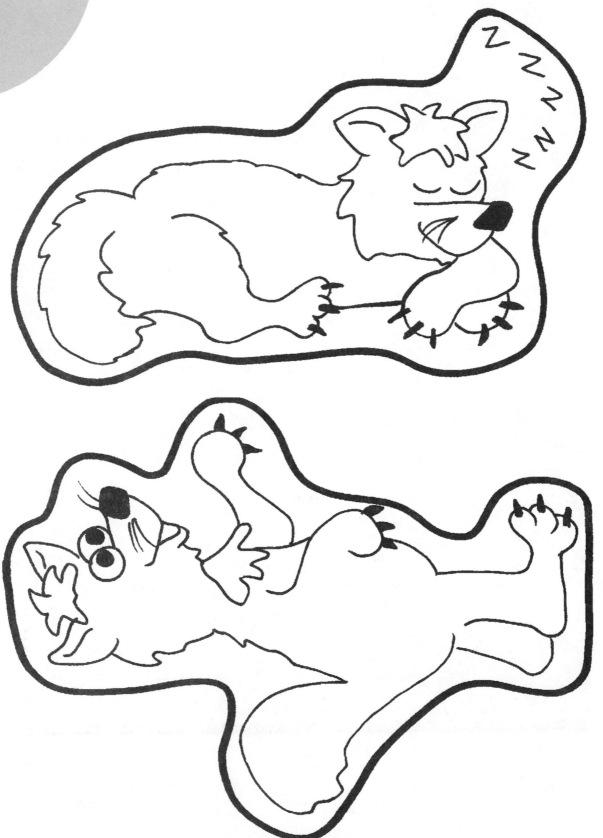

The Gunny Wolf

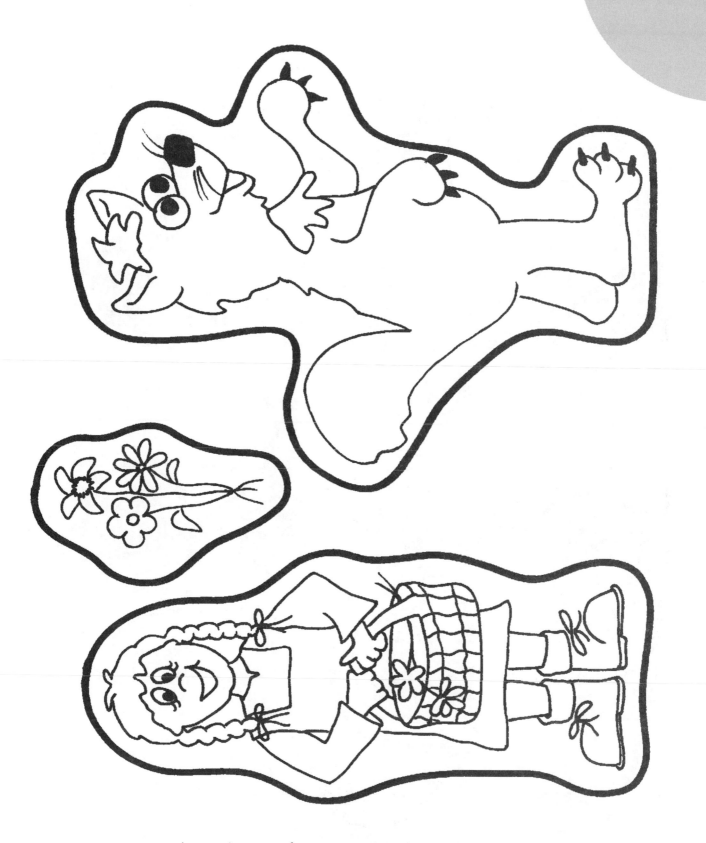

STORY PATTERNS: FLANNEL BOARD

Henny-Penny

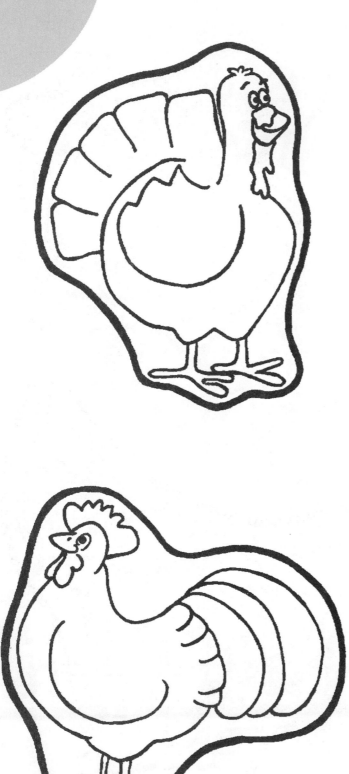

Henny-Penny

I Like Black

I Like Black

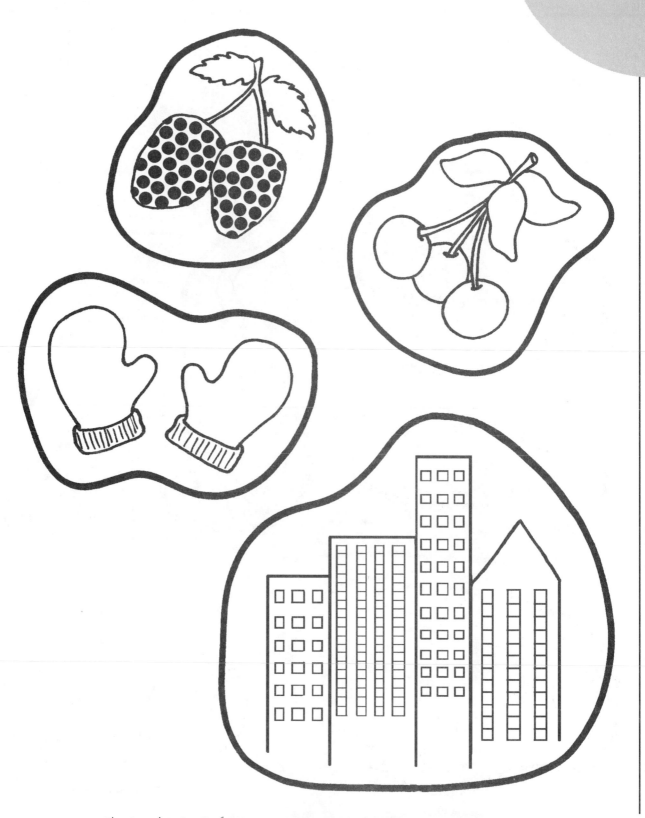

The Complete Book of Activities, Games, Stories, Props, Recipes, and Dances

STORY PATTERNS: FLANNEL BOARD

I Like Blue

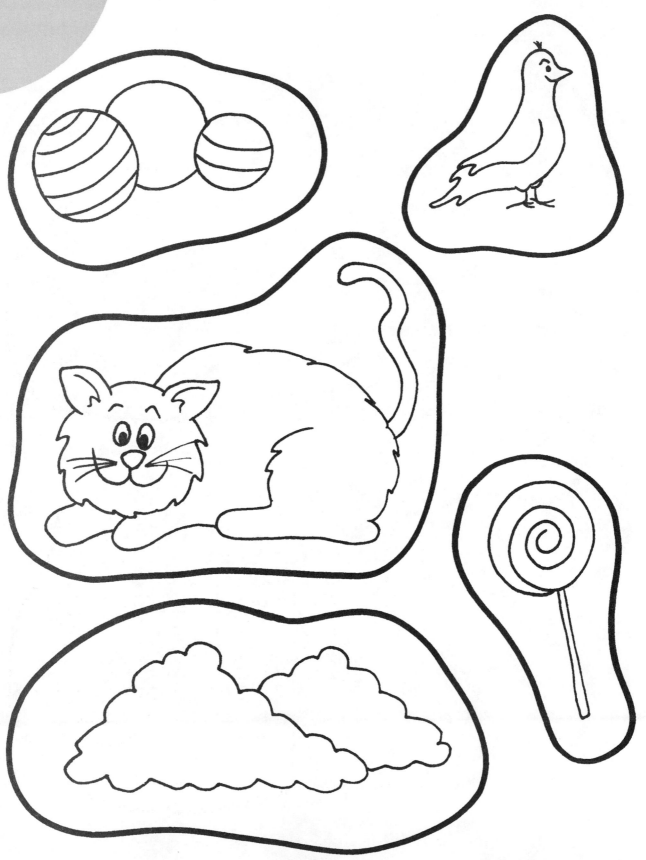

I Like Blue

The Complete Book of Activities, Games, Stories, Props, Recipes, and Dances

STORY PATTERNS: FLANNEL BOARD

I Like Blue

Lotion

I Like Green

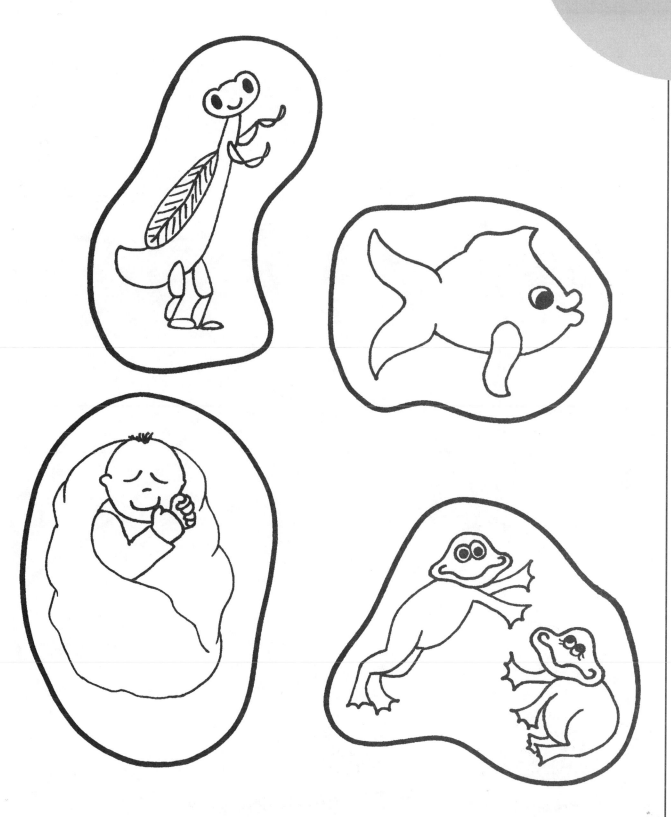

The Complete Book of Activities, Games, Stories, Props, Recipes, and Dances

I Like Green

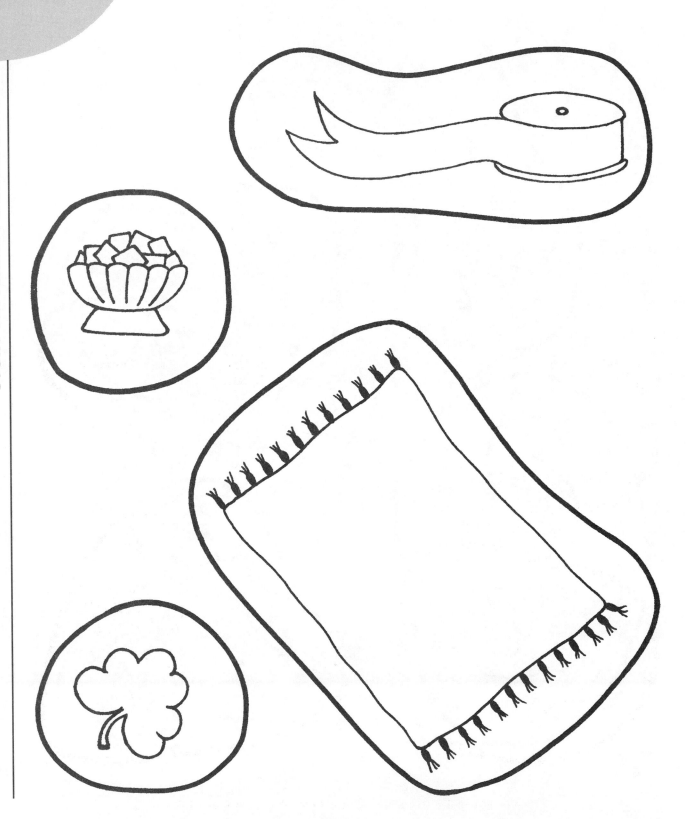

I Like Orange

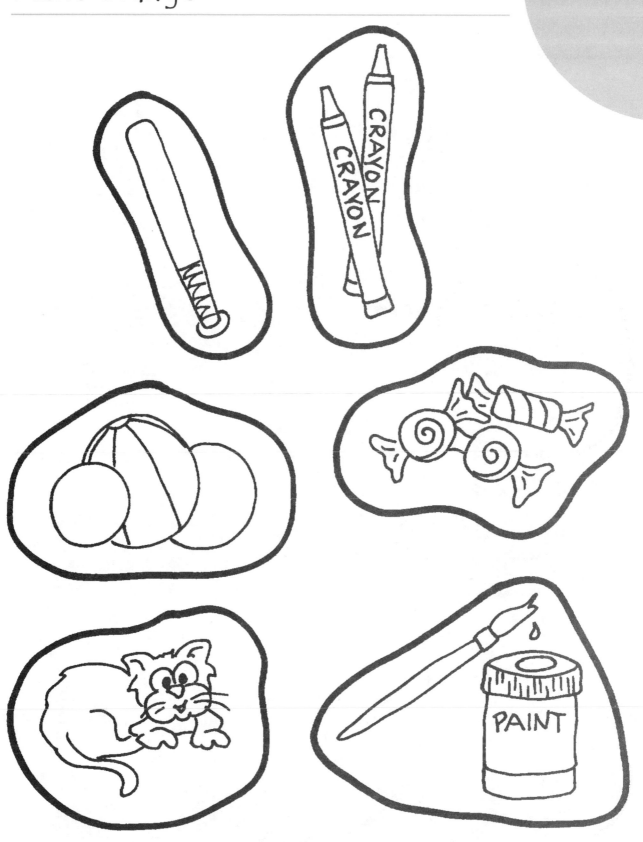

The Complete Book of Activities, Games, Stories, Props, Recipes, and Dances

I Like Purple

I Like Purple

INK

The Complete Book of Activities, Games, Stories, Props, Recipes, and Dances

I Like Purple

STORY PATTERNS: FLANNEL BOARD

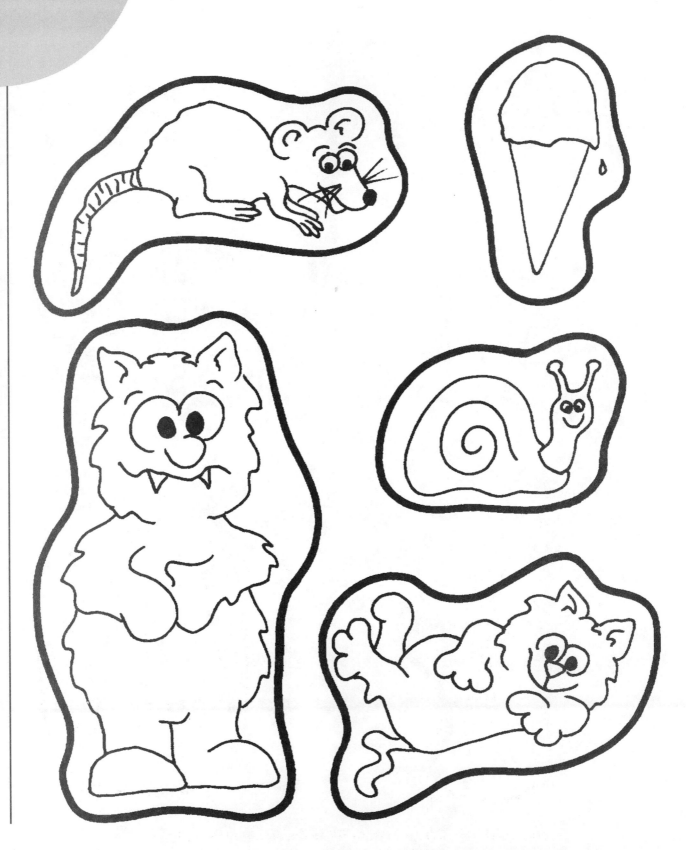

I Like Red

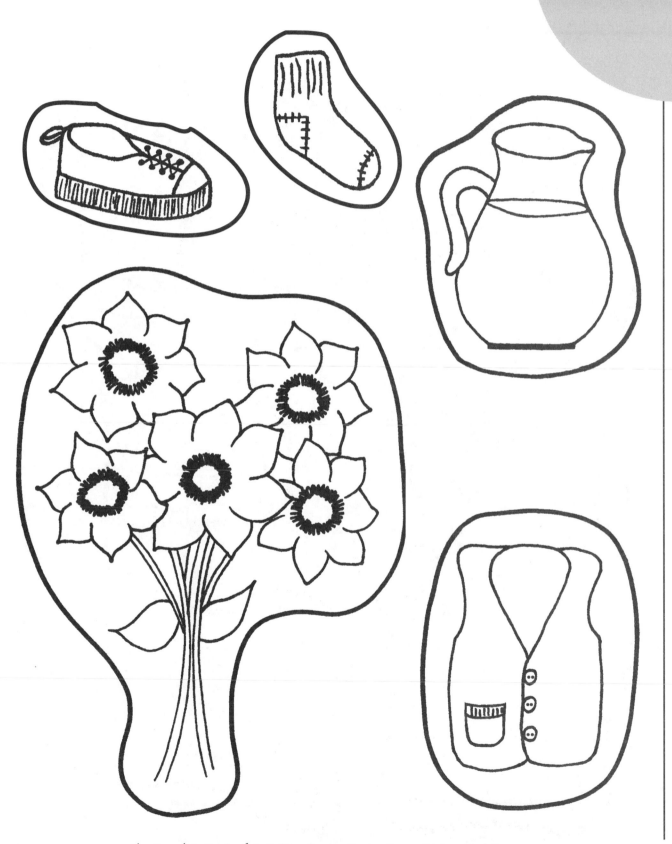

The Complete Book of Activities, Games, Stories, Props, Recipes, and Dances

STORY PATTERNS: FLANNEL BOARD

I Like Red

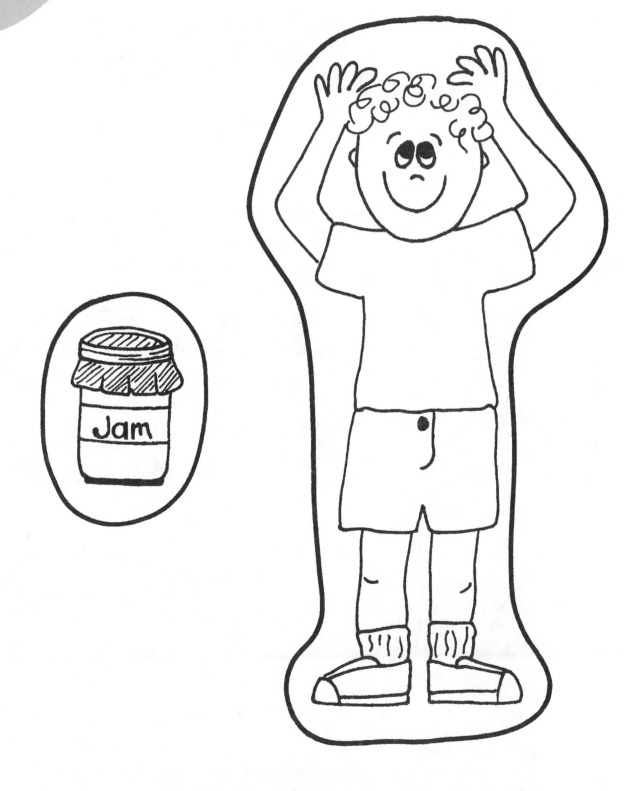

I Like White

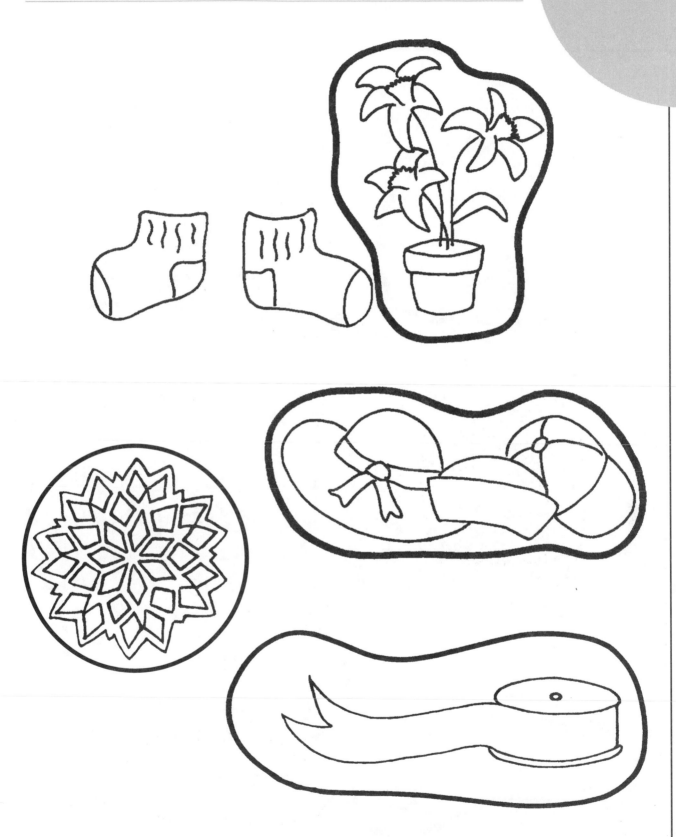

The Complete Book of Activities, Games, Stories, Props, Recipes, and Dances

APPENDIX

STORY PATTERNS: FLANNEL BOARD

I Like White

I Like White

The Complete Book of Activities, Games, Stories, Props, Recipes, and Dances

I Like Yellow

Nail
Polish

I Like Yellow

I Like Yellow

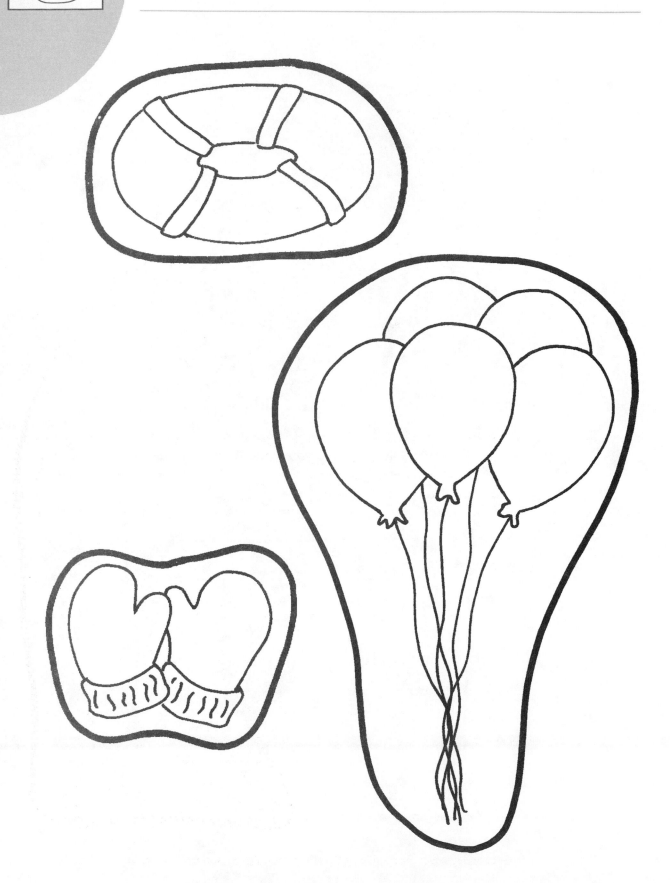

I Like Yellow

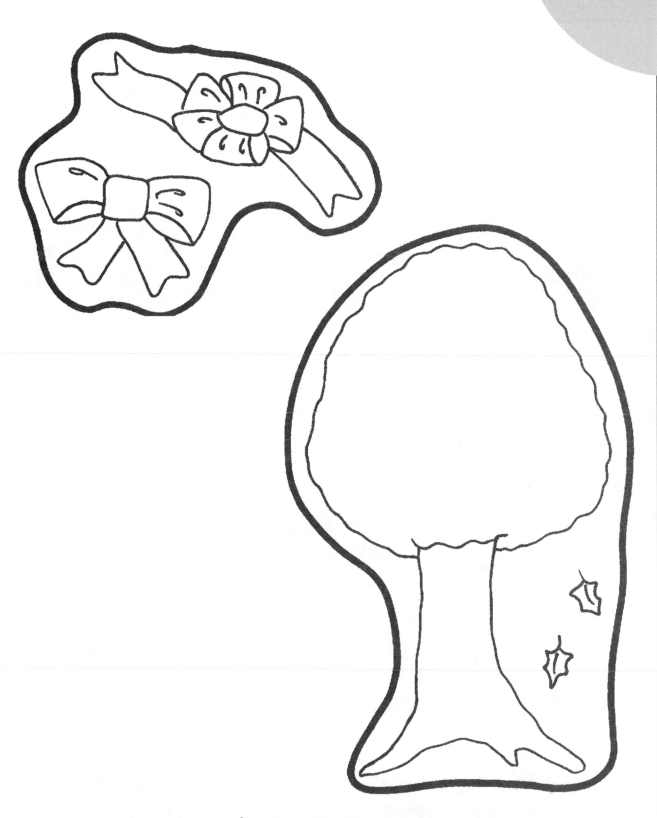

The Complete Book of Activities, Games, Stories, Props, Recipes, and Dances

STORY PATTERNS: FLANNEL BOARD

Issun Boshi

Issun Boshi

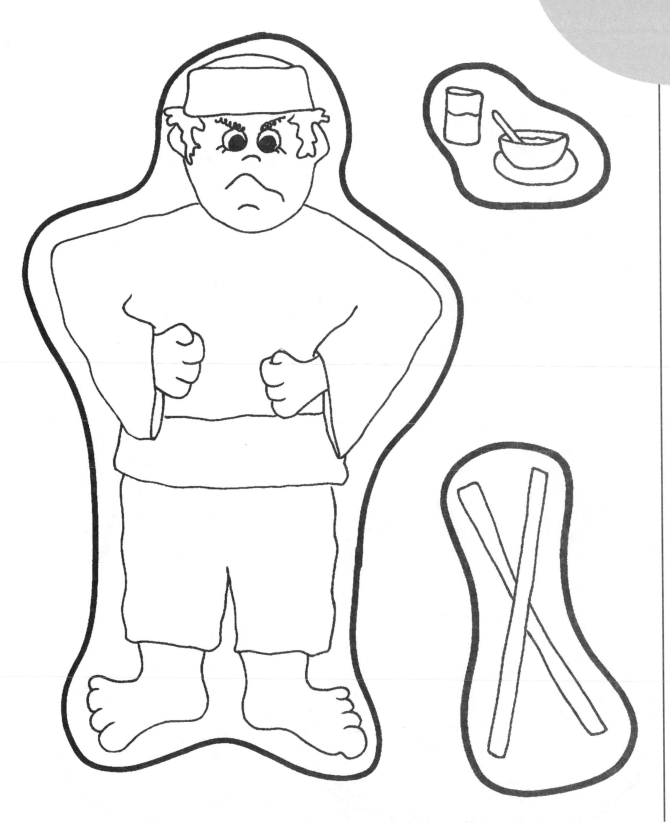

The Complete Book of Activities, Games, Stories, Props, Recipes, and Dances

Issun Boshi

Issun Boshi

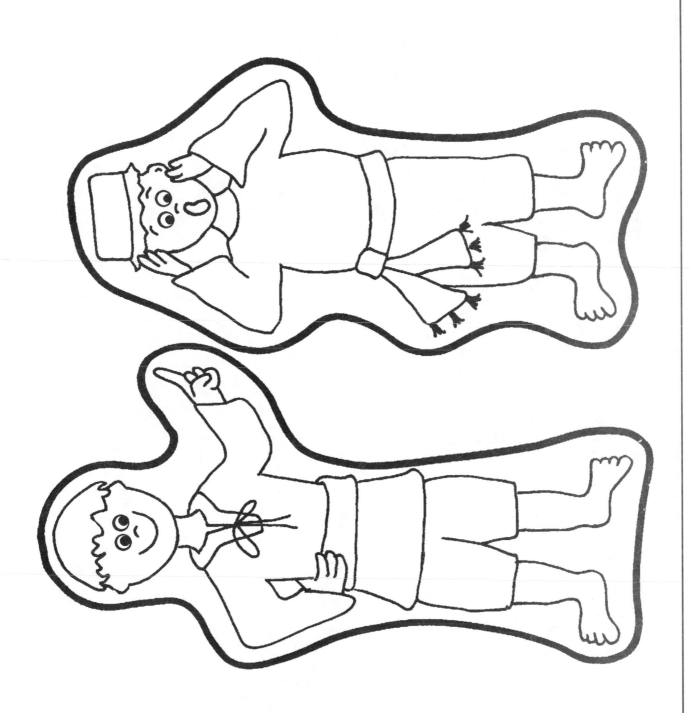

The Complete Book of Activities, Games, Stories, Props, Recipes, and Dances

Issun Boshi

Issun Boshi

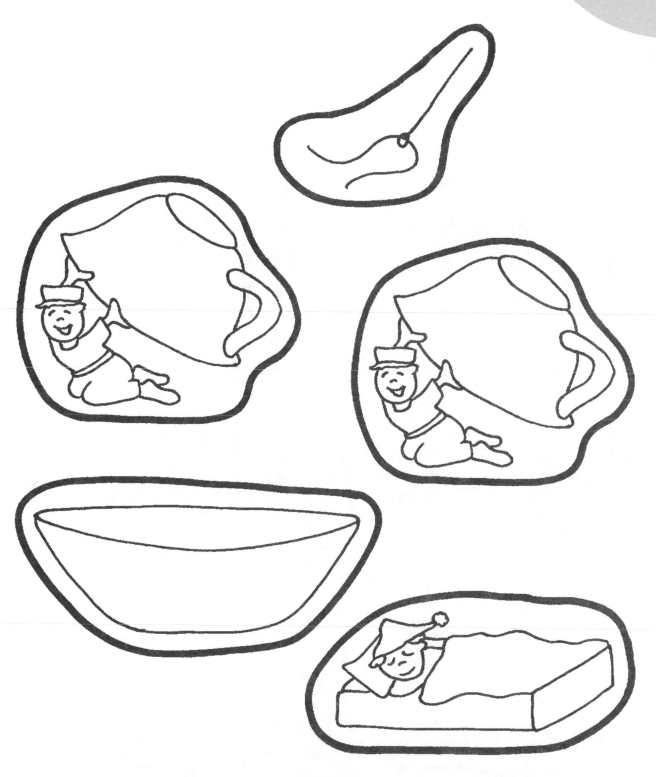

The Complete Book of Activities, Games, Stories, Props, Recipes, and Dances

Jack and the Beanstalk

Jack and the Beanstalk

The Complete Book of Activities, Games, Stories, Props, Recipes, and Dances

APPENDIX

STORY PATTERNS: FLANNEL BOARD

Jack and the Beanstalk

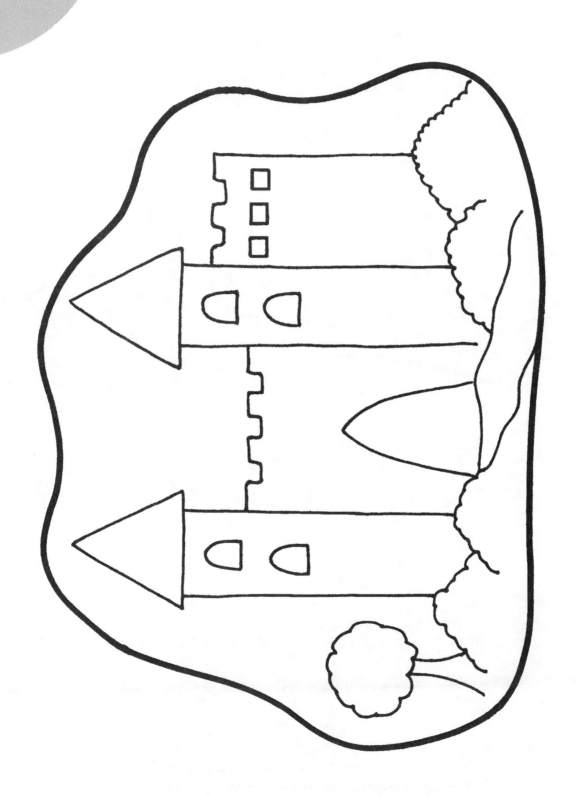

Jack and the Beanstalk

The Complete Book of Activities, Games, Stories, Props, Recipes, and Dances

Jack and the Beanstalk

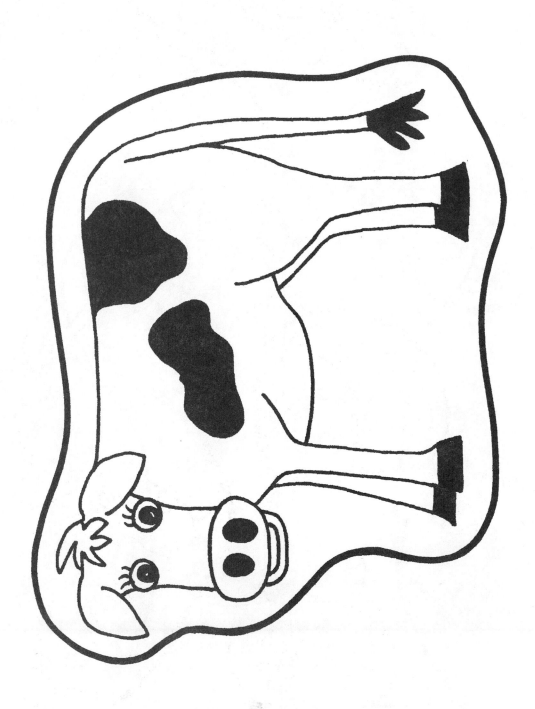

The Lazy Fox

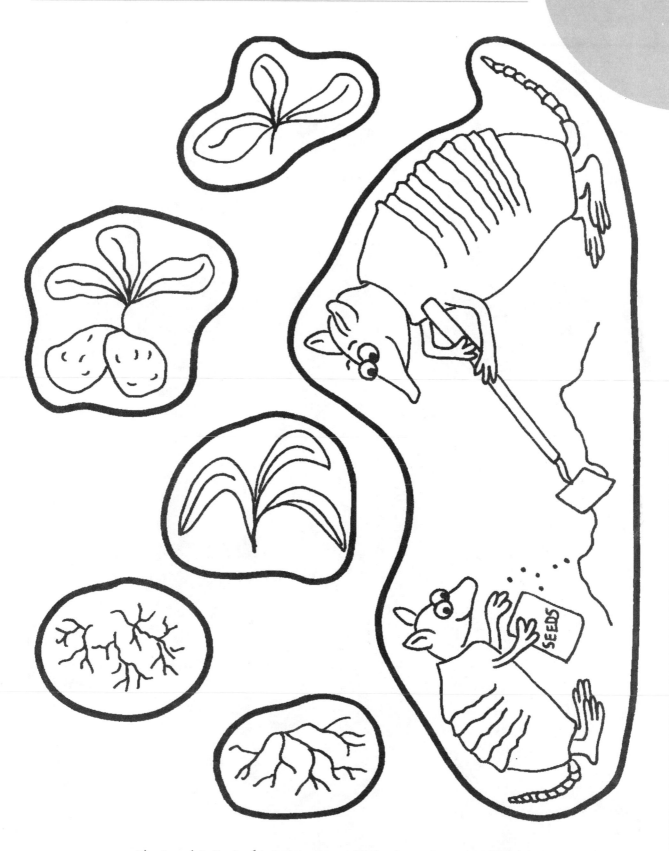

The Complete Book of Activities, Games, Stories, Props, Recipes, and Dances

The Lazy Fox

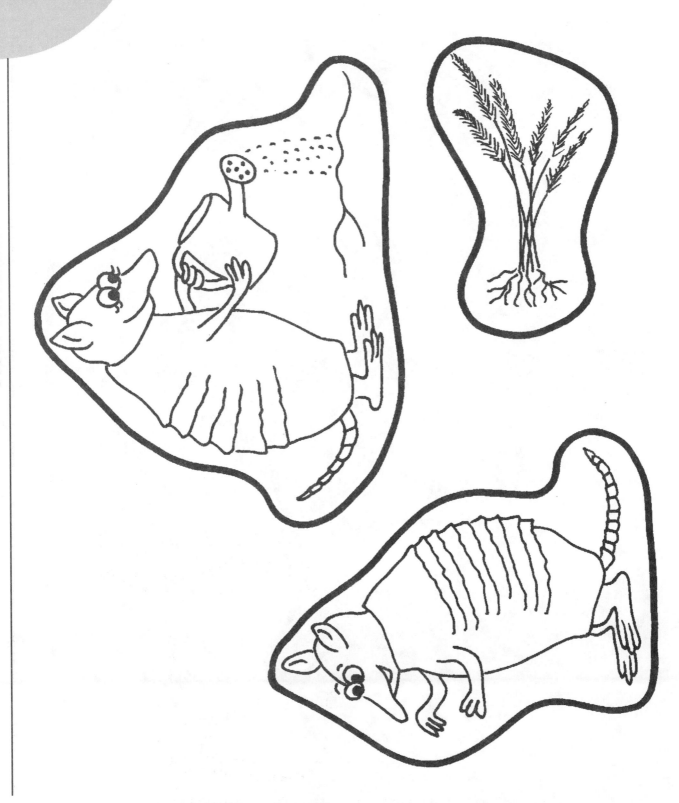

The Lazy Fox

Little Annie Oakley

Little Annie Oakley

The Complete Book of Activities, Games, Stories, Props, Recipes, and Dances

Little Annie Oakley

Official Annie Oakley Cowgirl Outfit

Little Engine Ninety-Nine

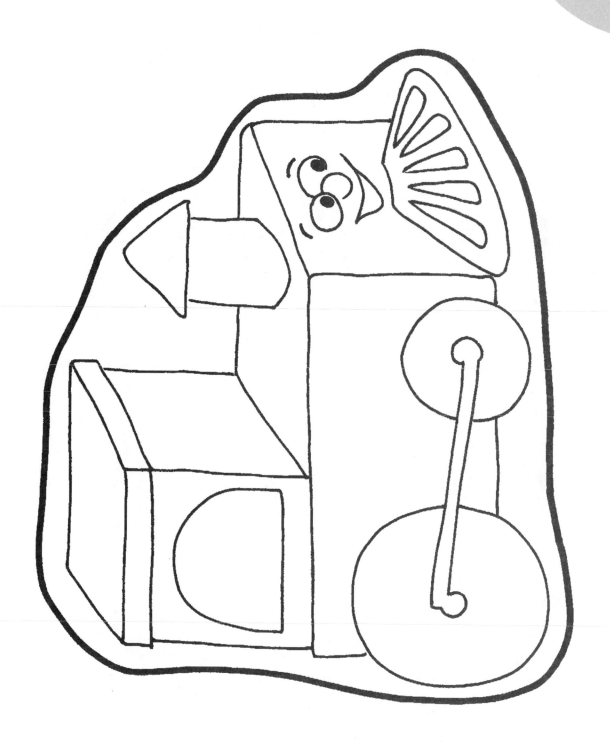

The Complete Book of Activities, Games, Stories, Props, Recipes, and Dances

Little Engine Ninety-Nine

Little Engine Ninety-Nine

Little Engine Ninety-Nine

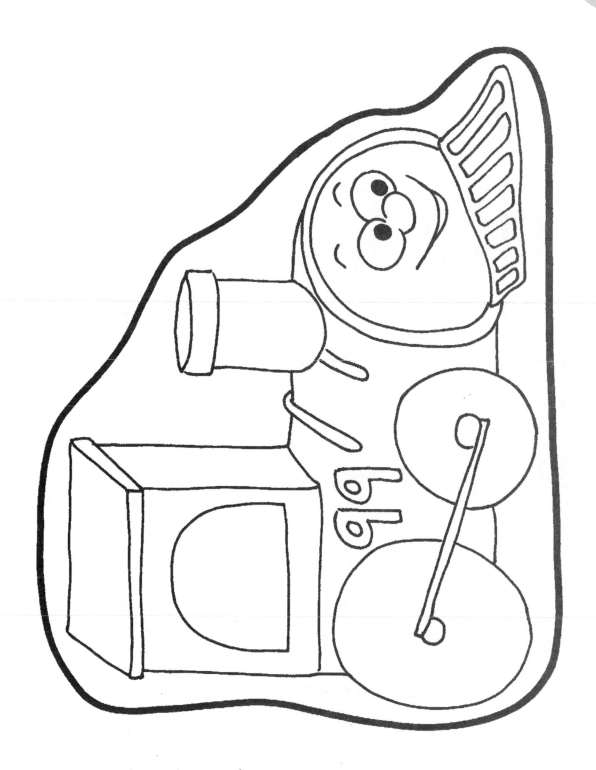

The Complete Book of Activities, Games, Stories, Props, Recipes, and Dances

APPENDIX

STORY PATTERNS: FLANNEL BOARD

Little Engine Ninety-Nine

Little Engine Ninety-Nine

Little Engine Ninety-Nine

The Little Old Woman Who Lived in a Vinegar Bottle

The Little Old Woman Who Lived in a Vinegar Bottle

The Little Old Woman Who Lived in a Vinegar Bottle

STORY PATTERNS: FLANNEL BOARD

The Little Old Woman Who Lived in a Vinegar Bottle

The Little Old Woman Who Lived in a Vinegar Bottle

The Complete Book of Activities, Games, Stories, Props, Recipes, and Dances

STORY PATTERNS: FLANNEL BOARD

The Little Old Woman Who Lived in a Vinegar Bottle

The Little Red Hen

The Complete Book of Activities, Games, Stories, Props, Recipes, and Dances

The Little Red Hen

The Little Red Hen

The Complete Book of Activities, Games, Stories, Props, Recipes, and Dances

Little Red Riding Hood
Caperucita Roja

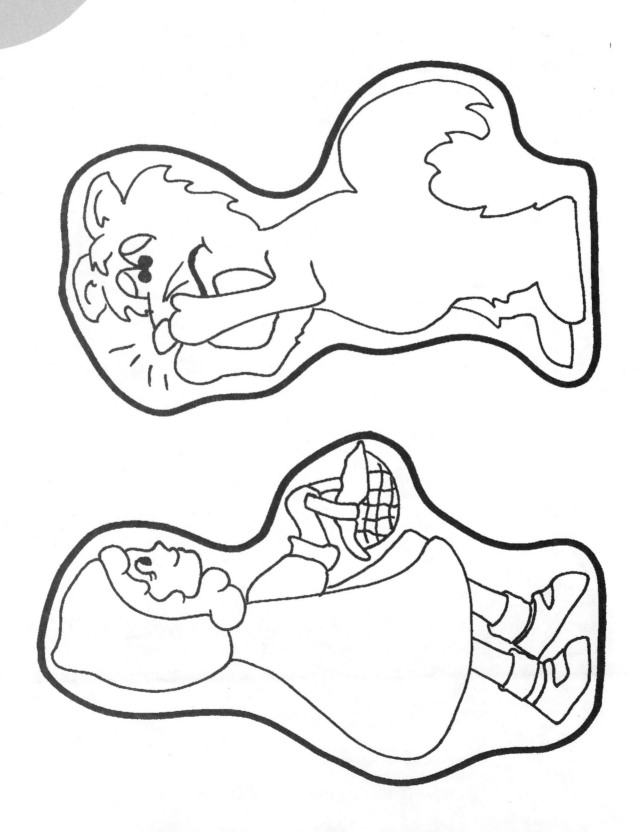

Little Red Riding Hood
Caperucita Roja

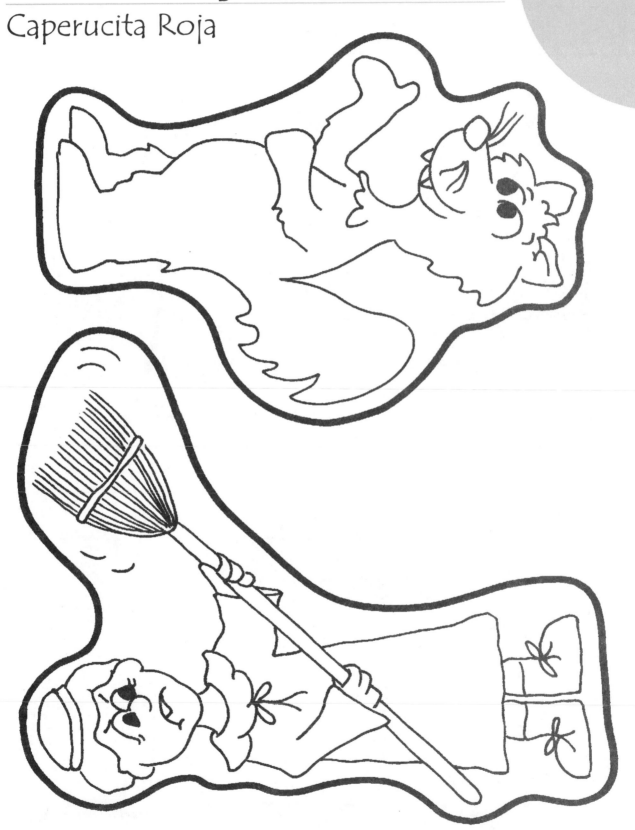

The Complete Book of Activities, Games, Stories, Props, Recipes, and Dances

STORY PATTERNS: FLANNEL BOARD

Little Red Riding Hood
Caperucita Roja

Little Red Riding Hood
Caperucita Roja

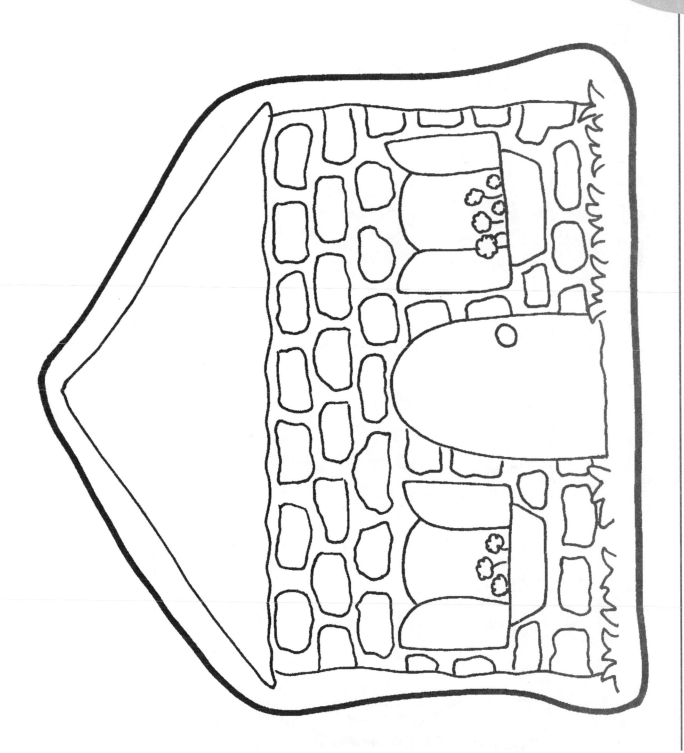

The Complete Book of Activities, Games, Stories, Props, Recipes, and Dances

Madison's Day

Madison's Day

The Complete Book of Activities, Games, Stories, Props, Recipes, and Dances

Miguel the Fearless

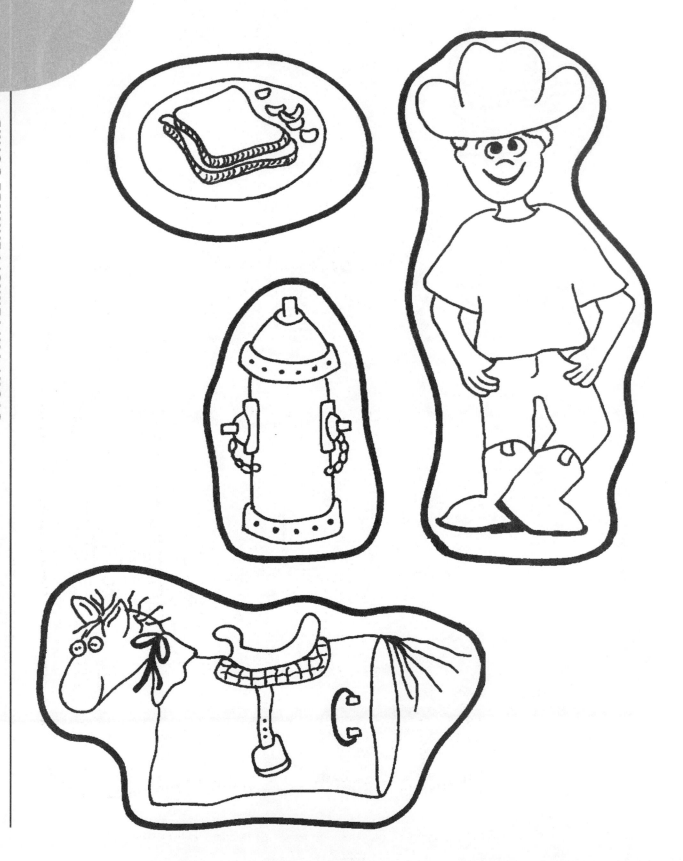

Miguel the Fearless

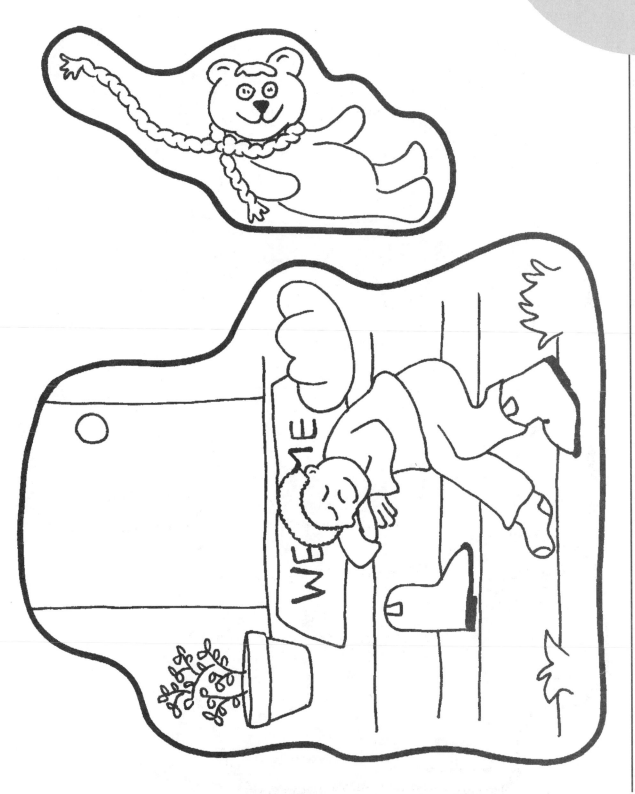

The Complete Book of Activities, Games, Stories, Props, Recipes, and Dances

Miguel the Fearless

My First Day of School

The Complete Book of Activities, Games, Stories, Props, Recipes, and Dances

My First Day of School

My First Day of School

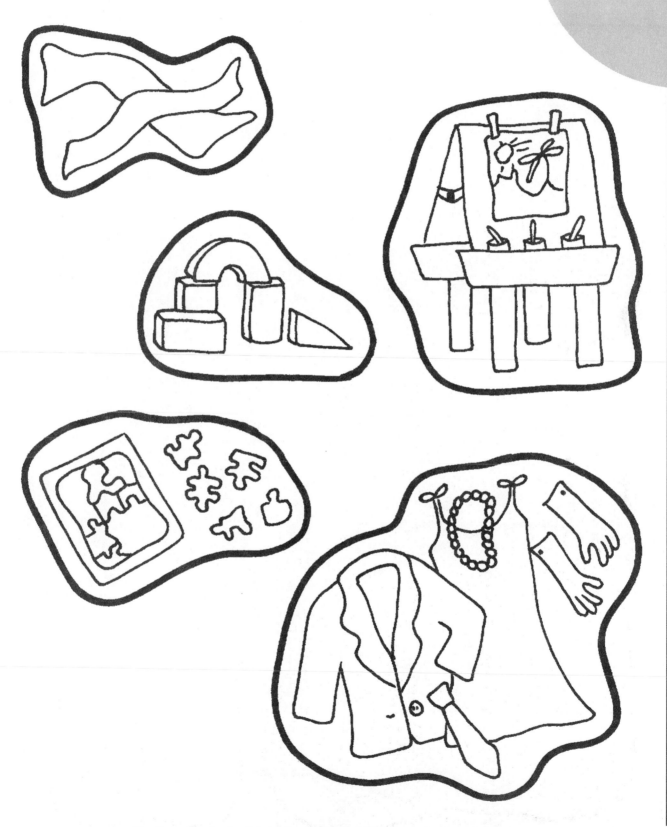

The Complete Book of Activities, Games, Stories, Props, Recipes, and Dances

My Shadow

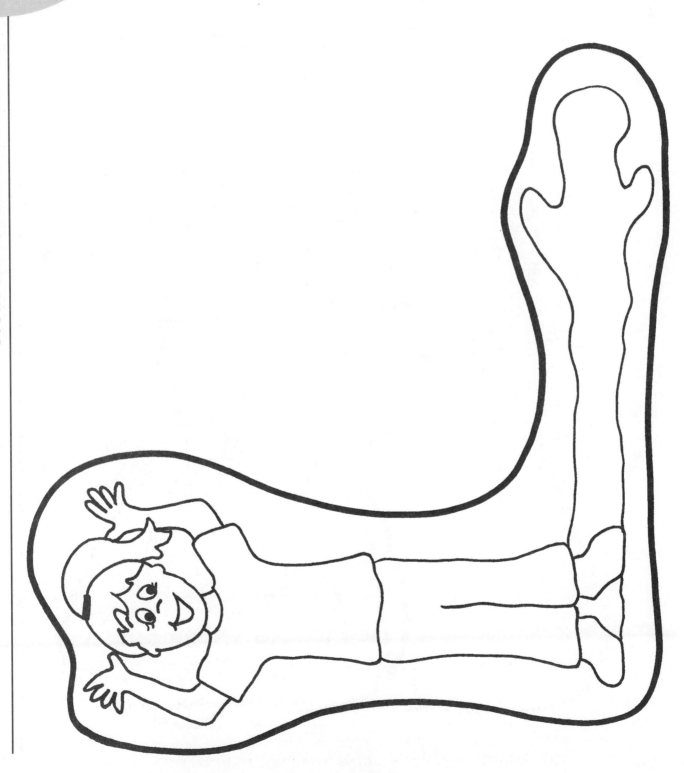

My Shadow

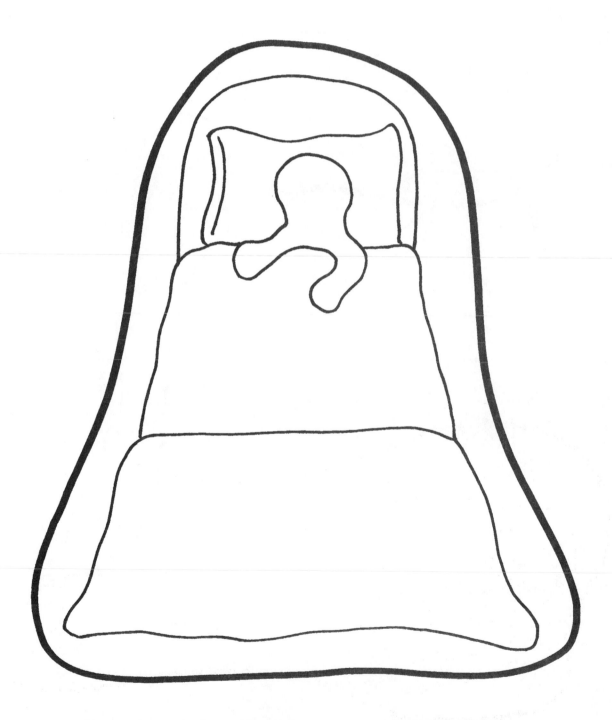

My Shadow

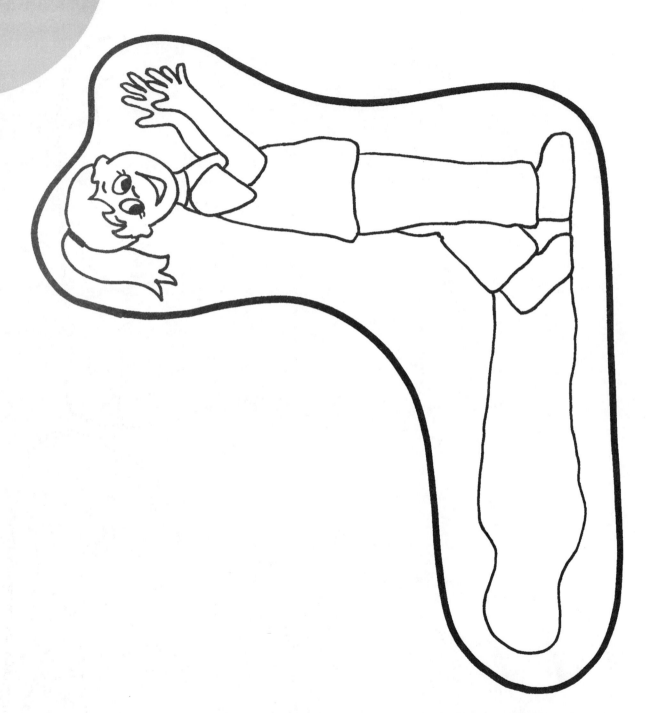

My Shadow

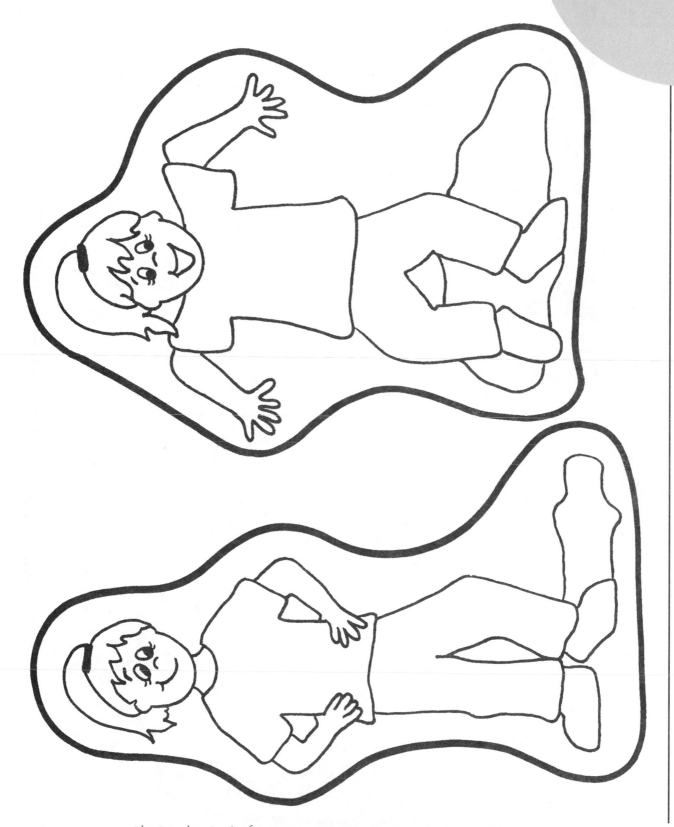

The Complete Book of Activities, Games, Stories, Props, Recipes, and Dances

My Sick Little Donkey
El Burrito Enfermo

My Very Own Pet

The Complete Book of Activities, Games, Stories, Props, Recipes, and Dances

Old MacDonald

STORY PATTERNS: FLANNEL BOARD

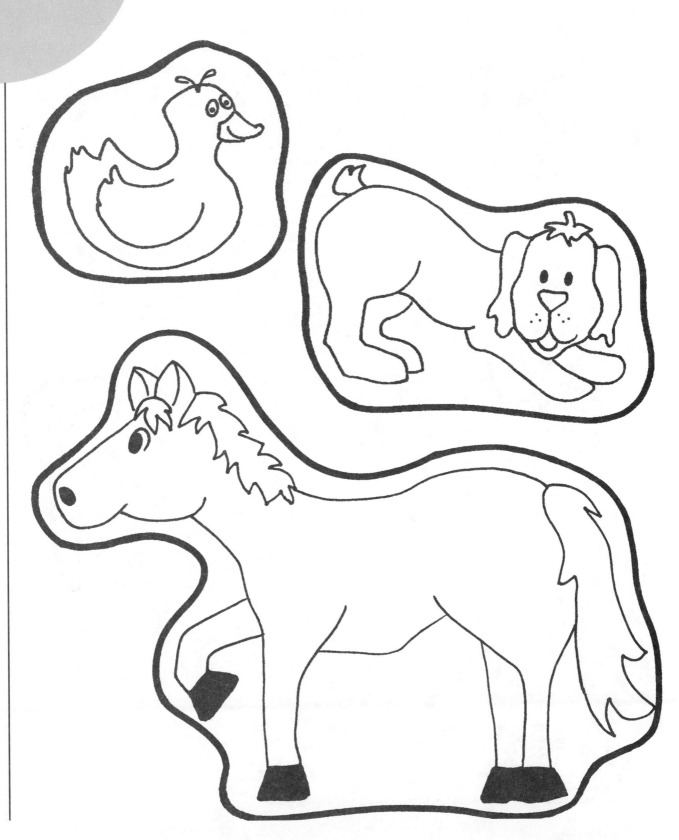

Old MacDonald

The Complete Book of Activities, Games, Stories, Props, Recipes, and Dances

Old MacDonald

The Pancake

The Pancake

The Pancake

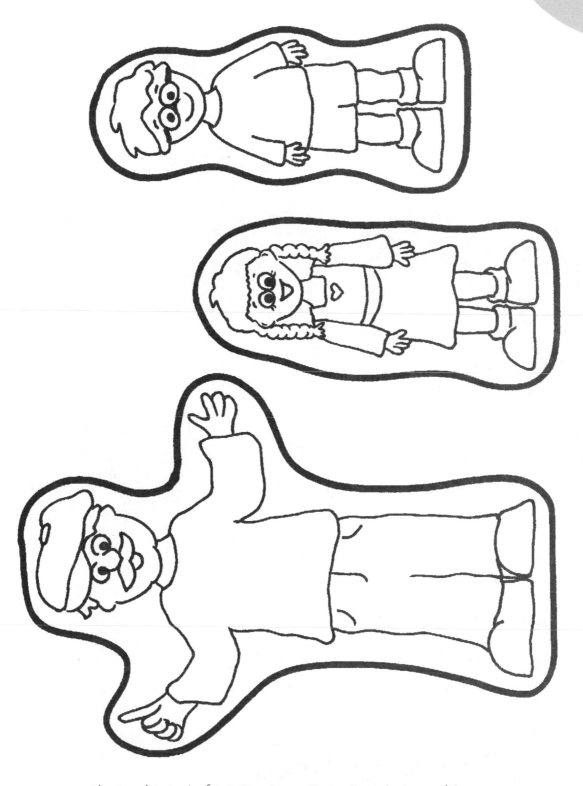

The Pancake

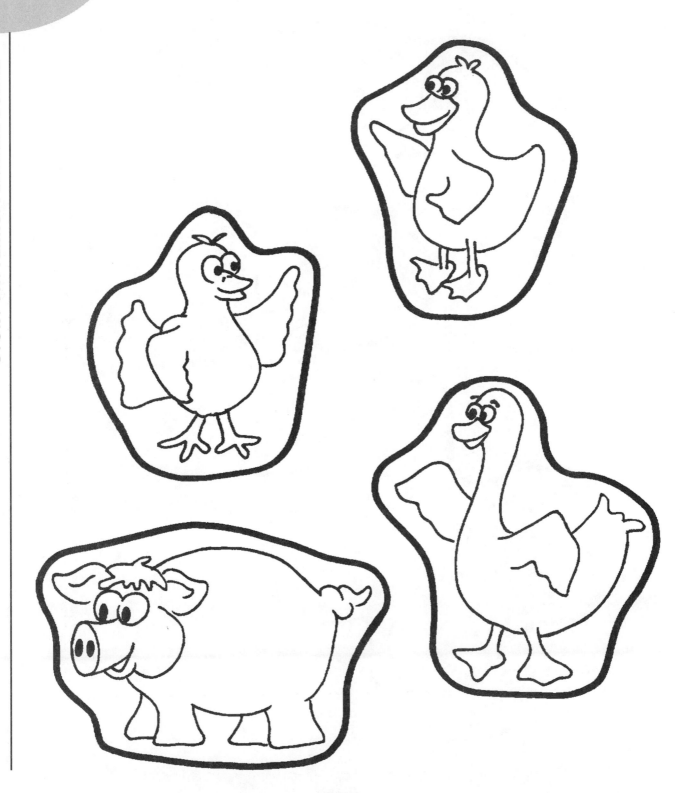

PeeWee, the Teeniest, Tiniest Pup on the Planet

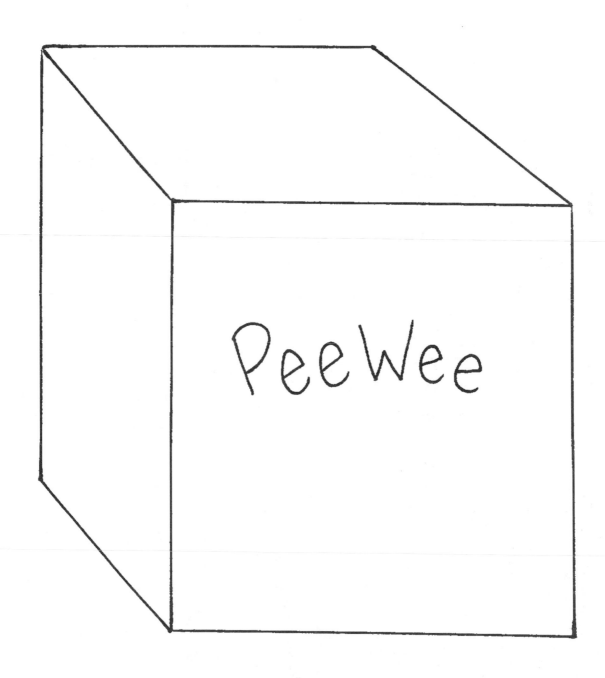

PeeWee

PeeWee, the Teeniest, Tiniest Pup on the Planet

PeeWee

PeeWee, the Teeniest, Tiniest Pup on the Planet

The Complete Book of Activities, Games, Stories, Props, Recipes, and Dances

The Princess and the Pea

The Princess and the Pea

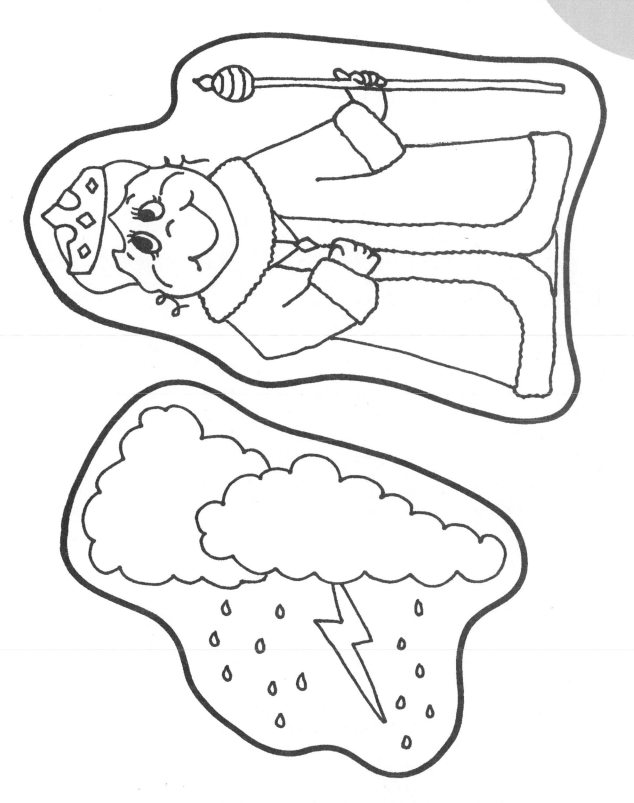

The Princess and the Pea

The Princess and the Pea

The Complete Book of Activities, Games, Stories, Props, Recipes, and Dances

The Ram in the Chile Patch

The Ram in the Chile Patch

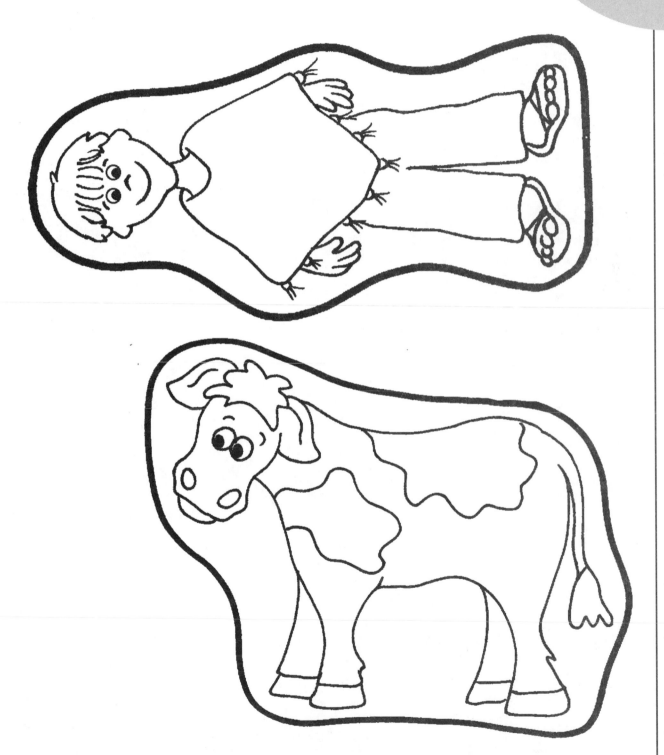

The Complete Book of Activities, Games, Stories, Props, Recipes, and Dances

The Ram in the Chile Patch

The Runaway Cookie Parade

The Complete Book of Activities, Games, Stories, Props, Recipes, and Dances

STORY PATTERNS: FLANNEL BOARD

The Runaway Cookie Parade

The Runaway Cookie Parade

The Complete Book of Activities, Games, Stories, Props, Recipes, and Dances

The Runaway Cookie Parade

Sammy, the Rodeo Seahorse

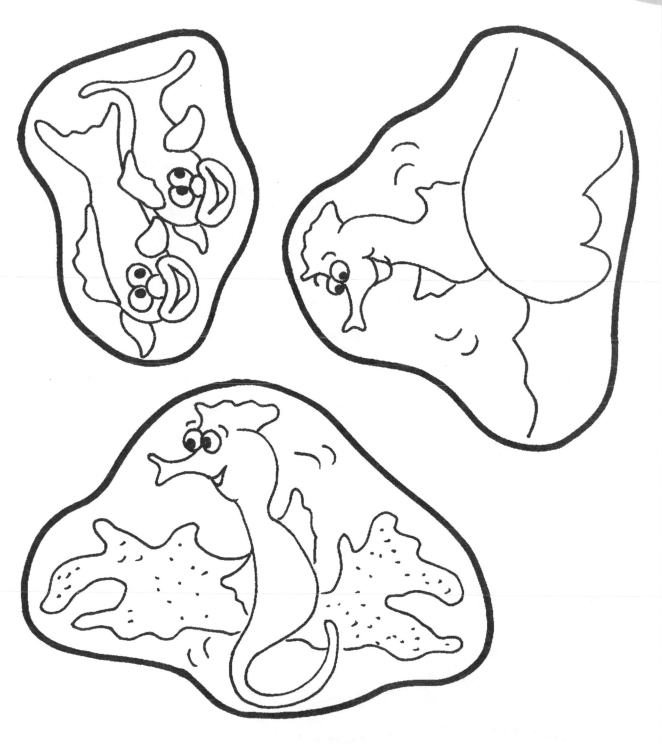

The Complete Book of Activities, Games, Stories, Props, Recipes, and Dances

Sammy, the Rodeo Seahorse

Sammy, the Rodeo Seahorse

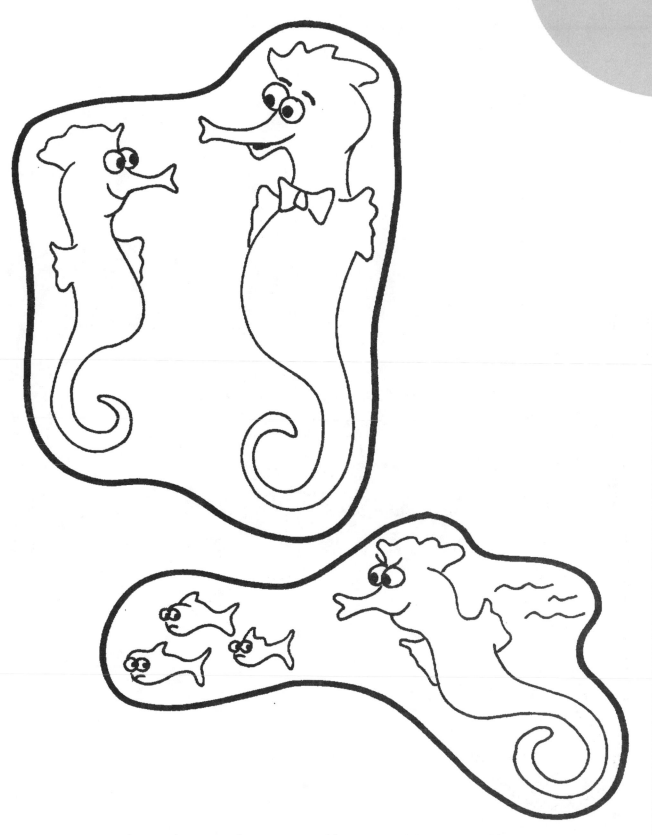

The Complete Book of Activities, Games, Stories, Props, Recipes, and Dances

Silly Jack

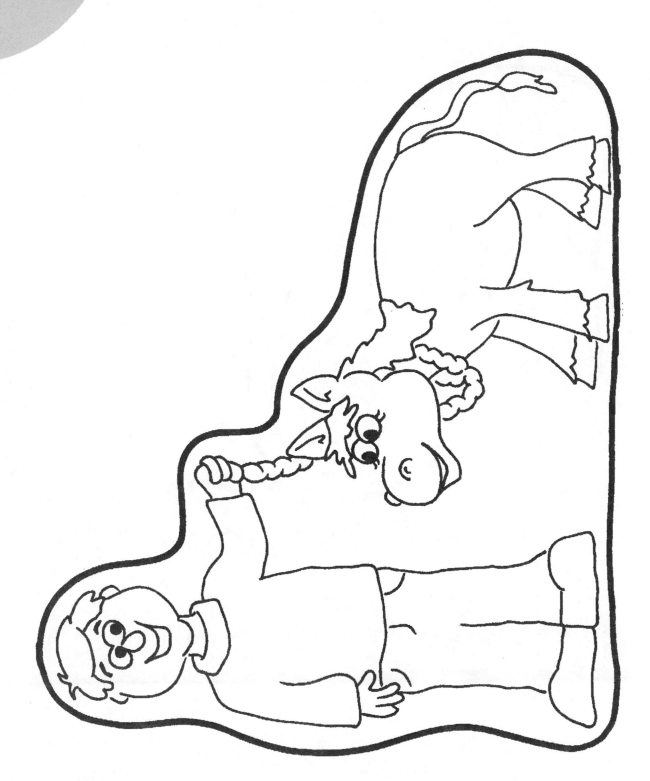

Silly Jack

The Complete Book of Activities, Games, Stories, Props, Recipes, and Dances

Silly Jack

STORY PATTERNS: FLANNEL BOARD

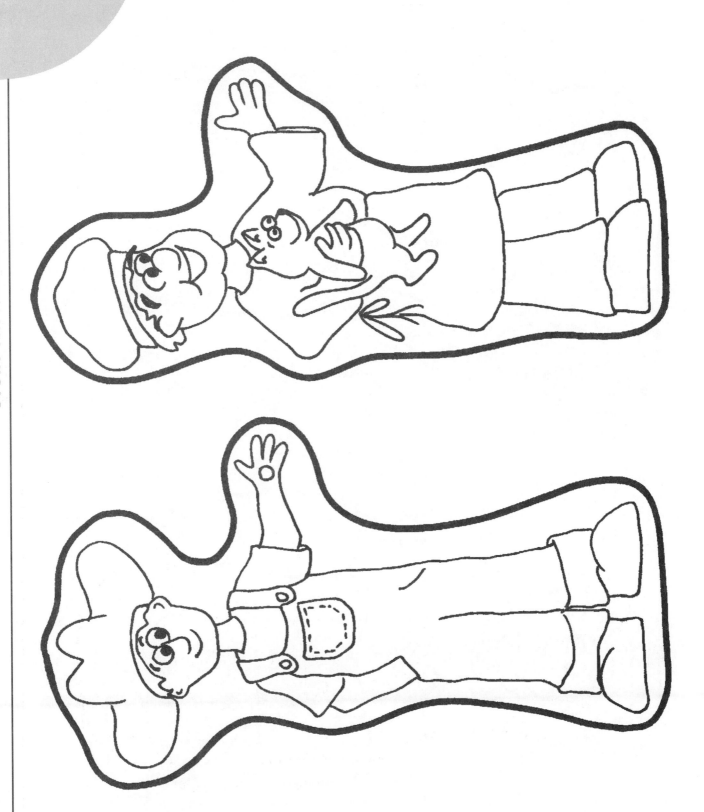

Silly Jack

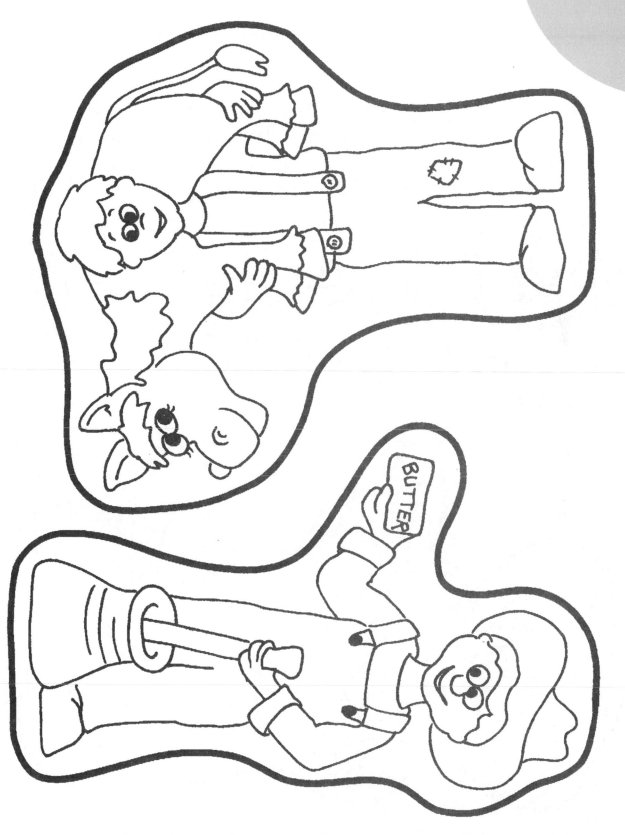

The Complete Book of Activities, Games, Stories, Props, Recipes, and Dances

Silly Jack

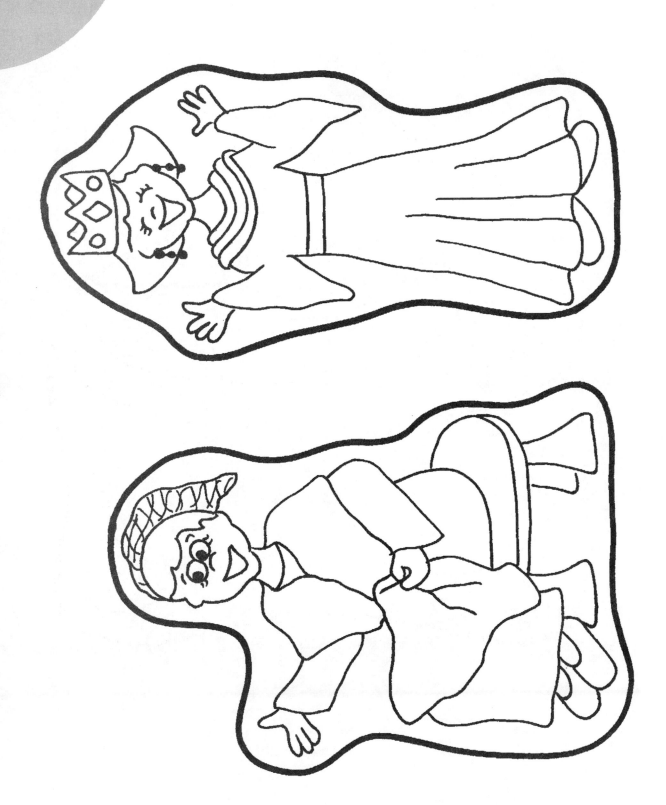

Sillie Millie

The Complete Book of Activities, Games, Stories, Props, Recipes, and Dances

STORY PATTERNS: FLANNEL BOARD

Sillie Millie

Sillie Millie

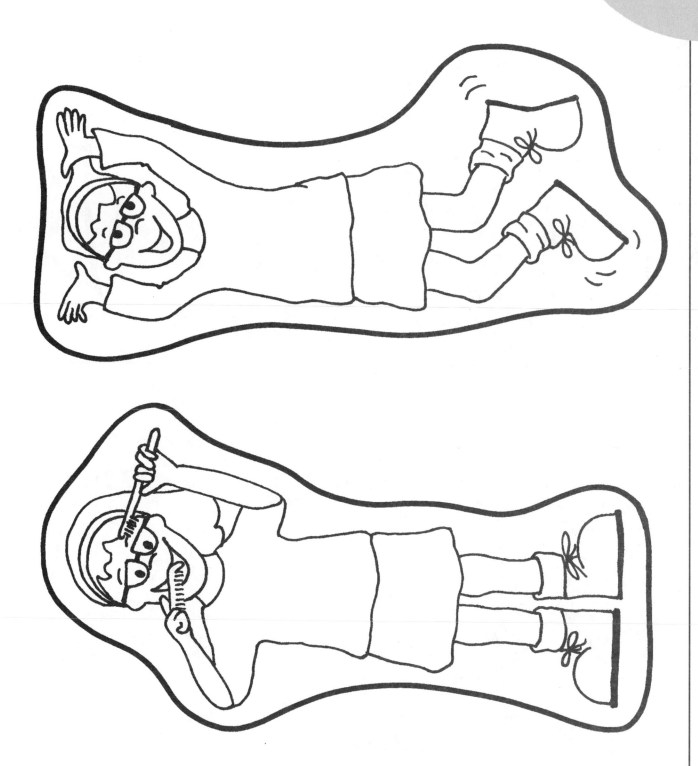

STORY PATTERNS: FLANNEL BOARD

Sillie Millie

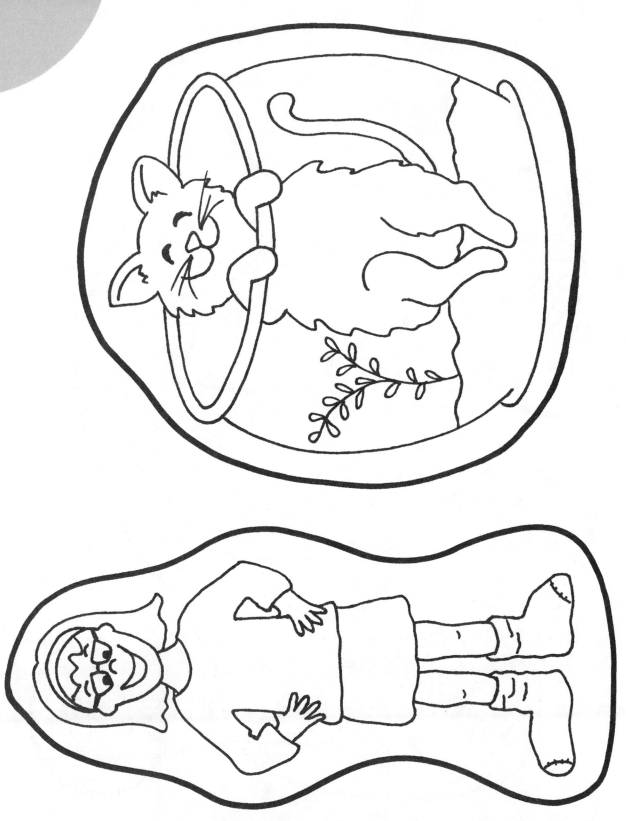

Silly Nellie: The Story of One Funny Turkey

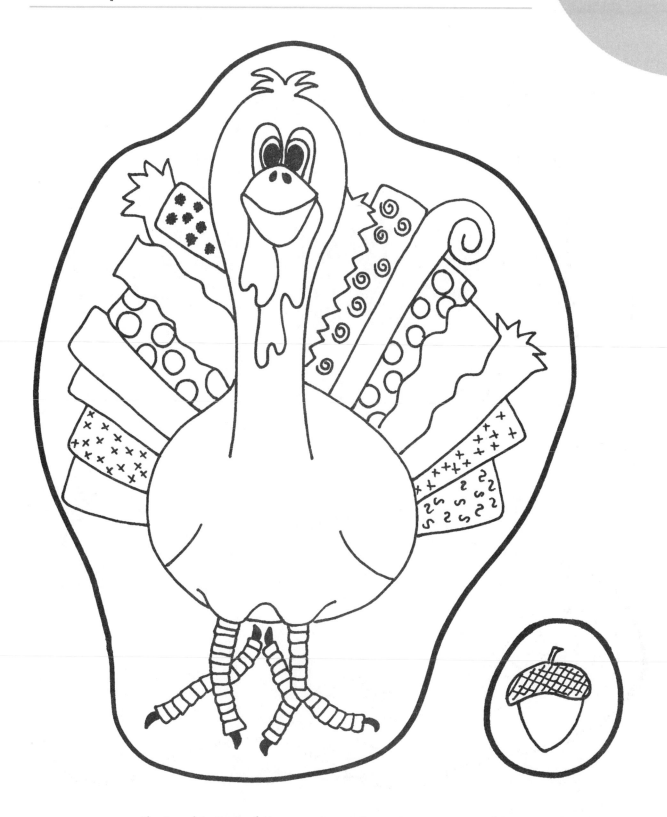

The Complete Book of Activities, Games, Stories, Props, Recipes, and Dances

Silly Nellie: The Story of One Funny Turkey

Silly Nellie: The Story of One Funny Turkey

Silly Nellie: The Story of One Funny Turkey

Silly Nellie: The Story of One Funny Turkey

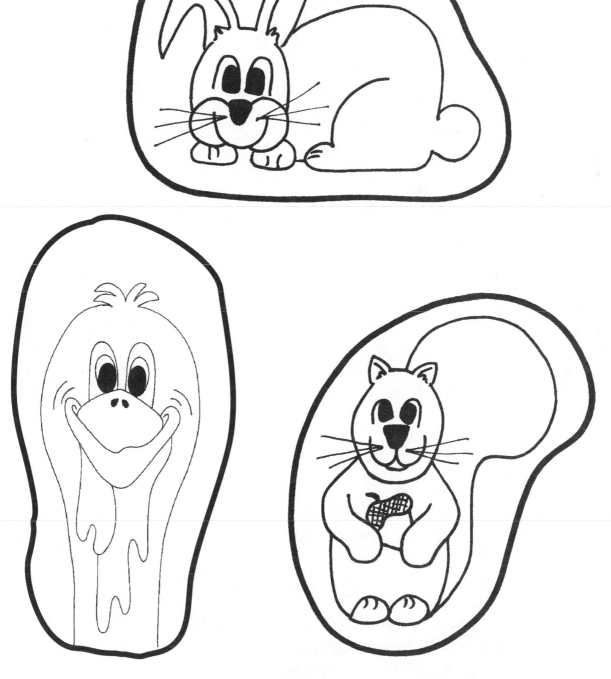

The Complete Book of Activities, Games, Stories, Props, Recipes, and Dances

STORY PATTERNS: FLANNEL BOARD

Sing a Song of Opposites
Un Cuento de Opuestos

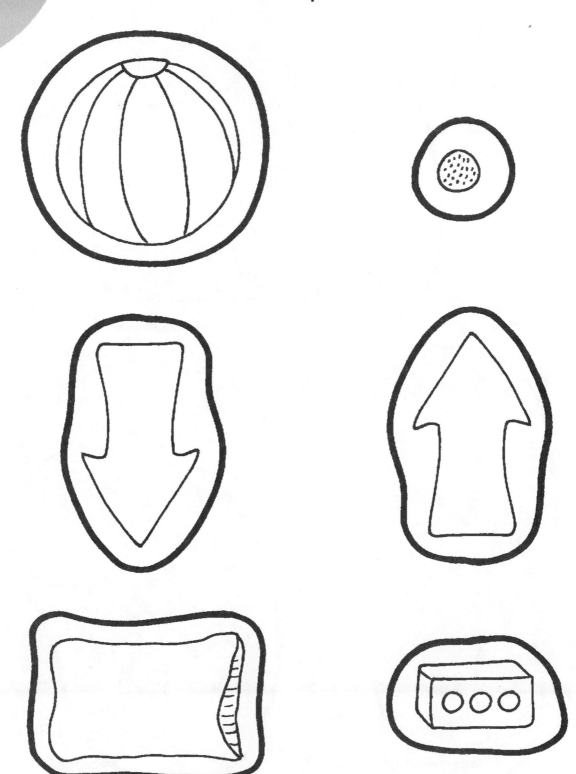

Sing a Song of Opposites
Un Cuento de Opuestos

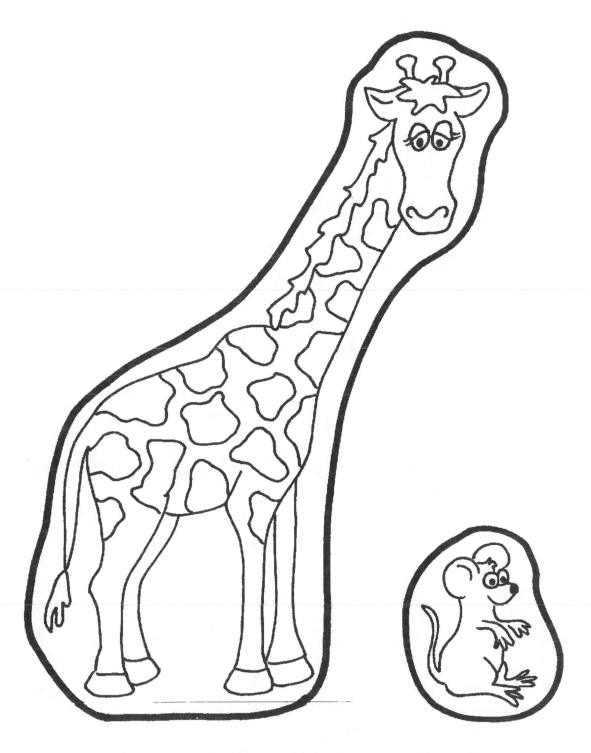

The Complete Book of Activities, Games, Stories, Props, Recipes, and Dances

STORY PATTERNS: FLANNEL BOARD

Sing a Song of Opposites
Un Cuento de Opuestos

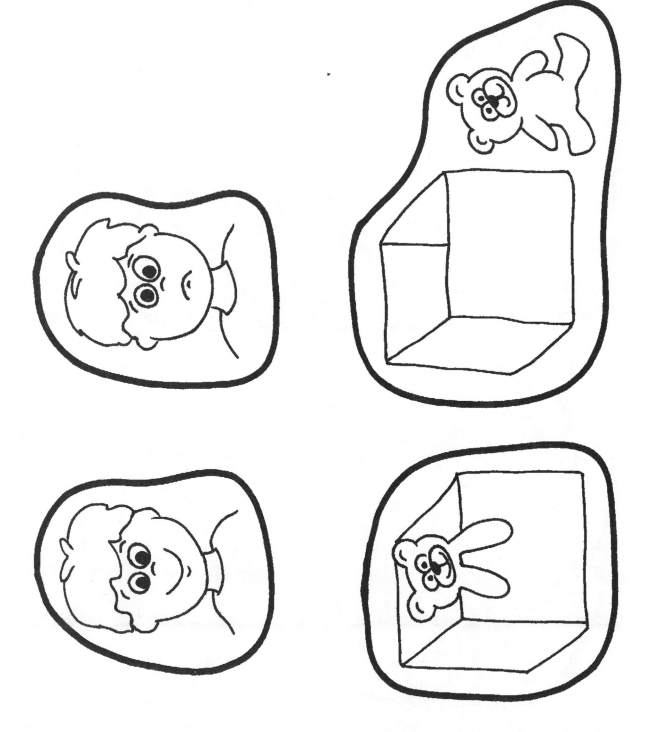

Smart Cookie's Best Friend, Gabby Graham

Smart Cookie's Best Friend, Gabby Graham

Smart Cookie's Clever Idea

The Complete Book of Activities, Games, Stories, Props, Recipes, and Dances

Smart Cookie's Clever Idea

The Snow Child

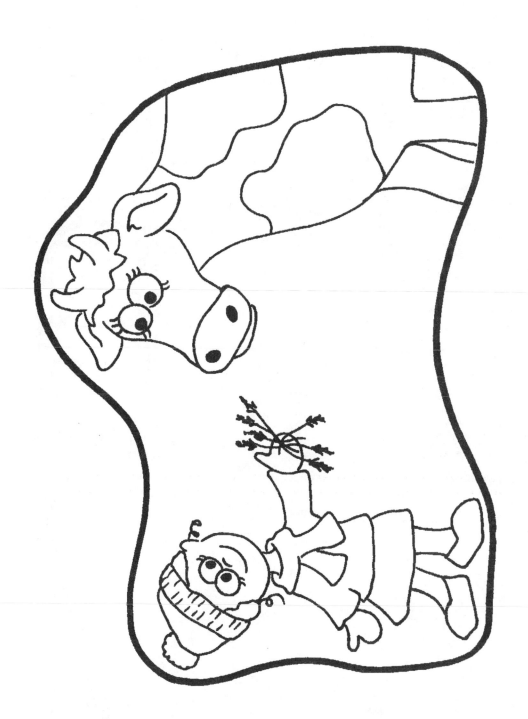

The Snow Child

The Snow Child

The Complete Book of Activities, Games, Stories, Props, Recipes, and Dances

The Sun and the Moon

The Sun and the Moon

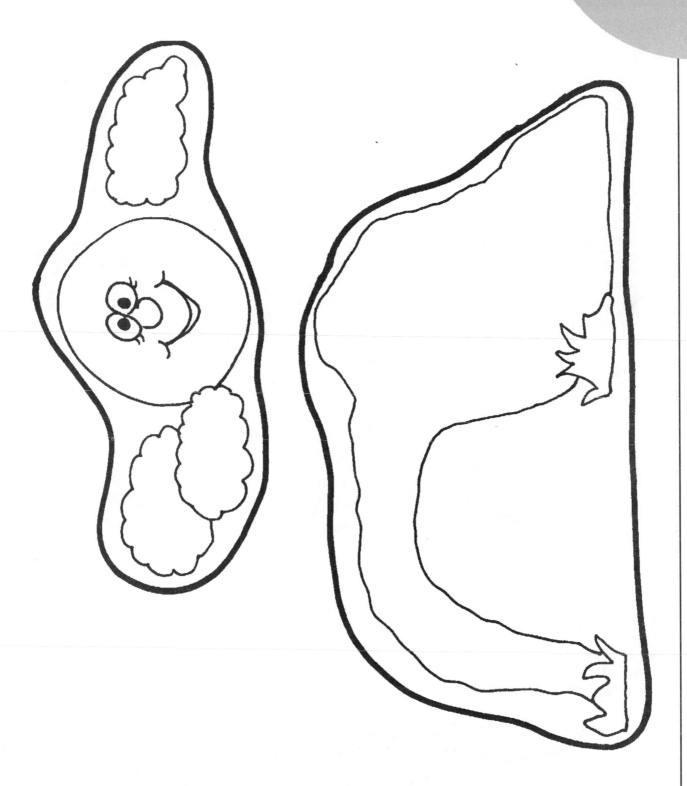

The Complete Book of Activities, Games, Stories, Props, Recipes, and Dances

This Old Man Is Rockin' On

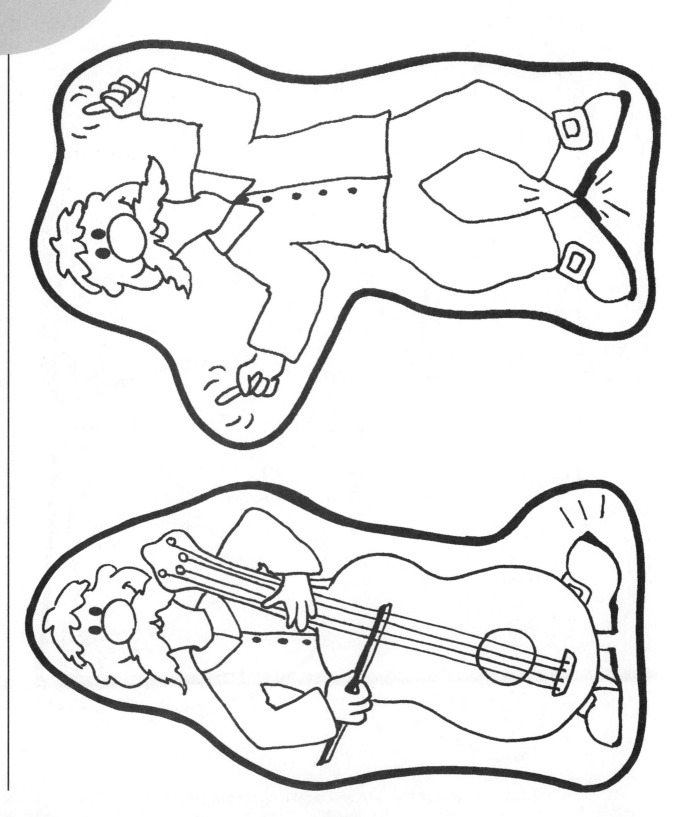

This Old Man Is Rockin' On

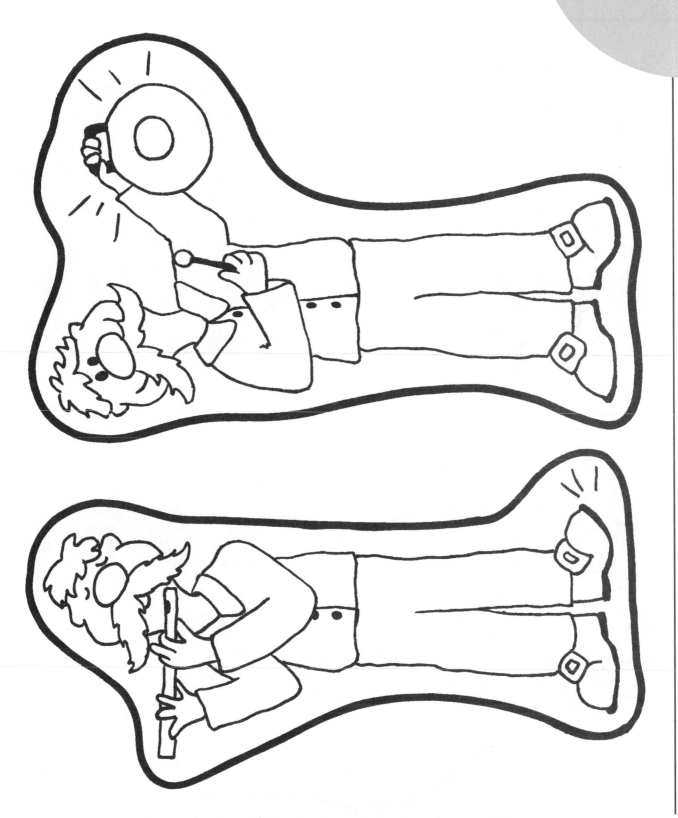

The Complete Book of Activities, Games, Stories, Props, Recipes, and Dances

STORY PATTERNS: FLANNEL BOARD

The Three Billy Goats Gruff

The Three Billy Goats Gruff

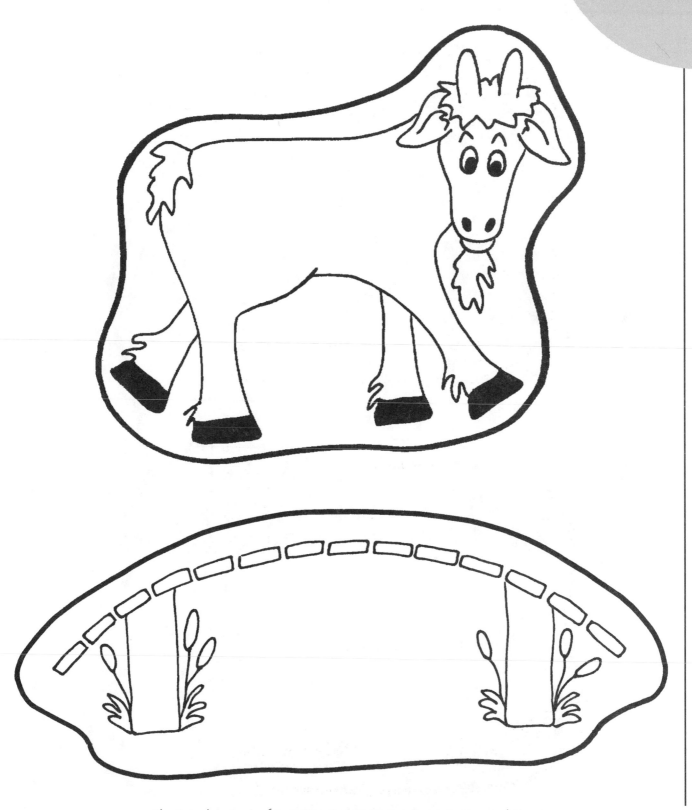

The Complete Book of Activities, Games, Stories, Props, Recipes, and Dances

The Three Billy Goats Gruff

The Three Billy Goats Gruff

The Complete Book of Activities, Games, Stories, Props, Recipes, and Dances

The Three Little Pigs

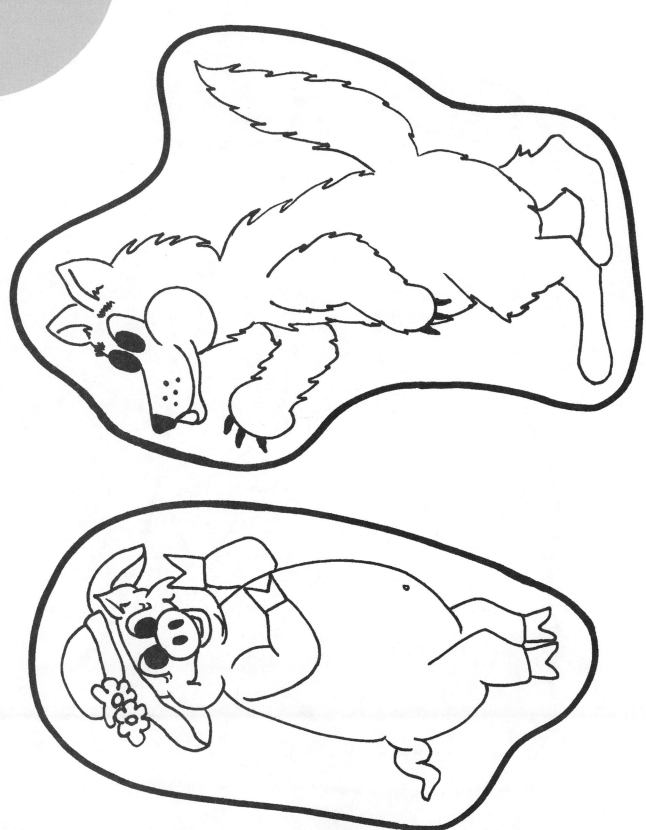

The Three Little Pigs

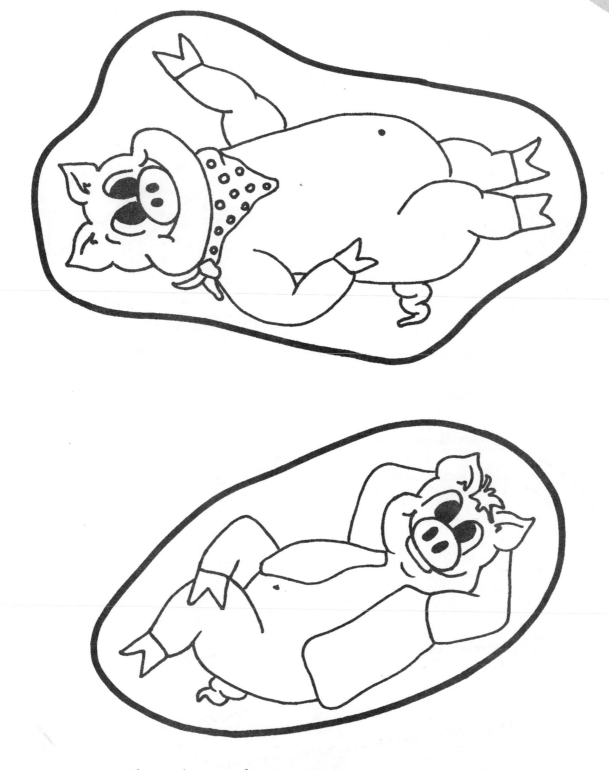

STORY PATTERNS: FLANNEL BOARD

The Three Little Pigs

The Three Little Pigs

The Complete Book of Activities, Games, Stories, Props, Recipes, and Dances

The Three Little Pigs

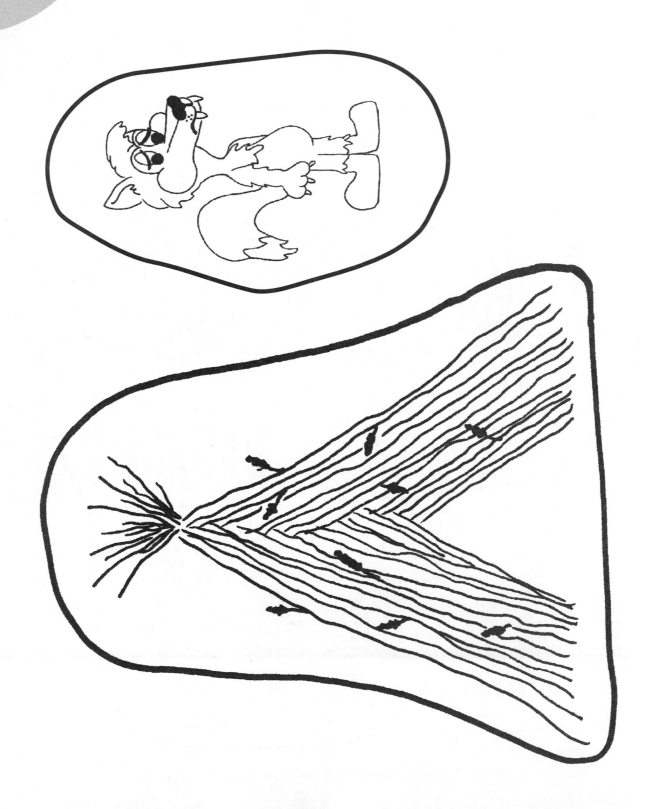

The Three Little Pigs

Victory!

The Complete Book of Activities, Games, Stories, Props, Recipes, and Dances

Three Wishes

Three Wishes

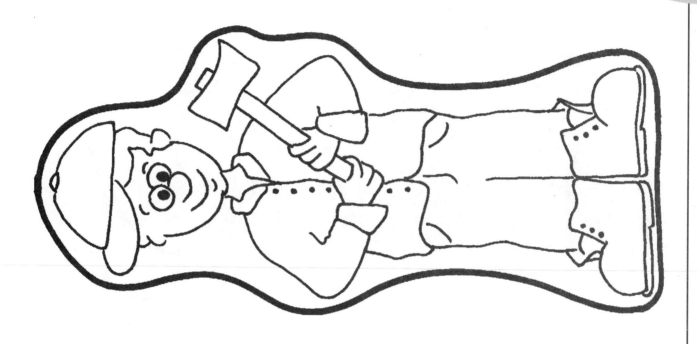

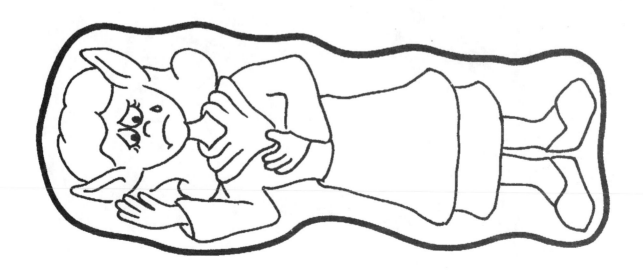

Tortoise Wins a Race

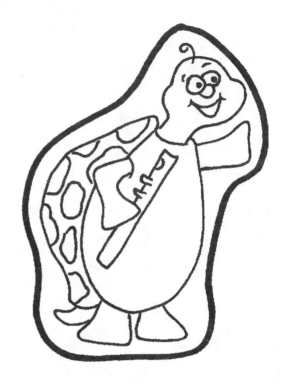

Tortoise Wins a Race

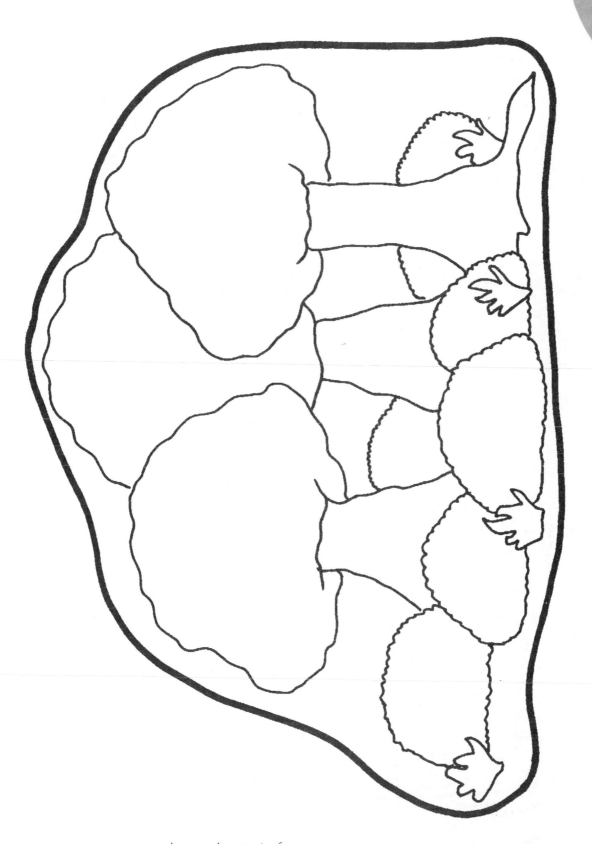

The Complete Book of Activities, Games, Stories, Props, Recipes, and Dances

Tortoise Wins a Race

The Traveling Musicians

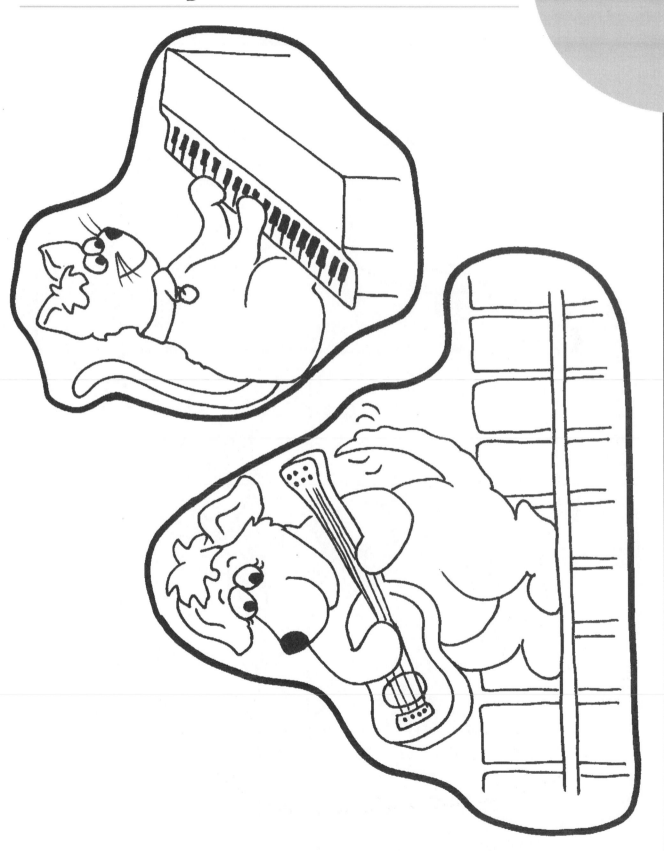

The Complete Book of Activities, Games, Stories, Props, Recipes, and Dances

The Traveling Musicians

The Traveling Musicians

The Complete Book of Activities, Games, Stories, Props, Recipes, and Dances

The Traveling Musicians

The Traveling Musicians

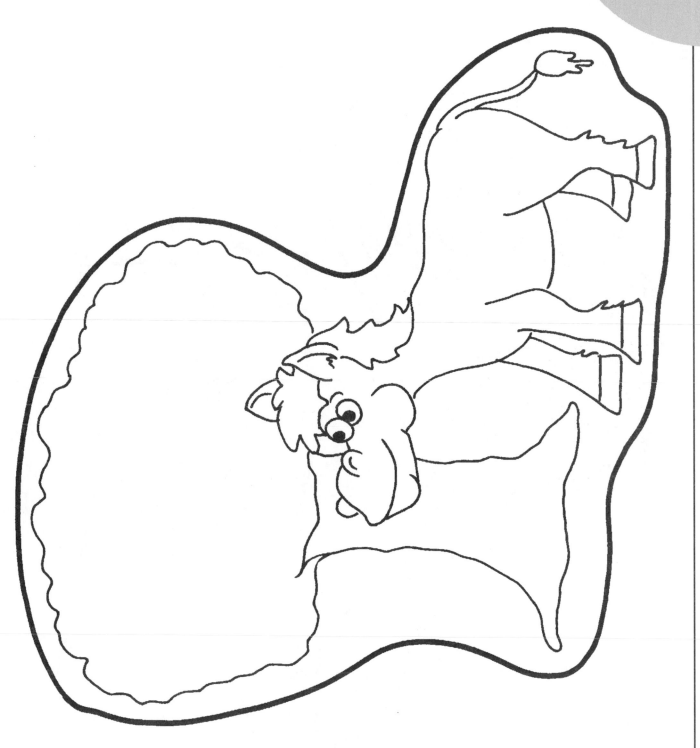

The Traveling Musicians

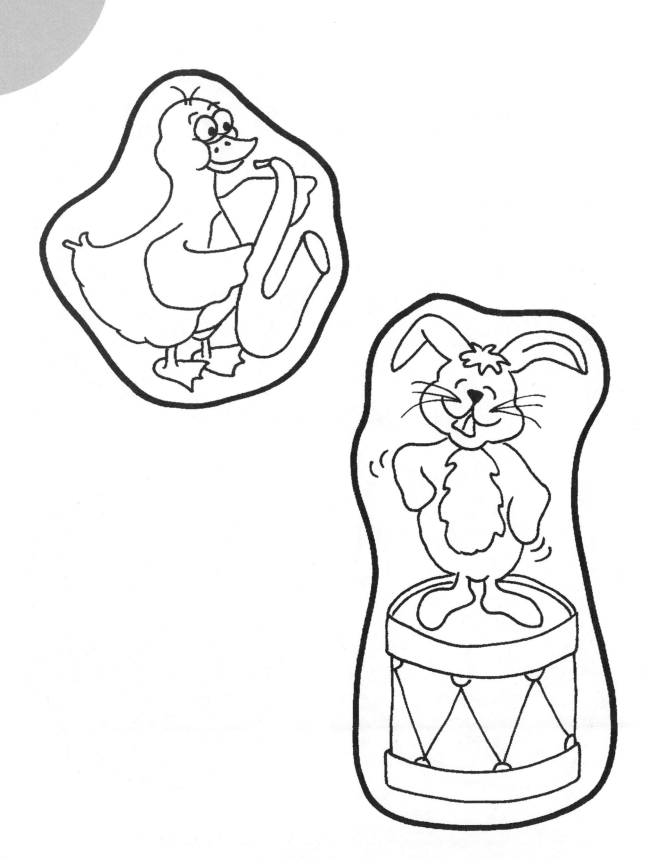

Valerie Valentine

The Complete Book of Activities, Games, Stories, Props, Recipes, and Dances

Valerie Valentine

Roses are red Violets are blue Sugar is sweet And so are you!

What's in the Box?

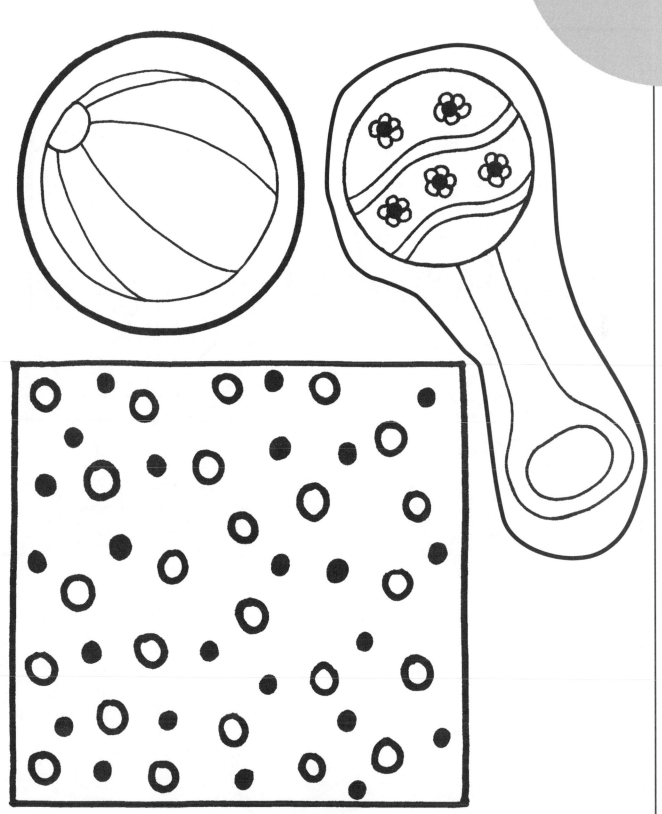

The Complete Book of Activities, Games, Stories, Props, Recipes, and Dances

What's in the Box?

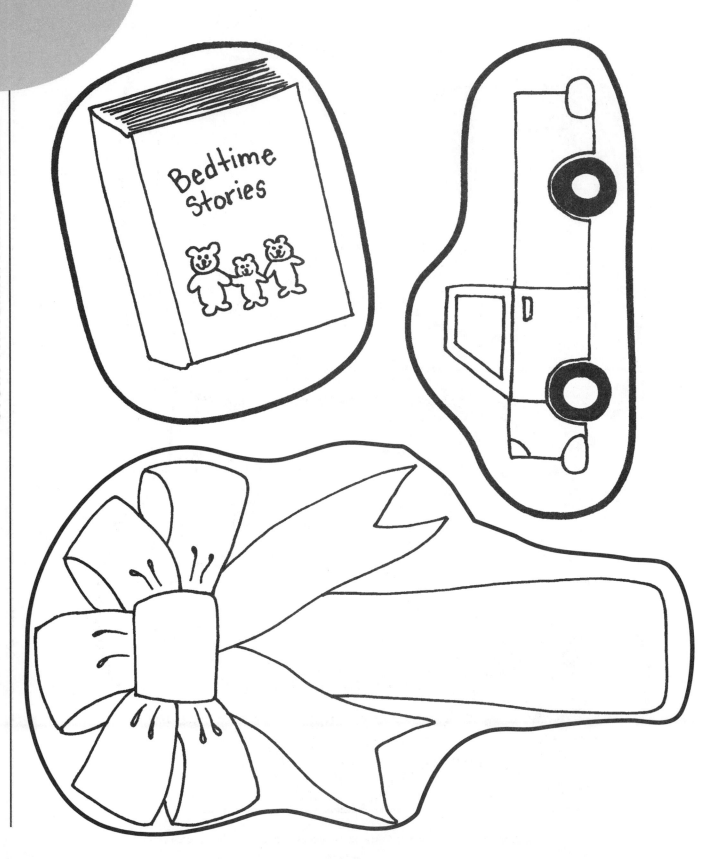

What's in the Box?

The Complete Book of Activities, Games, Stories, Props, Recipes, and Dances

What's in the Box?

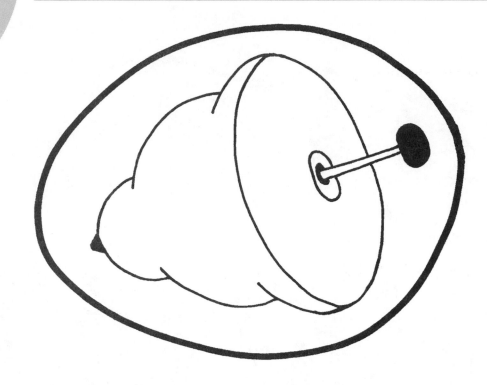

The Zebra on the Zyder Zee

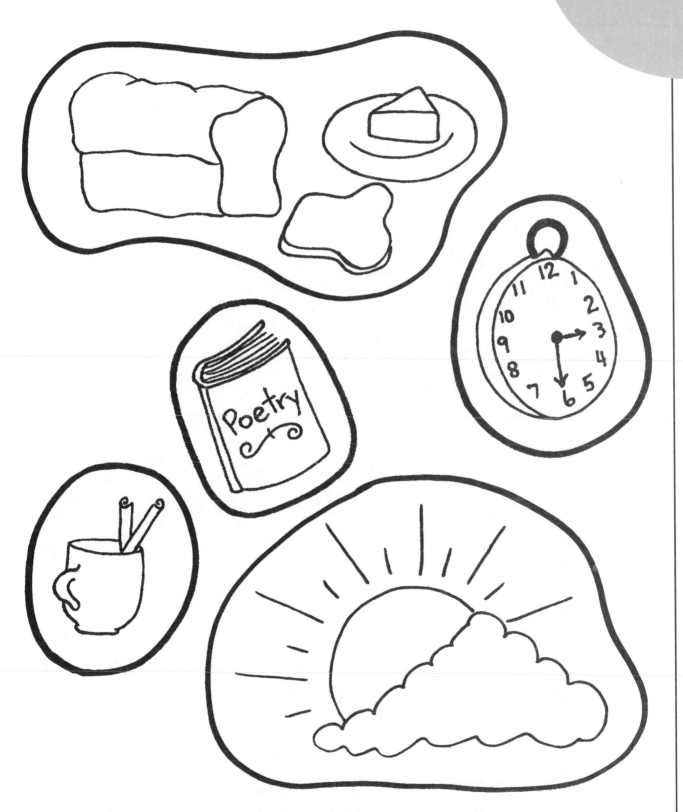

Poetry

The Complete Book of Activities, Games, Stories, Props, Recipes, and Dances

The Zebra on the Zyder Zee

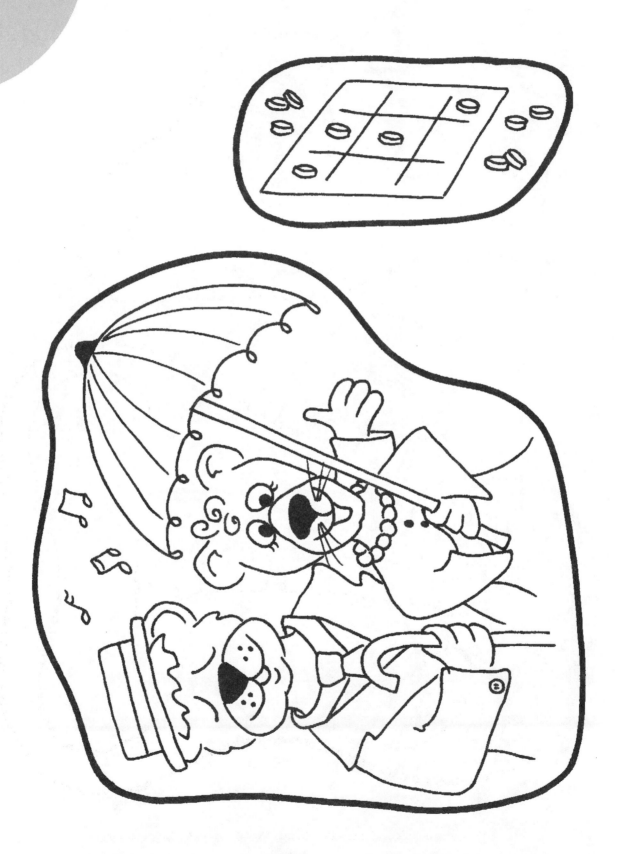

The Zebra on the Zyder Zee

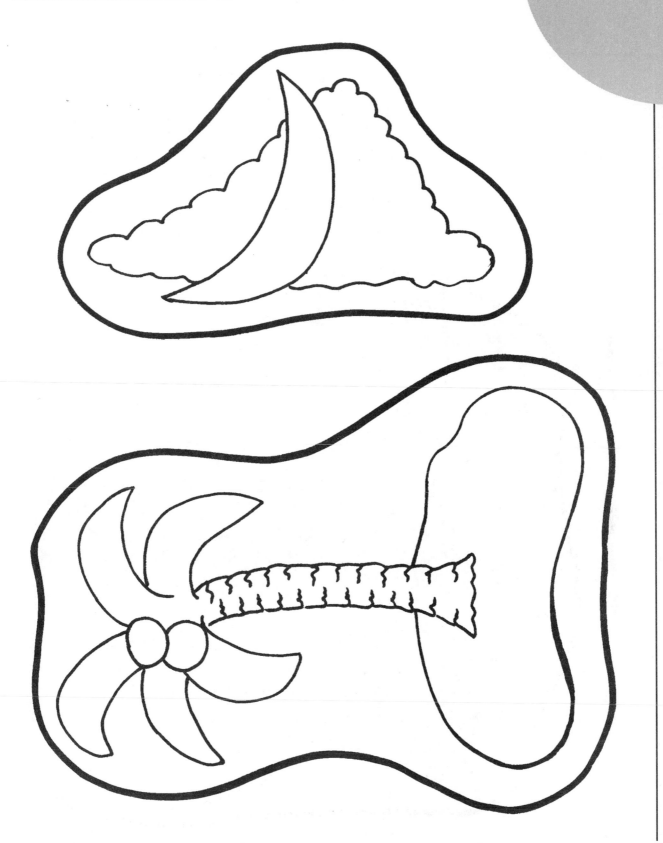

The Complete Book of Activities, Games, Stories, Props, Recipes, and Dances

The Zebra on the Zyder Zee

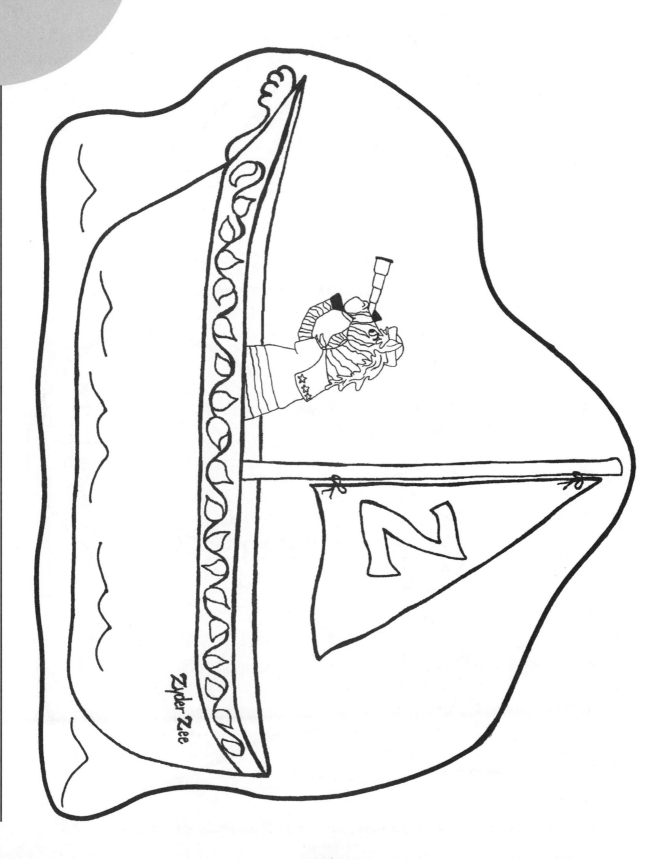

Zyder Zee

The Zebra on the Zyder Zee

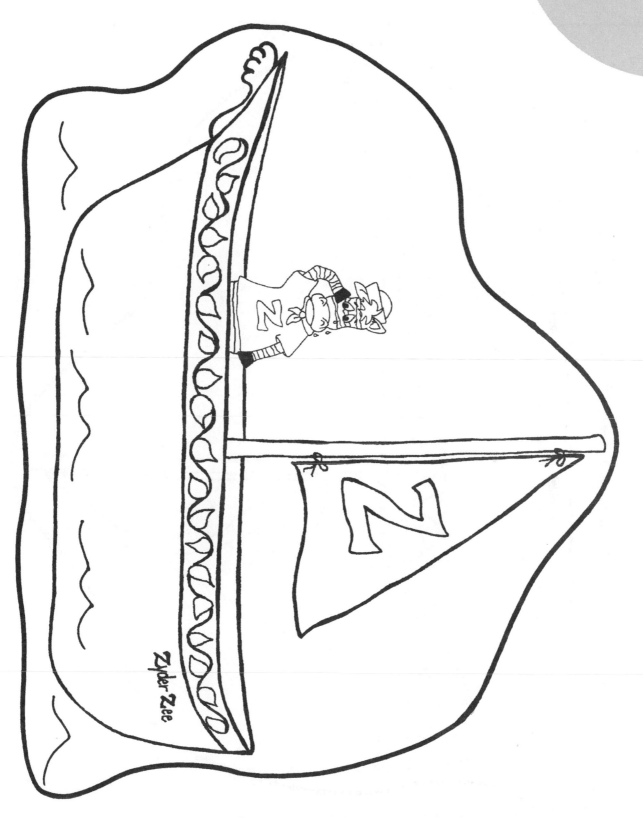

Zyder Zee

The Complete Book of Activities, Games, Stories, Props, Recipes, and Dances

The Zebra on the Zyder Zee

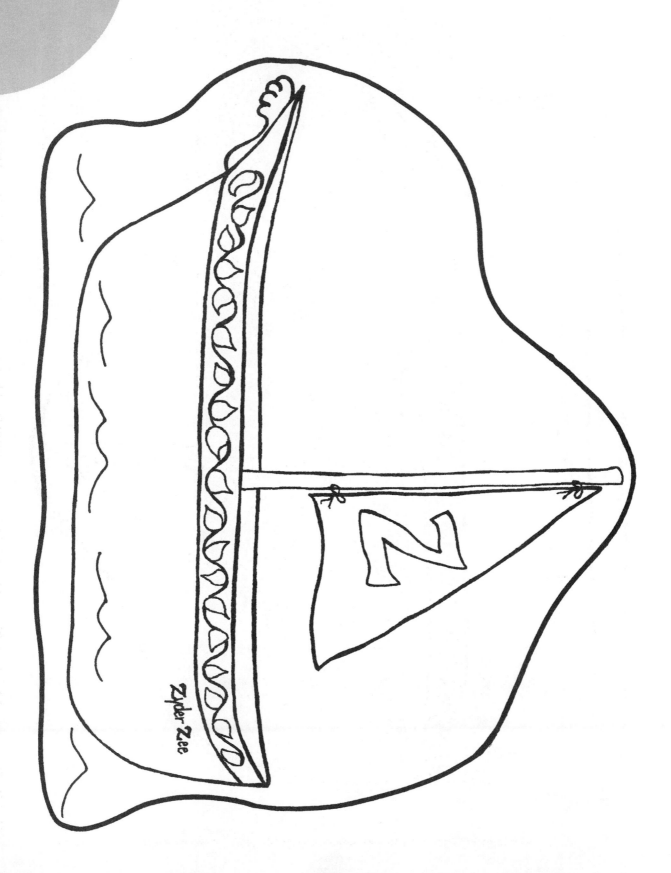

The Zebra on the Zyder Zee

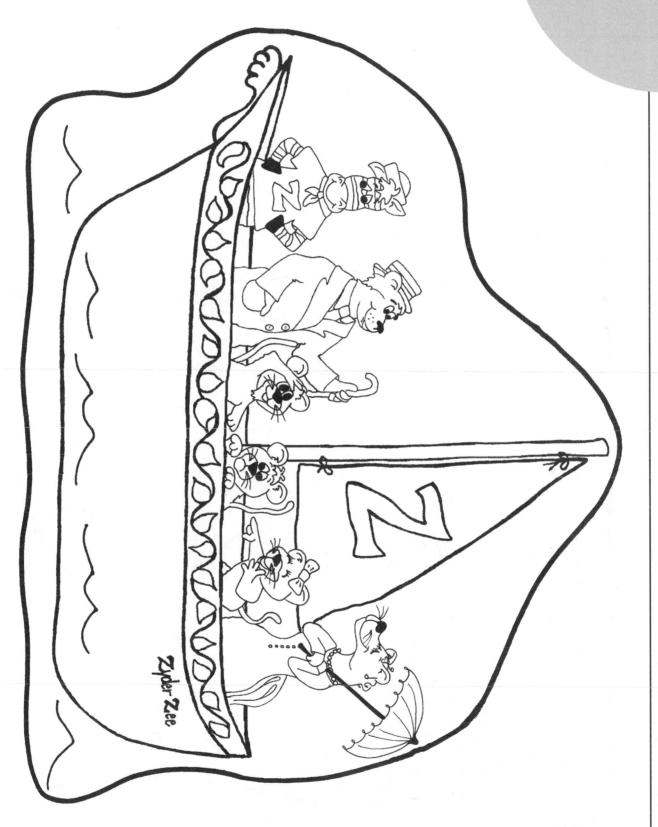

The Complete Book of Activities, Games, Stories, Props, Recipes, and Dances

Ellie's Party

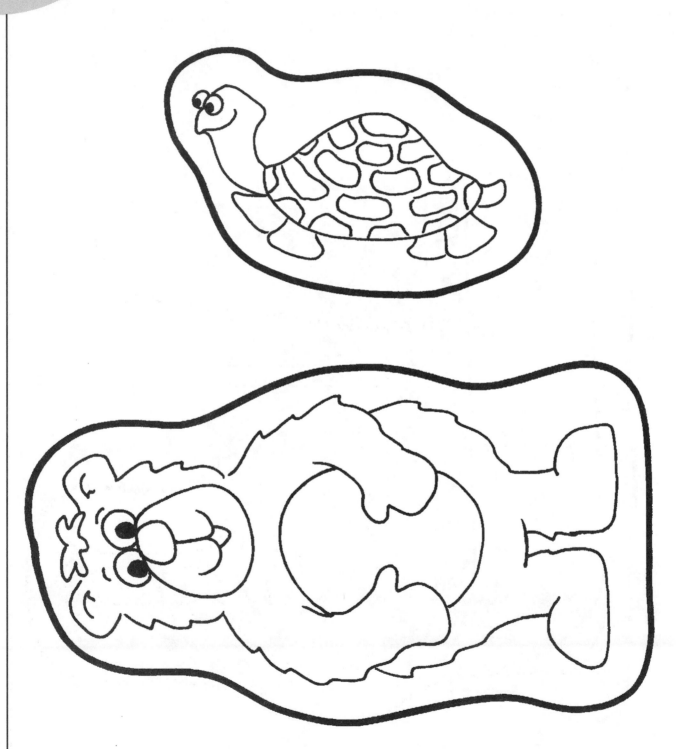

Ellie's Party

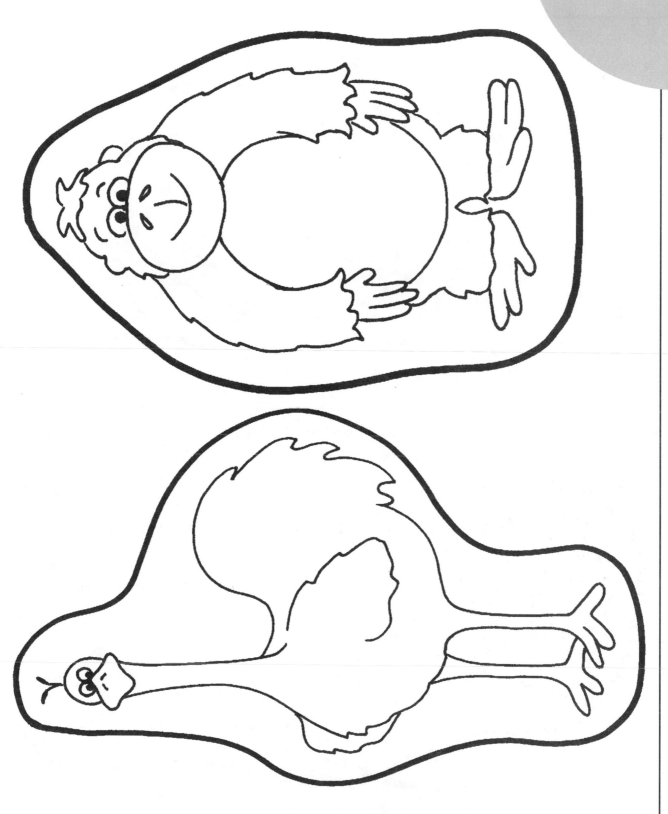

The Complete Book of Activities, Games, Stories, Props, Recipes, and Dances

Ellie's Party

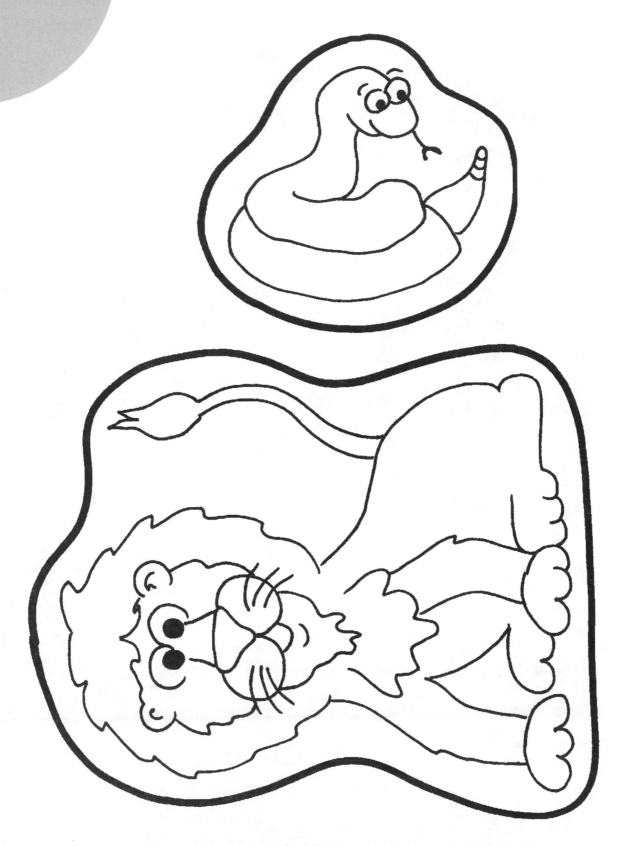

Ellie's Party

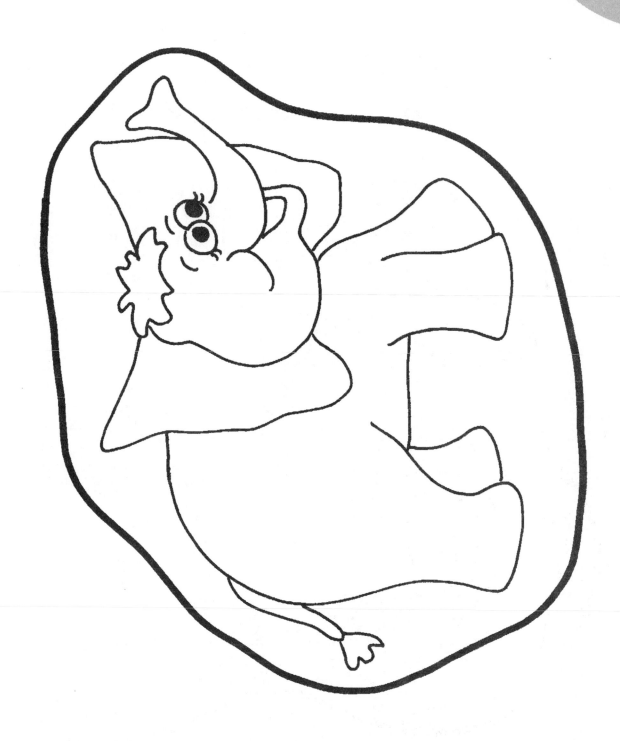

STORY PATTERNS: PROP STORIES

Ellie's Party

Little Red Hen Character Masks

The Complete Book of Activities, Games, Stories, Props, Recipes, and Dances

Little Red Hen Character Masks

Little Red Hen Character Masks

The Complete Book of Activities, Games, Stories, Props, Recipes, and Dances

Little Red Hen Character Masks

Five Dancing Dolphins

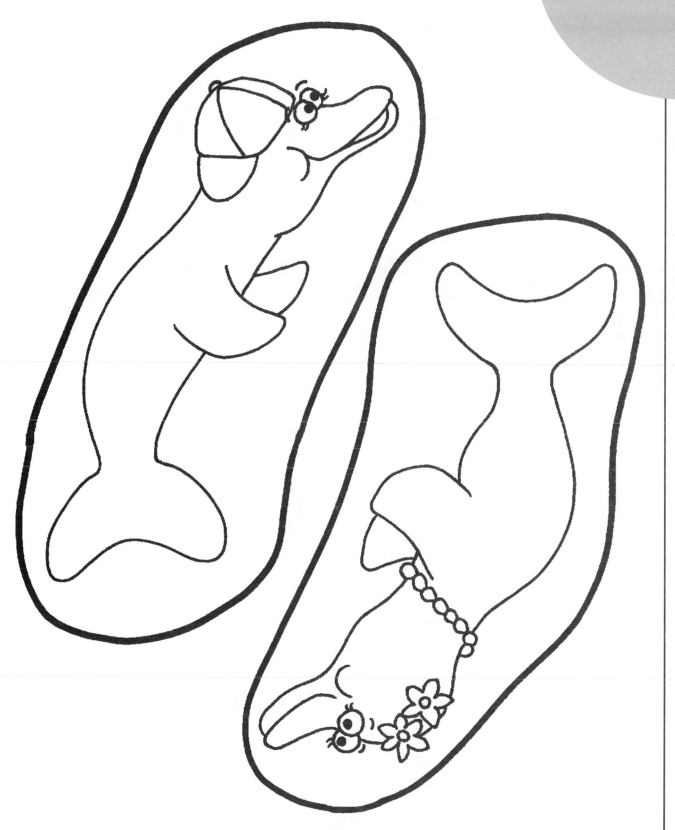

The Complete Book of Activities, Games, Stories, Props, Recipes, and Dances

Five Dancing Dolphins

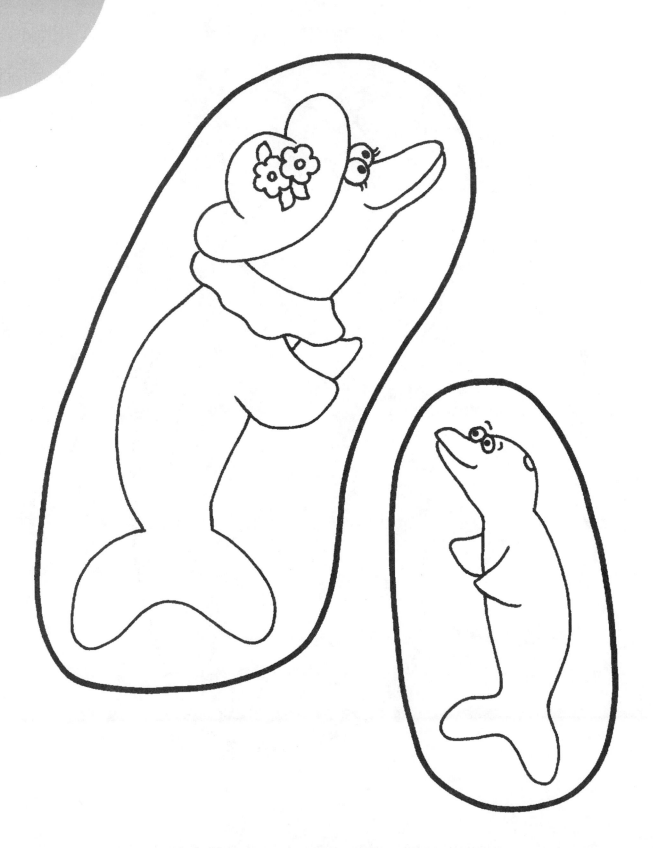

Five Dancing Dolphins

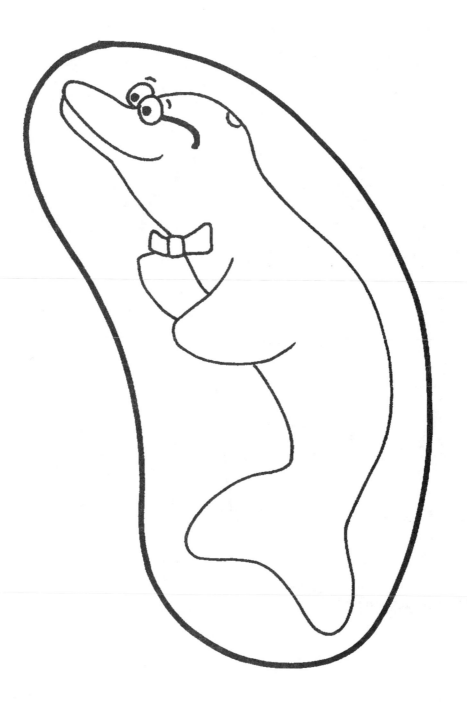

The Complete Book of Activities, Games, Stories, Props, Recipes, and Dances

Five Little Chickens

Frog Went a-Courtin'

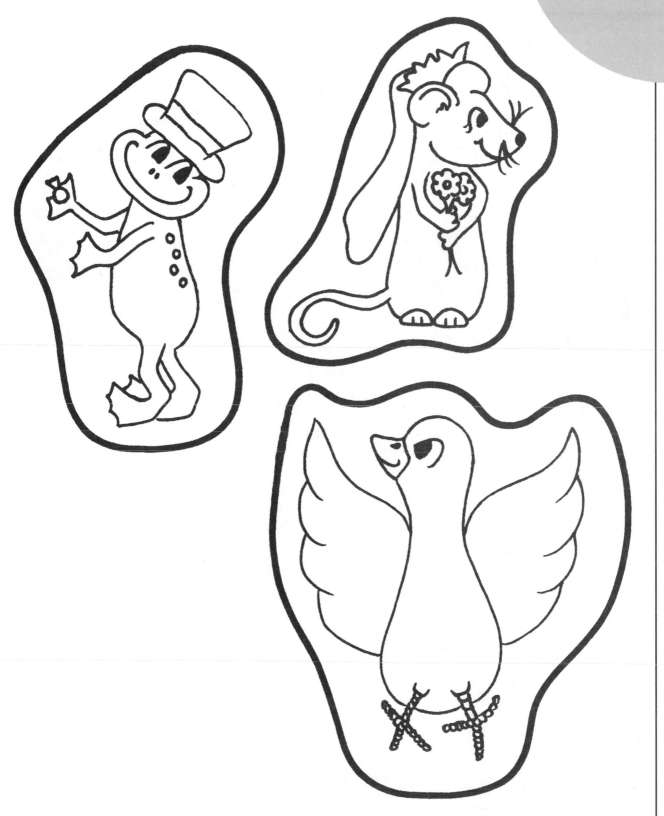

Frog Went a-Courtin'

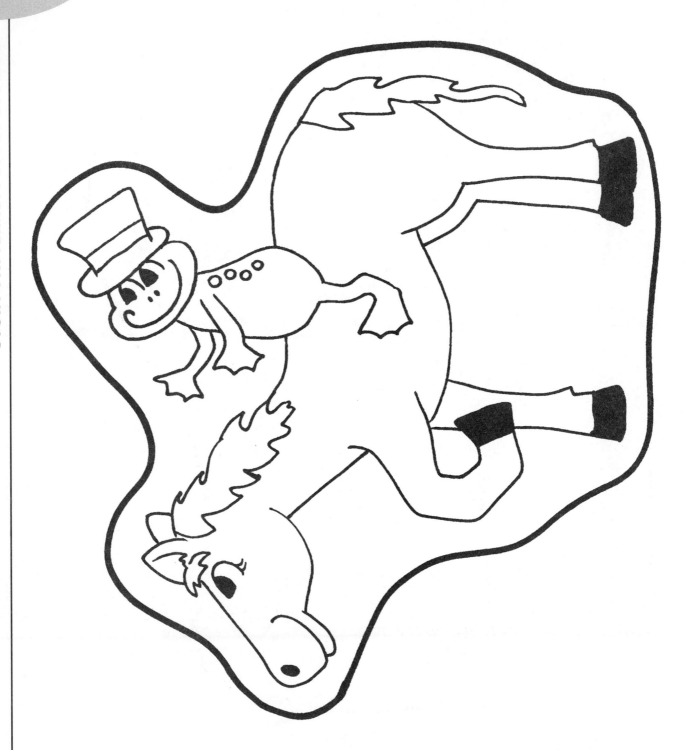

Frog Went a-Courtin'

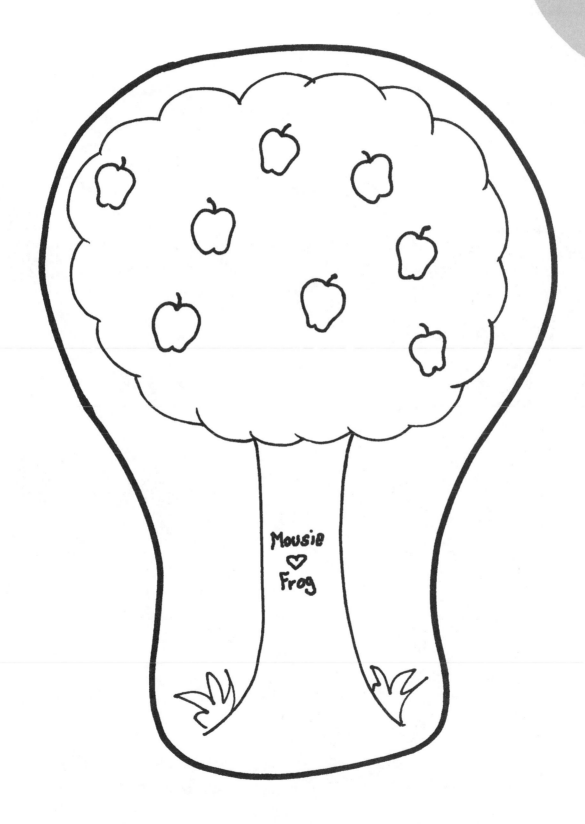

Mousie ♡ Frog

The Complete Book of Activities, Games, Stories, Props, Recipes, and Dances

Frog Went a-Courtin'

The Lion's Haircut

The Complete Book of Activities, Games, Stories, Props, Recipes, and Dances

STORY PATTERNS: PUPPET STORIES

Ms. Bumblebee Gathers Honey

Ms. Bumblebee Gathers Honey

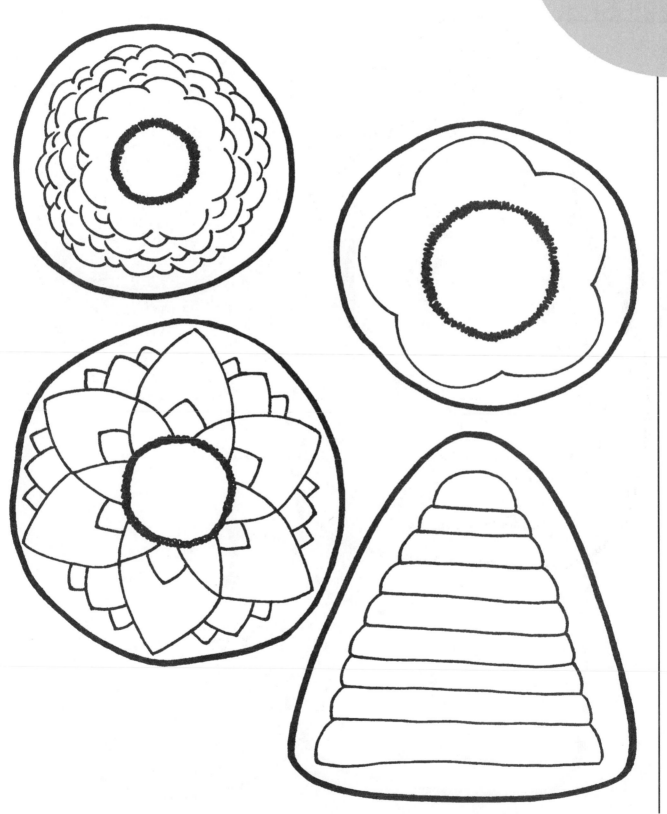

The Complete Book of Activities, Games, Stories, Props, Recipes, and Dances

The Old Woman and Her Pig

The Old Woman and Her Pig

The Complete Book of Activities, Games, Stories, Props, Recipes, and Dances

The Old Woman and Her Pig

STORY PATTERNS: PUPPET STORIES

The Old Woman and Her Pig

The Complete Book of Activities, Games, Stories, Props, Recipes, and Dances

The Old Woman and Her Pig

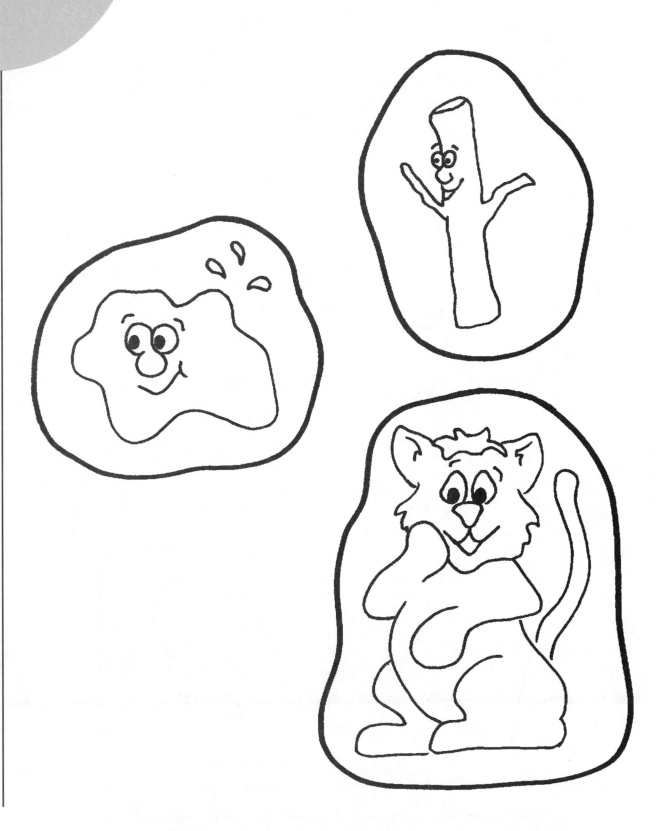

The Parade

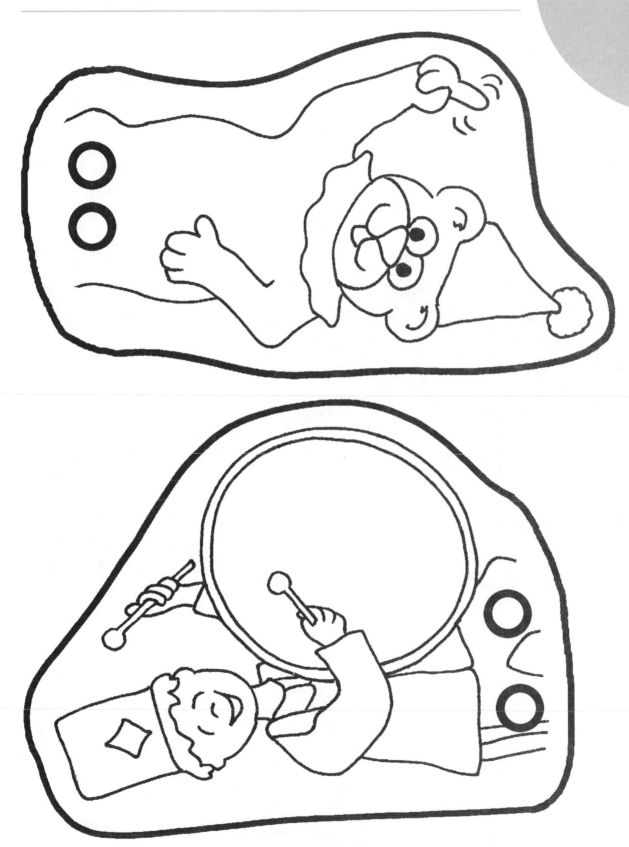

The Complete Book of Activities, Games, Stories, Props, Recipes, and Dances

STORY PATTERNS: PUPPET STORIES

The Parade

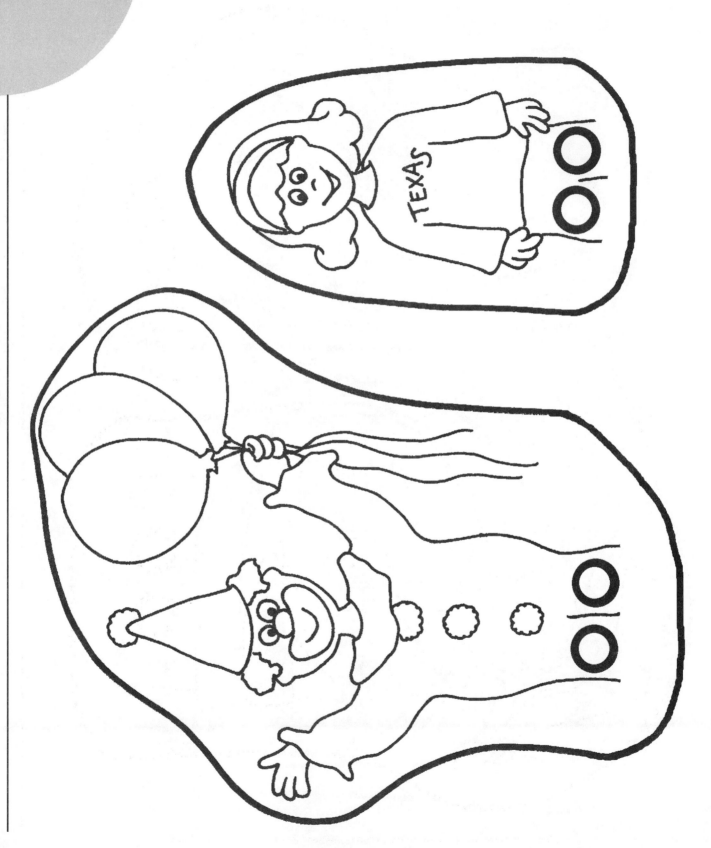

The Parade

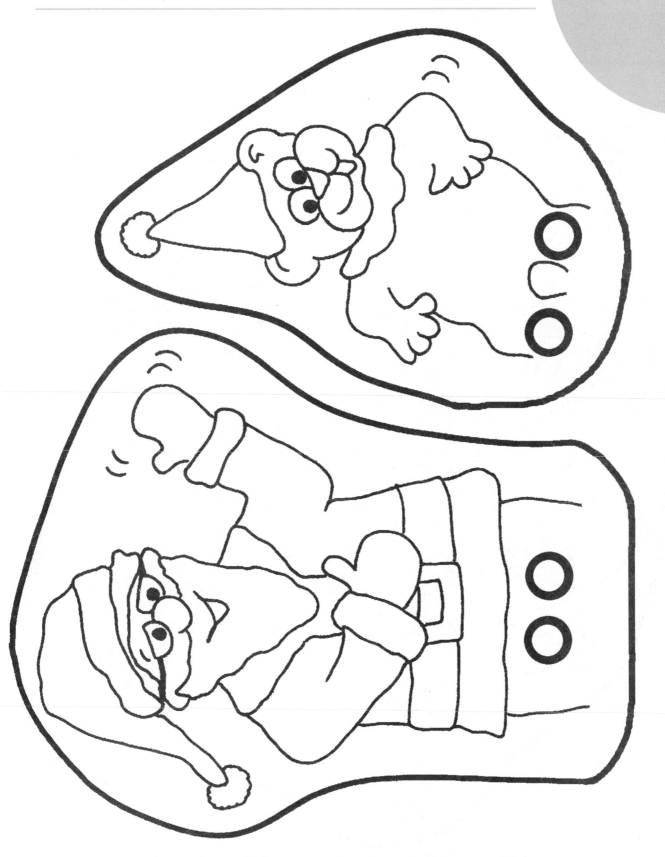

The Complete Book of Activities, Games, Stories, Props, Recipes, and Dances

The Parade

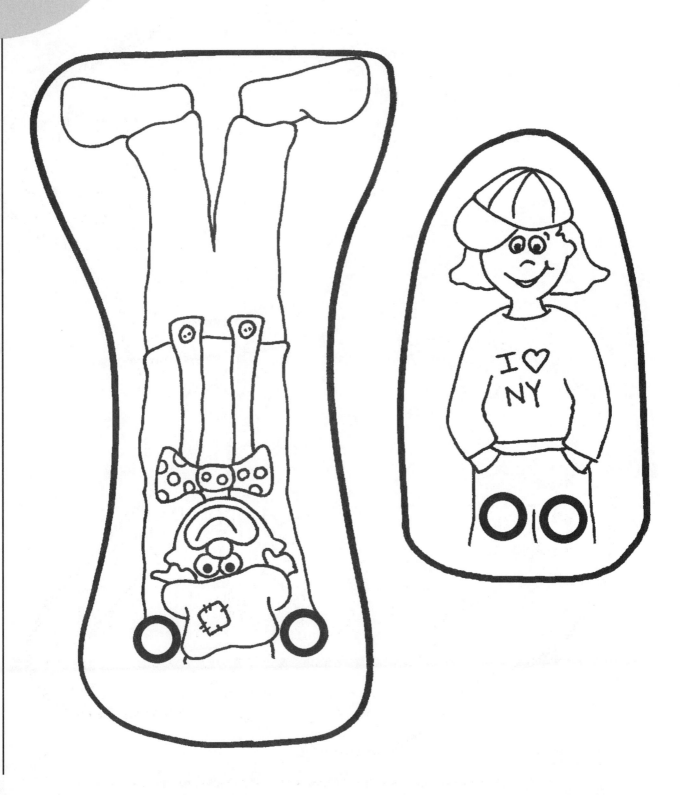

The Parade

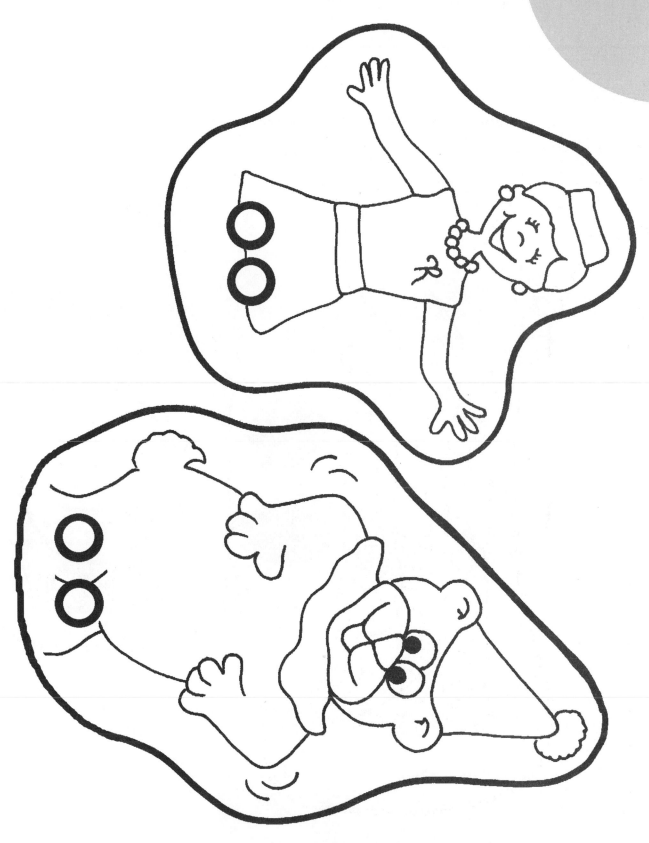

The Complete Book of Activities, Games, Stories, Props, Recipes, and Dances

There Was an Old Woman Who Swallowed a Fly

There Was an Old Woman Who Swallowed a Fly

The Complete Book of Activities, Games, Stories, Props, Recipes, and Dances

There Was an Old Woman Who Swallowed a Fly

The Three Bears Rap

The Complete Book of Activities, Games, Stories, Props, Recipes, and Dances

The Three Bears Rap

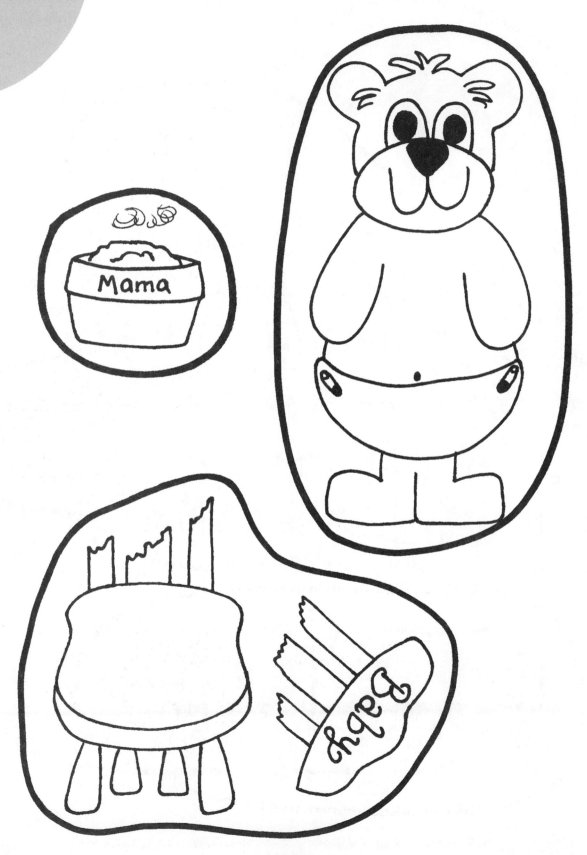

Mama

Baby

The Three Bears Rap

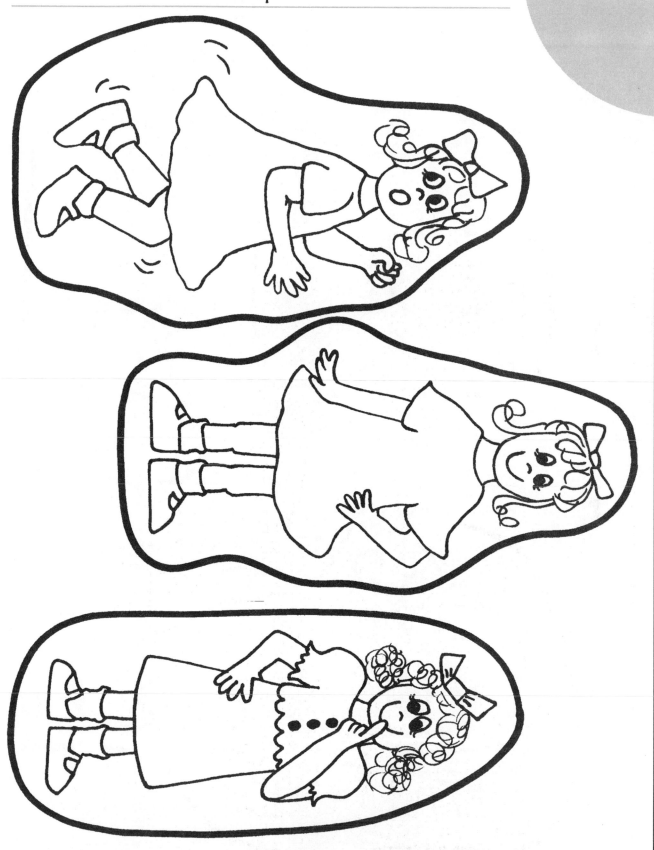

The Complete Book of Activities, Games, Stories, Props, Recipes, and Dances

APPENDIX

STORY PATTERNS: PUPPET STORIES

The Three Bears Rap

The Three Little Pigs

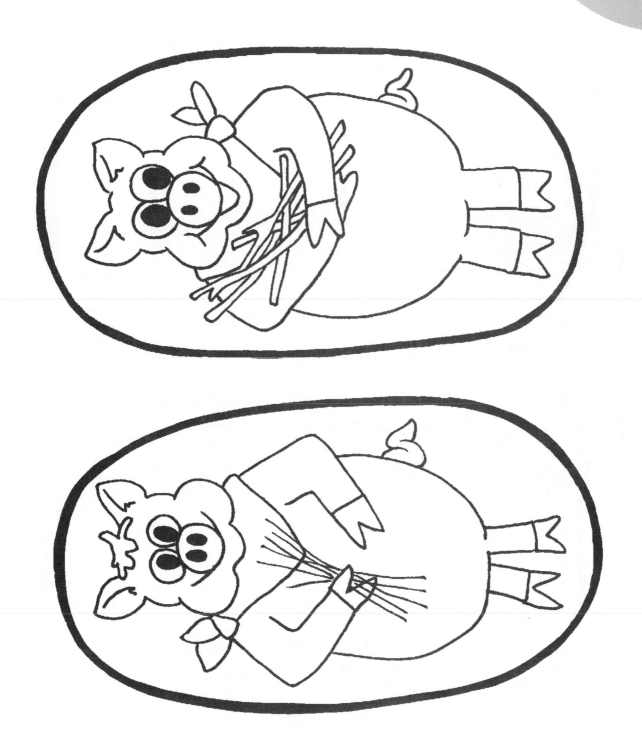

The Complete Book of Activities, Games, Stories, Props, Recipes, and Dances

The Three Little Pigs

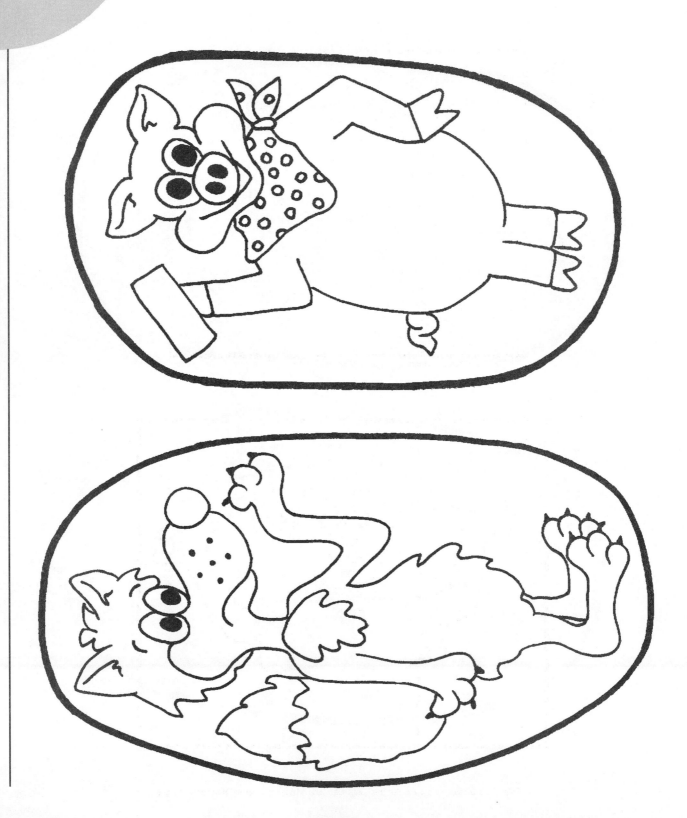

The Boy Who Tried to Fool His Father

The Complete Book of Activities, Games, Stories, Props, Recipes, and Dances

STORY PATTERNS: REBUS STORIES

The Boy Who Tried to Fool His Father

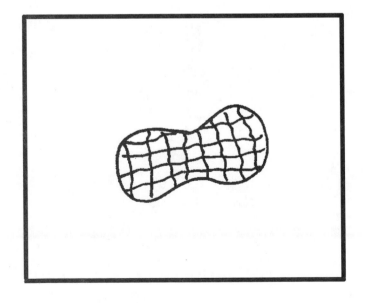

The Boy Who Tried to Fool His Father

The Complete Book of Activities, Games, Stories, Props, Recipes, and Dances

The Boy Who Tried to Fool His Father

The House That Jack Built

The Complete Book of Activities, Games, Stories, Props, Recipes, and Dances

The House That Jack Built

The House That Jack Built

The House That Jack Built

The House That Jack Built

The Complete Book of Activities, Games, Stories, Props, Recipes, and Dances

Hush, Little Baby

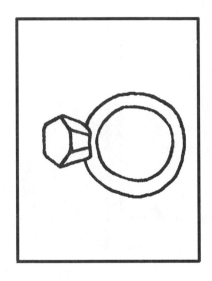

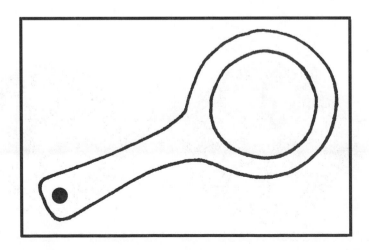

Hush, Little Baby

The Complete Book of Activities, Games, Stories, Props, Recipes, and Dances

Hush, Little Baby

Miss Mary Mack

Miss Mary Mack

Black

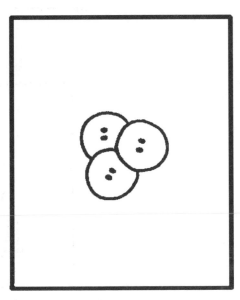

Buttons

The Complete Book of Activities, Games, Stories, Props, Recipes, and Dances

APPENDIX

STORY PATTERNS: REBUS STORIES

Miss Mary Mack

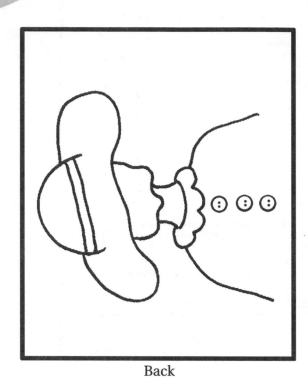

Back

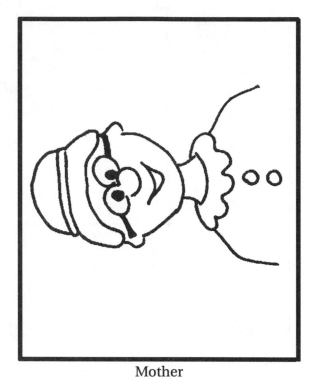

Mother

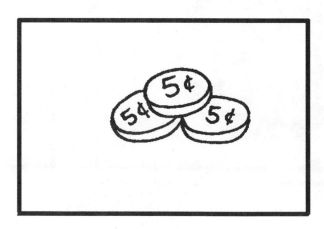

15 Cents

Miss Mary Mack

Elephants

Fence

The Complete Book of Activities, Games, Stories, Props, Recipes, and Dances

Miss Mary Mack

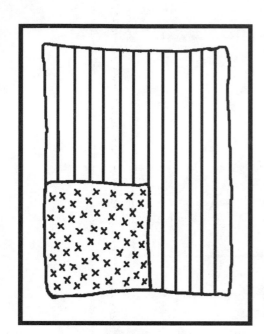

Fourth of July

High

Sky

Miss Mary Mack

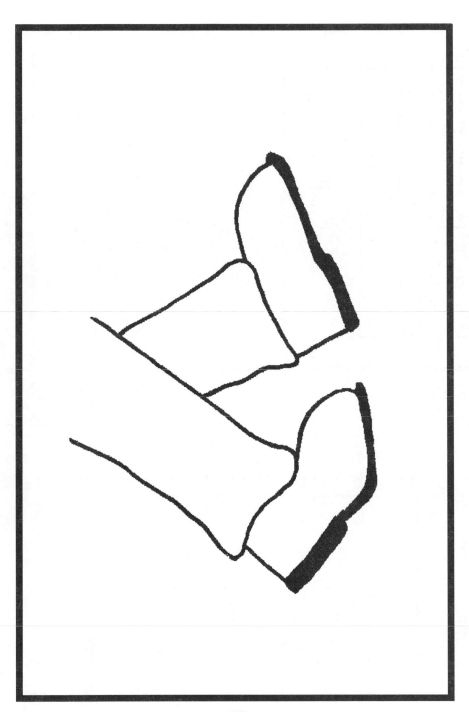

Walk

Miss Mary Mack

Talk

Knife and Fork

The Months

APPENDIX

STORY PATTERNS: REBUS STORIES

The Months

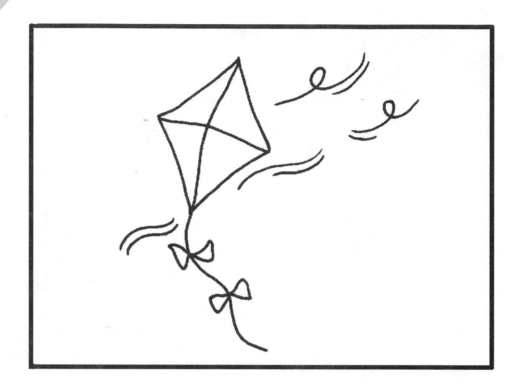

The Months

The Complete Book of Activities, Games, Stories, Props, Recipes, and Dances

The Months

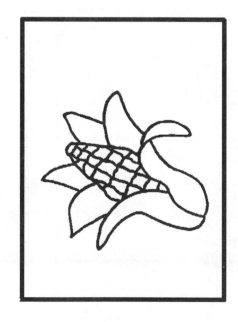

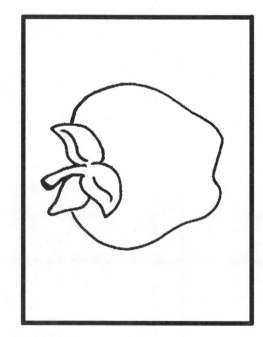

The Months

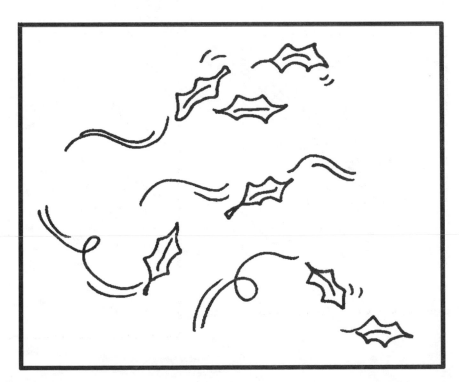

The Complete Book of Activities, Games, Stories, Props, Recipes, and Dances

On Top of a Hillside

On Top of a Hillside

The Complete Book of Activities, Games, Stories, Props, Recipes, and Dances

STORY PATTERNS: REBUS STORIES

On Top of a Hillside

On Top of a Hillside

On Top of a Hillside

SCHOOL

Santa's Workshop

Santa's Workshop

Santa's Workshop

The Complete Book of Activities, Games, Stories, Props, Recipes, and Dances

STORY PATTERNS: REBUS STORIES

Santa's Workshop

Santa's Workshop

The Complete Book of Activities, Games, Stories, Props, Recipes, and Dances

Santa's Workshop

Susie Moriar

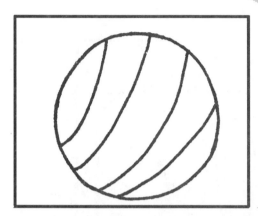

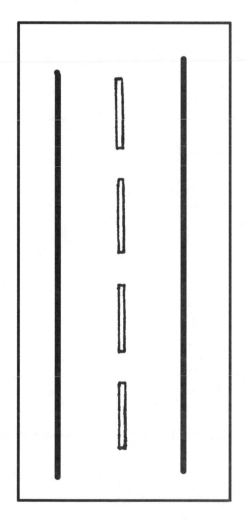

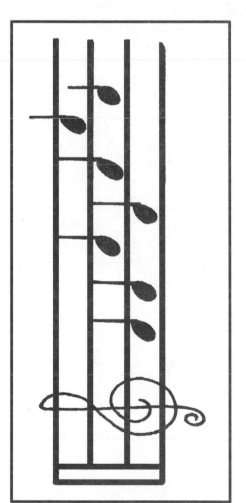

Susie Moriar

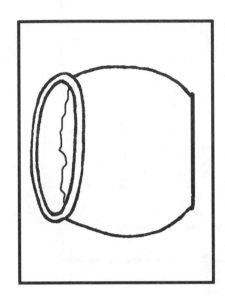

Tiny Tim

The Complete Book of Activities, Games, Stories, Props, Recipes, and Dances

Tiny Tim

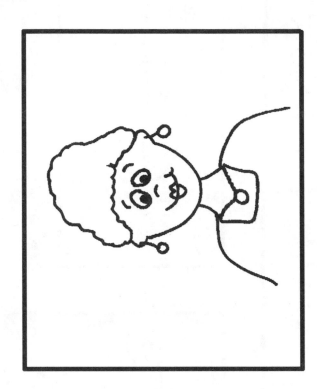

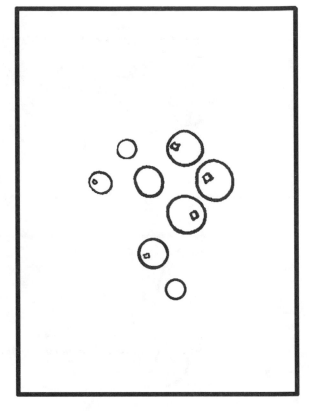

Tiny Tim

The Complete Book of Activities, Games, Stories, Props, Recipes, and Dances

APPENDIX

STORY PATTERNS: REBUS STORIES

Tiny Tim

The Wheels on the Bus

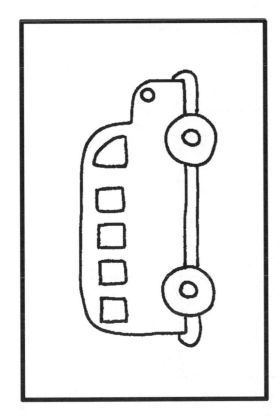

The Complete Book of Activities, Games, Stories, Props, Recipes, and Dances

APPENDIX

STORY PATTERNS: REBUS STORIES

The Wheels on the Bus

The Wheels on the Bus

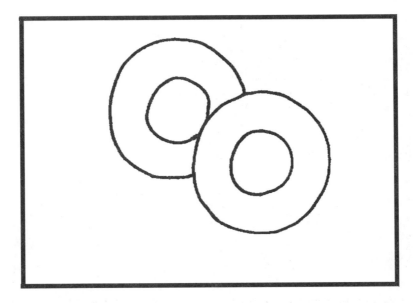

The Complete Book of Activities, Games, Stories, Props, Recipes, and Dances

Index

Theme Index

A

Alphabet

Animals

The Complete Book of Activities, Games, Stories, Props, Recipes, and Dances

The Complete Book of Activities, Games, Stories, Props, Recipes, and Dances

Friends

G

Growing Things

Growing Up

The Complete Book of Activities, Games, Stories, Props, Recipes, and Dances

The Complete Book of Activities, Games, Stories, Props, Recipes, and Dances

Occupations

Oceans and Seas

Opposites

Outer Space

P

Parts of the Body

R

Rhyming

S

School

Seasons

Self-Esteem

Senses

General Index

The Complete Book of Activities, Games, Stories, Props, Recipes, and Dances

The Complete Book of Activities, Games, Stories, Props, Recipes, and Dances

The Complete Book of Activities, Games, Stories, Props, Recipes, and Dances